⚖ NOLO Products & Services

⇨ Books & Software

Get in-depth information. Nolo publishes hundreds of great books and software programs for consumers and business owners. Order a copy—or download an ebook version instantly—at Nolo.com.

⇨ Legal Encyclopedia

Free at Nolo.com. Here are more than 1,400 free articles and answers to common questions about everyday legal issues including wills, bankruptcy, small business formation, divorce, patents, employment and much more.

⇨ Plain-English Legal Dictionary

Free at Nolo.com. Stumped by jargon? Look it up in America's most up-to-date source for definitions of legal terms.

⇨ Online Legal Documents

Create documents at your computer. Go to Nolo.com to make a will or living trust, form an LLC or corporation or obtain a trademark or provisional patent. For simpler matters, download one of our hundreds of high-quality legal forms, including bills of sale, promissory notes, nondisclosure agreements and many more.

⇨ Lawyer Directory

Find an attorney at Nolo.com. Nolo's consumer-friendly lawyer directory provides in-depth profiles of lawyers all over America. From fees and experience to legal philosophy, education and special expertise, you'll find all the information you need to pick the right lawyer. Every lawyer listed has pledged to work diligently and respectfully with clients.

⇨ Free Legal Updates

Keep up to date. Check for free updates at Nolo.com. Under "Products," find this book and click "Legal Updates." You can also sign up for our free e-newsletters at Nolo.com/newsletters.

3rd edition

The Complete Guide to Buying a Business

Attorney Fred S. Steingold

THIRD EDITION	AUGUST 2011
Editor	ILONA BRAY
Cover Design	SUSAN PUTNEY
Book Design	TERRI HEARSH
Proofreading	CATHERINE CAPUTO
Production	MARGARET LIVINGSTON
CD-ROM Preparation	ELLEN BITTER
Index	MEDEA MINNICH
Printing	BANG PRINTING

Steingold, Fred.
  The complete guide to buying a business / by Fred S. Steingold. — 3rd ed.
    p. cm.
  Includes bibliographical references and index.
  Summary: "Explains complex yet critical legal and practical details on choosing, investigating, and contracting to buy a business. The new edition includes updated tax laws and regulations."—Provided by publisher.
  ISBN-13: 978-1-4133-1267-6 (pbk.)
  ISBN-10: 1-4133-1267-5 (pbk.)
  ISBN-13: 978-1-4133-1287-4 (epub e-book)
  1. Business enterprises—Purchasing—Law and legislation—United States—Popular works. 2. Small business—Law and legislation—United States—Popular works. I. Title.
  KF1355.S74 2010
  346.73'065—dc22
                    2010008715

Please note

We believe accurate, plain-English legal information should help you solve many of your own legal problems. But this text is not a substitute for personalized advice from a knowledgeable lawyer. If you want the help of a trained professional—and we'll always point out situations in which we think that's a good idea—consult an attorney licensed to practice in your state.

Acknowledgments

I wish to thank Ilona Bray for her superb editing of the second and third editions of this book.

Thanks also to:

Emily Doskow for skillfully shaping up the first edition of this book

Marcia Stewart for building a strong foundation for this book through her skillful editing of *The Complete Guide to Selling a Business*

Jake Warner for his many helpful contributions and unflagging encouragement

Mark Hartley, CPA, for his analysis of tax issues

Glen J. Cooper for his insights regarding business brokers

Terri Hearsh for her production magic

André Zivkovich and the Applications Development Department for creating the CD-ROM, and

Susan Putney for designing the attractive cover.

About the Author

Attorney Fred S. Steingold is an expert on business law, advising entrepreneurs on how to start, buy, run, and sell businesses. He is the author of Nolo's *Complete Guide to Selling a Business, Legal Guide for Starting and Running a Small Business,* and *The Employer's Legal Handbook.* His monthly column, "The Legal Advisor," is carried by trade publications around the country.

Table of Contents

Part 2: Getting Ready to Buy

Part 3: Preparing the Sales Agreement

Part 4: Preparing the Promissory Note and Other Sales Documents

Part 5: Closing the Deal

Appendixes

Confidentiality Letter

Attachment to Sales Agreement

Amendment of Sales Agreement

Promissory Note

Security Agreement for Asset Sale

Security Agreement for Entity Sale

Escrow Agreement for Stock Certificates

Escrow Agreement for LLC Transfer Certificates

Bill of Sale for Business Assets

Statement Regarding Absence of Creditors

Assignment of Lease

Assignment of Contracts

Consent to Assignment of Contract

Assignment of Intellectual Property

Directors' Consent to the Corporation's Purchase of a Business

Shareholders' Consent to the Corporation's Purchase of a Business

LLC Members' Consent to the Company's Purchase of a Business

Partners' Consent to the Partnership's Purchase of a Business

Covenant Not to Compete

Independent Contractor Agreement

Closing Checklist for an Asset Sale

Closing Checklist for an Entity Sale

Asset Sale Agreement

Entity Sale Agreement

IRS 8594, Asset Acquisition Statement

Instructions, IRS 8594, Asset Acquisition Statement

UCC Financial Statement and Addendum

Your Companion for Buying a Business

You may be thinking about leaving a salaried job and becoming your own boss. Or maybe you already own a small business and would like to expand by buying a similar operation or a complementary business. Welcome to the world of entrepreneurs.

Don't be surprised if the process of buying a business seems intimidating at first. In fact, you probably have lots of legal and financial questions. Fortunately, whether you choose to handle the purchase wholly by yourself or you plan to work with lawyers, accountants, and other professionals, this book can help. It provides step-by-step guidance for doing it right—from evaluating available businesses to negotiating favorable purchase terms.

Each year, hundred of thousands of U.S. businesses change ownership—and even more are up for sale. A reported 20% of small businesses are for sale at any given time.

Most of these are small and midsized businesses: retail stores, beauty salons, quick-print shops, restaurants, tax preparation services, landscapers, electrical contracting firms, and modest manufacturing operations, to mention just a few. But no matter what kind of business you're looking for—a professional services company, a neighborhood bagel shop, or a home-based website that sells imported garden tools—there's likely to be someone out there who'd like to sell such a business. The key is to find the right business and buy it at a reasonable, affordable price. This book will help you get the job done with a minimum of hassle, worry, and expense. It provides step-by-step guidance, checklists, and all the forms you need, from the moment you start to consider buying a business to the day of the closing—and beyond.

Is This Book for You?

This book focuses on the purchase of small to midsized businesses. Though much of what you learn here will also be applicable to buying larger enterprises, this book definitely is not concerned with the sorts of mergers and acquisitions that you read about in *The Wall Street Journal*. It can help you if you fit this profile:

- You're looking to buy a business that costs tens or even hundreds of thousands of dollars or even several hundred thousand dollars, but probably not more than $2 million.
- You anticipate owning the business yourself or with one, two, or a handful of others.
- You'll consider an attractive business regardless of whether it's currently set up as a sole proprietorship, partnership, corporation, or limited liability company (LLC).
- You plan to play an active role in running the business and perhaps to make it your main source of income.

Does this sound like you? If it does, then this book has exactly the information you need to move forward with a smooth and financially sound purchase.

Chapter Number	What You'll Learn
Part 1 (Chapters 1-6)	**How to:** • decide whether buying a business is right for you • avoid acting on incomplete or inaccurate information • take the practical and legal steps involved in buying • find an available business that fits your needs • figure out how big a business you can afford • analyze the tax consequences • set a realistic price range for a particular business, and • choose and work with lawyers, accountants, and other professionals.
Part 2 (Chapters 7-10)	**How to:** • understand the alternatives for financing your purchase • negotiate for the best possible price and terms • structure your purchase • put legal protections in place to help assure you get everything you've bargained for • investigate the business, and • draft a letter of intent.
Part 3 (Chapters 11-17)	**How to put together a sales agreement, including:** • how you'll pay (lump sum versus installment payments) • which business liabilities the seller will remain responsible for • the seller's promise (if any) not to compete after the sale, and • arrangements (if any) to hire the seller for limited-term employment or consulting.
Part 4 (Chapters 18-20)	**How to create other needed sale documents, such as a:** • bill of sale • promissory note • security agreement, and • covenant not to compete.
Part 5 (Chapters 21 and 22)	**How to conduct a smooth closing and take over the reins of your new business.**

Will You Need to Hire Lawyers, Accountants, or Other Professionals?

Buying a business for a reasonable price may not seem like a job you want to tackle all on your own. But, fortunately, the process can be broken down into small pieces, each of which you can understand and master. With this book, you should be able to handle much of the work yourself. And if you call in a lawyer, accountant, or appraiser as needed, you'll be able to explain just what you need and why.

This book will alert you to specific situations in which you're likely to benefit from professional help. For example, because the business you're buying and the deal you strike with the seller are unique, it's a good idea to have a lawyer review your sales agreement before you sign it. Similarly, analyzing your individual tax exposure is a task best left to an experienced expert such as a CPA, after you've reviewed the tax material in the book.

By doing much of the work yourself and understanding the issues before you hire professionals, the fees you pay for professional services should be far lower than what you'd pay if you used experts to handle the entire purchase of a business. In fact, you stand to save thousands of dollars. Once you firmly grasp every step of the purchase process, you can act as a knowledgeable general contractor, with your professional advisers serving as your cost-efficient subcontractors. This book will help you along that path. ●

PART

Overview of the Process

Thinking About Buying a Business

A lot of people talk about buying a business, but relatively few actually take the steps necessary to make it happen. By consulting this book, you've taken the first step: learning about how the process works. This could be the beginning of an exciting and profitable adventure.

SKIP AHEAD

If you've already decided to buy a business, you're probably anxious to get on with it. That's fine. Skim or skip this chapter and move on to Chapter 2.

If, like many readers, your goal in buying a business is to earn a living working for yourself, you may be motivated by the opportunity to turn your back on being an employee and answering to a boss. But be forewarned: Independence does come at a price. By buying a business, you may be signing on for longer hours and more worries than you've ever experienced as a hired hand.

Then again, if the business succeeds, the financial and personal rewards are yours to savor. And of course, when you own your own business, no one can fire you. For many entrepreneurs, money may be a significant motivator, but it's not necessarily the most important. The simple joy of shaping an enterprise—almost always a creative endeavor—may stimulate your efforts far beyond the promise of financial independence.

Be Cautious and Be Prepared

Not everyone who wants to buy a business should. You need to consider carefully whether it will actually work for you. Many businesses fail or run marginal operations. How do you avoid that and become one of the winners instead? One way to be sure that you want to go ahead, and increase your chances of success, is to spend some time working in the industry you might enter. So, for example, if you think you want to open a restaurant, get a job working in one and learn the ropes. You'll see just how difficult it is—and, possibly, realize that it is exactly where you want to be—without taking on the risks right away. And it may be that you'll decide that it's not for you, and that it's better to save your nest egg and get a part-time job that will bring you less stress, less risk, and less heartbreak if you don't succeed.

In this chapter, you'll learn that not all buyers are cut from the same cloth; a number of different motivations and personality traits can lead someone to consider entrepreneurship. You'll see where you fall in the range of people who consider buying a business—and people who actually do become business owners. And you'll discover that if you decide owning a business is for you, buying an existing one is a great way to do it. You also have the options of starting a business from scratch or buying a franchise, and we'll discuss those options in this chapter. Each of these paths to business ownership has good and not-so-good features—but for many would-be entrepreneurs, buying a business is clearly the best choice.

Business-Buying Worries

Buying a business can be a heady experience, but, in addition to the adrenaline rush, you may also experience anxiety. You may have to get past a number of worries and concerns, including these things you might say to yourself:

- I can't afford a promising business.
- I may pay too much.
- The business may fail and I'll lose all that I have.
- The seller may conceal crucial information.
- Business trends will change and hurt the business I'm interested in.
- I'll have to work too hard—or I'll get bored—and then I'll have trouble selling the business.
- The sales agreement will contain tricky clauses that will lead to my financial ruin.
- The sales agreement will omit clauses that could protect me.
- Professional fees will add greatly to my costs.
- I'll wind up paying more income tax than I anticipated.

These are all important issues to consider, but you needn't lose sleep over them. This book will provide realistic information to help you deal with all these worries.

Which Kind of Buyer Are You?

People who think about buying a business tend to fall into the three basic categories described in this section. But while different buyers' needs and goals aren't the same, the process of buying a business—especially the legal procedures—is surprisingly constant. So whichever category you fit into, you can use this book as a roadmap to guide you through the entire transaction.

Let's look at the three types of buyers.

Buying a Business as a Livelihood

Many people buy a business where they intend to work each day, with the expectation that the business will provide a steady source of income. In a typical scenario, the buyer makes a down payment of between 10% and 25% of the sale price. Then, as the new owner, the buyer pays the seller the balance of the sale price in monthly installments spread over a number of years. The buyer, of course, will have other bills to pay each month—including rent, employee paychecks, utilities, insurance, and business taxes. Whatever is left over is income to the owner—though many business owners wisely keep some money in reserve to help them ride out slow periods.

EXAMPLE: Tired of working for someone else, Andy looks for and finds an attractive antique furniture store to buy. He's especially pleased that the business has built a loyal following in the community over a 15-year period. Andy plans to quit his job and run the business, which he believes will generate enough income to support him and his wife, Judy. He agrees to buy the business for $150,000. The seller is willing to accept a $30,000 down payment. Andy agrees to pay the balance—together with interest at a 6% annual rate—in 60 monthly payments of $2,320 each. Two years after buying the business, Andy is confident he made the right decision. He thoroughly enjoys talking antiques with his customers, and he looks forward to the buying trips that he and Judy take twice a year to replenish their inventory. Each month, after paying the seller, the landlord, and two employees, Andy is able to pay himself $6,000—and he knows that because of his hard work, he'll be able to sell the business some day at a handsome profit.

Andy, of course, could have tried to get a bank loan to buy an inventory of antiques and start a business from scratch. But he felt it was less risky to buy the existing business and get the benefit of the goodwill that the owner had built up over the years. He also liked the fact the business had an ideal location under a long-term lease that he could take over.

Buying a Business as a Strategic Move

Some people who buy a business are already in business and want to expand their current enterprise—both to increase their business and possibly to dominate a local market. Such people are often called *strategic* buyers because they're carrying out a larger business strategy.

Some of those who are looking to expand a business may be in the market for the same kind of business they're already in. There are enormous advantages to this, the biggest one being that the buyer already knows a great deal about the business and can value it appropriately at purchase and operate it more easily after the purchase is complete.

EXAMPLE: Emma owns a delivery service that primarily serves the east side of town. If she had a few more trucks and drivers, she could greatly expand her clientele and serve the entire city. She approaches Phil, a competitor who is reaching retirement age. They agree on terms that will let Emma expand by buying Phil's business. Emma will not only buy the additional trucks and drivers but will also benefit from the goodwill that Phil has built up over the years through consistently providing timely pick-ups and deliveries. She'll also protect herself from competitors who might have expanded in the same way had she not done so first. As frosting on the cake, Phil agrees to stay on for

90 days as a consultant so that the transition will go smoothly.

Others looking to expand an existing business may be seeking something that's not a mirror image of their existing business but would neatly dovetail with it.

EXAMPLE: Ernie and Paulette run a popular guitar studio. They realize there's a cap on how much they can earn by giving lessons, because there are just so many hours in the day. At a meeting of music educators, they hear a rumor that a guitar and drum store in a high-traffic shopping mall may be up for sale. They investigate and find that the rumor is true. Ernie and Paulette check out the facilities and discover to their delight that not only does the store deal in name-brand instruments but there is ample space in the premises to install four soundproof instruction rooms. They do the math and decide they've come upon an opportunity to greatly expand their income while continuing to work in a field they love.

Buying a Business as an Investment

Some people buy a small business simply as a way to round out their portfolios.

EXAMPLE: Doris is convinced of the wisdom of having diversified investments. She already owns stocks, bonds, money-market funds, and real estate, including two small apartment buildings. Some of her investments—like the bonds—are relatively conservative. Others—like some of her high-tech stocks—are more speculative. For additional balance in her portfolio, Doris feels she'd like to buy a small business that can be run by a full-time manager. Because she believes that small businesses are more risky than most of her other investments, she's hoping to find a business that's likely to return at least 15% annually on the money she pays for it.

This strategy, of course, is only available to folks with significant assets and the ability to bear the risk.

Three Ways to Become a Business Owner

If you decide you'd like to own a business, buying an existing one isn't the only way to accomplish your goal. You could, instead, start a business from scratch or buy a nationally branded franchise. As you'll see below, each of these options has its own pros and cons. For many would-be entrepreneurs, buying an existing nonfranchise business is the most attractive alternative. But this isn't always true, and it's important to consider all of your options before making such an important investment.

Starting a Business From Scratch

Whatever type of business you'd like to own—retail, service, manufacturing, or product distributorship—you always have the option of starting with a clean slate and creating a brand-new enterprise to your exact specifications. Here are some considerations to be weighed in assessing this option.

The Pros

Relatively low cost. You can typically start a business for less than it would cost to buy one. If the business you're thinking of buying is the least bit profitable, the seller will want money for goodwill: the intangible value that goes beyond the worth of the basic business assets. It represents, for example, the value of a loyal customer base and perhaps a good reputation in the marketplace. By contrast, when you start a business from scratch, not only do you avoid paying for goodwill, but you can assemble the exact assets you think you'll need. Goodwill is almost always overvalued, at least by the seller—for example, if you take on a popular restaurant but your food doesn't measure up to what customers are used to, loyalty will disappear pretty quickly. By contrast, a new restaurant with great food will generate buzz (and its own goodwill) pretty quickly—and you won't have paid for the existing customer base.

The joy of creation. You have the satisfaction of starting from scratch and making the business exactly what you want it to be. The business will have your personality indelibly imprinted in it. And if the business prospers, you'll feel the warm glow of pride.

Control. You'll be the only one to make decisions about how to start and run your business. You won't be obligated to stick with the practices of your predecessor or toe the line for a franchisor.

The Cons

Greater risk. Plunging into the great unknown carries greater risk than buying an existing business that has a good track record. At the beginning, you'll be engaging in an experiment to determine if your concept will work. And even if customers flock to your new enterprise, you'll have to deal with loads of issues such as pricing, hiring employees, setting up business systems, and so on, that would already have been addressed if you bought a going concern.

Difficulty of raising funds. You may have a hard time finding a bank or other lender to give you the funds you need for a business start-up. Lenders are often leery of brand-new enterprises.

Guesswork in making decisions. You'll need to make important business decisions without experience of your own, or the benefit of an existing business structure and possibly even the wisdom of the former owner. For example, how should you price your goods or services? What type of inventory should you maintain? What type of advertising will best support your business? This is the flip side of the positive element of having total control; being responsible for all the decisions means that you must figure everything out yourself.

No existing base of loyal customers or clients. You'll need to find ways to let people know you're around. Then you'll have to painstakingly convert them to loyal customers or clients who not only return to you time and again for your goods or services, but also tell others about you—the best way build your business.

No immediate cash flow. Since you have no ready-made base of customers or clients, it can take time for money to start coming in. And because you may be inexperienced at establishing systems, collecting debts, and managing inventory, it can take an even longer period for the business to start generating a profit.

Finding a suitable location. If location is important to your brand-new business—for example, if you need to be in a high-visibility, high-traffic location—you'll have to spend time and exert effort in finding just the right place to rent. Then comes the chore of negotiating a favorable lease, and possibly the expense of renovating the premises to suit your needs. If there's an existing business that has made a cheap or offbeat location work, you'll probably find this impossible to replicate.

No systems in place. You'll have to set up bookkeeping and accounting systems. How difficult this is will depend on your experience and comfort with tasks like this.

Even though excellent software is available to help you do this yourself with at most a little bit of professional help, it can be a time-draining diversion from running the business.

No employees in place. Unless you're going to be a one-person show, you'll have to find and train competent employees, which can be a more demanding task than you might imagine.

Hooking up with suppliers. With no established relationships, you'll need to seek out reliable and cost-effective suppliers.

Even though the list of negatives might seem long, through hard work and good fortune, you might find that starting a business from scratch will come closer to meeting your needs than the other means of becoming a business owner.

Buying a Franchise

Many people get started in business by buying a franchise from a franchisor. Some of these people are able to make a go of it, but others find the experience to be frustrating, disappointing, and even financially disastrous. In large part, this is because most franchises are overpriced when you figure in all the ongoing fees and costs. For most people who plan to own a business, the franchise route is probably the most problematic. But like the other methods of ownership, there are positive and negative factors for you to weigh.

Pros

Name recognition. A well-run franchisor—using its own money plus advertising fees from franchisees—can pour money into regional and national advertising to help consumers become familiar with the brand name. By becoming a franchisee, you get the benefit of this advertising. If the name has a good reputation, you begin to benefit it from the very first day you open your doors for business.

A precise plan for doing business. Typically, the franchisor will provide you with training and an operations manual. The franchisor will probably help you find a suitable location and order the necessary equipment. And if you're working with a good franchise, you can often count on the franchisor to offer advice if you run into a jam.

Credit is available. Franchisors frequently let you pay the bulk of start-up costs over a period of years, making it unnecessary for you to turn to a bank or other lender for money.

Territorial protection. You may have exclusive rights to a franchised business within a defined geographical area. But increasingly, territorial protections are nonexistent.

Cons

Lots of franchises are junk. Tens of thousands of different franchises are currently for sale. Many of these have little or no name recognition, high fees, and poor prospects. Starting a similar business on your own would be far cheaper and offer better chances of success.

Relatively high costs. Franchisors take money from you in many, many ways, often making it very difficult for owners of even well-known franchises to turn a decent profit. In addition to the basic fee to buy the franchise, you may have to pay the franchisor for required equipment and supplies and for a portion of the advertising pool. Also, you may have to send the franchisor a healthy share of your gross income each month. Franchise fees can often add up to more than 10% of the business's gross monthly income.

Very little flexibility. If you buy a franchise, you wind up marching to someone else's drummer. To the franchisor, it's the franchise way or the highway. If you don't mind taking orders about every detail of the business, being a franchisee may work out fine for you. But many entrepreneurs are independent types who bristle at the regimentation that often goes along with being a franchisee.

Long-term contracts. Buying a franchise almost always means signing a long-term contract in which every clause is tilted strongly in favor of the franchisor. Rarely are you able to negotiate more equitable terms. The franchise contract generally is offered on a take-it-or-leave-it basis.

Hard to escape. If the business doesn't live up to your expectations, it can be difficult to simply walk away, even if you're willing to give up the money invested so far. Not only is it likely that you'll have continuing financial obligations to the franchisor, but selling the business to someone else will be easier said than done. There may be few takers. And even if you find someone who is interested, that person may not be acceptable to the franchisor—who probably has reserved the right to approve or disapprove any sale of a franchise and to make changes in the franchise contract that might make it less desirable to a new buyer.

Given all these factors, it's a good idea to think twice before signing up for the cost and inflexibility of a franchise.

> **TIP**
>
> **Do your homework.** Before signing up for a franchise, get a copy of the proposed franchise agreement and review it carefully. If there are parts you don't understand completely, consult a lawyer. Also, contact a number of current franchisees and find out what they think of working with the franchisor you are considering. All of this information is crucial for your decision making.

Buying an Existing Business

Buying an existing business has its own set of positive and negative features. But you, like many others, may find that on balance, it's a desirable approach—and a goal you can attain with the help of this book.

Pros

No need to reinvent the wheel. An existing business has a history—a track record—so you can tell whether the concept is sound and profitable.

An existing customer base. You have a head start building up a roster of customers or clients—often the hardest part of establishing a business. (But to verify the bright picture the seller is likely to paint about how happy and loyal existing customers are, you'll want to talk to a good-sized sample.)

Immediate cash flow. Acquiring a healthy business usually means there's money flowing in right from the get-go. In the best-case scenario these funds will cover your expenses and leave enough to pay you for your time and effort in running the business.

Seller financing. You probably won't have to scrounge around for funds, other than for the down payment and a modest cash reserve. That's because most small business sellers will let you pay the bulk of the sale price over a period of three to five years.

An existing location. The business may have an established location that's protected by a favorable lease for several years. If so, you can continue operating from the same place. You won't have to reeducate customers about where to find the business, and you won't have to mount a search for suitable quarters.

Expert assistance. Many times, the seller will agree to stick around as an employee or consultant to help you learn the nuances of the business and make the transition easier. And if the seller isn't willing to help out for more than a month or two, you can probably still count on the help of long-time employees who will stay, giving you the benefit of their experience and knowledge. In short, if the transition is correctly managed, you won't be all alone with a new enterprise.

Contracts with suppliers and vendors. The business may have ongoing relationships and contracts with suppliers and vendors—perhaps on favorable terms. Often, you'll be able to benefit from such contracts and not have to form new relationships, which can be a time-consuming ordeal.

Reduced risk of business failure. Statistics show that established businesses are much less likely to fail than businesses started from scratch.

Cons

Using someone else's concept. When you pay a substantial sum for an existing business, you are by definition putting a high value on someone else's business concept. It follows that some of the thrill of creating something on your own will be missing. But it's also true that you'll be free to introduce your own good ideas to the already-successful business model over time. Or, put another way, you'll have plenty of chances to make a good business better.

Relatively high cost. Typically, to get the benefits of buying an existing business, you'll need to pay something beyond the value of the business assets: an intangible called goodwill. You can look at this as the price you pay to reduce the risks inherent in a start-up. It's also the seller's reward for

building a successful business. In business as everywhere else, there's no free lunch.

Possibility of hidden problems. The vast majority of business owners, including those looking to sell their businesses, are honest people. Especially if you patiently and diligently investigate all aspects of the business, the chances are excellent that you'll receive enough solid information to sensibly evaluate its prospects. Still, there's always the possibility that a shady seller will distort or withhold key facts. By following the suggestions in this book and consulting knowledgeable professionals before you buy, you can greatly diminish—but not eliminate—the chances of getting stung by a seller's dishonesty.

Because you are reading this book, you already believe that buying a business is an attractive option. The benefits listed above probably give you more reason to consider it.

The Basics of Buying a Business

Before we get into all the details, here are five basic principles that can help you buy a sound business at a decent price—and become a happy and prosperous business owner.

Understand all the steps in the purchase process. That's what this book is all about: making sure you've engaged in a thorough consideration of the practical and legal steps necessary to find and buy an existing business. Armed with this information, you can confidently take action on all aspects of buying a business, such as finding one that fits your needs, figuring out what it's worth, negotiating the price and payment terms, structuring the deal so as to save on taxes and protect your legal rights, and finding and using professionals to provide advice and review key documents. And you can also avoid the many pitfalls that are all too likely to trip up the naïve or poorly informed buyer.

Know yourself. If you've never owned a business before, you need to think about whether you're temperamentally suited to be a business owner. Are you able to tolerate risk? Deal with the unexpected? Work long and possibly erratic hours? Manage employees? Make important decisions quickly? If any of these things don't sound like you, maybe buying any business isn't the right course of action for you. At the same time, there's no reason to exaggerate the risks of owning a business. As you well know, working for someone is hardly ever risk-free. Companies fold or downsize. Benefits are cut. Working conditions change. So total security is an elusive goal. Because owning a business opens up the possibility of greater personal and financial growth than you can normally expect as someone else's employee, this risk can be well worth taking.

Be patient. At each stage of the purchase process, you want time on your side. Finding the right business to buy can take many months—or even a year or longer. If you try to rush the process, you'll almost surely end up buying a substandard business or

paying too much for a good one. And even after you've found the business of your dreams, you still face the meticulous work of investigating the business thoroughly and then negotiating the terms of your purchase. You can't accomplish these crucial chores overnight. Again, if you act impulsively and without adequate preparation, you are likely to make costly mistakes.

Budget wisely. You want to avoid the discomfort of extreme financial pressures that can lead to bad business decisions and cause hardship for you and your family. So you need to think carefully not just about the purchase price but also about the payment terms. You'll probably wind up buying a business on an installment basis, making monthly payments to the seller. Of course, you'd like to keep the down payment as low as possible. But because a relatively low down payment will mean relatively high monthly payments, this isn't always the best course. Will you be able to make the payments month after month, pay all the other expenses of doing business, and wind up with enough left over to provide adequate income for your family? To give yourself a little cushion, it's best not to sink every last penny into the business—even if that means purchasing a less-ambitious enterprise. What happens if you encounter unexpected expenses? Or if the business goes through a slow patch? Or a lawsuit or other unexpected problem adds to your expenses? You need to keep some money in reserve to ride out such periods.

Understand the limits of professional advice. Using this book, you should be able to personally handle much of the work involved in buying a business, but you may also need or want some professional help. For example, you may want to have an accountant look over the financial records of the business or offer tax-planning advice. Or you may want to have a lawyer draft or review the important legal documents (like the sales agreement and closing papers) that are part of every business purchase. This book alerts you to the times when professional advice can be especially helpful and explains how to work with lawyers and accountants on a cost-effective basis. But we will also remind you that there are limits to the kinds of advice the experts can offer. Most important, no expert—however experienced or well-intentioned—can make the decision on whether you should or shouldn't buy a specific business. That's your call and yours alone. That's not to say you should be a know-it-all. Many factors other than legal and financial concerns can and should influence your decision. You can often gain helpful insight by talking things through with your spouse or domestic partner—or perhaps a friend or relative who has owned a successful business.

We'll return to these suggestions periodically. For now, keeping them in the background, we'll turn to the key steps in buying a business, and then move on to discuss the key legal issues involved in the process. (See Chapter 2.)

Key Steps in Buying a Business

To buy a business on attractive terms, you must thoroughly understand and aggressively deal with a myriad of practical and financial details. To offer just a few examples, you must decide on the type of business you'd like to buy, find the business that will meet your needs, investigate its current situation and future prospects, come up with a workable plan to pay for it, and negotiate a sales agreement. And of course, each of these big steps has numerous smaller steps within it.

Understandably, if you've never bought a business before, thinking about all these tasks may feel overwhelming. But don't worry: Each one of these steps, and more, can be sensibly understood and dealt with when taken one at a time. That's where this book comes in. In the chapters that lie ahead, we'll take you through all the crucial details of the business-buying process. But before we delve into these many details, let's devote this section to understanding the big picture.

Coming Up With a Budget

No matter how eager you are to buy a business, you need to first take stock of your overall financial picture. Your enthusiasm for becoming a business owner can quickly turn into misery if you get in over your head. So plan to deal with dollar-and-cents realities right from the start.

The most likely scenario is that you'll buy a business on an installment basis. Typically, you'll make a substantial down payment to the seller and then pay the balance in monthly installments over a number of years. So, you first need to figure out where you'll get the down payment. Let's say you plan to take it from savings. Are you prepared to put every last cent of your savings into the business? That's probably a bad idea. It's far better to keep a comfortable reserve so you can deal with emergency expenses and not be forced to search frantically for money to meet unexpected bills.

If instead of raiding your savings for the down payment you plan to borrow the money, you must also use caution. Remember that you'll need to pay back the lender—and you may be making these payments at the same time you're making monthly installment payments to the seller. Where will all this money come from?

Looking beyond the down payment and the installment payments, you'll need to expect the unexpected: business expenses that perversely seem to crop up in periods when business income is at a low ebb. How will you deal with such expenses? Will you wind up even deeper in debt?

You also need to be clear on whether you're counting on the business to produce profits that you can use to pay for personal expenses: the mortgage on your home, the lease payments on your new car, the weekly grocery bills. If there's a second earner in your household, you're getting income checks from a trust fund, or you have substantial savings, this won't be a problem. But if you're expecting your business to immediately give you the wherewithal to cover personal living expenses each month, you need to consider the possibility that income from the business won't be as substantial as you think it will be.

If you're young and have no dependents and little or no debt, you can afford to take on more risk. But if loved ones are looking to you to bring home the bacon, you need to be a lot more cautious. This can translate into buying a less-expensive business, while keeping open the option of trading up to something grander when you're in a stronger financial position.

Perhaps you're not accustomed to thinking in broad financial terms. In that case, it can pay to talk matters over with an accountant—preferably one who thinks conservatively. As an entrepreneur, you can't afford to be wholly averse to risk. But you do need a dose of financial realism to prevent you from putting yourself into a painful financial bind.

Deciding on a Business and Finding It

The most time-consuming and frustrating part of buying a business may be your search for the right business to buy. Not that there's shortage of businesses on the market. In fact, it's likely that you will find many businesses up for sale that broadly fit your criteria. The key is to understand exactly what type of business you're looking for and then find an excellent one. Be patient. You can quickly buy a bad or merely average business. Buying an excellent one takes more time. It may take you a year or two of active searching to find a business with excellent prospects that you really want to own. So don't get discouraged if an attractive business doesn't pop up on your radar right away. And above all, don't let your own impatience cause you to make a poor decision.

In searching for a business to buy, it's essential to know early in the game what you want. You have surely heard the saying, "If you don't know where you're going, you probably won't get there." The business-buying corollary goes like this: If you don't know what you're looking for, you probably won't find it. You may already have a very clear idea of exactly the business you want. Especially if you've worked in the field for an extended period, you may even be able to describe it in detail. But if you're pretty sure that you want to buy a business but don't know what type, you'll need to narrow it down and then weigh the positive and negative features of the types of businesses that you might consider buying.

For starters, here are some questions to consider.

Are you mainly interested in owning a retail business, a service business, a distributorship, or a light manufacturing business? Each has its pros and cons. But on balance, well-designed service businesses often offer the best prospects of success, because it's usually easier to start or purchase them for a reasonable amount, and, once in operation, it's easier to establish and maintain robust profit margins.

What types of products or services are on your short list? Within the retail field, you may prefer dealing with food rather than bicycles, or vice versa. In the service arena, you may be interested in acquiring a landscaping business rather than a company that installs computer networks. Trust your intuition here. Only you can know what types of enterprises will fit you like a glove and which will feel like a handcuff.

What kinds of businesses would be a good match for your skills and experience and would give you pleasure? For example, if you're an avid sailor, you might be looking for a harbor-side business that sells, rents, and services small sailboats. Helping new sailors get started or an experienced one enjoy his or her hobby may be both financially and emotionally rewarding. Or, if you majored in art history and are an amateur artist, owning a workshop catering to amateur and professional local artists, complete with classes and exhibit space, might be right up your alley. Try for a niche that fits your personality and skills. But don't let your attraction to a particular activity, be it birds, bicycles, or begonias, drive all your decision making. You still need to find a business that is, or can quickly become, a profitable one.

The Bottom Line

Many people are attracted to retail or food service businesses—stores and restaurants, in particular. But the reality is that some service businesses (teaching teenagers to pass SAT exams, for example) have profit margins approaching 100% because they have almost no overhead. By contrast, many retail businesses reap almost no profits after overhead. In short, it's sometimes better to be the plumber than to sell tubs and showers.

Is physical location an issue? For any number of reasons, you may want to continue living in your current community. For example, your spouse may not want to give up his or her good job, or perhaps you're active in local civic affairs or have deep roots in your town. By contrast, if you're more flexible and can move anywhere in the country or perhaps anywhere within a certain region, this obviously will open up many more business possibilities. Figure this out first, and then you can narrow or broaden your search accordingly.

Realistically, how much can you afford to invest? It's important to start with a tight estimate of how much you can comfortably invest in a business. Still, because most businesses are bought largely or at least substantially on credit, you may be able to afford a bigger business than you might think. For example, to take over a $200,000

business, you may be able make a 10% down payment ($20,000) and pay the balance in installments over a five-year period using the profits the business generates.

On the other hand, you don't want to use every last cent of your savings. Keep something in reserve in case the business hits a rough patch.

Once you've thought through and answered these questions, you'll be in good position to start looking. In Chapter 4, you'll find practical suggestions for conducting your search.

Analyzing the Seller's Data

Even when you find a business that appears to have the right ingredients, you'll want to learn as much as possible about its history before making a commitment to buy it. Start by examining preliminary financial data from the seller—tax returns and balance sheets, for example—and then, if the business has some real possibilities, dig deeper. At that point, especially if you've never owned a business before, you might consider hiring a CPA or small business consultant to help you crunch and understand the numbers.

RELATED TOPIC

Chapters 4 and 5 have suggestions for investigating a business in depth, and Chapter 6 explains how to find and work with professionals.

Figuring Out What a Business Is Worth

In 1901, when Andrew Carnegie offered to sell his huge steel operations to J.P. Morgan, Morgan immediately asked, "How much?" Carnegie promptly picked up a napkin and wrote "$480 million" (perhaps $10 billion in today's dollars). Morgan said yes and the sale was made. Wow! How efficient.

Unfortunately, a quick agreement to a number written on a napkin won't be a good approach for you. In fact, chances are that before you get too far down the road in your discussions with the seller, you will need to devote a considerable amount of time and thought to the value of any business that you're considering buying. And this is true even if you think that you already have a ballpark idea of what the business is worth—either from your own experience in similar businesses, from talking to others in the industry, or from articles you've read in trade publications. Unless you've worked in a managerial capacity for the specific business you're considering, your seat-of-the-pants notion of the business's value may be wide of the mark. At the very least, you'll want to refine it based on a convincing method that you can use later in your negotiations with the seller.

If possible, it's advantageous to have a sense of what the business is worth before you even begin negotiating with the seller. That way, you'll know whether the price the owner has set is in a range that you'd even consider. If the seller has set the price way too high, you may decide that the gap between what you think the business is worth and what the seller thinks is simply too great to justify your spending more time in negotiations. Similarly, if you haven't done your homework and your opening offer is much lower than the low end of the business's value, the seller may not take you to be a serious buyer, and you may lose a good opportunity for the wrong reasons.

Valuing a business is both an art and a science. As you'll learn in Chapter 5, there are several textbook methods you can use: valuing the assets, basing the price on comparable sales, calculating return on investment, or using an industry formula based on sales or units. Whatever valuation approach you employ (and it's more likely you'll combine approaches), you'll probably end up with a range of values rather than one absolute number. And while it's essential to be able to defend the price that you offer to pay, in the last analysis, the number you name won't be nearly as meaningful as the one a willing seller agrees to accept.

Negotiating the Deal

When you find a likely business, even if you and the seller seem to come to a quick and enthusiastic meeting of the minds, there will be plenty of chances for the deal to fall apart as the details are worked out. For one thing, you'll be digging deeper into the business and learning more about what can be dozens of nitty-gritty operating issues. In addition, you'll be making sure you don't inadvertently assume liability for hidden problems, including lawsuits, toxics, and tax issues.

Because you'll probably want to pay the sale price in installments, you'll also need to convince the seller that you're creditworthy and have the necessary entrepreneurial skills and personal attributes to make a success of the purchase.

Obviously, it will take time to complete these steps. In addition, there will be many other legal and practical details to be worked out, including:

- **Structure of the sale.** Will you be buying the business entity (the partnership, corporation, or LLC) or just its assets?

- **Assets being transferred.** Will the seller keep some assets that are currently part of the business—accounts receivable, for example, or high-tech equipment?

- **Payment terms.** You probably won't pay the full purchase price in cash up front. But how much will you put down? And what payment terms and interest rate will the seller agree to?

- **Seller protection.** What kind of security interest will you give the seller to protect the seller if you stop making payments? For example, will you agree to give the seller a lien on your home as well as the business assets?

- **Buyer protection.** If the seller misrepresents some important details about the business or fails to take

care of existing business debts as promised, what legal recourse will you have to unwind the deal or get fair compensation?

- **Seller warranties.** What warranties will the seller make about the condition of the business or its assets? For example, will the seller guarantee that no environmental hazards lurk within the business premises? If hazards are found, will the seller be able to pay the cost of the clean-up?

- **Buyer warranties.** What warranties will you make? For example, until the seller has been paid off, will you be asked to agree to keep the business equipment in good shape, to maintain the inventory at presale levels, and to continue to operate from the existing location?

- **Liabilities.** How will you and the seller handle current business debts? Will responsibility for some current debts (and even potential lawsuits) be transferred to you? Or will the seller agree to stay liable for all presale obligations? And on the flip side, will you be adequately protected from future debts and lawsuits?

- **Ongoing connection to the business.** Will the seller perform any services for the business in the future? If so, for how long, and how will the seller be compensated? Will the seller be an employee or an independent contractor?

- **Ability to compete.** Will the seller be allowed to immediately invest in, own, or work for a similar business? If the seller will be restricted, how stringent will the restrictions be, and how long will they last? Obviously, if the seller is very elderly or ill, or is planning a move out of the area, this won't be a major issue. Conversely if the seller wants to stay active in a similar business or perhaps even sell just part of the enterprise, negotiating right-to-compete issues will be a crucial part of striking a deal.

These are all questions that will be very important in your negotiations, and this is just an outline. Later chapters provide the information and forms you need to negotiate the deal: Chapter 2 provides an overview of the legal issues. Chapters 8 ("Structuring Your Purchase"), 9 ("The Investigation Stage"), and 10 ("Drafting a Letter of Intent") will help you work toward a sales agreement.

Signing a Sales Agreement

The most important legal document used in the purchase of a business is a sales agreement. Correctly drafted, this legal contract should capture all the details of the sale. This, in turn, allows the seller to transfer the business entity or its assets to you smoothly on a specified date (called the closing). And if a dispute arises before or after the closing, the clear terms of your sales agreement will be the first place you'll look in an effort to resolve it.

Because the sales agreement is so crucial in the sale of your business, Part 3 of this book—Chapters 11 through 17—is devoted to a clause-by-clause analysis of the sample agreement we provide. Part 4 (Chapters 18 through 20) covers other important sales documents, including promissory notes. But before you draft and sign a sales agreement and related documents, it's essential that you carefully read the intervening chapters so that you understand the legal and practical import of every term and are sure that nothing significant has been left out.

Closing Your Purchase

After the sales agreement is signed, there's one more step before the business is actually transferred to you. This takes place at a meeting (called the closing) at which you pay the sale price, or at least the agreed-upon down payment, and sign documents such as a promissory note and security agreement. In exchange, the seller signs stock certificates or LLC documents (if an entity sale), or a bill of sale for the business assets (if an asset sale), plus all the other paperwork needed to turn ownership over to you. Chapter 21 provides details on the closing, including how to prepare for it and handle any last-minute problems that may occur.

The checklist below reiterates the main steps in buying a business. The rest of the book follows up on each of those major steps and gives you the details that will help you make the right purchase at the right price.

Checklist of Steps in Buying a Business

- ☐ Determine the kind of business you're looking for.
- ☐ Find the right business.
- ☐ Analyze the seller's data.
- ☐ Figure out what the business is worth— or perhaps a range of reasonable values.
- ☐ Negotiate a deal.
- ☐ Create and sign a sales agreement.
- ☐ Get ready for closing.

2

The Key Legal Issues in Buying a Business

B uying a business is one big legal transaction, made up of a whole slew of discrete legal issues. You'll need to master all these subsidiary legal issues to get the larger legal transaction right.

If you don't, you risk not getting all the benefits that you bargained for. For example, if the seller is going to remain responsible for some or all of the business's past debts and liabilities, you want to make sure you have legal recourse against the seller if he or she fails to pay creditors as agreed. And typically you'll want the seller to agree not to compete with the business once you become its owner. To get these and many other legal protections, you'll need to carefully craft a sales agreement and other legal documents. This chapter will introduce the key legal measures you can take to protect your financial interests throughout the sales process.

RELATED TOPIC

Later chapters will tell you more about how to deal with legal issues. You'll find clause-by-clause details of a sales agreement in Chapters 11 through 17 and examples of other necessary legal documents in Chapters 18 through 20.

SEE AN EXPERT

This book provides the information you'll need to handle all or most essential legal tasks yourself. But especially when lots of money is involved, it usually makes sense to have a lawyer review your handiwork. In addition, we'll alert you here to legally fraught or tricky situations in which professional help is especially important. For an overview of specific ways that lawyers can help with legal issues, see Chapter 6.

Understand the Differences Between Buying a Business Entity and Buying Just Its Assets

Any business you're considering buying is probably being operated as either a sole proprietorship, a partnership, a corporation, or a limited liability company (LLC). If a business is legally organized as a corporation or LLC, there are, broadly speaking, two principal ways to structure the purchase. The first method is to buy the corporate or LLC entity. The second method is to buy all or most of the entity's assets and let the seller hold on to the entity.

SKIP AHEAD

If you'll purchase a sole proprietorship or a partnership, you can skip this chapter. That's because with a sole proprietorship, there's no separate legal entity to buy; by definition, the seller, as the sole proprietor, will be selling just business assets. And although it's theoretically possible to buy a partnership by substituting new partners for old, a sale of a partnership is also almost always structured as an asset sale.

The importance of understanding the differences between asset and entity sales will come up repeatedly in this book. It affects everything from how you write off the sale price on your tax return, to liability issues and how ownership will be transferred. So although this material is seriously short on sex appeal, you'll want to master it.

How an Entity Sale Works

Let's assume that the business you're considering is either a corporation called Protobiz Inc., or an LLC called Old Stuff LLC. Here's how an entity sale will work. If you're buying Protobiz, a corporation, the shareholders will sell you all their stock in Protobiz Inc. In that case, you'll become Protobiz's owner and will have the right to control all the assets the corporation owns: furniture, fixtures, equipment, inventory, intellectual property, and so on. The corporation, under your ownership, will remain responsible for the debts and other liabilities of the business. Likewise, if you're buying Old Stuff LLC, the members of the company will sell you their membership interests, making you the owner of the LLC itself—again, with the right to control all its assets. The LLC, under your ownership, will remain responsible for the debts and other liabilities of the business.

How an Asset Sale Works

Now let's assume that you're considering buying the assets of Protobiz Inc., or an LLC called Old Stuff LLC rather than either entity. Here's how an asset sale will work. If you're buying the assets of Protobiz, the shareholders will arrange to have the corporation sell you all or most Protobiz Inc., assets, but not the corporation itself. That means the existing shareholders will continue to own what amounts to nothing more than the Protobiz corporate shell. The corporation will have no (or few) assets other than the promissory note you sign for the balance of the purchase price.

Similarly, if you decide to buy the assets of Old Stuff LLC, the company's members will agree to have Old Stuff LLC sell you all or most of the company's assets. The LLC members will continue to own the LLC shell. If the LLC sells its assets to you, its only remaining asset will probably be the promissory note you sign. When you buy the assets of the LLC, you won't automatically become responsible for the debts and other liabilities of the business, but you may agree to assume liability for at least some of them.

When you buy the assets of a corporation or LLC, you don't automatically become responsible for the debts and other liabilities of the business. You may, however, agree to assume liability for at least some of them as part of the sale contract.

It's important to understand that the assets that an entity sells to you may not be limited to physical property. You can acquire the entity's intangible assets as well, such as the company's goodwill and its trademark.

Why Sellers Usually Prefer Entity Sales, and Buyers Asset Sales

Why is the legal distinction between an asset or entity sale important if the result under either approach is that you end up owning your business? One important reason is that how your transaction is structured will affect how you write off the purchase price on your tax returns, and how the seller gets taxed. As you'll see in Chapter 3, you'll typically be able to begin getting depreciation benefits sooner if you acquire only the assets than if you buy the corporate entity or LLC. The flip side is that the seller will usually fare better from a tax standpoint selling the entity rather than its assets, because the seller will pay tax at the low long-term capital gain rate. By contrast, in an asset sale, part of the seller's tax bill may be computed at the ordinary income rate, which is higher. Sellers are especially skittish about using an asset sale for a C corporation, since they face the distasteful risk of double taxation.

Incidentally, this tax benefits issue is often resolved by a compromise between the seller and the buyer that's reflected in the sale price or the terms of payment. For example, you may prefer to buy a business on an asset basis so you can immediately begin to get tax benefits. The seller may have set the selling price at $500,000 based on the expectation of an entity sale and may face an additional $40,000 in taxes if there's an asset sale. To compensate, the two of you may agree to an asset sale, with an adjusted sale price of $520,000—a kind of middle ground.

Another reason why you, as a buyer, might prefer an asset sale is that it gives you the valuable opportunity to pick and choose among the assets you'll acquire. You'd like to negotiate a good deal for assets you want, leaving behind (and not paying for) those that aren't valuable to you.

Finally, the treatment of existing debts and other liabilities of the business is very different in entity and asset sales. Typically in an asset sale, you're not going to be responsible for existing debts of the business, unless you agree to accept responsibility. By contrast, in an entity sale, it's assumed that all the liabilities go along with the sale—though to make the deal happen, the shareholders or LLC members who are selling may agree to be responsible for some specified liabilities, such as a recent bank loan.

But again, as mentioned above, what's legally and financially best for you may not be best for the seller, who would probably find it most advantageous to transfer the entire corporation or LLC entity to you. That way, the seller gets favorable tax treatment, is less likely to have to keep any undesirable assets of the business, and shouldn't have to worry about paying existing business debts and liabilities. Still, even where your interests diverge, it may turn out that you have more clout than the seller when it comes to setting the terms of the deal, and you may be able to insist on an asset sale. This might be true, for example, if the business has been on the market a long time and the seller is anxious to unload it. Or you may be willing to make an unusually large down payment.

Still, in some situations, you may decide not to strenuously resist buying a complete entity rather than only its assets. This can be especially true, for example, if the business is highly sought after, putting the seller in a very strong bargaining position. Similarly, you may be quite willing to go along with an entity sale if the corporation or LLC has a valuable lease for the space where it does business, and the lease can't be assigned to you. By buying the corporation or LLC, the entity continues to be the tenant, so you get the benefit of the lease. (This won't always work, since some landlords state in the lease that a change in ownership of the entity will be treated as a forbidden transfer of the lease and cause a termination of the lease contract.) You'll learn more on this subject in Chapter 8. For now, just be aware that an entity sale can sometimes be the most practical choice even if it doesn't seem that way on the surface.

TIP

Not all entity sales are exactly the same. Important details may differ. For example, in buying a corporation or an LLC as an entity, you and the seller may agree that some assets will be transferred to the seller before the closing. You and the seller may also agree that the seller will assume personal responsibility for some of the existing debts of the business.

Consider Forming a Corporation or LLC to Buy the Business

If you're not buying a company that's already organized as a corporation or an LLC, you might consider creating one of your own, so you can have an entity to buy, own, and run the business. Of course, if you already have a corporation or LLC and that existing entity is buying the assets of another business, creating a new entity won't be necessary.

But let's say you're buying the assets of a business that's organized as a sole proprietorship or partnership and you don't now have a corporation or LLC. In that case, you face the same concerns as anyone starting a new business from scratch. If you alone own the business, you'll be a sole proprietor and have unlimited personal liability on all business debts, as well as any court judgments that are entered against the business. Likewise, if you and one or more other people own the business, you'll have a partnership and each of you will have unlimited personal liability for business debts and business-related court judgments. This means that with either a sole proprietorship or partnership, your personal bank accounts, your investments, and even your home will be at risk for business debts.

By contrast, if you form a corporation or LLC to own and run the business, you'll reduce the scope of your personal liability and that of your co-owners. For example, you won't be personally liable for the actions of employees or for business loans that you didn't personally guarantee. Because the cost of creating a corporation or LLC is fairly low and the paperwork burdens are minimal—especially with an LLC—many small businesses choose to set up one of these limited liability entities. Before you do, though, you should also become familiar with how taxes are computed and learn whether there are other benefits available that make a corporation or LLC an attractive choice.

TIP

You can safely defer your decision on whether or not to form a corporation or LLC. You can, for example, negotiate a deal for the purchase of assets and then form the entity before you sign a sales agreement. Or you can even wait until after the closing, create a corporation or LLC at that time, and then transfer the assets to the new entity. But while timing is not crucial, it does pay to begin considering this issue early on.

RESOURCE

For an in-depth look at the pros and cons of the various types of business entities: see *Legal Guide for Starting & Running a Small Business*, by Fred S. Steingold (Nolo).

Be Clear on What You'll Buy and What the Seller Will Keep

You and the seller may agree to an asset sale. (This will always be true when you purchase a sole proprietorship or partnership. It may

or may not be the case when you purchase a business that's run as a corporation or LLC.) In an asset sale, you'll want the sales agreement to state very clearly all of the assets you're buying. This may seem obvious, but a surprising number of sales agreements simply say the seller is selling, and the buyer is buying, "all the assets of the XYZ business." Including a specific list in the sales agreement is good common sense even if the seller plans to transfer every last asset to you. But a list is especially important if the seller will be keeping some of the assets, such as cash, accounts receivable, or perhaps even a desk and chair the seller has grown attached to. Or maybe the seller is going to license to you—rather than sell to you—some item of intellectual property like a proprietary formula, copyright, or patent.

Again, the point is that to avoid future arguments, you need to be specific in the sales agreement about what's being sold and what's not. Otherwise, you may get into a legal fight later over whether something as seemingly trivial as the business's phone number or trade name belongs to you or the seller. Or you might find yourself taking on responsibility for things you'd like to exclude, such as potential lawsuits or liability for later-discovered toxic damage.

If you're buying the seller's corporate or LLC entity, rather than the assets of the business, you usually don't have to worry about specifying in the sales agreement the assets being sold. By definition, everything the corporation or LLC owns that isn't specifically excluded will be transferred as part of the sale. But often there are some corporate assets that you and the seller agree won't be included in the sale. For example, the corporation may own the computer the seller uses, which is loaded with programs and data which the seller would like to keep. If you buy the corporate stock, the computer will automatically be transferred as part of the sale. To prevent that from happening, the seller will need to transfer the computer—and, in some instances, the software and information it contains—from the corporation to himself or herself before the closing of the sale. The sales agreement should make clear that the computer—and any other items the seller is keeping—won't be owned by the corporation when the stock is transferred to you.

Likewise, the sales agreement for an entity sale should exclude any items that the seller personally owns that are present on the business premises. Since personal items were never owned by the business entity in the first place, this may appear to be unnecessary. But you as the buyer may not otherwise know that the original Jackson Pollock painting on the seller's office wall and the handsome Oriental rug in the conference room are the seller's personal treasures and not owned by the business. To avoid a possible misunderstanding, a careful seller should mention these items in discussions with you and make sure they're specifically called out as exclusions in any listing of the property the company owns.

RELATED TOPIC

Chapter 12 helps you craft appropriate language in your sales agreement that clearly spells out what's being sold and what's not.

Pay Special Attention to the Transfer of Intellectual Property

A substantial number of small businesses own intellectual property—a legal term that covers copyrights, trademarks, patents, and trade secrets. Things that the seller or an employee has invented or material they've written are considered intellectual property and can be the most valuable asset that a business owns—even more valuable than tangible assets like goods or buildings. If a business has built a solid reputation for the high quality of its services or goods, then the business or product name will have positive associations among existing customers. If you're buying that business, you'll want to get the benefit of the reservoir of goodwill, knowing it will help ensure that current customers not only return, but also that they'll recommend the products and services to others.

TIP

Get the customer list. For most run-of-the-mill businesses, the customer list may be the most important asset you buy. It also may be considered a trade secret, so make sure the sales agreement says that you have the right to the entire customer database. (The noncompete clause could also state that the seller can't use the customer list after the sale.)

In preparing the sales agreement, you need to be clear about how intellectual property will be dealt with. In some cases, it may be appropriate for the seller to retain legal ownership of intellectual property but license you to use it. Let's say the seller owns a patent on a manufacturing process. You and the seller can agree that the seller will continue to own the patent, but that you'll have a license to use it—and that you will pay the seller a royalty fee for each item you make using the patented process. In other situations, the reverse may be the way to go: The seller can transfer the intellectual property to you but receive back a license to use it. So you might become the owner of the patent for the manufacturing process, but permit the seller to use the process; here, the seller would be paying you the royalty fee. Chapters 12 and 19 have more information about a business's intellectual property, including the type of paperwork you'd use to make agreements about the use of intellectual property.

SEE AN EXPERT

Intellectual property law is a legal specialty. Relatively few business lawyers have extensive training and experience in this field. If highly valuable intellectual property will be among the assets you're buying, consider consulting an intellectual property specialist for advice.

Know the Legal Consequences of Not Making Installment Payments on Time

Usually, when a small business changes hands, the seller doesn't receive the purchase price in one lump sum. Cash deals do occur—especially where the buyer is a larger corporation or can get third-party financing—but more typically, the buyer makes a down payment and gives the seller a promissory note for the balance. The promissory note usually sets up a schedule of payments to be made over a period of time, such as three or five years, with the buyer also agreeing to pay interest on the unpaid balance. This is called an installment sale.

With such arrangements, there's at least some risk that the buyer won't come through with all the required payments. How concerned a seller is about the possibility that you, the buyer, might default on the promissory note will probably be related to two things: whether the business itself is healthy, and what your management and credit record is. If the business is thriving and you're an experienced businessperson with good credit, the seller will probably feel reasonably confident that you'll pay on time and that all the money will be paid in the end. If your history isn't that great, or if the business is in trouble, the risk of default increases. Savvy sellers typically reduce their risk by insisting on selling to someone who is financially strong, has a good credit record, and has a proven record of entrepreneurial competence, ideally in the same field.

But no matter what the condition of the buyer, the reality is that the seller will be looking at protecting his or her own interests in case you default. The negotiations between you and the seller about what's being sold, and the price and terms of the sale, are primarily business, and not legal, matters. But when you start to put your deal in writing, the seller will want to build in legal protections, which you'll need to look at and understand the risks to you, your family, and perhaps even your guarantors.

Here are some common techniques that sellers use to reduce their financial risks:

- Getting a substantial down payment. The seller knows that a buyer with a good chunk of money already invested in the business has a powerful incentive to keep the business alive and thriving, and to pay off the promissory note.
- Having the promissory note cosigned by the buyer's spouse and possibly guaranteed by a parent, friend, or investor who's clearly financially solvent. When a second (perhaps wealthier) person is standing behind the buyer's promise to pay, it's much more likely that the seller will eventually receive the full sale price for the business.
- Getting the buyer to give a first or, more likely, a second mortgage or deed of trust on real estate the buyer owns that contains enough equity to cover the amount outstanding on the promissory note. Yes, that could mean your house!
- Having the buyer sign a security agreement allowing the seller to take back the business assets if payments aren't made.
- If the business operates from rented space, seeking the right to take back the lease as well so the seller can get back into business if necessary at the same location.

The seller's interest in protecting against your default may be understandable, but now let's look at the risks to which you're subjecting yourself—and possibly your family members and friends as well.

For example, if you personally sign the promissory note or guarantee its payment, you put your personal assets at risk if your business runs into financial trouble and doesn't produce enough income to meet the monthly payments. And adding your spouse as a signer or guarantor puts at risk the personal assets that you jointly own. Pledging your house as security means that if the business goes bad, you may lose your home. You need to figure, as best you're able, how risky the business is and how your family and friends will fare if the business takes a turn for the worse.

Sellers almost always want you to be personally liable for the sales price. You'll pretty much have to go along in order to do the deal. Fortunately, other protections that the seller might also want are subject to negotiation. For example, if you're wealthy and have a superior credit record, the seller may be less insistent on having you agree to more burdensome protections such as having your spouse cosign the promissory note or pledging your house as security for the sale price.

Assure That There Are No Liens on Business Assets

It's possible that either the seller of the business that you're buying, or the business itself, may owe money to another person or business. If so, it's likely that the creditor has established a lien on assets of the business. (A lien is a security interest in property—either real property or equipment or other business property.) If there's a lien on business property and the seller or the business fails to pay the debt, the creditor will have the legal right to seize and sell those assets. You'd hate to pay the seller for two trucks and a forklift, only to have them snatched away from you by a creditor whose debt the seller failed to pay or disclose. In short, it's important to not just take the seller's word about debts, but also to carefully check for undisclosed liens on the business assets.

Fortunately, it's easy to check for liens. Establishing a legally enforceable lien on property (other than real estate) requires that the lien holder file papers at a designated state office, such as the secretary of

state's office, following rules established by the Uniform Commercial Code (UCC). For a nominal fee, the filing office will search its records to see whether there are any UCC liens on the assets you're buying. If any liens do surface, you'll want to have the seller pay off the debts and then have the creditors notify the filing office that the liens have been canceled.

In addition, a handful of states still have laws called "bulk sales laws" that are intended to protect creditors when a business is sold. Where such laws are still on the books, they generally apply to the sale of retail businesses. If the business you're buying is in such a state and is covered by its bulk sales law, you'll need to notify creditors before the sale takes place or get an appropriate sworn statement from the seller, as explained in Chapter 14. Otherwise, business creditors may later surface and claim the right to seize certain assets,

Protect Yourself From Competition by the Seller

When you're buying a business, one nightmare scenario is that after the deal is completed, the seller begins competing with the business you've just bought—and your profitability is seriously affected. Of course, this isn't always a major worry. For example, the seller may be elderly, seriously ill, or subject to other circumstances that make it clear that his or her entrepreneurial days are over. But in most other cases, the possibility that the seller may start a competing business or go to work for a competitor is a legitimate concern. This means you'll want to structure the deal to limit the seller's ability to compete with you in the same field.

TIP

Don't take the seller's word that he or she is retiring. Many sellers will swear that they plan to retire for good. But a year later, lots of these same people get bored with golf and bridge games and want to get back into business. If they do—and if you don't have a strong noncompete agreement—they're likely to try to reenter the field they already know.

The best way to deal with the issue of competition is to ask the seller to sign a covenant not to compete (also called a non-compete agreement) that covers a period of years after the sale. Depending on the type of business you're buying, the covenant might limit the seller's competitive activity only in a certain geographic area. But in other instances—a publishing venture or an Internet-based business, for example—the covenant not to compete could prevent the seller from engaging in a similar business anywhere in the United States or, in rare instances, even worldwide.

The covenant not to compete can either be included in the sales agreement or consist of a separate document that's simply referred to in the sales agreement. How broadly the restrictions are worded is a matter to be negotiated between you and the seller. A seller who's retiring or going into a completely different line of work won't care much about how broadly the covenant not to compete is written. By contrast, a seller who may want to do something in the same or a closely related field in the future will look closely at how "competitive" activities are defined. For example, someone selling you a bagel store may never plan to set foot in a bagel shop again, but may want to keep open the possibility of investing in some other food-related business, starting a restaurant, or opening a catering firm.

Covenants not to compete are discussed in greater detail later in this book. Chapter 11 includes appropriate sales agreement language and Chapter 15 includes the covenant language.

Limit Your Legal Liability for Past Obligations of the Business

In addition to checking for liens on business property, you'll also want your new business to be free from old obligations that may not be secured by liens—that is, debts and other liabilities that the seller incurred. There are several kinds of liabilities you should look out for when you're studying a business:

- The business may owe money to a bank or other commercial lender.
- The business may owe money to a supplier or to a service company.
- The business may have unfulfilled contractual obligations.

- The business may owe money to someone who's been injured or whose property has been damaged by the negligence of the business.
- The business may have potential liability for injuries or damages in the form of pending lawsuits or lawsuits that may be filed later.

Whether you take on the obligations of the business will depend primarily on whether you buy the business entity or just its assets—as well as on the language you put in your sales agreement. Chapter 14 has more about liability issues and sales agreements.

The Liability Rules for Buyers

The basic rule is that after the sale of a business entity—a corporation, an LLC, or a partnership–the entity continues to be responsible for past liabilities. This means that if you buy an entity, you'll have to continue paying off the debts that the business has at the time you purchase it. By contrast, if you buy the assets of a business rather than the entity itself, you won't be responsible for old liabilities; the seller will keep them. (Sales of sole proprietorships are always asset sales. But as explained earlier, if you buy a business that's currently being run now as a corporation, a limited liability company, or a partnership, your purchase can be structured as either an asset sale or an entity sale.)

Even in an asset sale, it's possible to get stuck with old obligations of the business. Here's how that could happen.

There's an existing lien on business assets. A bank, a supplier, or some other creditor may have placed a UCC lien on business assets as security for a business debt. If the creditor doesn't release the lien at or before closing, you'll need to pay the debt or face the risk that the creditor will seize the assets to satisfy the debt.

The seller failed to comply with the bulk sales law. A handful of states still have bulk sales laws that apply primarily to the sale of a retail business. These laws require that creditors be notified before the business is sold. If the bulk sales requirements are not met, you face the possible loss of the assets if the creditor isn't paid. The bulk sales laws— and how to deal with them—are explained in more detail in Chapters 8 and 19.

Your business is subject to successor liability. This legal quirk applies primarily to someone who buys a manufacturing business—a rarity among small businesses. But if you are considering buying such a business, know that some states recognize a legal doctrine called "successor liability." If so, then in certain circumstances, even in an asset sale, you may be financially responsible if someone is injured by a product that was manufactured before you took over the assets. So if you buy a manufacturing business, you'll want to deal with this risk by getting appropriate insurance and having the seller agree to indemnify (protect) you from injury claims.

The seller left behind some toxic wastes. A gas station or dry cleaner may have caused environmental harm—knowingly or unknowingly—in, under, or around the business site, that you'll be expected to deal with when it's discovered. And in asbestos cases, lawyers will often go after everyone involved in the construction that included asbestos—including, for example, the current owner of a roofing company that installed a roof 40 years ago. Be extremely careful to include in your sales agreement a clause stating that the seller will indemnify you for any harm of this nature.

Ways to Deal With Past Liabilities

Whether you're buying an entity or its assets, you'll want to get as much information as you can about the business's obligations. This lets you evaluate the amount of risk you're exposing yourself to. Then you can negotiate with the seller over how those liabilities—actual or potential—will be handled. The seller may agree to remain responsible for some or all business liabilities, even in an entity sale—and your discussions may even result in an adjustment of the sale price. But a seller's commitment to stand behind business liabilities will work only if the seller has deep pockets. A promise to pay may be meaningless if the seller lacks the cash to make good on the promise because, in many

instances, the person with the lien or legal claim can then proceed against you.

Your arrangements with the seller about how to deal with past debts should be included in your sales agreement. That all-important document may say, for example, that the seller—and perhaps certain well-heeled guarantors as well—will be legally responsible for debts and obligations that arose before the closing, and that you'll be responsible for all debts and obligations that arise afterwards. These commitments can be accompanied by indemnification language in which, for example, the seller agrees to handle any lawsuit for past debts, and you agree to handle any lawsuit for future liabilities.

 TIP

Do a careful assessment of potential liabilities. Liens are easy to find because you can check on them quickly and easily. But for manufacturing businesses, those located in old industrial areas, or businesses that deal with toxic substances, you need to be more thorough. Guarantees by the seller are fine, but to be safe, you should also take soil samples and do whatever else is necessary to protect yourself.

If either the seller or your business is a corporation or LLC, you need to consider whether the individual owners (old or new) are personally agreeing to protect the other party from liability. Remember the general principle that a corporation or LLC is legally separate from the people who own it. An indemnification signed by a corporation or LLC doesn't personally bind the owners of the entity. The owners themselves must sign if they're to be held liable.

> **EXAMPLE:** Evelyn is buying the assets of The Pet Stop LLC, a limited liability company owned by Bill and Marvin. In the sales contract, the LLC agrees that it will indemnify, defend, and hold Evelyn harmless from any debts or claims arising in the period before the closing of the sale. Similarly, Evelyn agrees that she will indemnify, defend, and hold The Pet Stop LLC harmless from and against any debts or claims that arise after the closing. Wisely, Evelyn insists that Bill and Marvin personally join in the indemnification so that she has another place to turn for protection if the LLC becomes insolvent.

Sometimes, the simple formula for past and future debts needs to be tweaked slightly to fit the situation. In the pet supply example, suppose that The Pet Stop LLC is expecting a bill for $7,500 from a company that sells pet food to the store. If the parties have agreed that Evelyn will be responsible for paying that bill, the sales contract will need to refer specifically to that bill as an exception to The Pet Stop's duty to pay all past expenses.

Comply With State and Local Laws That May Affect Your Purchase

The sale of a business is not heavily regulated by state statutes or local ordinances. Within very broad limits, the courts will hold you and the seller to whatever contractual deal you agree to. But even though contract law usually controls in business sales, you may also encounter some state statutes or local ordinances. Here are the major areas of possible concern and the chapters where these are discussed:

- **Usury statutes** (Chapter 7). These are laws that limit the amount of interest that a lender can charge a borrower—or someone (such as the buyer of business) to whom credit is being extended. If you'll be signing a promissory note for the balance of the sale price, the interest the seller can charge will be regulated by the usury statute in your state.
- **Bulk sales statutes** (Chapter 8). These laws—on the books in a small and diminishing number of states—set out procedures for notifying creditors when a business that has an inventory of goods—usually either a retailer or a wholesaler—is about to change hands.
- **UCC-1 Financing Statement** (Chapter 18). This form is filed with a designated state office—typically the secretary of state's office—when a buyer has agreed to give the seller a security interest in

assets of the business. The seller can then grab the business back if the buyer fails to make payments.

- **Transfer of vehicles** (Chapter 19). In an asset sale, the seller may be transferring one or more vehicles to you. Usually this can be accomplished by completing forms provided by your state's motor vehicle department.

- **Transfer of real estate** (Chapter 19). Occasionally, the sale of a business includes the sale of real estate. Typically, this involves the seller signing a deed which you then file with the land registry office in the county where the land is located. There are precise technicalities to be followed, especially if the seller retains a security interest. You may want a lawyer's help. To learn more about the process, you can check with the land registry clerk or a knowledgeable person at a local title company.

- **Licenses** (Chapter 19). Most businesses don't need any license other than a city or county business license and, possibly, a sales tax permit. For the most part, only businesses that sell regulated products (like liquor), need to meet environmental laws (a dry cleaner or gas station), are subject to health laws (a restaurant), or must meet professional standards (a lawyer or doctor) need to worry about this. Even where a license is required, there's wide variation from state to state and from business to business about what licenses are required—and what needs to be done when a business changes hands. It's important to have the right licenses right from the beginning. Have the seller give you a list of the state and local licenses and permits currently held by the business. Next, contact each office that issued a license or permit and inquire about what, if anything, needs to be done when the business is sold. In most cases, this effort will suffice.

  But if you want to be extra safe, check with state, county, and local officials to find out whether there are any licenses or permits that the business should have but doesn't yet. At the state level, the department that works with small businesses can point you in the right direction. At the county and city level, the clerk's official is usually the best place to inquire. The state and local chamber of commerce are also useful resources.

- **Taxes** (Chapter 3). Check with your state revenue office to find out about any state forms you need to file when you buy a business. Also check with your county and city tax offices about local tax filings.

- **Entity matters** (Chapter 19). If the business you're buying is a corporation or an LLC, check with the state office —often the secretary of state's office— where the original corporate or LLC documents were filed. Depending on the shape of your deal, you or the seller may need to file papers for a change of registered agent, or to change or cancel an entity name. The clerk will also be able to tell you about any other documents you need to file. With a partnership or a sole proprietorship that uses an assumed or fictitious name, inquire at the county office where such businesses are registered.

RESOURCE

How to do your own legal research. If you have a specific legal question not covered in this book—for example, the requirements of the bulk sales law in your state (assuming that your state has such a law)—you may want to do some legal research on your own before calling your lawyer. Most states have a small business development office that can help you get started. Also, the closest branch of the U.S. Small Business Administration can be a useful resource. And the state and local chambers of commerce may have relevant information. Also check out Nolo's website at www.nolo.com, for general background information on a wide variety of legal topics, and access to statutes of all 50 states, plus federal laws. In addition, check out the official website of your state for links to relevant business and tax agencies, such as your state department of revenue. To find your state website, see www.statelocalgov.net. Finally, if you still need help, we recommend *Legal Research: How to Find & Understand the Law*, by Stephen Elias and Susan Levinkind (Nolo). This nontechnical book gives easy-to-use, step-by-step instructions on how to find legal information. ●

Tax-Saving Strategies

We don't have to tell you that tax deductions are a good thing. On a business tax return—as on a personal return—deductions reduce the amount of taxable income, meaning your tax bill is lower. Wouldn't it be great if you could take a tax write-off for the money you pay to buy a business? Well, in most cases you can—at least to some extent. But it takes knowledge and planning at the prepurchase stage to maximize your potential tax benefits. Structure your purchase one way and you can immediately start to benefit from generous tax deductions that help you recoup the purchase price. Structure your purchase another way and the tax benefits will be much smaller.

As you'll learn in this chapter, you need to focus on two primary strategies:

- **Strategy #1**—buying the assets rather than the business entity.
- **Strategy #2**—allocating most of the sale price to assets you can write off over a relatively short period.

This chapter summarizes the federal income tax principles that lie behind these strategies. Your own tax adviser can help you apply these rules to your specific situation. The rules for computing business taxes can be extremely complex—far more complex than simply preparing your typical Form 1040 tax return each year. So it's important that you seek good tax advice early in the purchase process. If you wait until after you reach an agreement with a seller, you risk missing out on tax-saving opportunities—or buying at a price that turns out to be higher than you expected because you assumed your business taxes would be tallied differently. Be sure to read Chapter 6, which covers how to work with accountants.

Understanding Business Write-Offs

Before we get into the details of the tax strategies involved in buying a business, you need to understand how business write-offs work under the federal income tax law. In brief, you can deduct some business expenses in the years in which you incur them. These are called current expenses. Other expenses must be spread over a number of years—these are called capitalized expenses. The business assets you acquire when you buy a business typically fall into the category of capitalized expenses.

Current Expenses

Current expenses are the everyday costs you pay to keep a business going. They include items like rent, electricity, salaries, postage, and janitorial services. You may deduct such expenses from gross income in the year they're incurred.

You and the Seller Will See Tax Issues Differently

When it comes to the tax implications of your purchase, the seller will be asking: *"How can I pay the least amount of tax on my sale?"* Given the likelihood that taxes will be owed, the seller would like to pay those taxes at the low long-term capital gain rate (generally, 15%) rather than the ordinary income rate (which can be as high as 35%). In many deals, some of the gain the seller receives will be taxed at one rate, while other parts of the gain will be taxed at another.

Unfortunately, the best tax strategy for the seller may not be the one that's best for you. For instance, in a sale that requires the allocation of the sale price by asset classes, the allocation will affect how much of the sale proceeds are taxed to the seller at ordinary income rates and how much at long-term capital gain rates. The seller, of course, will prefer to have as much of the price as possible allocated to assets that will lead to long-term capital gain treatment. But going along with the seller's wishes will reduce your opportunity to take large deductions for those assets in the year or years immediately following your purchase. Typically, if you purchase assets that give the seller the

benefit of long-term capital gain treatment, you'll have to depreciate those assets over 15 or more years, depending on the asset type. This translates into higher tax bills for you.

Another potential source of conflict is the seller's probable desire to reduce the amount of "recaptured" depreciation. Suppose the seller has fully or partly depreciated business equipment that's part of the sale. When you buy those assets, you'll have the opportunity to depreciate them all over again. But the tax law is designed to prevent the same depreciation being taken twice, so the seller will need to report (recapture, in tax parlance) as ordinary income the depreciation already taken. With that tax quirk in mind, the seller will normally want to assign a low value to the already-depreciated equipment so that there will be less depreciation to recapture and therefore less income for the seller to report and pay taxes on. But you'll want to assign a high value to such equipment so you can write off a larger amount once you own the business.

To reconcile differences like these, you and the seller may have to adjust the sale price up or down to reflect who takes the tax hit.

Capitalized Expenses

Capitalized expenses typically involve payment for assets that will have a useful life of a year or more. These purchases are treated as investments in your business. Generally, you can't write off the entire cost of a capitalized expense in the year of purchase but must spread the deduction over a number of years. This process is often called "depreciation" or, in some cases, "amortization."

The assets that you must capitalize may be tangible or intangible. *Tangible* items are things you can touch, like desks, trucks, and tools. *Intangible* items consist of things like trademarks, royalties, or business goodwill.

The tax law sets up depreciation categories for all business assets. Each category is assigned an arbitrary "useful life," meaning the period over which the cost of an asset can be deducted—for example, five years for a computer. IRS Publication 946, *How to Depreciate Property*, lists the categories and the depreciation periods for different assets.

Most of the tangible assets you're likely to buy in acquiring a business will fall into one of four classes, summarized here:

- **3-year property.** Molds, jigs, and over-the-road tractors.
- **5-year property.** Cars, trucks, small airplanes, trailers, computers and peripherals, copiers, typewriters, calculators, manufacturing equipment (apparel), assets used in construction activity, and equipment used in research and experimentation.
- **7-year property.** Office furniture, manufacturing equipment (except types included in 3- and 5-year categories above), fixtures, and personal property that doesn't fit into any other specific category.
- **Real estate (varying periods).** Business-use real estate is depreciated over 39 years. Some types of land improvement costs (sidewalks, roads, drainage facilities, fences, and landscaping) are depreciable over 20 years. Some leasehold improvements are depreciable over 15 years.

Intangible assets have different depreciation periods. For example, goodwill and the payments to the seller for a covenant not to compete must be amortized over a 15-year period.

The Section 179 Exception

There's an important exception to the rule that depreciation for capital expenses must be spread over a number of years. Section 179 of the tax code allows you—but doesn't require you—to deduct a generous sum for certain asset purchases in the year you buy the assets. The amount you can deduct is adjusted annually. In 2011, you can deduct up to $500,000 for the assets you buy during the year. This instant expensing can be used mainly for tangible personal property such as machines, equipment, and furniture. And yes, you can use this deduction for used equipment that you buy, because it's new

Computing the Amount of Yearly Depreciation Can Be Complex

Saying that an asset must be depreciated over, say, a five-year period doesn't necessarily mean that you'll make five equal yearly deductions. For starters, the tax code provides for two general methods for depreciating business assets: straight-line depreciation and accelerated depreciation. And to make it a bit more complicated, there are three kinds of accelerated depreciation— each of which lets you deduct more in the early years of the write-off. But all the methods result in the same amount of total depreciation in the end.

Even the simplest method—the straight-line method—isn't as simple as it sounds. Five years doesn't mean five years, because normally you can only deduct a half year's worth the first year. So if you use the straight-line method for a $20,000 machine, your depreciation will look like this:

Year 1	$ 2,000 (one-half year)
Years 2, 3, 4, & 5	16,000 ($4,000 per year)
Year 6	2,000 (one-half year)
Total deductions	$ 20,000

Another tax-code quirk can reduce the first year's depreciation even more if you buy over 40% of your total equipment purchases near the end of the year.

For an excellent introduction to the various depreciation methods, see *Tax Savvy for Small Business*, by Frederick Daily (Nolo). A tax pro can help establish the depreciation schedules that produce the best tax results for you. Software such as Intuit's *TurboTax for Business* can also compare and track depreciation under multiple schedules.

to you. This special deduction is well worth investigating. See IRS Publication 946, *How to Depreciate Property*, or speak to your accountant.

CAUTION

There's a phase-out that limits the amount you can deduct using the Section 179 deduction. It changes yearly, but in 2011, the phase-out starts at $2 million. For each dollar of

newly acquired property you purchase during the tax year that exceeds the current phase-out amount, the Section 179 deduction is reduced by $1. Most small business won't be affected by the phase-out rules.

RESOURCE

For further information on business write-offs, see *Tax Savvy for Small Business*, by Frederick Daily (Nolo).

Buying Assets vs. Buying the Entity

How depreciation rules will affect your tax picture will depend, to a great extent, on the way your purchase is structured. You won't always have a choice, but sometimes you will be able to negotiate to buy either the assets or the entity.

Basic Structural Differences

The distinction between an entity sale and an asset sale is covered in Chapter 2 and later in the book. Briefly once again, in an entity sale, you buy the seller's shares of a corporation's corporate stock or the seller's membership interests in an LLC. The business's assets (furniture, equipment, accounts receivable, real estate, inventory, and so on) continue to be owned by the entity, which is now owned by you.

By contrast, in an asset sale the corporation or LLC sells its assets to you. The seller continues to own the corporate stock or LLC membership interests. This means that the seller still owns the entity—though it may be nothing more than an empty legal shell.

SEE AN EXPERT

If you're buying an LLC that's taxed as a partnership, ask your accountant about a Section 754 election. Using this tax technique, you may be able to write off the market value of the LLC's assets. This gives you many of the advantages of an asset purchase, even though you're buying the entity.

Buying the Assets Is Usually Better

Given a choice, it's usually to your advantage (for both tax and nontax reasons) to buy the assets. In tax terms, an asset purchase lets you start depreciating the assets based on the amount you actually pay for them. If the sale price includes $50,000 for equipment, you can start depreciating the full $50,000 regardless of how much depreciation the seller has already taken on the same equipment.

By contrast, if you buy an entity (typically, a corporation or LLC), you're stuck with the entity's depreciation history. For example, let's say you buy the stock of a corporation, basing the sale price in part on equipment that's worth $50,000. If the corporation has already fully depreciated this equipment for federal income tax purposes, the corporation can take no further depreciation on this equipment even though the business has a new owner. Or if the corporation has taken $45,000 worth of depreciation, only $5,000 worth of further depreciation will be available after ownership of the entity is transferred to you. As you can see, your opportunity to reduce taxes through depreciation is diminished—or may not even exist.

Whether you have a choice between the two purchase methods depends on how the business you're looking at is currently organized.

- **Sole proprietorships.** A sole proprietorship is never treated as a legal taxable entity separate from its owner for federal tax purposes. This means that when you buy such a business, the sale is always treated as if you bought its individual items of property (that is, it's treated as an asset sale). So if you're considering buying a sole proprietorship business, you may choose to skip the rest of this section and go directly to the discussion of asset sales below.

- **Single-member LLCs.** For federal tax purposes, it's always an asset sale if you buy a single-member LLC whose owner pays taxes as an individual (in other words, he or hasn't filed the form electing to be taxed as a corporation). Such an LLC isn't treated as a separate taxable entity by the IRS.

- **Corporations, multimember LLCs, and partnerships.** If the business you're looking at is a corporation, a multi-member LLC, or a partnership, then you do have a choice of buying either the entity or the entity's assets—and the path you choose will determine the tax consequences.

Nontax Reasons for Preferring an Asset Purchase

There are also nontax reasons why an asset purchase usually is the better option. Here are some:

- **Limiting liability for past obligations of the business.** With an asset purchase, you're generally free of past liabilities of the business (whether known or unknown) except for liens on specific assets. An entity purchase is different: The entity, under your ownership, remains liable for past obligations, though the seller may agree to indemnify you for any bills or liabilities that crop up.

- **Picking and choosing the assets you want.** With an asset purchase, it's easier to say, *"I'll buy these assets but not those."* By contrast, if you buy an entity, you acquire *all* the assets it owns— unless the seller agrees to transfer specific assets out of the entity before the closing.

Buying an Entity Isn't All Bad

Despite the clear advantages of an asset sale, you may wind up buying the entity rather than its assets if the seller insists on it—a frequent scenario if the entity is a C corporation and the seller is worried about the possible double taxation that would result from an asset sale. And in some cases, you may actually prefer an entity sale. For example, the entity may have valuable contracts that can't be transferred—such as a favorable lease. Such contracts remain the property of the entity, so if you buy the entity, you get to benefit from the contracts. See Chapter 8 for more details.

Although you may not be able to write off the purchase price of an entity through depreciation deductions, you may realize some tax benefits if you sell the entity later. At that point, you'll be able to deduct the cost of the stock or LLC membership interests (in tax lingo, your basis) from the new sale price and pay tax on the difference at the long-term capital gain rate. This helps balance out the tax picture and may make you feel better about buying an entity—either because the seller insists on it, or because other economic factors are more important to you and outweigh the tax concerns.

> **TIP**
>
> **If you do wind up signing a sales agreement to buy an entity, you may be able work out terms that are more palatable to you.** One way is to agree that the seller will consult with you after you close on the business. You and the seller can then designate a substantial part of what you're paying for the business as a consulting fee. The entity will be able to deduct the consulting fee as a current expense, softening the loss of depreciation deductions you may be giving up.

Allocating the Purchase Price in an Asset Sale

When you buy assets, you'll need to allocate the sale price among the seven categories of assets established by the IRS. (This process isn't necessary if you buy an entity.)

To reduce the chance of tax complications, it's best if you and the seller agree on the allocation and put it in the sales contract. The IRS doesn't have to accept your joint allocation, but normally it will if the allocation is reasonable. You and the seller will each need to file an IRS Form 8594 (*Asset Acquisition Statement*). The tax laws don't require that the two forms match, but if they don't, it's a red flag inviting an IRS review. If that happens, the IRS may decide not to accept your numbers or the seller's numbers, and to make its own allocation instead. Again, to avoid trouble and unpredictability, you and the seller should agree on the allocation to be reported to the IRS so that your Forms 8594 are consistent. See Appendix C for the form and applicable instructions.

> **FORM**
>
> **Where to find the forms.** If you're reading a print copy of this book, you'll find a copy of the IRS Form 8594, *Asset Acquisition Statement*, and instructions on the CD-ROM at the back. If you're using an ebook version, you can download them on the Nolo website; the link is included in Appendix A.

The allocation of the sale price is important to you because it's used to determine the cost basis for each asset you buy. This lets you take the appropriate amount of depreciation (or amortization) for each asset. Obviously, you'd like to assign as much of the sale price as possible to items that will result—tax-wise—in rapid depreciation (three, five, or seven years, for example) rather than depreciation over a longer term (for example, the 15 years used for goodwill or the 39 years used for business real estate).

To do this, you'll want to assign relatively high values to certain items such as equipment and furniture. The seller, however, will be motivated by tax considerations to lump assets into categories that will result in long-term capital gain rather than ordinary income—buildings and goodwill, for example. The chart "Guidelines for Allocating the Sale Price to Keep Taxes Low," below, shows which assets sellers and buyers usually prefer to value relatively high and which they usually prefer to value relatively low. You and the seller should be able to arrive at an allocation you can both live with, though this may require help from tax professionals. (Allocation of the sale price in the sales agreement is covered in Chapter 13.)

The IRS Allocation Categories

The IRS rules establish seven asset classes for the allocation of the sale price.

Class I: Cash and Cash-Like Assets. This class includes:

- money, such as cash on hand, and
- bank and money market accounts.

The seller will probably be keeping the money, in which case there will be nothing to allocate to this class.

Class II: Securities. This category includes:

- certificates of deposit
- U.S. government securities

- readily marketable stock or securities, and
- foreign currency.

It's unlikely that you'll be acquiring items such as these in the purchase of a business.

Class III: Accounts Receivable. This category includes the amounts that customers owe the business. The accounts receivable are allocated here if they're included in the sale—which they may or may not be. Buying the accounts receivable typically shifts the burden of collection to you, which you understandably may be hesitant to take on. However, in exchange for your taking over these accounts, the seller may be willing to assign a discounted value to them so as to allow in advance for those that may not be collectible.

Class IV: Inventory. This category consists primarily of the goods the business keeps on hand for sale to customers. But remember that any goods that the business is holding on consignment from others are not considered to be part of the inventory.

Class V: Other Tangible Property. You can think of tangible as meaning anything you can touch. Inventory—one type of tangible property—is already covered by Class IV. The property in Class V typically includes:

- land and buildings
- furniture
- equipment, and
- fixtures (improvements that are permanently attached to buildings).

For land, buildings, and valuable equipment, it may be useful to get and rely on the

Guidelines for Allocating the Sale Price to Keep Taxes Low

Your tax adviser can analyze your assets and propose a plan to allocate the sale price among those assets to keep your tax bill low. The following chart provides general guidance on how sellers and buyers typically approach asset allocation issues—whether they prefer to allocate a low or high amount to a particular asset class or have no preference.

IRS Asset Class		Seller's Preference	Buyer's Preference
Class I	Cash and Cash-Like Assets	No preference	No preference
Class II	Securities	No preference	No preference
Class III	Accounts Receivable	No preference	No preference
Class IV	Inventory	Relatively low amount	Relatively high amount
Class V	Other Tangible Property	*Personal property:* Relatively low amount	*Personal property:* Relatively high amount
		Real estate: Relatively high amount	*Real estate:* Relatively low amount
Class VI	Covenants Not to Compete and Other Intangible Property	*Covenant not to compete:* Depends on type of business; see note below.	*Covenant not to compete:* Relatively low amount
		Other intangible property: Relatively high amount	*Other intangible property:* Relatively low amount
Class VII	Goodwill and Going-Concern Value	Relatively high amount	Relatively low amount

Note regarding covenants not to compete: When an individual (such as a shareholder) rather than an entity (such as a corporation) is paid for a covenant not to compete related to the sale of a business, the individual usually will prefer to assign a relatively low value to the covenant; this is because the fee received for the covenant will be taxed at ordinary income rates. But different principles will apply in an asset sale by a C corporation. In that situation, the shareholder will want to reduce the burden of double taxation and, for that reason, will prefer to assign a relatively high portion of the total payment package to the covenant and less to the asset being sold.

appraisal by a respected appraiser. This will reduce the chances that the IRS will later challenge the value that you and the seller assign to these items.

Class VI: Covenants Not to Compete and Other Intangible Property. Just as tangible means assets you can touch, intangible means property that you *can't* touch or physically possess. An intangible is typically a legal right—often recognized in a document. Here are some examples:

- covenant of a selling corporation or LLC that it won't compete with the buyer
- patents, copyrights, and trademarks
- trade secrets
- customer or client lists, and
- licenses or permits granted by the government.

Note that a covenant not to compete given by a sole proprietor, or by a shareholder or an LLC member as an individual, is not treated as an asset in the IRS asset allocation form. However, the covenant must be disclosed separately on line 6 of the form.

Goodwill and going-concern value are also types of intangible assets, but the IRS has given them a category of their own (Class VII). You'd prefer not to put much value on intangible assets, since it will take 15 years for you to fully amortize (write off) these items. The seller, however, will probably want to have more of the sale price allocated to intangibles, because these are capital assets and, for that reason, are taxed at the capital gain rate.

Class VII: Goodwill and Going-Concern Value. This class is a catch-all for any part of the sale price that doesn't fall into one of the first six classes. It recognizes the fact that a business with a good reputation and loyal customers who can be expected to patronize the business in the future may be worth more than the sum of its parts—and that this extra value is likely to be reflected in the sale price. You'd like to assign a relatively low value to Class VII items, as you have to amortize them over 15 years. But the seller will prefer to assign a relatively high value, because the proceeds from the sale of these items are taxed at the capital gains rate.

Applying the Allocation Rules

Obviously, the allocation of the sale price will vary widely from business to business, but the following example will illustrate how the system works.

EXAMPLE: Barbara, a certified personal trainer, is buying a successful exercise club from Steve for $500,000. Barbara and Steve also are signing a consulting contract under which Steve will provide consulting services to the business for two years and receive $50,000 for those services. And, in exchange for a $5,000 payment from Barbara, he agrees not to compete with the business. Barbara and Steve agree to allocate the total purchase price as follows.

Barbara and Steve's Price Allocation

Class	Allocation of $500,000 Sale Price	Reason
I. Cash and Cash-Like Assets	$ -0-	Steve will be keeping the money that's on hand.
II. Securities	$ -0-	The business has none.
III. Accounts Receivable	$ 10,000	There is $15,000 owing for club memberships, but collecting the full amount may be a problem for Barbara.
IV. Inventory	$ 2,000	For club T-shirts, power drinks, and pulse monitors on hand for sale to club members.
V. Other Tangible Property	$350,000	For the building and equipment.
VI. Covenants Not to Compete and Other Intangible Items	$ 50,000	For the club's membership list and all rights to Steve's copyrighted fitness manual.
VII. Goodwill and Going-Concern Value	$88,000	The rest of the sale price, reflecting the club's convenient location and its loyal membership base.

Because the consulting agreement and noncompete covenant are not assets of the business that Barbara is buying, they're not included in the allocation of the sale price. Instead, they're disclosed on Line 6 of the IRS asset allocation form.

Barbara will deduct the consulting fees as current business expenses when she pays them to Steve, and she'll amortize the noncompete fee over a 15-year period. Steve will report the consulting and noncompete fees as ordinary income when he receives them.

Writing Off Purchase-Related Expenses

So far, this chapter has summarized the tax treatment of many of the costs of buying a business, including:

- **The purchase price if you buy an entity.** Your tax basis is what you pay for the entity. If you own the entity for more than a year and then sell it, you'll owe tax on the gain at the long-term capital gain rate. During your period of ownership, the entity can take depreciation deductions for any of its assets that haven't already been fully depreciated.
- **The purchase price if you buy assets.** You and the seller allocate the sale price among different categories of assets. You can then begin to depreciate the assets based on what you paid for them. This is allowed even if the seller already depreciated the assets.
- **The fee you pay the seller for a covenant not to compete.** You amortize this fee over a 15-year period.
- **The amounts you pay the sellers for services as an employee or independent contractor.** You deduct these amounts as current business expenses in the years when you pay them.

Most of the money you spend to buy a business will probably fall into one of the above categories, but there may be other costs that do not. Here are some common ones and a bit on how they are treated for federal income tax purposes.

Professional Fees

In the process of buying a business, you may pay fees to a lawyer, an accountant, an appraiser, or other professionals. If you buy a business entity, these fees are added to what you pay for the entity, increasing your basis for income tax purposes:

EXAMPLE: Miriam and Dale buy all the shares of Carleton Park Enterprises Inc. for $200,000. In the process, they pay $1,500 to their lawyer for her help in negotiating the purchase and drafting sale documents. In addition, they pay $1,000 to their accountant for his analysis of the corporation's finances and tax guidance regarding their purchase.

For income tax purposes, Miriam and Dale's tax basis is $202,500 ($200,000 + $2,500). That figure will be used to determine the amount of capital gain tax owed if Miriam and Dale eventually sell the shares for a profit.

On the other hand, if you buy assets rather than an entity, professional fees are added to the basis of the assets and become part of the amounts you can depreciate. The fees are allocated among the various asset classes.

Start-Up Expenses

Other expenses associated with buying a business include the costs of investigating the business you're looking to acquire. If you're already in business and are buying a similar business, you can treat these investigation expenses as if you were simply expanding your existing business; in most cases you'll be able to deduct these incidental expenses in the current year.

If you *don't* already own a business—or if you're buying a business that's not similar to one you own—you can immediately deduct up to $5,000 of start-up expenses in the tax year in which you start doing business. You can also immediately deduct up to $5,000 for your costs of creating an entity such as a corporation or partnership to buy the business. If you use these immediate deductions, any start-up and organizational costs that exceed the $5,000 limits must be spread over a 15-year period.

Interest

Many people who buy a small business use credit to pay for at least part of the purchase price. This is so, for example, when you buy a business on an installment basis in which the seller extends credit to you, or you borrow funds from a bank or other lender for the purchase price. In either case, you'll undoubtedly be paying interest. Almost always, the interest you pay is tax-deductible when you pay it, but "investment interest" is only deductible to the extent you have investment income. You may need an accountant's help in sorting this out.

Costs of Not Buying a Business

You may spend money looking into buying a business but then decide not to buy one. If you make just a general search or preliminary investigation, you can't deduct these expenses.

> **EXAMPLE:** Alice thinks she might like to buy a restaurant business. She hires Eric, a business broker, to come up with restaurants that are for sale in her city. She pays him $1,500 for his services. Eric comes up with six prospects. After Alice reviews the information, she decides to drop the idea. She can't deduct the money she spent for this general search.

What's more, unless you're an investor (typically, someone who has other investments), you can't deduct the costs of attempting to acquire a specific business. But if you *are* an investor and you decide not to acquire a specific business that you've been considering, you can deduct the costs as investment expenses. You'll itemize these expenses on Schedule A of your individual tax return.

EXAMPLE: Albert—who regularly invests in stocks and bonds—is interested in broadening his investment portfolio by buying Eddie's Memphis-Style Barbecue Shack. He hires an accountant to review the business's books, a construction expert to check out the building that houses the business, and a lawyer to draw up a sales agreement. Unfortunately, Albert and Eddie can't come to terms, so no deal is made. Albert can deduct the money he spent for these services, since he's an investor and the expenses were related to a specific business.

Checklist for Saving Taxes When Buying a Business

- ☐ Learn the rules for business write-offs for both current expenses and capitalized items.

- ☐ Understand the tax differences between an asset sale and an entity sale.

- ☐ Buy assets rather than a business entity whenever possible.

- ☐ Carefully allocate the sale price among assets for the best tax results.

- ☐ Evaluate all the elements of your purchase for tax effect: sale price, covenant not to compete, and payments for the seller's post-closing services.

- ☐ Keep track of legal and accounting fees connected to the purchase sale, since they may be tax-deductible.

- ☐ Agree with the seller on figures for the IRS asset allocation form.

- ☐ Consult a tax professional early on.

TIP

Consider forming a corporation so that you can write off the expenses of investigating a business purchase. Have the corporation pay these expenses. If it turns out you don't buy a business, you can abandon the corporation and then claim a Section 1244 loss or a capital loss for the expenses that the corporation incurred. See an accountant for details.

Tax Law Resources

Federal Tax Law

The federal tax code contains thousands of pages of fine print—and it changes often. So, in many cases, going straight to a tax expert is your best bet. But if you'd like to see IRS forms and official instructions, or if you have a specific tax question you'd like to research yourself, here are some useful resources on the federal tax consequences of buying a business.

The IRS website, www.irs.gov. This is a good starting point, where you'll find tax forms, instructions, and numerous publications that explain tax law—although in gray areas of tax law, the information reflects only the IRS perspective. The following publications are especially helpful: IRS Publication 535, *Business Expenses*; IRS Publication 537, *Installment Sales*; IRS Publication 544, *Sales and Other Dispositions of Assets*; IRS Publication 551, *Basis of Assets*; and IRS Publication 946, *How to Depreciate Property*.

CCH Standard Federal Tax Reporter, published by Commerce Clearing House, www.cchgroup.com. This multivolume work is the gold standard for tax research but may be more than you need.

Tax Guide for Buying and Selling a Business, by Stanley Hagendorf, published by Knowles Publishing Inc., www.knowlespublishing. com. This is a focused treatment of the tax complexities and perhaps your best bet for learning about this subject in depth.

PPC's Guide to Buying and Selling a Business, published by Practitioners Publishing Company, http://ria.thomsonreuters.com. This book is written primarily for accountants and has excellent coverage of the tax issues.

State Tax Law

In addition to the federal income tax implications of buying a business, you need to understand the state tax rules as well. While many states follow the federal tax pattern, some do not. A good starting point for learning about the tax system in your state is *All States Tax Handbook*, published by Thomson/RIA, www.riathomson.com. Your state's department of revenue can provide further specific guidance. To find yours, go to your state's home page (see www.statelocalgov.net).

Finding the Right Business for You

Looking for a business to buy is probably different from anything else you've ever done. It's more like looking for the ideal house than looking for the right car, but even more difficult, as there are no lawn signs or Realtors' multiple listings to consult. So be prepared for a long and possibly arduous search. True, if you're lucky, the perfect fit may fall into your lap—for example, your Aunt Martha may decide to get out of the diner business at the exact time that you're looking for a restaurant to buy. Or Marvin, the owner of the antique furniture store that you've managed for ten years, could decide it's time for him to retire, and offer to sell the business to you. But don't count on the process being this quick and easy. More likely, your search for a business to buy will extend over several months, or even a year or more. This chapter will help you make your search more productive.

Before You Begin

Your search for the right business is likely to be more efficient and, ultimately, more successful if you've narrowed down what you're looking for. The "I'll know it when I see it" method can work in some cases, but being too open-minded about what you want will probably make your search more difficult rather than easier.

The first step is to take stock of your skills, education, experience, talents, and interests—especially your interests. Finding a business that involves something you're passionate about means that you're likely to stick with it and work hard to make it successful. No need for your work life to be boring, humdrum, or even painful—especially if, like many small business owners, you wind up working 50 or 60 hours a week. So if you're deeply interested in food or cooking, you might focus on buying a specialty food store, a bakery, a restaurant, or a wholesale food distribution business. Similarly, your interest in gardening may tilt you in the direction of a garden shop or floral business. Or as an avid runner, you might consider buying a business that sells running shoes and apparel as well as other goods for the athletically inclined.

Your strong interest in—or your experience with—a certain type of work is a good starting point for identifying the general industry you might be looking for. The next step is to consider whether to apply your energies to a retail business, a service business, a manufacturing business, or a distributorship. For most people hoping to buy a small business, the choice usually boils down to either a retail or a service business—or, in some cases, a combination of the two, such as a shop that sells draperies and shades and also provides design and installation services.

Another decision you'll need to make is whether to focus on a business that deals primarily with the general public, or one that deals primarily with other businesses and institutions. Some businesses deal with both types of customers or clients—for example, a business that sells and installs both residential and commercial alarm systems.

Finally, think about the size of the business you're looking for. A bigger business can sometimes offer the potential for greater profit, but it might cost more than you can afford, and you might get bogged down with unwanted management headaches if you have to supervise lots of employees. Sometimes smaller is better—at least until you get your feet wet.

Attractive Businesses May Be Nearer Than You Think

You may be able to find a business just by looking around you. Often the best prospects are businesses owned by people you already know—including friends, family members, and possibly even your current employer. Finding a business close at hand is good news for several reasons. Perhaps the most important is that you can then eliminate much of the sweat and anxiety of a wide search. Another is that because you already know the business and the person who owns it, you'll be better positioned to weigh the business's strengths and weaknesses than you might be if you were buying from a stranger.

Your Employer

If you're working for a small business, you already know the good, the bad, and the ugly about it. If there's any chance that the owner may be thinking of bailing out, you might tactfully broach the possibility of your buying the business. Since the owner knows a great deal about you, including your work habits and probably your financial resources as well, your early expression of interest may rapidly culminate in a sale to you.

EXAMPLE: For 15 years, Al has owned Town & Country Footwear, an upscale shoe store in a small city. For the last ten of those years, Ellen has worked alongside him selling shoes and helping to manage the store. When Al goes on a buying trip or takes a vacation, Ellen does an excellent job of running the store—and realizes how much she enjoys being in charge. Ellen learns that Al, an avid golfer, has an opportunity to improve his lifestyle by opening a shoe store in a new shopping plaza located 400 miles away near several expanding golf resorts. But Ellen sees that Al is hesitant to make the move because he can't efficiently own and manage two stores a day's drive apart. A light goes on in Ellen's head. She suggests to Al that he sell the existing store—to her. Al mulls it over. Knowing that Ellen is honest, reliable, and frugal, and that customers like and respect her, Al is receptive and discussions ensue. But much as Ellen would like to buy the business, there's a hitch. Although she's carefully saved money over the years, Ellen can only put down 15% of the sale price. Al, who needs money to invest in his new store, prefers 30%. Fortunately, when Ellen's parents step forward and agree to invest 10%, Al is willing to reduce the down payment requirement to 25% and a deal is struck. Ellen will pay Al the remaining 75% of the purchase price over four years in 48 equal installments carrying 7% interest. Both Ellen and Al are confident that the store will enable Ellen to meet the note payments and still take a modest but adequate salary for herself. The sale is concluded within 60 days, and Ellen is the proud owner of a small business she already knows very well.

If the business where you're employed is too big for you to buy alone, maybe a few fellow employees would like to become co-owners. You and a colleague or two can join together to buy and run the business.

Friends and Family Members

Sometimes, a friend or family member has a business that would be ideal for you to buy. Let's say your uncle owns a successful small business and is thinking of retiring. Maybe you've just received an MBA, have a strong entrepreneurial bent—and can raise a $50,000 down payment from the trust fund that your grandmother set up for you. Your uncle may be delighted to sell the business to a family member.

Friends, too, may have a business that fits your needs perfectly.

EXAMPLE: Chuck, age 50, has been considering a buyout retirement package offered by his large employer, which is downsizing its operations. He has never been completely happy working in the corporate environment but is unsure about how to make a transition into being his own boss. One afternoon, over a post-tennis snack, Chuck's buddy Pete casually mentions that he and his wife Joan (now in their early 60s) are thinking of selling the profitable self-storage facility they've owned for 20 years. Pete and Joan would like more time to travel and get involved in volunteer activities. Chuck immediately expresses interest, and a plan begins to crystallize. Chuck decides to accept his employer's buyout package and retire in three months, using part of his lump sum payment as a down payment on Pete's self-storage business. Meanwhile, to get some hands-on experience in a business that's new to him, Chuck arranges to come in every Saturday to work at the storage facility. In addition, Joan and Pete agree that they'll be available as consultants and trainers part time for six months after Chuck takes over.

Joan and Pete also own five acres of vacant land next to the self-storage facility. Chuck would like a chance to buy that land as well so that he can eventually build more storage units. But because he doesn't have the cash now, he offers Joan and Pete $10,000 for an option to buy the extra land within five years for $200,000. (The $10,000 is to be applied toward the price of the land if Chuck buys it.) Joan and Pete agree and the deal is done.

You'll be fortunate if a family member or friend has a successful small business and is thinking of selling at the same time you're thinking of buying. But before you rush into a deal with someone who is part of your social or family network, carefully consider the downsides. For example, what will happen to the personal relationship you now enjoy with a close friend if it turns out that the friend didn't disclose some negative facts about the business, or if you run into hard times and can't come up with the cash to make monthly installment payments? Would you become embroiled in litigation? Would your friend suffer a financial loss? Might your larger social network be damaged as people take sides?

With family members, the fallout from a deal gone sour can have even more wrenching effects than a troubled deal with a friend. Think about how relatives may behave if, after buying your aunt's business, you and she end up battling in court. Let's say you attend a family reunion or a wedding the month your aunt sues you for missing six installment payments. Some relatives may stick up for you because your aunt left the business in a shambles when she turned it

over to you; others may take your aunt's side and treat you like an irresponsible deadbeat.

There's no hard-and-fast rule that says you should never buy from a friend or relative. But it's crucial that you and the friend or family member frankly discuss all the financial issues—and especially the risks— well before you sign a sales contract.

TIP

Keep it professional. If you decide to buy a business from a friend or family member, it's essential that you and the seller sign a sales contract, as well as all the same papers you'd sign if this deal were between you and a stranger. And to help make sure you'll really be happy running the business, it can be a good idea to work for the seller for six months before finalizing the sale.

Think about having the business appraised before you buy from a friend or family member. That way, if your friend or relative later decides that you paid too little, you can point to the appraisal as evidence that you acted fairly and honestly.

SEE AN EXPERT

See that your parents get tax advice before selling a business to you. Perhaps the sale can be integrated with their estate plan, for maximum tax savings. Also, a tax pro can help evaluate whether the sales price, the allocation of the price (in an asset sale), and the interest rate (in an installment sale) will pass muster with the tax collector.

Businesses That You Patronize

Occasionally, purchase lightning can strike in the form of business you've come to know by being a regular customer or client. For example, maybe your hobby is building model vintage airplanes from kits. The niche store you've where you've been buying kits for the past five years may fulfill your dream of owning a small business. Or perhaps you have a passion for sailing and have found yourself drawn to a shop that rents and repairs sail boats; you frequently watch and sometimes help as the owner installs new rigging on customers' boats. Or possibly you're an art teacher and you often spend time at an art print and framing store, where you chat with the owner and check out the new stock. In these and other situations, a business that fits your interests and your budget may be available for sale—and you'll never find out unless you ask.

If the owner doesn't decisively reject your inquiry about buying the business, take that as a good sign. See if the owner is willing to prepare a fact sheet that summarizes the business and contains an overview of profits and losses for the past several years. If there continues to be mutual interest, you can seek more information.

> **EXAMPLE:** Over a period of a year, Stan, a freelance writer, has become a regular customer at The Daily Grind, a coffee shop that Laura owns. Stan often spends the morning in the shop working away on his laptop while consuming several lattés and a couple of scones. At some point, Stan finds himself eyeing the flow of business and begins asking Laura about coffee suppliers, popular selling items, and how one gets started in the coffeehouse business. One day, he musters the courage to ask Laura if she might consider selling her business. As luck would have it, Stan's timing couldn't be better. It turns out that Laura has been thinking of selling to enable her to be able to finally go back to finish her Ph.D. Stan explains to Laura that he and his wife Cheryl moved to the area so that Cheryl could begin work as chief of ophthalmology at the big teaching hospital in town. Stan, who is tired of hustling articles for business publications, has concluded that now that Cheryl has a good income, it's his chance to own a business rather than just write about them. Laura realizes she has a serious prospective buyer in Stan, and that her desire to complete her education can now become a reality. Stan and Laura are both excited about putting a deal together. When Stan asks for detailed financial data, Laura quickly complies, providing him with full information about the five years the store has been in operation. They work out a deal that allows Laura to give up the shop and return to school the following September—and lets Stan become the entrepreneur he's been longing to be.

You May Be a Strategic Buyer

Of course, these stories aren't all that common. There are limits to looking for a business by approaching a friend, family member, employer, or business owner at a place you patronize. This approach may not be right for you, especially if you're already in business and want to add to your existing business, rather than buying a business to run as a standalone operation. In other words, you may be a "strategic buyer" who might fall into one of the following three categories:

- You're looking for a business that's the same as or similar to the one you already own.
- You're looking for a complementary business that neatly dovetails with your current business.
- You're looking to buy a business that you currently sell to or buy from.

Strategic buyers see the acquisition of a business as a logical extension of their already-existing business. Generally the purchase fits into a larger business strategy. For example, if you already run five successful pizza shops in your city, you may reap significant economy-of-scale benefits by acquiring another pizza shop, or even a family-style Italian restaurant.

As a strategic buyer, here are some businesses that you may want to consider.

Businesses That Are Like the One You Now Own

If you have a thriving appliance repair shop and are looking to expand into new markets, it may be less costly, more profitable, and, above all, less risky to pick up a successful existing shop rather than develop a new location from scratch. In addition, if competition from another business that resembles yours has been keeping your prices artificially low, buying the competitor's business may be a quick way to fatten profit margins. Of course, the owner of a competing business may be reluctant to disclose much information to you early on, fearing that your interest in buying is just a ruse to get your hands on sensitive information. Don't be surprised if the owner of the other business asks you to sign a confidentiality agreement in which you promise not to use or reveal insider information if you don't wind up buying the business.

Let's look more closely at why you might consider buying a business that's similar to yours.

You Can Benefit From Acquiring an Additional Location

You may be interested in adding a new location—but reluctant to build it from the ground up. If you purchase an existing business, you don't have to find a new space, negotiate a lease, prepare the new space for business, or perform dozens of other labor-intensive tasks. And best of all, the existing business, if it's already successful, comes with a built-in pool of paying customers.

There can be many good economic reasons for you to add another location—whether by opening a new one or by buying a similar business that's already up and running. For one, certain fixed expenses that you're already paying can be spread over a larger enterprise, thus reducing the overhead portion of each product or service sold. For example, a business with $750,000 in annual gross sales may spend $75,000 a year for bookkeeping and administrative services. Buying a business of similar size would produce $1.5 million in annual gross sales—but the $75,000 for bookkeeping and administrative services might only go up to $100,000. Promotional dollars may also go farther, since one campaign may draw customers to two locations. And equipment may be used more efficiently. A flower shop may own a delivery truck that's being used only four hours a day. Add a second location and the truck will be used eight hours a days—cutting the average delivery cost of each flower order and increasing profits.

For retail businesses, adding a second location often allows the business to buy goods at a lower price, as increased volume means it qualifies for a bigger discount. For example, a motorcycle shop that buys and then sells 150 high-end motorcycles annually may be eligible for an additional discount if it buys at least 250 units a year, something that would be possible with a second shop.

You Can Instantly Acquire New Customers and Clients

An existing business that's similar to yours may have built up a long roster of loyal customers or clients. This can be a very attractive aspect of buying the business. With a good business plan, you should be able to retain most of those customers and clients. And assuming you're already well-established in your field, picking up a new customer list or client base gives you the opportunity to become a bigger player.

> **EXAMPLE:** Statewide Reporting Service LLC, a court reporting firm in Washington and Jefferson counties, has been gradually expanding and has captured more and more of the market for legal depositions. Statewide's owners would like to expand into nearby Lincoln County, but they're afraid of competition from the long-established Court Reporter Associates LLC (CRA). Competing with the well-entrenched local firm may mean low or no profits for Statewide. But Statewide's owners realize the owners of CRA are nearing retirement age so, with some trepidation, they decide to schedule a friendly lunch meeting. Their hunch pays off. It turns out that CRA's owners had been talking amongst themselves about how to sell their business, but the only local buyers were two young court reporters who were financially strapped and would

need eight years to pay off the sale price. At the lunch, the Statewide people say that if their investigation goes well, they can pay the full asking price—and pay it in just three years. A month later, after the seller and buyer check each other out, they sign a sales agreement, including a commitment from CRA's owners to stay on for a year's transition period so that current customers have a chance to get used to Statewide. The deal is closed 45 days later.

Sometimes, by acquiring a similar business, you can go beyond merely expanding your base of customers or clients. You can become the leader in a particular market niche. When a business achieves such a leadership role, the vast majority of potential customers or clients automatically will think of that business first when in the market for that type of goods or services. As you might imagine, sales can then grow exponentially.

EXAMPLE: Italia Imports LLC has built a profitable business importing distinctive tile from the Tuscan and Umbrian regions of Italy to the U.S. West Coast. The company's main competitor west of the Mississippi is Tile and Stone Surfaces Inc. So when Antonio, the owner of Italia Imports, decides to expand his business, he approaches Maria, the owner of Tile and Stone Surfaces. He is aware that Maria

not only can offer a warehouse full of unusual tiles (some of which are no longer produced), but could also transfer Italia Imports' exclusive contracts with small producers in Italy plus the extensive roster of building supply and specialty tile retailers that carry its wares. Antonio offers an attractive price and equally attractive terms to Maria. After six weeks of negotiations, they sign a sales agreement. Upon closing, Antonio becomes the biggest importer of high-end Italian tile in the western part of the U.S., with the opportunity to realize ever-increasing profits.

Businesses That Are Related to Yours

There are likely to be many businesses that, while not directly competitive with yours, are involved in related activities. This possibility is worth paying attention to as another way to expand your business. For example, the other business may provide a way for you to offer a wider range of goods or services to its existing customers—or to your own. Or, because the customers of the other business will begin using your services or purchasing your goods, acquiring the related business may provide an easy way for you to acquire new customers. And sometimes buying a related business will make for an efficient use of your space or workforce.

Here are a few examples of this comple-mentary relationship between two businesses.

Business #1	Business #2
Alarm system company	Security guard service
Bicycle store	Exercise equipment store
Taxi service	Local delivery service
Upholstery business	Interior decoration service
Poster shop	Picture-framing service
Tree-cutting service	Landscaping business
Women's clothing boutique	Women's shoe store
Restaurant	Catering service

As you've probably already figured out from the match-ups suggested above, once you establish a logical synergy, either business can be the buyer or the seller.

Coming up with a logical synergy may require some imagination and creativity, but it's well worth the effort. For example, if you own a Mediterranean-style restaurant, you may come up with the idea of approaching the owner of a respected catering service to see if that business might be for sale. You may conclude that with your commercial kitchen, you can easily integrate the catering service into your business and, by hiring just a few more workers, add greatly to your profits. The goodwill from your restaurant can build up the catering operation and vice versa.

Commercial Customers and Suppliers

You may be interested in buying a business that your existing business is currently buying from or selling to. Often referred to as vertical integration, the idea is that one business enterprise decides that it's economically efficient to control several levels of the production or distribution system. For example, a boat manufacturer engages in vertical integration when it owns its own dealerships. Similarly, a retailer of archery equipment engages in vertical integration when it acquires a small manufacturer of bows and arrows.

To see how this can work, consider two local businesses that have had a long-term and productive relationship. Berkshire Bakehouse, located in low-cost space in an industrial park, produces bread, rolls, bagels, and pastries for a number of commercial clients, including hotels, restaurants, and the locally popular Dora's Deli. Viewed from Berkshire's perspective, Dora's is a customer. Viewed from Dora's perspective, Berkshire is a supplier. Following a vertical integration approach, either business might sensibly consider buying the other.

- Dora, the owner of Dora's Deli, may seek to buy Berkshire Bakehouse. The Deli already buys more than one-third of the baked goods Berkshire produces. This means that buying Berkshire's Bakehouse would allow Dora's to enjoy all the profits earned by the baked goods she sells. And perhaps Dora can use the Berkshire brand, sales contacts, and distribution network to build up her deli business by selling her popular hummus, tabbouleh, and other freshly made products to hotels and restaurants.

- Phil Berkshire, the owner of Berkshire Bakehouse, may seek to buy Dora's Deli. He knows that there's a large retail demand for Berkshire's products that Berkshire can begin to tap by expanding the bread counter portion of Dora's Deli to become a small bakery outlet. Berkshire can also use the deli as testing ground to check out the potential market for new products.

One good thing about approaching a supplier or commercial customer is that you already know a lot about their business. A second is that you have a relationship with them. However, these potential sellers may not be actively looking to sell and may not even have considered the possibility. Your offer will need to be attractive to get their attention and keep the dialogue going.

Finding a Business by Word of Mouth

Assuming you've exhausted your A-list of the close-to-home prospects, you'll need to look further. It often makes sense to tap the extended network of people you can reach through word of mouth—unless you need to keep secret your interest in buying. For example, you might not want your employer

to find out that you're considering becoming an entrepreneur.

Assuming that's not a problem, though, letting financially savvy friends and business associates know that you're thinking of buying a business is a good strategy. Think about it: You probably have dozens of everyday contacts, each of whom could be the link between you and a possible seller. For example:

- At his daughter's soccer game, Ed mentions to Nina (another parent who runs a prominent local business) that he's thinking of buying a vending machine business. Nina tells Dave, one of the sales reps who calls on her business, about Ed's interest in buying a vending machine business. Dave, who's been thinking of moving out of state, phones Ed that night to discuss a possible deal.

- Connie mentions to the 15 members of her book club that she's looking for a profitable small business to buy. One of the members, Edna, says that she and her husband have some interest in selling their dry cleaning business.

- While Joe is doing volunteer work to clean up a local beach, he mentions to Bill (another volunteer worker) that he's hoping to buy an insurance agency. Bill says his neighbor's mother has an insurance business and he's heard that she'd like to get rid of it so she can spend more time with her three grandchildren.

Just talking to people can open up a vast network of potential buying opportunities. The person you talk to may not have a business to sell but may have a friend, relative, neighbor, or business associate who does.

Finding a Business Through Advertising— Yours and Theirs

Another way to get leads for a business to buy is through advertising. This can work in two ways: You can look for ads placed by businesses that are up for sale, or you can advertise that you're in the market for a business. If you follow the second course— placing your own ads—you'll want to be sure your ads are going to reach enough potential buyers to justify the cost.

Local Papers

If you're interested in buying a business in a specific location or area, a logical place to look—and to advertise—is the classified section of the local newspaper, and perhaps also papers serving nearby communities. There's often a "Businesses for Sale" classification in the paper, and there may also be a section for people seeking businesses ("Business Wanted"). Classified ads in local papers often appear in the paper's online edition as well. Also consider the ad sections of local business publications, the regional

editions of the metropolitan dailies, and community papers serving a specific area of the city.

If you place an ad of your own, remember that you're aiming for a small, targeted audience. For that reason, a classified ad will likely be more effective and appropriate than a larger, more costly display ad. Here are a couple of examples of how your ad might read.

> **SEEKING RESTAURANT TO BUY.**
> Downtown or College Park area. Liquor license preferred, but beer and wine license will suffice. Can make substantial down payment. Inquiries to P.O. Box 456, Centreville, NY 55555.

> **ATTENTION PRINT SHOP OWNERS.**
> If you have a history of high-volume and consistent profits, I'd like to talk to you about buying your business—especially if your clientele is largely commercial. I can move quickly to acquire the right shop. Send information, including asking price, to Box 789, Daily Herald, 222 Herald Plaza, Sun Center, CA 55555.

Remember, less is more. Your ad needs to just hit the highlights: type of business and general location. You could also include a ballpark price (such as "$400,000 range") to help weed out businesses that will be too expensive for your pocketbook. But be aware that suggesting a price or range can be counterproductive, because any top price you mention may forever serve as a floor on offers you might make later.

To try to keep things anonymous at this stage, you can ask readers to reply to a post office box or a box designated for you by the paper's ad department. Or you can route phone calls to an intermediary—a friend or your lawyer, for instance—who won't divulge your name until you're sure a caller's business is a good prospect. Another option is to ask readers to respond to an anonymous email address.

National Papers

Sellers and buyers often reach out to one another on a national or regional basis through classified ads in the three main national papers: *The Wall Street Journal, The New York Times,* and *USA Today.* Placing an ad in the regional edition covering your extended area will reach the most likely sellers, so there's no reason to spring for a 50-state ad.

Business Publications

Publications aimed at business readers may have a limited circulation, but they're useful because they're more targeted than other media. Business publications fall into one of two general categories.

General Business Publications

In some metropolitan areas, you'll find weekly or monthly business publications that serve an entire region. Local chambers of commerce may also put out a publication that accepts advertising. (For a directory of state and local chambers of commerce, go to www.uschamber.com.) These publications are a good place to find businesses for sale and can be a surprisingly affordable and effective way to reach possible sellers.

Trade Publications

Sellers sometimes advertise in trade publications that serve their industry. You're probably already aware of the specialized publications in the industry that most interests you, but if you're not, go to the reference desk of your local library and ask to see the *SRDS Business Publication Advertising Source*—a directory that lists thousands of trade publications, categorized by industry. To learn more about this directory and order a copy if you want one, go to www.srds.com. Another reference work is the *Gale Encyclopedia of Associations,* which can lead you to trade association publications. Further information is available at www.gale.cengage. com. If you prefer to do online research, check http://dir.yahoo.com/business_and_ economy/organizations/trade_associations, where you'll find links to a number of trade association sites. You can consult trade publications for leads on businesses, or you can place your own ad. But when you place an ad in a trade publication, don't expect that the ad will appear immediately. Although the publication may be put out monthly, it quite possibly will have a relatively long lead-in time for ads, such as three months after you place the order.

Some trade organizations put out regional and statewide publications—often in the form of a simple newsletter. These publications can be good places to look and attractive places to advertise, since they reach the businesses that are closest to where you're located.

Websites That List Businesses for Sale

These days, buyers of everything from books and CDs to cars and houses turn to the Internet. For that reason, an alert seller is likely to list a for-sale business on a website devoted to such listings. And some sites also run listings for people like you who are interested in buying a business. Among the many sites used for the sale and purchase of businesses are:

- bizbuysell.com
- businessesforsale.com
- businessbroker.net
- bizquest.com
- mergernetwork.com
- startupjournal.com (operated by *The Wall Street Journal*), and
- bizben.com (featuring California businesses)
- Craigslist.org.

You can use a search feature like Google to find even more sites.

If you do place an ad on an online site, know that some sites will be more effective than others. Select the ones that, in your opinion, will be the easiest for prospective sellers to navigate. It's a plus, too, if all initial communications can be handled through the site to assure confidentiality.

Some sites have business brokers' and "Business Wanted" listings—features that may be helpful to you.

Direct Mail

A direct mail approach involves putting together a list of prospective sellers—usually no more than 100 or possibly 200 names, and often far fewer—and mailing each of them a letter expressing your interest in buying a business such as theirs. Realistically, the odds of finding a business with this approach are long, but very occasionally it works. Compiling a good list is the key to success. You need to start with a decent idea of the kind of business you're looking for and where, geographically, you'd like to be located. You can then consult the yellow pages directories for the regions you're interested in and peruse as many other lists of businesses as possible. For example, see if the local chamber of commerce will sell you a list of its members. These lists often divide businesses into categories, making it easy to identify businesses that may meet your criteria. Similarly, national, state, and local trade associations may be able to provide you with the names of their members in your area.

Once you've identified the businesses you want to contact, it's better to address your package to the owner rather than just the business—which means you'll need to do some further digging to identify the owner. If the business is a corporation or an LLC, it's likely that you can get this information from your state's secretary of state office. Ownership information for partnerships and sole proprietorships should be available from the local office where fictitious business names are registered or business licenses obtained.

Your letter to prospective sellers should include as specific a statement as possible about what you're looking for and a summary of your education, jobs you've had, and business experience. To have any chance of getting the attention of a business owner, you need to establish right off the bat that yours is a serious inquiry—that you have the background, drive, and resources to move forward with the deal and to make all the payments that you and the seller agree on.

Even under the best of circumstances, the response rate to direct mailings can be abysmally low—sometimes just one or two percent. So you may also want to plan a follow-up phone call to some of the best prospects.

Business Brokers Can Help Find Sellers

Sometimes a seller lists a business with a broker who earns a commission from the seller for helping to sell the business. You have nothing to lose by asking several brokers about businesses they're handling that may be of interest to you.

 CAUTION

The seller's broker will be loyal to the seller. The broker's job is to put together a deal at the highest possible price. He or she won't be looking out for the buyer's interests at all. So be very cautious, and make sure you have a lawyer review the sale documents before signing on the dotted line in a broker-assisted sale.

While brokers usually represent sellers, it's possible to find one who will work exclusively for you—an option worth considering if you're stymied in your search for a business to buy. You may be able to hire a broker on either an hourly or a fixed-fee basis. The broker's role will be to give you the benefit of his or her expertise and to guide you in your search. You can also agree on arrangements under which a broker will actively seek a business for you to buy. But if you do, the broker will undoubtedly want financial protection in the form of a retainer and some commitment from you to pay a commission if you buy a business and the broker's commission isn't fully picked up by the seller. Arrangements vary widely, but brokers do expect reasonable compensation for their time and effort.

For more on finding and working with brokers, including getting piecemeal help in finding a business, see Chapter 6.

What Sellers Want to Know About You

Understandably, sellers don't spend much time talking to people who are only casually interested in buying a business—the tire kickers—or those who are unlikely to come up with the money to buy. So your job, right from the get-go, is to leave sellers with as positive an impression of you as you can. You're a buyer, but you're also selling something: yourself. To help you get your foot in the door, especially with a business that might be attractive to numerous potential buyers, here are some of the things a seller will want to know about you:

- **Identification.** Most obviously, a seller will need to know exactly whom he or she is dealing with, so be prepared to provide your full name, address, email, and phone numbers.
- **Employment, career, and educational history.** A seller will be looking for detailed information about what you're doing now and what you've done in the past. You can give this information in a resumé, just as if you were applying for a key position at the business.
- **Why you're interested in buying the business.** The reasons why you're inquiring need to make logical sense to the seller. If an engineering professor says, "I don't know anything about business, but I've always thought it would be fun to own a restaurant," the seller may (understandably) conclude that the potential buyer may be a kook. By contrast, if the owner of a small, successful catering company expresses interest, the seller might keep talking.
- **Preliminary information about your financial resources.** A seller will probably require much more information up front from someone who works as a clerk at the local discount store than from someone who's just taken early retirement from a good job at a local manufacturing company. Again, the seller will want to get enough information to eliminate people with inadequate financial resources or skills.
- **References.** A seller may ask for references from employers, bankers, and business associates to be reasonably confident you're telling a straight story.

After you've provided the basic information, a seller who's concluded that there's a reasonable prospect of doing a deal may want to dig deeper. Here are some further sources of information the seller might consider:

- **Other people who know you.** The seller may believe that the people you name as references are almost sure to paint a positive picture, so, in addition to contacting the named references, the seller may look further. For example, a seller may tap his or her own extended personal network to find other people who know you and possibly have done business with you. In addition, the seller may inquire of former employers and colleagues.

- **Bankruptcy history.** A seller may check with the federal bankruptcy court in your district to see if you've ever filed for personal or business bankruptcy.
- **Educational background.** If your educational or professional background is important for success in the business, a seller may ask you for written permission to check with colleges and professional associations.

Trusting their intuition, some sellers may be willing to have more extensive discussions with you before checking you out in much depth. But sooner or later, a savvy seller will want to learn as much as possible about you before signing a sales agreement.

Of course, you'll also want to check the seller out thoroughly—both personally and in terms of the claims he or she is making about the profitability and condition of the business. Some of the information you'll want is the same as what's listed above, and some is specific to investigating a possible purchase. For more about how to do a thorough investigation before making a commitment, see Chapter 9.

The checklist below reiterates the main tasks you'll need to undertake at the beginning of your search for a business.

✓ Checklist for Finding a Business to Buy

- ☐ Identify potential sellers close to home—family members, friends, and your employer, for example.

- ☐ If you own a business now, identify businesses similar to yours or that complement yours.

- ☐ Develop a search plan that includes word of mouth, advertising, and/or direct mail.

- ☐ Consult a broker if you need help in finding available businesses.

- ☐ Know what sellers look for in a buyer so that you can put your best foot forward.

What's the Business Worth?

Valuing the business you are considering buying is a key concern. Of course, you don't want to overpay. But, equally important, if you have unrealistic expectations and you persistently try to negotiate for a bargain price, you may find yourself spinning your wheels as seller after seller concludes that you're not a serious buyer.

Figuring out what a business is worth isn't as precise a process as you might want it to be. There's no secret pricing formula, expert estimate, or clairvoyant that can provide you with just the right figure. Still, you can arrive at a reasonable price range that you will use in your negotiations. Depending on the business, the low end of the range will probably be little more than the liquidation value of the physical assets. The high end is likely to be based on income projections, and what you think it's reasonable to pay for the right to receive (and hopefully increase) those earnings in the future.

If you're looking at a healthy business—especially one with a well-established customer base and positive reputation—the seller will probably start the negotiations by stating an asking price toward the top of the range of possible values for that business but may back off a bit in negotiating the final price. In valuing any business, you'll need to take into account the general economic climate, as well as trends in the industry. And, of course, a seller who has to sell quickly will likely accept a lower price than if there was no rush on the sale.

This chapter explains the main factors that influence the worth of a business and suggests ways for you to arrive at a realistic price range to use in your negotiations. It also offers you help in figuring out your own bottom line for buying a business if you're buying it as an investment—a calculation that isn't only about what the business might be worth in terms of its fair market value, but also clarifies what you, specifically, are willing to pay for it.

There's No Universal Pricing Formula: Many Factors Affect Price

It would be logical to think that there's some simple, widely accepted formula to determine what a business is worth. You may even expect that you can plug some numbers into a long-established valuation formula to get a reasonable idea of what the sale price of a given business should be. Unfortunately, no magic formula exists. Instead, there are multiple approaches to figuring out the value of a business—all of which are subject to exceptions and caveats relating to factors in and outside the business. For example, the presence of a major new competitor or a lingering economic downturn may make the best formulaic price estimates irrelevant.

Several factors go into pricing a business, including terms of payment, the type of buyer you are, market demand, and the seller's personal needs. Let's look at each of these.

Terms of Payment

The price that you feel comfortable paying is often tied directly to the terms of payment. Chances are that you'll find a seller willing to let you finance the purchase of a business on an installment basis in which you pay the seller over time.

It follows that the terms of the deal, such as the amount of the down payment, the repayment period, and the interest rate, can all affect what you're willing to pay and what the seller is willing to accept. For example, if you'll be paying for the business over five years rather than three, the seller may insist on charging you more because of the longer-lasting risk that you'll default. And you may be willing to pay a bit more for the privilege of lower payments and a longer payment period.

 TIP

Installment payments may also favor the seller. Installment payments may put the seller into a lower income tax bracket than would apply if you paid in a lump sum.

Type of Buyer

Especially when you'll be relying on the business for a livelihood, the sale price and the terms of payment need to result in cash flow sufficient to cover not only operating expenses and monthly installments, but also enough to pay you a decent salary for the hours that you work. So if you're intending to work in the business on a daily basis and it will be your primary source of income, you must factor those needs into your thinking about what price you're willing to pay for the business.

If you're a different kind of buyer—for example, one who's looking to buy a business as an investment and will have a manager running the place—your considerations may be different. You'll then need to be sure the business can support the necessary number of employees and still be profitable enough to yield a decent return on the money you invest in it. And if you're buying a business as a strategic addition to a similar business you already own, you may be able to reap the benefits of scale, and for that reason you may be willing to pay a bit more up front knowing that you'll earn it back through increased profits in the next few years.

Market Demand

A fact of life in buying anything of value, including a business, is current demand: what other buyers may be willing to pay for what the seller has to sell. As you probably know from buying a house or other valuable property, timing can be crucial. The seller may present you with a price or range that—based on all available evidence and the best evaluation approach—is quite fair. But forces beyond the seller's control may enable you to buy the business at a much lower price. For example, if a number of similar businesses have just been put on the market or there's been a recent spate of factory closures in your area, the seller may feel pressure to lower the sale price—or, on the other hand, might opt to take the business off the market and wait until conditions create a demand at a higher price. In other words, factors outside of either party's control may affect the sale price, and the sale itself, in many ways.

The Seller's Personal Needs or Preferences

Poor health or financial pressures may force a seller to sell a business quickly—within months, or possibly even weeks of making the decision to sell. If for these or other reasons the seller needs to sell quickly, you'll probably be able to acquire the business at much less than the top dollar the seller might otherwise have been able to command.

Similarly, if the seller is unable or unwilling to work for you—even for a short time after the closing—that fact may justify your putting a lower value on the business because you lose the potential benefit of a smooth transition and the transfer of knowledge. Conversely, the seller's willingness to help with the transition for, say, six months may be a plus that tips the scale toward a higher price.

Sales of Comparable Businesses

A great way to set a value on a business is to see what similar small enterprises have

sold for. This happens all the time in the housing market, where it's called looking at "comparables" or "comps." But unlike real estate sales, where it's usually not too difficult to find recent sales of homes more or less like the one you're considering, in the business world there may have been few, if any, recent sales of similar businesses. What's more, since small businesses tend to be unique, even a business that's similar on the surface probably won't be the same as the one you're considering. Location, sales volume, number of employees, and a host of other important factors can make comparisons difficult.

Even in the unlikely event that you can find a recent sale of a company that very closely resembles one you're thinking of buying, you may not be able to get access to accurate figures relating to the sale. Unlike sales of real estate, which often leave a public paper trail, reliable business sales numbers can be hard to come by—especially since rumor, exaggeration, and just plain blarney often obscure the facts.

CAUTION

Watch out for incomplete sales information. Go to any event with people in your field—or just attend a service club meeting—and you're sure to hear that so-and-so bought a certain business for such-and-such dollars. For example, at a Kiwanis lunch, you may learn that Ed paid only $100,000 for a thriving dry cleaning business. Even assuming this number has some truth to it (and it may not), you may not be told other important details. For example, the reports of the sale price may not mention that Ed agreed to pay the former owner a salary of $75,000 a year for three years to stay on as an employee, that Ed had to immediately replace deteriorating equipment at a cost of $60,000, and that, as part the deal, he bought the old building that contains the business for a whopping $500,000.

Despite these difficulties with comparable sales, if you're able to use information from a number of sources, including trade publications, business brokers, the Internet, and personal contacts, you should be able to come up with a reasonably accurate ballpark estimate for what businesses like the one you're considering are selling for.

 RESOURCE

How to research comparable sales. A good place to look online for comparable sales information is the Business Valuation Resource site at www.bvmarketdata.com, where you'll find information on the company's BizComp service.

The Asset-Based Approach

Another commonly used approach to putting a price on a business is to tally up the value of the assets, starting with the tangible ones, such as furniture, equipment, and inventory—using resale rather than replacement numbers. An appraiser can help

you. The figure you arrive at will probably be the smallest amount the seller will accept for a business. But if you're looking at a money-losing or otherwise troubled business—or if the seller is under pressure to quickly sell a tiny business that depends primarily on the seller's efforts—then the value of the physical assets may be the most the seller can hope to get and should be the most you're willing to pay.

EXAMPLE: Carl owns a T-shirt shop in a resort town. He has a month-to-month lease. Lately, Carl's business has barely broken even, because other T-shirt shops have opened and because a scare from a large forest fire left the town less popular than it once was. Carl has a chance to take a full-time, year-round job in another city and wants to sell his business. Marlene, a prospective buyer, adds up the value of the tangible assets, including the shelving, counters, display cases, furniture, computer, T-shirt printing equipment, and inventory. She arrives at a figure of $22,500. This is the most that Marlene is willing to pay, especially since she knows that Carl needs to sell quickly in order to take the job elsewhere.

Even a business that's been performing poorly may be worth more than the value of its tangible assets. For example, the business may have favorable long-term contracts with customers or suppliers or other intangible assets that translate into additional value. A long-term lease for a good location with below-market rent is one especially valuable intangible asset. If the lease can be transferred to you, the seller may be justified in seeking more than just the value of the tangible assets.

Similarly, the seller may be able to demonstrate that there's value in a business name or in patents, copyrights, or customer lists the business owns. Employees, too, can be an important intangible asset.

But just as intangible assets can add value to a business, negative factors such as unresolved lawsuits can reduce its value. However, business liabilities, whether known or unknown, will be significant only if you'll be assuming responsibility for them. If the seller agrees to be solely responsible—and you're convinced that the seller has the financial resources to follow through—the liabilities are unlikely to affect the asset pricing of a business.

! CAUTION

Don't confuse asset pricing with an asset sale. These two terms are similar but have very different meanings. The asset method of pricing a business can be used whether you buy a corporate or LLC entity, or only a laundry list of its key assets. The same, incidentally, is true for all the other methods of valuing a business. In short, the method used to value a business doesn't depend on how the sale is structured.

The Income Valuation Approach

The income valuation method assumes that you're looking at a business as just one more type of investment, competing for your dollars with stocks, bonds, real estate, and other business opportunities. The question then becomes, "What kind of return would you expect from an investment in this business?" Once you arrive at this number, you can work backwards to determine the price you're willing to pay. And this method also assumes that you won't buy a business that doesn't give you the return you want on your investment. Rather than determining what the business is worth on some objective level, this method helps you determine what the business is worth *to you*, given what you hope to accomplish by purchasing it.

Here's how it works. As you know, if you're seeking a conservative investment, you might look into U.S. government bonds. The money you invest in those bonds will be about as safe as you can imagine. In return for that safety, you'll probably be satisfied with a relatively low interest rate—say, 5%. If you invest $10,000 in a 5% government bond, you're confident that for the duration of the bond, you'll receive $500 each year in interest. When the bond matures, you know you'll get back your $10,000 investment.

But most any business is more risky than U.S. government bonds or other conservative investments. So if you're looking to buy a business as an investment, you'll reasonably want your expected annual rate of return to be higher—at least 10%–12% for an extremely stable business, but 15%–20% or more for a riskier small enterprise. This is where the income valuation approach comes in.

If you've evaluated a business that earns about $10,000 in profit each year and you're quite sure it will continue to earn at the same level in future years, and you want to earn 10% on your investment, you can figure out that $100,000 is the right price for you to pay (10% x $100,000 = $10,000). But if you want to earn 20% on your investment in that same business, you'll only be willing to pay $50,000 (20% x $50,000 = $10,000.) Note that the $10,000 profit figure is constant in both instances. The desired rate of return and the price are the variables. In a moment, we'll see how you can apply this method of setting a price to almost any business you're considering.

 CAUTION

Before you use the income valuation—or investment—method of determining the right price for you to pay: You need to be convinced that you can predict the business's profits for the next three to five years with a reasonable degree of accuracy. Otherwise, you have nothing solid on which to base your computations—it's all speculation. This chapter and Chapter 9 tell you how to evaluate the financial information that the seller provides you, to determine whether you're able to make these predictions.

Here are a couple of examples of how you can use your prediction of future profits and your desired rate of return to come up with a value for a business.

EXAMPLE 1: Let's say that based on your research, you reasonably expect a particular business will produce annual profits of $50,000 for each of the next several years. Let's also say that you believe the business is relatively risky. For that reason, you'd want a high return on your investment, perhaps 20% a year. So how much is the business worth? Let's start with the following formula:

Business Value x Desired Rate of Return = Expected Annual Profits

Here, we know two of the three variables, so we can plug those numbers into the equation:

Business Value x 20% = $50,000

As you'll remember from high school math, another way to state this is:

$$\text{Business Value} = \frac{\$50,000}{20\%}$$

Now, using a calculator, let's divide $50,000 by .20 (the decimal equivalent of 20%). The answer is a value of $250,000.

If everything goes according to plan, you can invest $250,000 in the business, receive a return of $50,000 a year, and then at some point sell the business for—you hope—at least the original $250,000.

EXAMPLE 2: Now let's say that if because of the business's long history of profitability you'd be happy with a 15% rate of return. Here's how the formula would play out:

Business Value x 15% = $50,000

Let's restate the equation this way:

$$\text{Business Value} = \frac{\$50,000}{15\%}$$

Now, using a calculator, we'll divide $50,000 by .15 (the decimal equivalent of 15%). The answer is a business value of $333,333. If everything goes according to plan, you'll invest $333,333 in the business, receive a return of $50,000 a year, and then at some point sell the business for—you hope—at least the original $333,333.

As you can see, deciding on the rate of return you expect to receive is crucial. In these examples, the difference in what you're willing to pay if you use a 15% return rate rather than a 20% rate is significant. At the 15% rate of return, you'd value the business at $333,333, but if you're counting on a 20% rate of return, you'd value it at only $250,000.

You can't rely solely on this type of income formula to arrive at the value of a business. For one thing, you'll need to factor in an estimate of how future inflation or deflation might affect the business and its income. Even more important is the fact that you'll probably be looking at the business not just as an investment, but also as a way to earn a living. The cash flow of the business will need to be sufficient to adequately reward you for your work.

Industry Formulas and Rules of Thumb

In some specific areas of business, such as bakeries, tax services, and publishing, certain valuation formulas have gained credence. For example, you might be told that a certain type of business commonly sells for ten times profits or two times sales. Unquestionably, such formulas promise a quick and easy way to price a business. The problem is that these formulas are almost always too simplistic to serve as anything more than a very rough guide for the sale of real businesses, with their unique quirks and characteristics.

Formulas Based on Sales or Earnings

Insiders in some industries suggest that you can arrive at a sales value by multiplying either gross sales or net earnings by a number that's generally accepted in that business community. So, for example, in some niches of the publishing business, you may read in a trade journal that profitable companies commonly change hands at from 1.2 to 1.5 times annual sales. In theory, these formulas are derived from industry experience over a number of years, as represented by data covering lots of previous sales. In reality, such formulas may be based on little more than industry lore and may not accurately reflect current market conditions or the particular business niche you're in. Thus, in the real world of book publishing, textbook publishers tend to sell for a higher multiple of sales than the industry average (because the textbook backlist tends to have more value and discounts are lower). By comparison, publishers that concentrate on popular fiction must settle for a lower multiple (because even a long string of bestsellers is no guarantee of future success).

If you're considering buying a business in a field where formulas like this are part of the culture, go ahead and look at what the figure would be using that formula. But then make sure you carefully consider all of the factors that might cause the sale price to deviate from the number you reach with that calculation. And be prepared for the seller to do the same.

Formulas Based on Units

In some industries, there are also pricing formulas based on the number of customer contracts in place, or the number of machines in operation. For example, you may read that a company that sells and monitors security alarm systems can be priced based on a widely recognized sum for each customer currently under contract for alarm monitoring services. Similarly, a food and beverage vending machine business may be priced based on a sum for each vending machine currently owned by the business and in operation at a money-making location.

Again, at best, formulaic approaches like these are extremely rough guides. Because in any real sale there are so many other variables to be accounted for—from competition and location to consumer trends and general economic conditions—it's a poor idea to apply a formula uncritically to the business you're considering. Still, almost everyone tosses these numbers around, and they may have some utility in determining whether the price you're thinking of offering is within a normally accepted range. If you're way off the mark, it may be a sign that you should take a second look at your calculations and assumptions.

How Appraisers and Other Experts Can Help You Decide on a Fair Price

This chapter covers the general principles of business valuation, but it can't deal with the dozens of often complex and conflicting factors that go into pricing a particular business. Unless you already have some specialized knowledge or experience valuing businesses, it often makes sense to pay a reasonable amount for the opinion of a small business accountant, experienced business broker, or appraiser.

Accountants

An accountant can help organize and evaluate the financial data of the business you're looking at, and then apply whatever pricing formulas might be available. Also, the accountant can help you present the pricing information in a format that will make sense to the seller and to the seller's own accountant. See Chapter 6 for advice on finding and working with accountants.

Business Brokers

A broker can help by tracking down elusive information about sales of comparable businesses and then tailoring that information to current market conditions in your community. If you'll be handling most of the purchase yourself, including finding a business to buy, make it clear at the outset that you just want the broker's opinion on pricing. See Chapter 6 for advice on finding and working with brokers.

Appraisers

In general terms, an appraiser is someone who routinely puts a value on things such as real estate, equipment, and businesses. Some appraisers are—or started out as—accountants. Others are, or were, real estate agents. And still others have simply attended some seminars on appraising. If you decide to hire an appraiser, be very careful to choose the right one. Historically, appraisers have excelled in assigning a value to tangible property such as land, buildings, and equipment. However, in most cases, a business is worth more than the sum of its assets, so you need to pick an appraiser who understands and has had experience in factoring in nontangible elements, such as a long-term lease (which can add to value) or increasing competition (which can detract from it).

A banker or real estate broker may be able to suggest a good local appraiser. You can also find appraisers through such organizations as the American Society of Appraisers (www.appraisers.org) and the Institute of Business Appraisers (www.go-iba. org). But before you sign on with someone, make sure that he or she has training and experience in appraising small businesses— ideally in the same industry as the business under consideration, and in the same general geographic location that you're considering. Ask for the names of past clients, and then call these references to learn what you can about the appraiser's competence and communication skills.

Once hired, a careful appraiser will insist on seeing a whole raft of information, including the business's tax returns, financial statements, asset lists, and leases and other contracts. The appraiser will use this information to write a comprehensive report explaining how he or she reached an opinion as to value. Expect to pay several thousand dollars at a minimum for a thorough appraisal and an informative written report. Assuming that the appraiser has good credentials, you can use the appraisal report to help convince the seller that you're offering a reasonable price for the business.

Books and Seminars on Valuing a Business

Another excellent option for tapping into expertise on value is to read up on the subject in greater detail. Specialized books offer information on the various pricing methods and provide examples of how the theories can be applied to actual businesses. You might start with *Valuing Small Businesses and Professional Practices,* by Shannon P. Pratt (McGraw-Hill), which is the clearest and most comprehensive treatment that you're likely to find.

Other less-expensive choices include *What Every Business Owner Should Know About Valuing Their Business,* by Stanley J. Feldman, Timothy G. Sullivan, and Roger M. Winsby (McGraw-Hill), and *The Small Business Valuation Book,* by Lawrence W. Tuller (Adams Media).

Occasionally, business brokers or appraisers present seminars on valuation methods, and a community college or business school in your area may offer a short course on the subject. Your local Chamber of Commerce also may have information about such offerings.

Putting Together All the Information

This chapter offers just a brief introduction to an enormously important and complex subject. Obviously, to feel anywhere near comfortable with your conclusions about the price range for a business, you'll need to tap into other resources such as professionals, books, and seminars. You'll quickly discover that most accountants, business brokers, and other experts prefer to blend the results of several methods to arrive at a range of values for a business.

No price you offer for a business will mean much if it doesn't make sense to the seller, who, after all, is just as interested in a good deal as you are. And remember that you'll probably be paying for the business on an installment payment plan. Your ability to pay the full sale price over the long run should be more important to the seller than whether you agree to pay the highest possible price. If you have an excellent credit history and can convince the seller that the business will almost certainly succeed under your ownership, you may be able to pick up a business at a very low price.

From the seller's point of view, the sale won't be complete until you've paid all the money you've agreed upon, typically in three to five years. The seller is well aware that much can go wrong in the meantime, and even the best security arrangements may not guarantee that the seller will get all that you've agreed to pay. For example, if two years after the closing the seller takes back the business because you can't keep up the installment payments, the seller may wind up with a much-deteriorated business that isn't worth what's still owed on your promissory note. To make matters worse, the seller will be forced to run the business again until another buyer can be found. So it's in the seller's interest—as well as yours—to not set the price so high that you can't make a decent living while also paying the balance you owe on the business.

TIP

Wiggle room can be built into the sales price. If you're not convinced that the business is worth as much the seller thinks, see if the seller will consider an earn-out arrangement. It works like this: You and the seller agree to a base price that's lower than what the seller wants. You also agree that if the business meets a stated earnings level during the first year, you'll pay the seller additional money. Understandably, however, the seller may be hesitant to leave the sales price unsettled—especially if the seller will no longer be substantially involved in running the business.

Below is a checklist reiterating the key factors you'll need to consider in valuing the business you are considering buying.

Checklist for Pricing a Business

☐ Obtain a list of the business's assets—both tangible (such as equipment) and intangible (such as your company's goodwill)—and put a value on those assets.

☐ Learn all you can about the sale prices of comparable businesses.

☐ Evaluate the current business climate in your community.

☐ Determine the rate of return you'd expect, if you're buying the business as an investment.

☐ Consider whether the sale price and installment payment terms would let you earn a decent living by working in the business.

☐ Learn the formulas and rules of thumb used in the industry that the business is a part of—but use the resulting numbers as a rough guide only.

☐ Read books and attend seminars on business valuation.

☐ Get professional help as needed from your accountant, or hire a business broker or appraiser.

Working With Lawyers, Accountants, and Brokers

As you start the process of looking for a business to buy, and then move into negotiating and closing a deal, you'll need to decide how much of the work you want to delegate to others and how much you're prepared to do yourself. If your purchase is fairly straightforward and you want to limit expenses, you may decide to perform many routine tasks yourself, using occasional expert help from a lawyer, an accountant, or perhaps a business broker. Armed with the information in this book, many buyers will find that to be a feasible arrangement. Not only will you have the legal and practical information necessary to handle the purchase mostly by yourself, but you should also be able to save considerable money in professional fees. But to make this approach work, you'll need to find professionals who are willing to offer advice, serve as objective sounding boards, and do some technical chores without trying to take over the whole job.

This chapter discusses your relationships with the main professionals you're likely to hire in the process of buying a business. See Chapter 5 for information about working with an appraiser to help you determine an appropriate price to pay for the business you're looking into.

You May Need More Than Occasional Professional Help

The subcontracting-coaching model of working with lawyers, accountants, and other professionals suggested in this book may not be optimal for everyone. Here are some situations when you may decide to rely much more heavily on professional assistance, doing little if anything yourself:

- You've never owned or managed a business before.
- You're buying a business from a sophisticated seller who's aided by a team of seasoned professionals.
- You anticipate there will be unusual legal or financial complexities.
- The deal involves a substantial amount of money.
- You're buying a business that owns—and will be transferring to you—real estate or significant intellectual property.
- You're unsure about the best way to include cobuyers in your purchase.

Even if you decide to rely heavily on outside professional help, take the time to read this book carefully. By doing so, you'll better understand all that needs to be done and will have the information you need to effectively supervise the people who will do it.

Lawyers

If you're already in business, you've probably hired a lawyer from time to time. Your attorney may have helped or advised you in the creation of a partnership, corporation, or LLC. And perhaps your lawyer reviewed your lease, drafted a contract between you and an independent contractor, or represented you in a lawsuit or at an arbitration hearing. If so, you're already familiar with the kinds of things an attorney can do for a small business.

But if you're not now in business or this is the first time that you're buying one, you may not know the many places in the transaction where a lawyer can assist you.

How a Lawyer Can Help

Here are some of the tasks for which the help or coaching of an experienced small business lawyer can be valuable:

- making sure the seller's partnership, corporation, or LLC documents are complete and up to date
- assisting you in forming an entity to buy a business
- helping you prepare an agreement with people who will co-own the business with you
- figuring out whether or not the seller's lease and other contracts can be readily transferred to you, and making the transfers happen

- identifying relevant state and local laws that apply to your purchase, such as bulk sales laws
- analyzing the pros and cons of buying a business's assets versus buying the entity
- reviewing any agreement you sign with a broker
- negotiating terms of the sale
- preparing a nonbinding letter of intent summarizing the deal terms
- drafting or reviewing a sales agreement, including important clauses on the allocation of responsibility for liabilities
- drafting or reviewing other important documents such as assignments of the seller's intellectual property rights or an employment contract describing the arrangements for the seller to work for you
- making sure that a consulting agreement or noncompete agreement protects you adequately
- preparing or reviewing transfer documents if you're buying a building or land
- creating your closing checklist and otherwise preparing paperwork for the closing, and
- conducting a smooth and thorough closing.

In addition, a lawyer with tax expertise can advise you on the tax consequences of your purchase.

The key point here is not necessarily that your lawyer should do everything; it's that you should understand that your lawyer can help you with the important steps in the purchase process on an as-needed basis. Just how much legal help you buy is your call. Especially if a lot of money is involved in the purchase, so that in the overall scheme of things professional fees will be a relatively small item, you may find it cost-efficient to ask your lawyer to do much of this work. By contrast, if you're counting every penny, you'll be inclined to do the lion's share yourself.

EXAMPLE: Lori and Toni have been negotiating with Tom to buy Tom's food supplement and vitamin business. They agree on major terms, and Lori and Toni try their hands at preparing a sales agreement. With the help of this book, they understand most of what they're doing but get hung up on exactly how to word the sections of the agreement dealing with who's liable if a disaffected former employee sues. They also have questions about how to draft some of the terms of a one-year employment contract under which Tom will continue to work for the business. To get help, Lori and Toni take the sales agreement and employment contract to their business lawyer, Sheila. They talk for 45 minutes. After they part, Sheila spends an hour and a half revising the two agreements. They talk again for 15 minutes and then jointly make the final changes. Lori and Toni thank Sheila and make sure she'll be available to look over the closing documents later on. Sheila bills them $700 for three and one-half hours of her time. Given the value of the help they received, Lori and Toni consider this to be a bargain.

As you read this book, you can prepare a running list of legal tasks for which you'd like a lawyer's help. By doing this, you'll reduce the chances that you'll omit any needed legal coaching or services. An experienced business lawyer should be able to deal with most aspects of a small business purchase, but you may need more specialized legal help in some cases—for example, if there are intellectual property or environmental issues.

Finding or Selecting a Lawyer

You may already have an ongoing professional relationship with a business lawyer, or at least have a lawyer you've occasionally consulted in the past. If you're happy with that person's services and the fee arrangements, great.

But if you've gotten by without a lawyer's assistance, or feel that the lawyer you know best doesn't have the right experience to help you with a business purchase, you'll need to do some searching. Finding a good lawyer to assist you in the purchase of a business may take a bit of doing, but it's important to persist and find the right person to help you.

Special Business Situations That Require a Lawyer's Help

Here are three special situations when consulting a lawyer is almost always necessary:

- **You're buying a business that's operating under a franchise.** The procedures are considerably more complicated than those for buying an independently owned and operated business. The franchise agreement almost certainly will limit the seller's freedom to negotiate the terms of a sale in a number of significant ways, all of which must be allowed for. A lawyer can help make sure that your purchase will be consistent with the terms of the franchise agreement and will be acceptable to the franchisor. (See Chapter 1 for cautions about getting into a franchise deal.)
- **The business owns a building.** If you're buying the building along with the business itself, you'll need state-specific information on how ownership should be transferred to you so that you acquire good legal title. This book doesn't go into depth on the mechanics of transferring ownership in all 50 states. But for a lawyer, preparing and reviewing real estate documents is a routine task.
- **The business needs a license or permit issued by a state or local regulatory agency.** The procedure for transferring a license or permit to a new owner differs from locale to locale. So while this book explains the role of licenses and permits in some detail, you'll need additional information or help to have them transferred to you. If you have trouble navigating the bureaucracy on your own, a lawyer may be able to cut through the red tape.

Begin your search by compiling a list of lawyers who are already expert in the field. The last thing you want is someone who will use your purchase to learn the ropes while charging you. Seek out recommendations from people who have successfully bought businesses—ideally businesses similar to the one you're considering. Also, check with people in your community who own or operate high-quality independent businesses, even if they're not the same type you're planning to buy. These people obviously understand quality in other ways, so why not in lawyers?

People who provide services to the business community can also help you identify lawyers to consider. For example, a banker, accountant, insurance agent, or real estate broker you respect and trust may frequently come into contact with lawyers who represent businesses. They're in a prime position to make informed judgments. Friends, relatives, and business associates can also provide names of possible lawyers. But ask them specifically for the names of lawyers who've had experience working for business clients.

Checking Out Lawyers

For more information about the lawyers on your preliminary list, check out the Martindale-Hubbell Law Directory at www.martindale.com. This resource contains biographical sketches of most practicing lawyers and information about their experience, specialties, and education and the professional organizations they belong to. Another source of information about lawyers is the Nolo Lawyer Directory at www.nolo.com, which contains personal profiles of lawyers by geographical area.

If you want to expand your search, the director of your local chamber of commerce may be able to provide a list of likely prospects. Or ask a local law librarian to give you a list of lawyers who have written books or articles on your state's business law and practices. And the director of a trade association may point you in the direction of a lawyer in your area who has experience working with businesses in the industry that you're interested in.

Interviewing Prospects

After you've narrowed your list, take the time to talk to your top prospects. Especially if a fair amount of legal work may be involved, many lawyers will be open to talking to you about your needs as part of an initial consultation—either for free or for an agreed-on nominal fee. Call each lawyer on your list and try to set up a short meeting at which you can explain your business needs, assess the prospect's experience, and evaluate how the two of you get along. Also try to judge how accessible the lawyer will be when you have questions.

Trust your instincts in deciding whether the lawyer's personality and business sense are compatible with yours. And be sure the lawyer is comfortable with working at least to some degree as your coach while you take care of important aspects of the purchase yourself. If a lawyer seems more inclined to take charge of every aspect of your purchase, look elsewhere, unless that's what you want and need.

Understanding Lawyer Fees

Most likely, the lawyers you speak to will charge by the hour—often in the range of $200 to $300 an hour or more, depending on where you live and how experienced the lawyer is. Cheaper isn't always better, as more-experienced lawyers who charge higher rates may be more efficient and cost you less in the long run. Based on what you want the lawyer to do, try to get an estimate of what the total legal fees will likely be for the services you need. But realize that most lawyers will be reluctant to commit to a firm price, because the hours of service you'll ultimately use are inherently unpredictable. The time spent will depend on how much help you need and how quickly your sale comes together— and whether there are any big glitches in the course of the purchase. Still, a ballpark estimate is better than nothing.

To keep your legal costs under control, be well organized. Gather all important documents before you meet with your lawyer, and come prepared with a written list of questions and discussion items. Also, insist that you be given an itemized bill each month. If for any reason your initial bills are for more than you expected, don't just bite your tongue and pay; call the lawyer and discuss your concerns.

 RESOURCE

Find out more about hiring and working with a business lawyer. Check out the *Legal Guide for Starting & Running a Small Business*, by Fred S. Steingold (Nolo).

Accountants

You know, of course, that accountants deal in numbers and are steeped in the mysteries of the tax laws. If you're already using an accountant in an existing business—for example, to prepare your tax returns and financial statements—or for personal financial matters, you have some idea of what he or she can do for you. But if you've never bought a business before, you may

not be fully aware of how an accountant can participate at this stage of the game. An accountant may be able to help you in carrying out the following important tasks:

- reviewing the seller's tax returns, and making sure that there are no outstanding disputes with the IRS or state taxing authorities
- looking over the past financial records of the business to see how the business has performed
- allocating the sale price among the various assets being sold and completing IRS Form 8594, *Asset Acquisition Statement*
- checking the restated versions of the seller's income tax figures in which the seller legitimately tries to demonstrate that the business is more profitable than a mere perusal of the tax returns would suggest
- reviewing the seller's business plan (if any) to see if projections of future profits seem realistic
- estimating the federal and state tax consequences of buying the business under various scenarios—for example, buying the assets versus the entire entity, paying the seller in one lump sum versus installments, and whether your estate plan should be factored in
- reviewing documents that show your financial status
- determining a reasonable price range for the business

- developing sensible interest and payment terms for the promissory note you'll sign, and
- preparing future tax returns associated with the sale, including appropriate depreciation schedules.

Your best source of accounting help is likely to be a Certified Public Accountant (CPA), because of the rigorous requirements for earning that designation. But a word of caution: Not all CPAs are qualified to provide all of the small business purchase services suggested above. That's because many CPAs specialize in preparing individual tax returns but don't routinely assist in business purchases. It follows that you'll need to probe a bit to see whether the CPA you're considering has depth in the kind of work you need help with. And especially if you're looking for a CPA to help in determining the value of the business, find out whether the CPA is a Certified Valuation Analyst. A CPA with this certification is more likely to have the valuation skills you're looking for than one who lacks that certification. (To learn more about these specialists, check the website of the National Association of Certified Valuation Analysts, www.nacva.com.)

The process of finding the right CPA is roughly parallel to that of finding a suitable business lawyer. Your best bet is to compile a list of prospects by talking to other business owners—especially ones who've had a CPA's help in buying a business. Lawyers, bankers, real estate brokers, and insurance agents can often provide good leads as well.

CPAs are listed in the yellow pages under "Accountants." You can also use the Internet in your search, starting with the site of the American Institute of Certified Public Accountants at www.aicpa.org and www.cpadirectory.com.

Interviewing your short list of accountant prospects will help you size up the likelihood that you will work well with one of them. For obvious reasons, when checking out a CPA, try to avoid the weeks just before April 15.

Just as it does when you are working with a lawyer, it pays to develop a collaborative relationship with your CPA so that you can decide the exact level of services you want or need. If you have a reasonable facility with numbers, you can certainly save money by doing a lot of the work yourself. But even if you're very good with numbers, you may want to turn to your accountant for help with the tax aspects of your purchase.

Like lawyers, accountants typically charge for their services on an hourly basis, as illustrated in the example below.

EXAMPLE: Marian is considering the purchase of a computer repair business. She requests and gets the seller's financial and tax records and discusses an installment payment plan. Now Marian is ready to negotiate the terms of the purchase. But before doing so, Marian wants to be 100% sure that she's correctly interpreted the federal tax rules that will apply to her purchase and that the plan she's put together for allocating the sale price among the business assets is appropriate. To this end, she schedules a one-hour conference with Mark, an experienced CPA, at which Marian fills Mark in on the background of her intended purchase and how she hopes to pay the sale price. After the conference, Mark reviews the draft sales agreement and the promissory note that Marian has left with him. When they meet again the following week, Mark explains precisely what Marian's tax liability will be and how she can allocate the sales price for quicker write-offs on her income tax returns. And for further advantage, he recommends reducing the amount Marian will pay for the seller's covenant not to compete and slightly increasing the sale price instead. Mark charges Marian $150 an hour for two and a half hours of his professional time. The total bill ($375) is well worth it. Realizing what a big help Mark has been, Marian decides to hire him to prepare her business and personal tax returns in the future, since she knows she'll be facing some complex and unfamiliar tax issues.

Business Brokers

With this book and appropriate coaching and assistance from your lawyer and accountant, you may not need any other professional help with your purchase. But, if you're searching for a highly specialized business or any kind of business that might be difficult to find, you can also use a business broker to help you locate the business you want.

If you do turn to a broker, keep one important fact in mind: Business brokers almost invariably work for sellers, not buyers. This is completely different from brokers who operate in the area of residential real estate, but that hasn't always been the case. Once upon a time, all real estate agents worked just for sellers. But today, it's possible for a buyer to engage a buyer's agent to help find land or a building to buy, or suitable commercial space to lease. Professional practices are firmly in place to make this work.

Business brokers have not yet moved in this direction. They feel that working for buyers can be an unproductive use of time. One business broker explains that of the people who call to inquire about available businesses to buy, only about 2% actually wind up buying one. By contrast, among people calling a real estate agent to ask about available houses, probably 80% will wind up buying one in the local market.

But don't write off business brokers entirely. A business broker who has lots of businesses listed for sale may have one that interests you and may be able to present your credentials to the seller in an attractive package. The broker may also help in working out the terms of a deal. But the broker's primary interest will be to see that a deal is concluded and the seller gets the best possible price. The seller pays the broker's commission, and the broker's duty of loyalty is to the seller alone. Before you sign any documents prepared or presented by a broker, read them carefully. And get a lawyer's help if there's anything you don't understand or if you need more assurance that everything is on the up and up.

Although business brokers typically have little or no experience in working for buyers, you may find one who's willing to break out of the usual mold and work for you alone. An experienced broker will be familiar with the current business-for-sale market in the industry or location you're interested in. It's highly unlikely that any professional other than a business broker will have this kind of information available.

If you decide to approach a business broker to find a business for you, you'll need to reach agreement on how the broker will get paid. There are no hard-and-fast rules. Here are some possibilities to consider:

Flat fee. You pay a fixed amount (such as $3,000) for the broker's efforts in looking for a business for you, regardless of whether the broker is successful or not.

Fee based on success. You pay a fixed fee, but only if you buy a business as a result of the broker's efforts.

Hourly fee. You pay by the hour for the broker's time.

To repeat a key point, if you find a broker willing to work for you, you'll be entering new territory. There are no established norms for how business brokers work for buyers and get paid for their efforts. You should feel comfortable negotiating whatever kind of deal will work for you and the broker.

 Checklist for Working With Lawyers, Accountants, and Brokers

☐ Read this whole book, so that you're clear on the legal and financial tasks involved in buying a business.

☐ Keep a running list of tasks you feel comfortable handling yourself and those that may require professional help.

☐ Identify possible lawyers, accountants, and brokers to help with your purchase based on your own personal contacts and recommendations of other business people.

☐ Interview prospects and select ones you want to work with after checking references and agreeing on fees.

☐ Remember that many well-qualified professionals are willing to work on a piecemeal basis and to coach you on the tasks that you can largely handle yourself.

☐ Be aware that business brokers traditionally have represented only the interests of the seller, though you may be able to find one willing to work exclusively for you.

☐ Keep careful track of your expenses for professional services, since you can almost always deduct or amortize these costs on your tax return.

PART

2

Getting Ready to Buy

Financing Your Purchase

Before you can negotiate the purchase of a business, you'll need to have some idea of how you're going to pay for it. You can, of course, pay the whole amount at closing, if you have the cash and want to use it that way. More likely, however, you'll make a down payment of perhaps 20% or 25% and then pay the balance over a number of years—this is called an installment sale. This chapter will help you identify good ways to round up your cash for a down payment or lump sum purchase and explain how an installment sale works.

Lump Sum Purchase

What circumstances would make it necessary or desirable to pay the full price for a business at the closing? One possibility is that the business is very attractive to you and the seller is unwilling to finance the purchase but, instead, insists on full payment. Another possibility is that the seller offers you an attractive discount on the sale price if you pay the whole amount up front. If your business sense tells you that a lump sum purchase will pay off in the long run, you might be willing to go along. Under either of these scenarios, of course, you'll have to figure out how to come up with the cash to make it happen.

If you already own a larger business and have accumulated a cash reserve, you're in a good position to use cash to buy a smaller business. Similarly, you may be sitting pretty if you've inherited a large sum or received a large buyout or retirement payment from an employer. But if you're like most people who buy small businesses, and you don't have funds for a full-fund purchase stashed away in a bank account, you'll need to consider other sources, which we'll address later in this chapter. First, we'll look at the most common way of financing a purchase: an installment purchase.

Installment Purchase

Chances are, you'll pay for your new business by making a down payment at closing and signing a promissory note in which you'll agree to pay the balance in installments over a number of years. The terms of the promissory note will be spelled out in your sales agreement—most likely you'll attach the form for the actual promissory note that you're going to sign. (In Chapter 18, you'll find detailed information on preparing the promissory note.)

There are a number of variables that you'll need to negotiate with the seller so that you're sure you can comfortably meet the payment terms of the promissory note. There's no hard-and-fast formula for what your financing has to look like. Just make sure that you don't agree to an impossible payment schedule or any other terms that will make the payment plan unworkable for you.

Keep the Down Payment as Low as Possible

Given a choice, it's usually better to make a down payment of 10% than one of 30%. By making a relatively small down payment, you should be able to keep some cash in reserve to help you deal with unexpected expenses in the early months of ownership. And having cash on hand can help you ride out slow periods.

A small down payment also gives you greater protection if you get stuck with old bills that the seller failed to mention—fortunately, an infrequent scenario. Assuming that the seller has agreed to pay past bills but doesn't follow through, you can pay them and deduct those payments from installments you owe to the seller. With a low down payment, you have more money on hand to pay old bills.

Another advantage of a small down payment is that it may allow you to work with what you have, rather than borrowing money for the down payment as well as financing the bulk of the purchase. If you have to borrow money to make the down payment, you'll wind up owing monthly payments to both the seller and the person who loaned you money for the down payment.

EXAMPLE: Clementine agrees to pay 40% down on a $200,000 business. To raise the required $80,000, she uses $20,000 from her savings account and borrows $60,000 from her Uncle Clem. Two months after the closing, she realizes that it will be a struggle each month to pay the seller and her Uncle Clem and come away with a reasonable salary for herself. She regrets having agreed to make a large down payment, but it's too late.

There is a downside to making a small down payment. Assuming that your payoff period would be the same regardless of how much you put down, the monthly payments on a larger balance will be higher, and you'll end up paying more interest over the life of the deal.

TIP

The down payment doesn't have to consist solely of cash. You may have assets other than—or in addition to—cash that the seller would be willing to accept as part of the down payment. Maybe you own a sailboat like one the seller has been yearning for, a timeshare interest in a prime vacation condo in the Caribbean, or even a serviceable truck. As long as they're not encumbered by debt, assets like those could be transferred to the seller as part of the down payment. Similarly, services can sometimes be used in place of money. For example, if you have home improvement skills that the seller lacks, maybe you can repaint the seller's house, build a deck, or do other needed work in exchange for paying less cash.

Avoid a Short Payoff Period

Most typically, the promissory note will obligate you to pay the balance of the sales price by making equal monthly payments over two or three years, or perhaps a bit longer. Each payment will consist partly of interest and partly of principal. The amount of each payment is simply what it takes to pay off the entire balance and interest in the time agreed. The calculations are easily arrived at by consulting amortization tables available online.

What if the seller asks for a short payoff period? You might run the numbers and then explain that the business won't produce enough profit to let you make the relatively high payments and still have money for you and your family to live on. No matter what, make sure the repayment plan is realistic. If you don't, you're not doing anyone any favors by agreeing to something you can't follow through with.

> **EXAMPLE:** Tracy has been trying for six months to sell her shoe repair business, when Nelson appears on the scene eager to buy it. Tracy and Nelson agree on a sale price of $150,000, but Nelson is able to raise only a 10% down payment. This would leave $135,000 to be financed under a promissory note that Nelson would give to Tracy at closing. Tracy tells Nelson she'd like to get all of her money out of the business within two years. Nelson carefully goes through the math for Tracy and convinces her that,

given how much money the business nets each year, it's unlikely that he can come up with the relatively large monthly payments while still supporting his family. Tracy thinks it over and agrees that Nelson can have four years to pay off the balance—a more realistic schedule with significantly lower payments.

Pay Close Attention to the Interest Rate

Because an installment sale means that the seller is extending credit to you, you can expect to be charged interest, in keeping with the normal commercial practice. Think of it this way: If you paid the full sale price at closing, the seller could invest that money in securities, a money market account, real estate, a certificate of deposit (CD), or even another business, so the capital would earn money for the seller. Thus, it's reasonable for the seller to look for interest on any portion of the sale price that's deferred.

The rate you pay is mostly open to negotiation between you and the seller. Usury laws in many states cap the rate of interest that a seller can charge an individual (including a sole proprietor). Often, the maximum rate is 10% to 12% per year for individuals. (Institutional credit grantors, such as banks and credit card companies, are allowed to charge higher rates.) It follows that as a general rule, a seller who requires interest at 10% per year or less will have no usury law problems.

An accountant in your community can give you a reasonable range of interest rates to use in negotiations with the seller.

How Sellers Try to Protect Themselves in an Installment Sale

In any installment sale, the seller is taking a risk by extending credit to you. You may know that you're a good credit risk, but the seller may not have history with you and most likely will be anxious to be protected from the possibility that you might default on the promissory note you sign. To try to mitigate some of the risk, there are a variety of strategies that the seller may suggest.

While you can appreciate why a seller might seek maximum protection, some of the available protective measures will expose you—and possibly even your family members and friends—to a level of risk that may be unacceptable to you. This section will help you understand the extent of such risk so that you can negotiate effectively about the terms of the credit agreement.

The specific forms (such as a security agreement) and legal language (including personal guarantee and attorney fee clauses in a promissory note) that you and the seller might decide to use are set out in Chapter 18.

Personal Guarantee

You may be buying a business through a corporation or an LLC that you own—maybe one that's been formed just to acquire and run the enterprise. If only your corporation or LLC signs the promissory note, then only the corporation or LLC is responsible for making the payments. The seller will only be able to aim collection efforts at the legal entity if you don't make payments.

Many small corporations or LLCs have few assets, and especially if the seller knows that the entity doesn't have much beyond what was transferred in the sale, he or she may realize that trying to collect from the entity will be an exercise in futility.

For that reason, the seller may insist that you (and any co-owners of your corporation or LLC) personally guarantee payment of the promissory note. This is exactly what a bank or other commercial lender does on loans to small corporations or LLCs. A personal guarantee allows a lender to go after your nonbusiness assets should there be a default in paying the note. This means that the seller will be able to seize your personal assets such as bank accounts and cars if you don't pay as promised. You'll no longer be protected by the business entity, so consider carefully before agreeing to a personal guarantee.

Guarantee by a Spouse

Whether the purchasing entity is a sole proprietorship, partnership, corporation, or LLC, it's also possible that the seller may seek personal guarantees from the spouses of the people involved. In most states, if your spouse signs as a guarantor, his or her assets as well as property owned jointly by the two of you will be available to pay a judgment in favor of the seller if the business defaults.

> **EXAMPLE:** Phyllis agrees to sell her dress boutique to a new one-person LLC formed by Kari: Smart Style Enterprises LLC. It's an installment sale, with a 20% down payment and the rest of the sale price to be paid over a three-year period. A promissory note will be given by Smart Style Enterprises LLC for the unpaid balance and signed by Kari on behalf of the company. But Phyllis also conditions the sale on Kari and her husband George personally guaranteeing the note. Since George has a good job as a radiologist, Phyllis knows that if the LLC has trouble keeping up the payments, she can look to Kari and George for the money. If they don't pay, Phyllis can sue them as well as the company and get a court judgment against the couple. She can then force a sale of their house and vacation cabin, as well as their other investments, to satisfy any judgment. With Kari's and George's guarantees, Phyllis feels well protected. For their part, Kari and George feel confident that Kari will make the boutique work and also know they have money to make the payments even if it doesn't turn a profit right away, so the guarantee doesn't feel like too big a risk for them.

Guarantee by a Third Party

Sometimes a seller will conclude that getting a personal guarantee from the buyer and the buyer's spouse won't provide enough additional protection. Typically this is because neither the buyer nor his or her spouse owns real estate or securities or has a good job or other source of income that makes the guarantee meaningful. Suppose, for example, that a buyer has no valuable personal assets beyond a few bucks in the bank, a five-year-old car, and a rented flat full of thrift-shop furniture. If the business fails, the fact that the buyer signed a personal guarantee won't help the seller.

In this situation, the seller may seek the personal guarantee of a third party with lots of assets, such as the buyer's parents, a financially successful friend, or the proverbial rich uncle. Legally, this third party may be called a guarantor or a cosigner. While there are some minor technical differences between them, the legal outcome is the same: If the debt isn't paid by the primary signer, the backup signer is on the hook for it.

Obviously, a friend or family member who agrees to guarantee your promissory note puts his or her personal assets at risk. If you don't make payments to the seller as promised, and the seller looks to a friend or family member for payment, this can strain your relationship with the unlucky guarantor.

Security Interest in the Business Assets

If you've ever financed the purchase of a car, you know that even though you became the car's owner, the bank or other lender retained the right to repossess the vehicle if you didn't keep up the payments. That's because, in legal parlance, the lender retained a lien (often called a security interest) on your car until you made all your payments. A similar legal mechanism is available to the seller when you buy a business.

Here's how this works: First, the sales agreement will provide that you're buying the business assets subject to the seller's continuing security interest in them. At closing, to give legal effect to this provision, you and the seller will sign a security agreement and fill out a Uniform Commercial Code (UCC) Financing Statement. The seller will then file the financing statement with your state's secretary of state (or other designated office) to create a public record that he or she has a first lien on the business assets should you fail to pay. If later you miss payments or otherwise fail to meet the terms of the security agreement, the seller can repossess the assets.

Security Interest in Real Estate or Other Property

The seller may request that you give a security interest in other valuable property you own, such as a home or other real estate.

Typically, this means you'll give the seller a mortgage or deed of trust as security for the amount of the unpaid balance owed for the business. The lien is canceled only when you've paid the seller in full.

Putting your home at risk is a drastic step, as it can jeopardize the well-being of your family. Think long and hard before agreeing to do it.

Term Life Insurance

What happens if you die before the promissory note is paid in full? The seller may have to try collecting the money from your estate. To avoid this complicated and distasteful procedure, the seller may ask you to take out a term life insurance policy that, in case of your death, will provide money to pay off the promissory note. This type of life insurance is relatively inexpensive, and it can give the seller enormous peace of mind. If you die and the insurance proceeds exceed what's owed on the promissory note, the remaining money will go to your family—or whomever you designate as a backup beneficiary.

Acceleration Clause

For additional protection, the seller will probably insist on including in your promissory note something called an acceleration clause. An acceleration clause says that if you fail to make a payment on time, the entire unpaid balance of the debt becomes immediately due.

This is a pretty extreme consequence for simply missing one payment. To avoid it, you should negotiate for an additional provision in the promissory note that the seller must give you written notice and a chance to make the missed payment before the acceleration can take effect. That way, if you or your bookkeeper forgets to make a payment, or if you've been distracted by a personal crisis, the roof won't fall in on you.

Attorney Fee Clause

Buying a business isn't cheap, and any promissory note you sign will likely have a large balance. If you default, the seller probably will need to hire a lawyer to file suit. To keep from having to bear this substantial cost (and to put additional pressure on you not to default), the seller may want the promissory note to say that you'll be responsible for all expenses—including court costs and lawyer's fees—needed to collect the note balance. If you agree to such a clause, you may want to say that you'll be responsible only for *reasonable* costs and fees.

Escrow Arrangements

When the business you're buying is a corporation or LLC and you've agreed to buy the entity and not just its assets, the seller may ask you to agree that the corporate stock certificates or LLC membership certificates won't actually be turned over to you until the promissory note has been fully paid. Before you agree to this, make sure the agreement also states that you'll get these documents promptly when all contractual obligations have been met. You and the seller can agree that the corporate stock certificates or LLC transfer documents will be held by a third party—an escrow agent—until you've made all the payments. The escrow agent will have instructions to return the papers to the seller if you default.

Show Me the Money: Where You Can Get Funds for a Lump Sum Purchase or Hefty Down Payment

This section suggests a number of financial sources to which you might turn when you need to raise money for a lump sum payment or a large down payment. Just remember that if you borrow money for all or part of a down payment, you'll probably have to pay back those funds at the same time that you're making installment payments to the seller. Be very cautious. Making two large payments each month can become a back-breaking burden.

Personal Savings

Using your own money is the simplest way to buy a business. You avoid entanglements with others, keep your business affairs private, and steer clear of possible legal complications. If the business takes off, you'll own the business assets—such as inventory, equipment, and furniture—free of debt, making it easier to borrow money later or to bring equity investors into the business.

Your money may come from savings that you've carefully accumulated over the years. Or it may come from a large sum of money that's available all at once, like an inheritance from a relative or a severance package from a job you've just left. Or perhaps you've sold your house and will be living in a less-expensive one or in rented quarters. Using this money to buy a business may yield a bigger return than you could ever expect to receive by simply investing it.

CAUTION

Try to keep some cash in reserve. No business is risk-free and the cash flow is often unpredictable, so it makes sense not to commit every last dollar to the purchase. Yes, this can be hard. But if you can plan well enough to keep a reasonable amount of cash on hand—enough to cover several months' worth of living expenses plus some for emergencies— you'll improve your odds of succeeding. And you'll get the added bonus of not having to worry constantly about how you'll pay your personal bills.

Equity in Your Home

If you own a home, you may be able to tap into a portion of the equity—the difference between what the home is worth and the amount left on the mortgage—to raise cash. For example, let's say you bought your home several years ago for $150,000 by paying $30,000 down and getting a $120,000 mortgage. Today, the house would sell for $200,000 and the mortgage balance is down to $100,000. You have $100,000 in equity— some of which you can use to help finance your business.

There are two ways to get your hands on a portion of the equity. One is to get a new, larger mortgage that will pay off the earlier one and yield some cash. For example, if you get a new mortgage for $160,000— which is 80% of the home's current value and likely to be approved by a conservative lender—you'll have $60,000 after the earlier mortgage balance of $100,000 is paid off. Unfortunately, the actual amount you'll end up with will be significantly less, because the bank will require you to pay some hefty costs for processing the mortgage. These transaction costs typically include an application fee; document preparation fees; closing costs known as points; fees for a personal credit check; an appraisal of the home; and mortgage title insurance.

CAUTION

Plan carefully before you apply for a new mortgage. If your purpose in getting a new mortgage is to raise a relatively small amount of money for a down payment on buying a business, make sure you understand all of the costs involved. Unless it's your only way to raise money, you don't want to plunk down $4,000 in expenses to get your hands on $20,000. Before applying for a mortgage, ask the lender to itemize the costs involved. And if you're planning to quit your job or cut back your hours to run the business, wait until after your mortgage loan has been approved, so that you look like a good risk to the mortgage lender.

The second way to get money from the equity in your house is to apply for an equity line of credit. The bank will then have a second mortgage on your home. Using the assumptions in the example above, you may be able to obtain a line of credit for $60,000. Typically, the bank will give you a checkbook which you can use to write checks against the line of credit. Your monthly payment to the bank will depend on how much of the credit line you've used.

A line of credit will likely cost less to set up—perhaps there will simply be a $250 up-front fee rather than a few thousand dollars in closing costs for a mortgage—but the interest rate will likely be higher. And if the loan has a variable interest rate, the bank will have the right to increase the interest rate if interest rates in the overall economy rise.

> **TIP**
>
> **Don't overborrow on your home equity.** Whichever method you use to get money out of your house, don't forget that you're putting your home at risk if you can't meet the repayment schedule. You don't want

to lose your house to the lender or be forced to sell under the threat of foreclosure. So don't borrow more than you absolutely need—and take the time to figure out how you'll make the mortgage payments if the business is slow to flourish or you end up having to close it down. It sometimes makes sense to find a loan with a lengthy repayment schedule. If your business does well, you can always repay the loan early, but the lower payments offer you some flexibility in the meantime.

Retirement Savings

If you have—or had in the past—a job through which you contributed money to a retirement savings plan, you may be able to borrow some of that money. As you know, income tax on the money you contribute to an IRS qualified plan—such as a 401(k) plan—is deferred, allowing your retirement savings to grow faster. Check the plan language to see if loans are allowed for business purposes. If so, you should be able to borrow up to one-half of what you have in the plan, up to $50,000. Also check other conditions, such as the maximum term allowed for a loan (typically, five years), the interest rate, and the loan fees. You will have to pay interest on the money you borrow from your plan, but that's not all bad. Because the money you're borrowing is yours, the interest goes back into your plan.

Generally, unless you've reached the age of 59½, you'd be wise to borrow money from the tax-deferred plan, rather than simply taking it out. Early withdrawals are subject to a penalty tax. After age 59½, however, IRS rules allow you to withdraw funds without paying a penalty tax.

CAUTION

Don't borrow from an IRA. Unfortunately, if you borrow money from an Individual Retirement Account (IRA), it will be treated as a withdrawal and you'll have to pay a penalty tax if you haven't reached age 59½.

Credit Cards

Credit cards can be very useful to help finance certain business expenses, but they're usually not a wise source of funds for purchasing a business.

Plastic can quickly get you a computer and fax machine—and probably other business equipment and furniture as well. And for expenses such as rent, phone bills, or even money to pay employees, you can usually get a cash advance. Credit cards are a convenient way to arrange for short-term financing because they're so easy to use. Over the long haul, however, they're less attractive—mainly because the interest charges are relatively high, often as much as 20% or more per year. If you're going to succeed in business, you shouldn't need to be told it's unwise to borrow very much for very long at those rates.

Friends, Relatives, and Business Associates

You may be fortunate enough to have close friends, relatives, or colleagues who can lend you money or invest in your business. This helps you avoid the hassle of pleading your case to outsiders and enduring extra paperwork and bureaucratic delays—and can be especially valuable if you've been through bankruptcy or had other credit problems that would make borrowing from a commercial lender difficult.

Some advantages of borrowing money from people you know well are that you may be charged a lower interest rate, may be able to delay paying back money until you're more established, and may find the lender more lenient if you get into a jam. But once the loan terms are agreed to, you have the same legal obligation to meet the terms of a loan from friends or relatives that you would have with a commercial lender.

Borrowing money from relatives and friends can have a big downside. There's always the possibility that if your business does poorly and those close to you end up losing money, you'll damage a good personal relationship. So in dealing with friends, relatives, and business associates, be extra careful to establish clear terms for the deal and put it in writing—and make an extra effort to explain the risks. In short, it's your job to make sure your helpful friend or relative won't suffer a true hardship if you're unable to meet your financial commitments.

CAUTION

Don't borrow from someone on a fixed income. It's fine to borrow needed money from your Mom if she's well enough off that losing the $20,000 she loaned to you won't put her in the poor house. But if she lives on Social Security, don't borrow her last savings no matter how badly you need it. If you do, and your business fails, you'll be about as miserable as it's possible to be.

Supporters

Many types of businesses have loyal and devoted followers—people who care as much about the business as the owners do. A health food restaurant, a women's bookstore, an import car repair shop, or an art studio, for example, may attract people who are enthusiastic about lending money to or investing in the business because it fits in with their lifestyle or beliefs.

A supporter's decision to participate is driven to some extent by feelings and is not strictly a business proposition. The rules for borrowing from friends and relatives apply here as well. Put repayment terms in writing—and don't accept money from people who can't afford to risk it.

Banks

Banks are in the money business, so it's natural to look to a bank when you're in need of funds to buy a business. It's hard to predict, however, whether the banks you approach will be willing to lend you money on reasonable terms. Some banks are eager to establish a banking relationship with those just becoming part of the business community, and with a little luck you may be able to locate an enlightened, small business-oriented bank in your community. As you might imagine, banks offer their best terms to businesses that appear the least risky and that are likely to maintain sizable deposits as the business grows.

Generally, banks respond more favorably to loan applications when the requested loan is guaranteed by the Small Business Administration (SBA). Check out the SBA's Express loan program. It requires only minimal paperwork, and the SBA says that it will respond to an application in less than 36 hours—a far cry from other programs in which the document review can take weeks or months.

The Difference Between Loans and Equity Investments

When you're seeking funds from outside sources, it's important to understand the two main categories of such funding and the differences between them. The two types of funding you can get are loans and equity investments. This section explains each money source.

Loans

As you know, a loan is based on a simple idea: Someone provides you with money and you promise to pay it back, usually with interest. Since you must pay back the lender whether the business is a fabulous success or a miserable failure, the entire risk of buying a business is placed squarely on your shoulders.

Of course, nothing in business—or in life, for that matter—is without risk. Nevertheless, a commercial lender will be unwilling to lend you money if it looks like there's much chance the money won't get repaid. And to help keep the risk low, a lender will very likely ask for security for the loan—for example, a mortgage on your house so that the lender can take and sell your house if you don't keep up your loan payments.

Of the sources of funds listed above, most are loan-related. When you accept money from your friends, relatives, business associates, and supporters, you'll need to negotiate with them about whether the money they are offering you is a loan or an equity investment.

Equity Investments

Equity investors buy a piece of the business. They become co-owners and share in the fortunes and misfortunes of the business. Like you, they can make or lose a bundle. Generally, if the business does badly or flops, you're under no obligation to pay them back their money. However, some equity investors would like to have their cake and eat it, too; they want you to guarantee some return on their investment even if the business does poorly. Unless you're really desperate for the cash, avoid an investor who wants a guarantee. It's simply too risky a proposition for someone buying a small business.

As compared to bringing in others to invest in the business you're buying, there's an obvious plus side to borrowing money from a bank: If the business succeeds as you hope and you pay back the lender as promised, you reap all future profits. There's no need to share them. In short, if you're confident about the prospects of the business you're buying and you have the opportunity to borrow money, a loan is a more attractive source of money than getting it from an equity investor who will own a piece of the business and receive a share of the profits. Again, the downside is that if the business fails and you've personally guaranteed the loan, you'll have to repay it. By contrast, you don't have to repay equity investors if the business goes under. ●

Structuring Your Purchase

Once you and the seller have agreed on the sale price and payment terms (see Chapter 7), you might think you're in the home stretch. Not so. While you've taken important steps, there's still a lot more to do. In purchasing all but the tiniest businesses, there are a number of other legal and financial issues for you and the seller to work out and capture in a sales agreement.

This chapter covers four major issues that you and the seller should consider and negotiate after you have a basic agreement on the sale price and payment terms. For you to be able to negotiate, you need to have an idea of how you'd like to have them resolved, even though you know that after the give and take of negotiations, you may not wind up with everything you want. This chapter will help you figure out what will work best for you, what the seller might want, and where you can compromise, all in the service of getting a deal that works for you in the long run.

The four major issues we'll help you work on are:

- **Asset vs. Entity Sale.** Will you buy the assets of the business (its inventory, equipment, and customer lists, for example) or the entity that owns the assets (the corporation or LLC)? As you'll see below, the route that you and the seller choose can have enormous legal, financial, and tax consequences.
- **A Continuing Relationship With Seller vs. Making a Clean Break.** After the sale, will the seller work for the business as an employee or consultant? Staying connected to the business for a few months or even several years gives the seller a chance to earn additional money. And it can help assure you that the change in ownership will go smoothly with customers, employees, and other key people. Still, you may prefer to have the seller cut all ties to the business.
- **Limits on the Seller's Work Life vs. Complete Career Freedom After the Sale.** After the closing, will there be limits on the seller being able to do similar work elsewhere? A seller who plans to retire, go into a different line of work, or make a major life change will probably be willing to sign a strict noncompete agreement. But if there's a chance the seller may want to do some work related to the business he or she is selling to you, expect intense negotiations over the precise wording of any noncompete agreement you want the seller to sign.
- **Retaining Key Employees vs. Making a Fresh Start.** Will key employees stick around after the sale? The current staff may be an important factor in your decision to acquire a particular business. If so, you'll want to work out arrangements to keep them on board. But that won't be a concern if you prefer to start with a clean slate.

Later chapters (Parts 3 and 4 of this book) provide specifics about how to deal with these issues in a sales agreement and related documents, such as a promissory note, noncompete agreement, and employment contract.

Asset Sale vs. Entity Sale

We've already looked at this issue generally; now it's time to get down to the particulars. When you think about buying a specific business, you need to understand exactly what you're buying. Sometimes, that isn't entirely obvious. Especially if you've never bought or sold a business before, your notion of how a business is defined for purposes of a purchase may not be exactly in line with prevailing legal and commercial concepts. Let's start with the basics. That way, by the time you're ready to negotiate with the seller and put together a sales agreement, you'll have a good working knowledge of the major ways business sales can be structured.

A Business Is a Collection of Assets

Almost every business can be viewed as a collection of property called assets—some that you can see and touch, and others that are more abstract. Here are examples of each type of asset.

Tangible Assets

Assets you can see and touch are called tangible assets. Here are a few examples:

- cars, trucks, forklifts, and pallet jacks
- computers, copiers, and fax machines

- repair and manufacturing equipment
- counters and other point-of-sale fixtures
- inventory of goods for sale (excluding consignment items), such as clothing, wine, electronic equipment, kitchen supplies, fishing rods, and so on
- office and other supplies
- desks, furniture, and rugs
- specialized equipment—for example, for a veterinarian's clinic or a tanning salon, and
- cooking and serving equipment (for restaurants).

Intangible Assets

More abstract assets are called intangible. Here are a few examples:

- copyrights and patents
- trademarks (the name of a product or service)
- phone numbers
- business name
- right to occupy leased premises
- trade secrets (confidential recipes, customer lists, business methods)
- accounts receivable
- favorable contracts with suppliers
- business reputation and goodwill, and
- employee relationships, including employment contracts.

Estimating a Business's Assets

Whether you're buying the assets or the entity, ask the seller for a list of all assets—both tangible and intangible. That way, you can more accurately assess the value of what you're buying. And if you'll be buying the business assets rather than the entity, a basic list can give you a running start on preparing the asset portion of your sales agreement and any related attachments. See Chapter 12 to learn how the assets might be treated in a sales agreement for an asset sale.

The Two Ways to Transfer Business Assets

For the purchase of most types of businesses, you're legally free to follow either the asset sale or the entity sale approach. The big exception occurs if the seller runs the business as a sole proprietorship: a one-person business that hasn't been organized as either a corporation or LLC.

The Sale of a Sole Proprietorship Is Always an Asset Sale

If the seller is a sole proprietor, by definition he or she hasn't formed a separate business entity such as a corporation or an LLC. It follows, then, that the seller personally owns all the assets and that a sale of the business will always be an asset sale. This is true even though the sales agreement will normally mention the business's name, as well as that of the seller—for example, *Margaret Chen, doing business as Sunshine Daycare Center.*

In addition to its assets, a sole proprietorship may have liabilities: the debts the business owes and the legal claims that someone may bring against it. A sole proprietor is personally liable for those liabilities; selling a business doesn't automatically relieve the owner from responsibility for the liabilities incurred before the sale. You and the seller, however, may negotiate a deal in which you agree to take over at least some of the liabilities. Chapter 14 explains how this is done.

The Sale of a Partnership, Corporation, or LLC Can Be Either an Asset Sale or an Entity Sale

If the business you're considering isn't a sole proprietorship, it's most likely a partnership, corporation, or LLC. A crucial distinction between a sole proprietorship and the other types of businesses is that the law treats partnerships, corporations, and LLCs as legal entities separate from their owners. Unlike a sole proprietorship, in which business assets belong directly to the proprietor or owner, when people do business through a partnership, corporation, or LLC, the business entity legally owns the assets. Stated another way, the people who formed and now operate the business don't own its assets. This is true even though a person may own 100% of the corporate stock or LLC membership interests.

The fact that the business entity owns the assets means that you and the seller have a choice in how you structure the purchase of the business: You can structure it either as an asset sale or as a sale of the legal entity. In an asset sale, the partnership, corporate, or LLC entity sells its assets to you. By contrast, in an entity sale, the owners sell the entire entity (for example, all the stock in a corporation) to you, in which case you'll own the assets (furniture, inventory, intellectual property, and so on) by owning the entity. Compared to an asset sale, where assets are listed and transferred one by one, in an entity sale you have less opportunity to pick only the most desirable assets.

If you buy only the assets of a business entity, you don't become responsible for the business's liabilities except to the extent you agree to do so. In contrast, when you buy the entire entity, its liabilities (debts, legal claims against it, and even future lawsuits based on presale conduct) are typically included in the sale and become your responsibility. In an entity sale, the seller isn't personally responsible for liabilities unless he or she agrees to be.

However, in the real world of business sales, where nearly everything is negotiable, you can bargain to omit some assets from an entity sale (aging equipment, for example) or to require that the seller retain a particular debt or liability (say, the balance owed by the entity on a promissory note). In short, a seller who wants to reach a deal with you may be willing to combine some of the major characteristics of an entity and an asset sale.

How Liabilities Affect the Sale

In addition to having assets, a business may also have liabilities such as debts or claims against it that may result in lawsuits. How concerned you need to be about liabilities will depend in large part on whether you'll be acquiring the entity or just its assets. There are relevant sales agreement clauses to deal with these liability issues in Chapter 14. Here's an overview of the differences in asset and entity sales as they relate to liabilities.

Entity Sale

If you're thinking of buying a business entity, you'll need to find out what the entity's liabilities are. The corporation or LLC that you buy will be responsible for paying any existing debts and resolving any existing claims, regardless of who owns it, so you need to know exactly what you're taking on. Payments on existing debts can be a significant financial burden on the business's cash flow. To reduce that burden, you may insist that the seller pay some or all of the known liabilities before the closing and agree to be responsible for any unknown or undisclosed liabilities that might pop up later. Another way to factor in liabilities is to negotiate for a lower sale price to reflect the fact that the entity will have to spend money on debts that already exist.

Asset Sale

If you're looking to buy the business assets rather than the entity, you needn't be quite as concerned about liabilities, which normally don't follow the assets. There are, however, a few exceptions—situations that are uncommon but in which you could become responsible for past liabilities.

Bulk sales laws. A dwindling number of states have bulk sales laws that apply when you buy the assets of a retail business—a business that sells goods from stock (for example, a store that sells small appliances). In those states, creditors can void the sale if you and the seller don't give the notices specified in the statute. Giving the notices is a big nuisance, filled with legal technicalities. If you're in a state with a bulk sales law, there's a simple solution: Just agree that the seller will pay off the debts before or at the closing. That way, there will be no creditors with rights to affect the sale.

Here are the states that still have a bulk sales law:

| California | Maryland |
| Georgia | Virginia |

Chapter 19 provides suggestions for complying with bulk sales laws in these states.

Successor liability. Some states recognize a legal doctrine called successor liability in relation to manufacturing businesses. Let's say you're buying a business that manufactures dangerous products. You buy the assets and, two years later, someone is injured by a product that was made before you bought the business. Even though you bought the business in an asset sale, there's a chance that you may be held liable. The courts will look at whether you:

- kept the same employees
- kept the same managers
- kept the same product facilities in the same locations

- continued to produce the same product or product line
- used the same business or product name
- used the same business assets
- continued the general business operations, and
- represented yourself as the successor to the business.

When most of these factors are present, there's a risk that you'll be burdened by liability for the products previously made. You may be able to protect against this risk by insurance (which can be expensive) and/or by asking the seller to personally indemnify you against liability claims (a topic discussed in Chapter 14). Fortunately, this will be not be an issue for many readers, as most small businesses don't manufacture products.

 SEE AN EXPERT

If you're thinking of buying a manufacturing business, consult a lawyer about the successor liability rules in your state. This will help you weigh the risks and come up with a plan to reduce your potential exposure.

The Tax Consequences of Your Purchase

The distinction between an asset sale and an entity sale may at first seem oppressively technical. Since you wind up owning the assets of the business either way, why do you really care how they're transferred?

You've already learned that the type of sale affects liability issues, as discussed above. In addition, the type of sale can make a huge difference in terms of taxes.

As explained in Chapter 3, from the seller's perspective, there are almost always tax advantages to an entity sale, whether the business is a corporation, an LLC, or a partnership. By contrast, as a buyer, you'll prefer an asset sale; it will allow you to more quickly take deductions for the money you're paying to buy the business. To convince the seller to accept an asset sale, you may have to increase the sale price to partly offset the additional taxes the seller will have to pay.

Unless you're unusually savvy about taxes, it makes sense for you to discuss your specific tax situation with a CPA or other tax professional.

Try to Buy the Assets Rather Than the Entity—Usually

For a number of reasons, it's to your advantage to persuade the seller to offer you an asset sale:

- An asset purchase can make it easier for you to acquire only the most valuable assets of the business, leaving the less desirable ones behind.
- The tax consequences of buying individual assets are usually more favorable to you than for buying the entity. In an asset sale, it's easier for you to start writing off large chunks of the sale price.
- If you buy a business's assets, you're usually not responsible for the business's liabilities unless the sales

Comparison of Mechanics for Asset Sales and Entity Sales		
Entity	**Asset Sale**	**Entity Sale**
Corporation	The corporation sells most or all of its individual assets to the buyer. The corporation normally retains the liabilities.	The shareholders sell their shares of corporate stock to the buyer. The corporation, under its new ownership, continues to own the assets and remains responsible for the existing liabilities.
LLC	The LLC sells most or all of its assets to the buyer. The LLC normally retains the liabilities.	The members sell their LLC membership interests to the buyer. The LLC, under its new ownership, continues to own the assets and remains responsible for the existing liabilities.
Partnership	The partnership sells its assets to the buyer. The partnership normally retains the liabilities.	The partners sell their partnership interests to the buyer. The partnership, under its new ownership, continues to own the assets and remains liable for the existing liabilities (Entity sales of a partnership are rare.).

agreement specifically says so. There are some exceptions to this rule, including product liability and environmental contamination claims that can follow problematic assets. For example, if you purchase a building full of asbestos you may get stuck with the legal responsibility to clean up the problem.

If you have more negotiating leverage than the seller does regarding the structure of the deal, you may wind up with an asset sale. By contrast, if the business is well-known in your community or industry, and doing an asset sale means having to laboriously transfer lots of intangible assets (the business name, goodwill, customer lists, supplier relationships, and the like), you may be willing to buy the entity—especially if you believe that all problems are out in the open. And if a corporation, LLC, or partnership business has a favorable lease or other contract (to supply services on very profitable terms, for example) and that contract can't be assigned to a new entity without the other party's consent, you may have a further incentive to purchase the business entity.

EXAMPLE: Excel Products Corporation signs a five-year lease for a building owned by Realty Associates LLC. The lease contains options giving Excel the right to renew the lease for two additional five-year periods at a very moderate increase. As the years pass and the neighborhood becomes far more desirable, Excel's rental rate turns out to be well below the market rate. Four years into the lease, Jean—the owner of Excel—decides to sell the business. For tax reasons and in an effort to avoid any hidden business liabilities, Tom, an interested buyer, first proposes buying Excel Corporation's assets, leaving Jean owning the corporate entity. But Tom changes his mind when he learns that if he buys Excel Corporation, he takes over its favorable lease, but if he buys just Excel's assets, he doesn't. After a thorough investigation that discloses little likelihood of hidden financial or legal claims, Tom agrees to buy the entire corporation. Of course, as an alternative Tom could have offered to buy just Excel's assets while also asking the landlord to let him separately take over Excel's current lease. But the landlord, who can rent the building for more if Excel leaves, is unlikely to agree unless Tom is willing to pay market rent.

The Seller's Future Role

Assuming that yours is an installment purchase, you'll have an important connection to the seller at least until you've made the last installment payment. But you may also want to have the seller maintain a more active relationship with the business as a consultant, part-time employee, or adviser. And you may want to condition your purchase on the seller's staying involved during a transition period—for, say, a year or two. Although you and the seller can adopt a let's-wait-and-see attitude about the possibility of the seller staying in the business, it's usually a better idea to make it part of your negotiations and include your agreement in your written sale documents.

It's often desirable to keep the seller active in the business, at least on a part-time basis. The seller can provide valuable assistance with details of the business operations—such as teaching you the intricacies of the bookkeeping system or how to order the right kinds and amounts of merchandise. Even more important, the seller's continuing presence in the business can be reassuring to employees, suppliers, and long-time customers who might otherwise be wary of a new owner.

The exception to this general rule is where you believe the business has enjoyed less than a stellar reputation. In that case, you'll understandably want to keep a distance from the seller, preferring instead to post a sign that proclaims, "Under New Management."

From the seller's standpoint, there can be several advantages to an agreement in which he or she continues to work for the business after it changes hands. First, the seller may want to stay on deck until you've made all the installment payments. Second, unless the seller has serious health problems or for some other reason no longer wants to work, arranging for additional income may seem desirable. Third, the seller may have strong emotional ties to the business that may make

it satisfying to stay involved at least part time.

From a legal standpoint, there are two ways that you can arrange for the seller to perform future services you: as an employee or an independent contractor.

An Employment Relationship

The seller can go on—or stay on—the books as a full- or part-time employee, and receive a fixed weekly or biweekly salary or an hourly wage. As with any other employee, the business will withhold income tax, Social Security, Medicare, and other taxes. The seller may also receive benefits, depending on the arrangements that you negotiate. For example, the business may pay for the seller's health insurance coverage and offer paid vacation or sick leave.

If you and the seller agree that the seller will become an employee, it makes sense to sign an employment contract stating what he or she will do for the business. In addition to covering job duties, the contract should state how much time the seller will put in, what the payment arrangements are, and what benefits (if any) you'll be providing. You'll also want to cover how long the employment will last—it can be anywhere from a few months to several years—and what happens if the seller wants to leave or you want to cancel the arrangement before its full term. You can also sign a contract that *doesn't* include a date or conditions for termination. In that case, it will be an "at-will" employment relationship that either of you can end at any time without giving a reason. This may suit you just fine, since it means you have no obligation to continue to hire the seller for an extended period if you find that the two of you don't get along.

RELATED TOPIC

Chapter 20 contains more information on what might go into a written employment contract between you and the seller.

SEE AN EXPERT

Get legal advice before signing an employment contract. Employment law can be complex. A lawyer can help assure that the contract fully protects your business.

An Independent Contractor Relationship

In an independent contractor relationship, the seller is paid by the assignment, typically either on a flat-fee or time-related basis. So, for example, you might agree to pay the seller a fixed sum for working as a consultant to the business for 20 hours a week for three months. Or you could agree to pay the seller a flat fee to be available to perform a list of specified tasks. Or you could pay a certain amount per day for each project you ask the seller to perform on an as-needed basis.

Unlike an employment relationship, if the seller works as an independent contractor,

you won't withhold taxes. Income taxes and self-employment tax will be the sole responsibility of the seller. And, unless separately negotiated, you won't pay for health insurance, vacation, or other benefits that the business normally provides employees.

Complying With IRS Criteria for Independent Contractors

Before agreeing to an independent contractor relationship, you'll want to make sure the IRS won't second-guess the arrangement and later require you to treat the seller as an employee for employment tax purposes. The IRS assumes that a significant number of independent contractors fail to pay all the taxes they owe, and believes that it stands to receive more money when workers are classified as employees. Consequently, the IRS may someday challenge you to prove that the seller really meets the criteria to be considered an independent contractor (discussed below). This means the arrangements for the seller's work and the payment arrangements will need to be carefully structured. You can't just call the seller an independent contractor and be done with it.

Preparing an Independent Contractor Agreement

If the seller will be working for you as an independent contractor, it's crucial that you put the details of your agreement in writing. That way there will be a clear understanding about how much work you'll assign to the seller and how much you'll pay for that work.

Chapter 20 contains a sample form that you can use as a starting point in preparing your own independent contractor agreement.

There are several major topics that your independent contractor agreement should cover, including:

- **The services that the seller will perform.** You want to be clear about what the seller is agreeing to do for the business in the future. For example, if you've promised that the seller will earn at least $10,000 per year for three years, the agreement should describe the work that the seller will perform that will allow him or her to bill the business for at least that amount.

- **How much you'll pay—and when.** Payment may be by the hour, by the day (or week, month, or even year), or by the project. Perhaps your agreement will call for the seller to submit periodic invoices (a common practice for independent contractors) and will say that you'll pay within ten days after an invoice is sent.

- **The expenses for which you'll reimburse the seller.** Depending on the type of work the seller will be doing, you may want to provide for reimbursement for necessary expenses. These might include travel, entertainment, communications costs, and supplies.

- **Who will own any intellectual property that the seller produces.** If the seller will be creating copyrighted material or doing innovative work that can form the basis of a patent or be treated as a trade secret, it will be important to clarify who owns the material.

- **How long the agreement will last.** Typically, neither you nor the seller will want to make a commitment that lasts longer than a few years, though there may be exceptions.

- **How the agreement can be terminated.** You may want a provision that allows either you or the seller to end the agreement by giving a certain amount of written notice, such as 60 or 90 days. But if the seller is counting on receiving income for an extended period, it may be hard to get agreement on a clause that gives you an easy way to end the deal early.

- **A statement that the seller is an independent contractor.** This may help you convince the IRS that the seller isn't an employee (which would subject you to additional tax obligations). But such a statement will not by itself assure that the IRS will classify the seller as an independent contractor. The working arrangement must in fact meet the IRS criteria—for example, you can't have too much control over how the seller performs the duties assigned. For more about the IRS criteria, see *Working With Independent Contractors,* by Stephen Fishman (Nolo). Also, see IRS Publication 15-A, *Employer's Supplemental Tax Guide,* available at www.irs.gov.

- **Who will pay local, state, and federal taxes on the seller's earnings.** In an independent contractor relationship, this is the responsibility of the contractor; the business doesn't withhold taxes. Mentioning this in your agreement may help establish that the seller really isn't an employee if the IRS or a state agency challenges you.

- **How any disputes will get resolved.** You can provide for mediation or arbitration as a way to avoid going to court.

EXAMPLE: Clara, a certified commercial real estate appraiser, has built up a profitable appraisal business: Consolidated Appraising. After 25 years, Clara is offered both a job teaching appraising at a business school and a contract to write a book on practical real estate appraising. She offers to sell the business to three long-time employees who are also appraisers. They jump at the chance, but as part of the deal, they want Clara to stay involved with the business part time to help maintain Consolidated's strong relationship with several large real estate brokers who send a large chunk of business to Consolidated. This suits Clara fine—at least while she is working on her book, she'd like to keep her hand in the actual practice of appraising. So as part of the sale, Clara and the buyers agree that for two years, Clara will be available to consult with them on business issues and to review their more

difficult appraisals. The buyers agree to pay her $125 an hour for her work. She won't be required to provide more than 20 hours of services in any one month and will be able to do the work on her own schedule and mostly from her home office.

 RESOURCE

For complete guidance on independent contractor relationships, see *Consultant & Independent Contractor Agreements,* by Stephen Fishman (Nolo). The book and accompanying CD-ROM will explain the difference between hiring an employee and dealing with an independent contractor and lead you through the preparation of an independent contractor agreement. Also see *Working With Independent Contractors,* by Stephen Fishman (Nolo).

Restrictions on the Seller: Noncompete Agreements

Another important element of purchasing an existing business is ensuring that the seller won't promptly go into a competing business that might cut into your income. For example, if you were to buy a successful florist shop, and the seller opened a similar business down the street, you'd rightfully be upset. To guard against the possibility of such unfair competition, it makes good sense to require the seller to sign an agreement (also called a covenant) not to compete.

RELATED TOPIC

Chapter 15 offers appropriate language for a sales agreement that includes a covenant not to compete. Chapter 20 includes a form and instructions for completing it.

EXAMPLE: Luigi has built a hugely profitable business, Bella Italia Ristorante, by selling pizzas, calzones, lasagna, and other Italian food prepared from old family recipes. Now, Rosa is looking to buy the business (including its wonderful recipes), but she's concerned that Luigi may grow bored after a few months in retirement and open another shop in town that would draw away customers from hers. To guard against this, she requests that Luigi agree to a noncompetition clause in the sales contract in which he promises that for three years, he won't own, work in, or invest in any restaurant within 15 miles of Bella Italia Ristorante. Luigi feels this is fair. Rosa and Luigi agree that $1,000 of the sale price will be treated as payment to Luigi for his agreement not to compete.

In a few states, including California, employers can't legally require that their employees agree not to compete in the future. In most other states, to be enforceable, such agreements must be strictly limited by time, geography, and scope. The reason is that judges are leery of restricting someone's right to earn a living. But the situation is different when someone sells a business. The law takes the position that it's legitimate for those buying and selling businesses to bargain freely over covenants not to compete. So if the seller does agree to sign a covenant not to compete, you can assume that it will be legally enforceable.

In negotiating a noncompete agreement, you need to consider how much you'll pay the seller for the agreement and how the agreement will restrict the seller in terms of:

- the kind of work the seller can do and can't do
- the geographical area or where the seller may work, and
- the length of time the agreement is in effect.

You'd prefer to place very broad limitations on the seller's future activities. A seller who is planning to retire or go into a completely different line of work will probably not have a problem accepting stringent limitations. But a seller who has a possible expectation of doing related work—or even the very same work in another part of the country—may want to bargain for something less drastic.

Fortunately, there's usually a compromise that will meet your needs and those of the seller. In the example above, Luigi might feel too restrained if he couldn't be involved in any restaurant for three years. But since Rosa, the buyer of Bella Italia, really only fears that he'll open another Italian place, chances are she'd be willing to accept his covenant not to compete only in this specialty. Accordingly, they could design a covenant not to compete that allows Luigi to enter any type of food business where his offerings do not include a list of the 20 most popular Italian dishes.

A noncompete agreement is a personal commitment that the seller makes to you. That promise should be included in or attached to the sales agreement. For the seller's promise to be legally binding, you must pay the seller something of value in exchange. (In legal parlance, this is known as consideration.) A few dollars will meet this technical legal requirement—and that's a good thing, because you can't write off the payment for the noncompete covenant as quickly as you can write off the amounts you pay for most of the assets you buy. So you'd like to keep the payment as low as possible. But, especially if you're buying the assets of a C corporation, the seller may have tax reasons for wanting a more substantial payment. Be prepared to negotiate about this until both sides are satisfied.

The Future of Key Employees

Many businesses have employees, so think about what will happen to employees of the business if you buy it. You have a number of options depending on the business and your own inclinations.

You May Have No Interest in Keeping Employees

Perhaps you're not at all interested in keeping any current employees, preferring instead to bring in your own team or hire from scratch. This is especially likely in a small business that needs only a few workers. You may be thinking of bringing in family members, friends, or workplace colleagues to help run the business.

You May Be Undecided About Keeping Employees

You may be primarily interested in keeping the business's name, favorable lease, or other assets. You may not really care if current employees stay on or leave. In that case, you may want to meet key employees so you can size them up, and they can do the same. Then, if there's mutual interest in a continuing relationship, you can work out the details.

You May Be Very Interested in Keeping Employees

In some situations, you will consider it quite important that one or more key employees stay on after you buy the business. This is especially likely if you haven't worked in the field in which you're buying, and retaining a key employee—such as a head chef, chief mechanic, or sales manager—will help you to feel more confident in your new business.

If the seller has signed employment contracts with current employees, guaranteeing a decent wage for a set period in exchange for a promise to continue to work for the business for a year or more, you may be able to take over those contracts and be secure that the employees will stay. Whether you get the benefit of the contracts will depend on whether your purchase is an entity sale or an asset sale. If you buy a corporation or LLC, preexisting contracts with employees will automatically be part of the deal, and both the business entity and the contracting employees will continue to be legally bound.

The process is different, however, in an asset sale. Here, the employment contracts won't automatically be transferred to you, unless the sales agreement says so. However, in this situation you can certainly negotiate with the employees to continue to honor the existing contract or to sign a new contract with you. If the existing contract provides for yearly salary increases and a bonus at the end of the contract period, you can feel pretty confident that the employees will honor the deal. Consider it a bonus if, in an employment contract, a key employee pledges not to compete with the business for several years after their employment ends.

 SEE AN EXPERT

Figuring out the noncompete rules in your state can be complicated. In most states, noncompete promises from employees are legally enforceable if they're reasonable and if payment is adequate. But in a few states, such as California, noncompete agreements that attempt to bind employees are not enforceable. You may want to seek advice from a business lawyer.

One additional technical detail in an asset sale: At closing, you'll list the employment contracts in a formal assignment document. (See Chapter 20 for details.) That way, you'll have the legal authority to step into the seller's shoes as the employer.

Checklist for Structuring Your Purchase

- [ ] Reach agreement with the seller on whether you'll buy the assets or the entity.
- [ ] Work out the terms of how the seller will work for you as either an employee or an independent contractor.
- [ ] Negotiate a noncompete agreement to protect against unfair competition by the seller.
- [ ] Agree on arrangements for what will happen to key employees.

The Investigation Stage: How Buyers and Sellers Check Each Other Out

Before you really get really serious about a particular business—and certainly before you and the seller sign a sales agreement—you'll need to do a lot more than kick the tires and open the hood. Just how extensive an investigation you'll make will depend on the nature of the business and the extent of your business experience. Consider, for example, the contrasting approaches of two buyers.

Buyer #1—The Old Hand

Ben, the savvy owner of a lawn maintenance company, is looking to buy a similar business across town so as to be king of the local turf. He's primarily interested in just three things beyond the seller's routine financial statements: the terms of major contracts with office complexes and shopping centers, the quantity and quality of the business's trucks and equipment, and the percentage of customers who use the business's services on a month-to-month basis without long-term contracts. Armed with these facts, Ben figures he'll have a pretty good handle on the seller's operation.

Buyer #2—The Newcomer

Marjorie, who's never owned a business before, is interested in buying a bar-and-grill business. She wants to see piles of financial detail in order to evaluate the potential for profit and growth. Because Marjorie doesn't understand the key business indicators that can predict future profitability, she asks the seller to provide three years' worth of monthly financial statements, sales tax records, income tax returns, and a raft of other material. In addition to looking at these materials herself, she'll ask both her accountant and her good friend who owns a similar business to go over the information and give her feedback. She also expects the seller to educate her about how the business works.

You'll want to devise an investigation strategy that meets your own emotional and financial needs and is appropriate for the circumstances. Whatever approach you take, though, at the very least you'll probably conduct a physical inspection to size up the condition of any business equipment (as in the lawn maintenance example, above) as well as the business premises. In a retail operation, you'll also want to carefully assess the condition of the inventory. Obviously, if you'll have to spend money to upgrade the business space, replace old equipment, or acquire up-to-date inventory, this will significantly affect the negotiations over sale price.

You'll also want to learn about the growth of the customer base and the loyalty of customers—whether they're happy and likely to continue to patronize the business. But physical inspections and evaluations of customer loyalty are just part of the story. You'll definitely want to perform a broader investigation starting with the seller's paperwork, such as tax returns and financial statements.

See "Your Investigation of the Seller's Business," below, for general pointers on how to investigate a business before agreeing to buy it. Then see the next section, "Paperwork the Seller Should Provide." Because much of the paperwork the seller shares with you may contain sensitive information, the seller is likely to be concerned about what happens to that information if the sale falls through. One fear is that this information may give you an unfair advantage if you're now a competitor, or that you may decide to open a competing new business instead of buying this one. Another is the risk that you'll divulge sensitive information to outsiders—again creating the possibility that the seller's business could be harmed. To help protect against the misuse of information you acquire during the investigation stage, the seller may require that you sign a confidentiality agreement (also called a nondisclosure agreement), as described in "The Role of Confidentiality Agreements," below.

Beyond the information you receive from the seller, you may want to go further and look to third-party sources that have the potential to provide more objective data. The section called "Information to Garner From Other Sources," below, suggests ways to do this.

And you may not be the only one who conducts an investigation before signing a

sales agreement. It's a two-way street: The seller may want to learn more about you, as explained in the section called "Why and How the Seller May Check You Out," below.

TIP

Even if you're a full-cash buyer, the seller may want to look into your background. A seller who's built a decent reputation among employees, customers, and others in the community would hate to have that reputation destroyed by a feckless successor. With that in mind, the seller may want to take reasonable steps to assure that you're someone who's likely to remain solvent and who'll treat people fairly. Otherwise, the seller's legacy may be tainted.

Your Investigation of the Seller's Business

While the seller understandably may value the privacy of the business's accounts, customer lists, and key proprietary information, you need full access to this information before you commit to a deal. Evaluating the business in detail is the only way you can rationally decide whether or not to buy it and on what terms. In fact, such investigations are so routine and expected that lawyers and accountants have given it the name due diligence, as in the phrase, "The buyer is doing his due diligence."

In your investigation, you'll want to see not only the seller's internal profit and loss numbers, but also those that the seller has provided to the IRS, as described in the next section. You need these data so you can put together a picture of how profitable the business has been—and how profitable it's likely to be under your ownership. You'll want to focus first on how much money the business has made in the last year or two and the trend of its earnings over as many years as possible. The longer-term profits perspective is particularly important since it's often possible for a business to manipulate expenses to produce an artificial profit for a year or two (by reducing the number of employees or cutting the amount of new product development, for example), but it's much harder to pull this off over a three- or five-year period.

Obviously, if a business has been losing money of late, the paperwork the seller provides will put a damper on your interest in buying. But the seller may be able to demonstrate to your satisfaction that the business has suffered just a temporary downturn. Perhaps, for example, the business has recently incurred unusual expenses to greatly expand its product line and it will take a while for sales to catch up. Or maybe the business is caught in a short-term economic downdraft that's affecting a whole market segment or the entire geographical community. Naturally, you should maintain a healthy skepticism when a seller tries to explain away the business's losses. But sometimes the explanation is logical and convincing, and you should trust your own knowledge and experience in evaluating the situation.

Sometimes it's reasonable for you to consider more than the raw profit and loss data. The seller may try to put the numbers in perspective for you through a process called a restatement. Typically this involves removing a number of discretionary expenditures from the expense side of the balance sheet to show that the business is actually more profitable than it may at first appear to be. The salary the business is paying the seller or a member of his or her family, for example, may be higher than what you'd need to pay for replacement services. Or the seller may have expensed several business trips, vehicles, or club memberships that, while legitimate business expenses, weren't essential. This can be useful information, but you'll need to carefully study any restated figures the seller prepares to make sure you agree with the underlying assumptions and are not being subjected to a slick snow job.

 TIP

Sellers have an incentive to disclose all facts. While "buyer beware" is always a useful admonition, it may be reassuring to know that a seller has an incentive to act ethically by giving you full and accurate information about the business. Basically, a seller who is less than honest may wind up in deep legal trouble. You might, for example, be able to sue such a seller for fraud and misrepresentation. And the seller's dishonesty might entitle you to stop making installment payments, or at least to deduct sums to cover losses reasonably attributable to the misrepresentations.

Paperwork the Seller Should Provide

Let's look at some of the paperwork you should consider requesting from the seller before buying a business. Your own list, of course, will depend on the type of business involved. And unless you've had a great deal of business experience, you may want to bring in a lawyer or accountant—or both—to help evaluate the information the seller gives you.

> **TIP**
>
> **Get it in writing.** It's all too easy for an unscrupulous seller to tell you things orally and then later claim that the statement was never made, or that you misunderstood. You rely on oral statements at your own risk. If you and the seller ever become embroiled in a legal dispute that turns on what the seller represented to you about the business, you're not likely to win unless the representations were in writing.

Tax Returns

Ask to see the income tax returns for the business going back at least three years. One reason to review tax returns, of course, is that a business owner has a powerful motivation not only to be accurate in providing numbers to the IRS, but also to come up with a low bottom line to keep taxes at a minimum. Stated another way, for tax

purposes, the seller will want to show profits at as low a figure as is legitimately possible.

But as a savvy seller may point out to you, what's a legitimately low bottom line for income tax purposes may not represent the true profitability of the business. For example, on a tax return, the seller may legally deduct certain items from gross income that are discretionary, not essential, expenses of running the business.

Let's say the seller enjoys travel. If so, the seller may have the business pay for travel to useful trade shows and conventions that just happen to be held near locations where the fishing or skiing is so terrific he or she can't help staying over a few extra days. As long as the seller allocates the cost of air travel and hotel accommodations between business and pleasure in accordance with IRS guidelines, the deduction of the appropriate portion on a tax return is absolutely legitimate. So the seller may point out to you that some travel expenses can best be looked at as discretionary costs that you can choose to eliminate in order to fatten the bottom line. Assuming there are a number of similar items, the business may be more profitable than it appears to be when you only review the tax returns. Your accountant can help you sort this out.

> **CAUTION**
>
> **Be wary of a seller who suggests that you can make money "off the books."** It's a very bad sign. Someone who engages in

tax fraud will probably have no qualms about cheating you as well.

Detailed Financial Statements

Financial statements showing income and expenses, especially if they're prepared on a monthly or weekly basis, can help you understand the cash flow of the business. And the statement can contain important clues about the business. For example, if the records show that the cash flow is uneven—such as is often true for a campus-related business in a college town or retail businesses that do a lot of business at holiday time—you'll know that you'll need to have enough cash on hand to carry you through the slow months.

Another way a financial statement can be useful is if you ask for financial statements and the seller hands you a shoebox filled with deposit slips and canceled checks; that can tell you that the business is being run in a slipshod manner.

The Lease

For many businesses where location isn't critical, you won't care about trying to keep the lease, assuming the seller even has one. For example, a business that very profitably sells American antiques from the Revolutionary War period may consist of a website headquartered in the seller's converted garage. Or the seller may be an electrician, plumber, or contractor operating on a month-to-month tenancy from low-cost digs that few customers ever visit.

But if the business is more location-sensitive and operates under an existing lease—as would normally be true of a restaurant or retail business—you'll surely want to examine the lease closely for essential information such as:

- the length of the tenancy
- whether there are options that allow the seller or a new owner to renew the lease for additional time periods and, if so, for how long, for how much money, and under what additional conditions
- the rent and scheduled rent increases
- other tenant costs such as property taxes, insurance premiums, utility bills, and repair and maintenance expenses, and
- landlord and tenant responsibilities.

Beyond these basics, a key issue is almost always whether the lease requires the landlord's consent for you to take over and continue to run the business in the same space. Usually, this is less likely to be a problem when you're buying an entity rather than assets, because the existing corporation or LLC will continue to be the tenant and there will be no assignment of the lease. The entity was the tenant when the lease was signed and will continue to be the tenant after the sale. But occasionally, leases to a corporation or LLC do require the landlord's consent for new owners to take over the lease. If the business is a corporation or an LLC, and the lease doesn't say anything about getting the landlord's consent if someone buys the entity, you don't have to be concerned about whether the landlord can object to a change in the ownership of business.

If you're buying a business through an asset sale, there are a few different ways that a lease may deal with the issue of whether a new business owner can continue as the tenant under the former owner's lease. The following sections discuss the principal types of lease clauses that might be relevant.

Can't Assign Without Landlord's Consent

The lease may simply say that the business can't assign it, meaning give up the space to someone else, without the landlord's written consent. If it's a tenant-friendly lease, it may go on to say that the landlord won't unreasonably withhold that consent. Even without that language, courts in many states have ruled that the landlord must be reasonable. Still, even a landlord who has an obligation to be reasonable under the lease or according to state law has a fair measure of discretion. So if a landlord's consent is necessary, it will almost always make sense for the seller to talk to the landlord in advance to try to agree on a reasonable standard for approving a new tenant.

If the seller can tell the landlord that you're a prospective buyer, so much the better. The landlord may agree to an assignment if your business credentials make it very likely that the rent will be paid promptly and you won't do anything to diminish the

value of the property. In some instances, you and the seller may want to propose—or be ready to agree to—a small rent increase as an incentive for the landlord to accept you.

EXAMPLE: Tom, a sole proprietor, owns a profitable sports paraphernalia shop located near a PAC 10 football stadium in a building that Tom leases from Franz. Just before putting his business up for sale, Tom exercises an option to renew his lease for an additional five years at a rent of $2,000 a month. Since the rent is significantly below the current market rate, Tom enjoys a good deal. Unfortunately, the lease specifically prohibits an assignment to a new owner without the landlord's consent—and the courts in Tom's state haven't ruled on whether a landlord needs to be reasonable in deciding whether or not to give that consent. A well-financed partnership wants to buy the business from Tom, but the partners are concerned about being able to take over the lease. To encourage the landlord to consent to the partnership (which in all respects would be an ideal tenant), Tom arranges a meeting so Franz can meet the partners. At the meeting, Franz quickly realizes that the partnership would make a first-class tenant, and rather than scare the partnership away with a demand for full-market rent, he proposes that the rent be increased to $2,400 a month for the remainder of the lease—still a fairly long period of time. This modest increase is acceptable to the partnership in return for Franz's consent to the lease assignment.

Can't Assign, Period

The lease may flat-out say that the seller can't assign it. In most states, that prohibition is legally binding. The landlord, of course, is free to waive that provision, so it can't hurt to discuss the issue. Again, faced with a responsible new tenant (such as yourself) who's ready to take over and perhaps even agree to a modest rent increase, the landlord may say, "Fine, go ahead." And in an entity sale, this may not be a concern, because the entity continues to be the tenant and there's no assignment of the lease. But some leases anticipate this situation and state that if 50% or more of the entity ownership changes, the no-assignment clause applies.

Nothing Said on the Subject

The lease may not say anything on the subject of whether the tenant can assign it to a new business owner. In most states, the seller would be free to assign the lease to your buyer. But it's still a good idea to get the landlord involved—and cooperating—early in the process.

The Seller's Concern About Personal Liability

Besides wanting to be sure the lease is assignable, the seller will be concerned about whether the lease releases him or her from responsibility for the rent if a new owner takes over the business. In most states, even those where a tenant has the right to assign the lease, the tenant may still be liable for paying the rent and meeting other obligations under the lease if the new occupant fails to do so. So if the lease doesn't specify that the seller will no longer be liable to the landlord in case of an assignment, the seller may want to negotiate with the landlord for a release.

> **RELATED TOPIC**
>
> **Chapter 16 explains how to make a sale contingent on getting the landlord's consent to a lease assignment.** The contingency can also refer to the landlord releasing the seller from personal responsibility once the closing occurs.

> **RESOURCE**
>
> **For more on lease clauses and assignments,** see *Negotiate the Best Lease for Your Business,* by Janet Portman and Fred Steingold (Nolo).

Paperwork Concerning Real Estate Ownership

While most small businesses rent the space they occupy, a significant number own their own building and perhaps even some surrounding land. If that's true of the business you're considering, and the seller is willing to sell you the building along with the business, special paperwork will be needed. Because real estate laws and procedures vary greatly from state to state (and many business owners establish separate legal entities to own real estate), this book can't provide in-depth information covering the purchase of a building or other real estate. You'll need to seek guidance from a lawyer who's had experience with the transfer of real estate in the area where the business is located.

RESOURCE

For an introduction to the legal side of commercial real estate sales, see *A Practical Guide to Real Estate Practice*, by Joshua Stein (ALI-ABA). You can order the guide at www.ali-aba.org. Another useful resource is *A Practical Guide to Commercial Real Estate Transactions*, by Gregory Stein and others, which you can order at www.abanet.org. Also, check with the continuing legal education organization in your state for state-specific resources.

Before you proceed to buy a business and the building it's in, you'll want to see clear evidence that the seller owns the building— usually in the form of a deed, an existing title insurance policy, or a recent title search prepared by a title insurance company. If possible, also ask to see any mortgages, deeds of trust, or other liens or debts that may presently affect the title. But don't worry if the seller doesn't have these documents immediately available; they'll surface when

the title company does a careful search in preparing a "commitment" for a new title insurance policy to be issued in your name. The commitment is a document that spells out what needs to be done legally to transfer ownership of the building to you. For example, because of the due-on-sale clause in a mortgage or the presence of a lien stemming from a recent lawsuit, the seller may need to pay off a mortgage loan or other lien at or before closing.

Environmental Reports

Because of the danger of lawsuits based on the presence of asbestos, lead, or other environmental hazards, you may also want to see something called a Phase I environmental study. Environmental issues are important, because you can sometimes become legally responsible for the potentially huge cost of a cleanup even if the problem existed before you even bought the business. Although true horror scenarios are rare, you're sensible to be concerned about environmental hazards and to require a full investigation into any possible environmental problems.

The seller should have already thought through the possibility of environmental hazards. The vast majority of businesses don't have any, as would be true, for example, of a consulting business that operates from rented space in a new building. But some other businesses, such as dry cleaners and gas stations, may have real environmental concerns, especially if they've been in business for many years. Potential environmental issues could include any of the following:

- A dry cleaning business uses drums of volatile cleaning fluids that may have leaked from their containers.
- A lighting store is located on property which years ago was occupied by a gas station and may have tanks buried underground or have soil contamination problems resulting from leaking tanks or midnight dumping.
- A retail store occupies an older building that may contain asbestos insulation or lead-based paint.
- A garden supply business repairs power lawn mowers; the gasoline-oil fuel sometimes drips into soil behind the shop area.

In these and similar situations, the seller may have consulted an environmental expert and obtained a Phase I study to check on possible environmental hazards: air pollution, contaminated soil or water, asbestos, and so forth. In a Phase I study, the consultant researches the history of the site and neighboring sites; this typically includes interviewing people familiar with the area, looking at aerial photos to check on past uses of the site, and reviewing government documents that might disclose hazards. If the findings show a need for further investigation, a Phase II study may be in order; this often involves having engineers and chemists actually test the soil, air, structures, and groundwater for signs of contamination.

Depending on the nature of the problem and how it got started, the cost of a cleanup may be shared by the seller, the landlord, the government, and perhaps a former building occupant or business owner.

If you think there's a possible environmental issue, it's reasonable to ask the seller to come up with a Phase I study or explain to your satisfaction why such a study isn't necessary.

Contracts Other Than the Lease

A lease for business space is just one type of important contract that a business is likely to have. Others may include:

- equipment leases for cars, trucks, computers, phone systems, photocopiers, and machines used for manufacturing or repair
- contracts with suppliers—for example, a contract with a company that supplies chemicals for a dry cleaning business
- contracts to supply goods or services to customers or clients—for example, a contract that requires a heating and cooling company to inspect and maintain a large corporation's HVAC systems, or
- employment contracts with key employees.

If contracts such as these exist—and if they're important to the business and its operations—you'll probably want to see the contracts themselves, not just hear about what they say. This is especially true if you're thinking of buying the business entity, and not just its assets. In that case, you'll be bound by or will receive the benefits of those contracts, so it's particularly important that you know what's in them. Of course, you'll be pleased if you find that many of the contracts contain favorable terms—for example, if you stand to inherit an equipment lease calling for payments well below current market rates or a contract to provide goods or services to a customer or client for an amount that produces a handsome profit.

On the other side of the coin, you'll be dismayed to discover disadvantageous contracts—for example, one that obligates the business to make hefty payments for equipment that's no longer needed or to provide goods or services to others at a low price. If you buy the entity, you'll pretty much have to accept the bad along with the good.

This section looks at how the transfer of business contracts works, keeping in mind the distinction between an entity sale and an asset sale, which we've discussed at length in Chapters 2, 3, and 8.

Transferring Contracts in an Entity Sale

In the sale of a corporation or an LLC, the contracts usually go along with the business as a matter of law. With no need for separate paperwork, the business entity, under new ownership, gets the benefits and bears the burdens of the contracts the company signed under previous ownership. However, there are two situations in which a contract may not remain valid in an entity sale:

- The contract itself says that it will be or can be terminated if the corporation or LLC changes ownership. However, the law in some states requires the other party to the contract to be reasonable in deciding whether or not to continue the contract with the company under new ownership.

- The contract involves the performance of personal services that require special skills, so that it's clear that the contract is tied to the services of a specific person. For example, let's say that an architect has an LLC and someone hires the LLC to design an office building. Without the consent of the person who retained the architect's services, the architect normally is not free to transfer the contract to an architect who buys the practice.

EXAMPLE: Marge and Phil are the sole owners and employees of Web Eyes LLC, a small ad agency that writes ads for companies that run websites. They have a two-year contract with Topside Corporation which, for a substantial fee, obligates Marge and Phil to write a series of ads each month for Topside's website. Halfway through the contract, Marge and Phil sell their LLC to Wendy. Topside may decide not to honor the contract now that Wendy is the owner and is writing the ads. Topside signed up to get the special skills of Marge and Phil—and not the unknown skills of an unknown buyer.

Typically there's no legal requirement that a buyer notify vendors, suppliers, and customers when a sale occurs and an entity is under new ownership. Still, it usually makes sense for you and the seller to give the other parties a heads-up so that the transition is smooth. Especially on major contracts where the other party may be nervous about an unannounced substitution, you and the seller will want to put energy into convincing suppliers and customers that you're equipped to honor all existing obligations.

Transferring Contracts in an Asset Sale

Most commercial contracts contain a clause requiring the consent of the other party before the seller can assign the contract to you. So in most asset sale situations, the seller will first need to obtain the written permission of the other party to each contract and then formally transfer each contract to you by an assignment document. (Chapter 19 explains how to do this.)

If the contract doesn't require permission, the seller is free to transfer it—unless the contract clearly contemplates the rendering of services by a specific person. Assuming there's no clause requiring consent to assignment and the contract doesn't involve personal services, the seller is free to transfer a contract so that you can reap its benefit.

During the investigation stage, you'll want to review all existing contracts, analyze the transfer or assignment situation, and decide whether you and the seller need to contact the other contracting party about keeping the contract in force after you take over the business.

If you decide that contacting the other party is required or appropriate, it's usually best for the seller to start out with a phone call or meeting to discuss the likelihood that the business will be sold to you and explain that the seller would like to transfer the contract. If the other party is agreeable to the transfer, the seller may press further and try to get released from future liability on the contract. From your point of view, you'd like to see written proof that the seller has received permission to transfer the contract. Ideally, you'd like to see a formal agreement or amendment in which the other contracting party approves the transfer, but a letter to that effect will normally be enough.

Information About Accounts Receivable

Lots of businesses conduct important business dealings without formal written documents. For example, a business might ship orders expecting to be paid in 90 days, keeping no more than records of order and shipment. If you expect to receive payment for orders that are shipped prior to closing the sale of the business, you'll want to review these accounts carefully so as to be reasonably assured payment will be forthcoming.

To facilitate this review, see whether the seller can provide information about what is called the "aging" of each account (how long it has previously taken for that customer to pay, such as 30, 60, or 90 days). Where customers reliably pay on time, you'll normally feel comfortable stepping into the seller's legal shoes. But you should ask for a reduction in the sales price for accounts that have a history of paying late or paying only after repeated dunning. Or, depending on how bad they are, you and the seller may agree to delete those accounts from the sale entirely.

Chapter 13 explains how you can deal with accounts receivable in the sales agreement.

Corporate or LLC Records

If you're buying the business entity—not just the assets of the business—you and your lawyer will want to see the records that relate to the entity.

Purchase of a Corporation

Before purchasing the stock of a corporation, you'll want to examine the corporate record book, which should contain such things as the original incorporation papers (called articles of incorporation in most states), documents concerning registration of business names, and any trademarks, bylaws, list of shareholders, minutes of board of directors' meetings, or written documents (called consents) showing legal actions taken by shareholders and directors on paper in the absence of a physical meeting. You should also ask to see copies of the annual reports the business has filed with the state authorities.

If, like some small business owners, the seller hasn't created any corporate minutes, board resolutions, or written consents to actions taken without a meeting since the day the corporation was formed, the seller will have some catching up to do. At the very least, this means the seller will have to create records of the actions usually taken at annual meetings of shareholders and directors. At a minimum, the shareholders' annual meeting records should document the election of people to serve on the board of directors. Similarly, the board of directors' annual meeting records should document the election of officers. And the seller should prepare records of any important corporate decisions customarily taken by the board, such as leasing real property or borrowing money.

You may be nervous about accepting corporate documents prepared after the fact. But fortunately, there's a perfectly legal and accepted way for the seller to create current records for actions that should have been taken at meetings that never took place: The seller simply prepares current written documents (consents) that ratify (approve) past activities. Let's say, for example, the corporate shareholders didn't hold an annual shareholders' or directors' meeting for the last three years and didn't sign timely written consents in place of these meetings. To fill in this gap, the current shareholders can sign a "Written Consent in Lieu of Shareholders'

Annual Meetings" for the years in question. The written consent might state that the shareholders acknowledge that Joe Brown and Mary White were selected to serve as the corporate directors for 2011, 2012, and 2013 and that the shareholders are ratifying the services of these two as the corporate directors for those years. The seller would then put the current date on the written consent. He or she can prepare a similar written consent for the directors to sign regarding the corporate officers and any other major corporate decisions that need to be ratified.

RESOURCE

If the seller is flummoxed about how to create corporate records, suggest that he or she look at *The Corporate Records Handbook: Meetings, Minutes & Resolutions,* by Anthony Mancuso (Nolo). This highly recommended resource explains the kinds of corporate decisions that should be documented through minutes or written consents and will show the seller exactly how to do it. And just as important, it will show the seller how to legally fix holes in the corporate records.

Purchase of a Limited Liability Company

If you're buying an LLC, you'll technically be buying the membership interest of each owner. It follows that you'll want to see the organizational records of the LLC. The seller may or may not have a formal records book that resembles the ones maintained by a corporation; the law allows LLCs to opt for minimal paperwork. But at the very least, you'll need to see the document that created the entity—called the articles of organization in most states—and a formal operating agreement if there are two or more members of the LLC (maybe even if there's only one member). And, if a multimember LLC conducts its affairs with the same formality as a corporation, you'll also want to see the minutes of membership meetings or written consents of members for actions taken by the company.

RESOURCE

If the seller needs help with LLC records, you can recommend *Your Limited Liability Company: An Operating Manual,* by Anthony Mancuso (Nolo). It's addressed to LLC owners who'd like to maintain—or create—the same types of entity records that corporations have traditionally kept. Scores of examples cover a wide variety of situations.

Licenses and Permits

In many localities, all businesses must obtain a basic business license. In addition, many businesses, from restaurants and gun shops to home repair services and hair-styling salons, require specialized licenses and permits from state and/or local authorities, and occasionally from the federal government. Some types of licenses can easily and legally be transferred—especially if you're buying an entity. But others—especially those that are based on an owner's personal skills or training—may be harder to transfer or may not be transferable at all.

For example, if you're buying a civil engineering firm that's set up as a professional corporation, state law may require that each purchasing shareholder have a civil engineer's license. Similarly, if you're buying an LLC that operates a restaurant and bar, it may be necessary to have a state liquor board investigate and approve you and any other new members of the LLC before your ownership permit can be approved.

You'll certainly want to know about all current licenses and permits, both for figuring out transfer issues and to be sure that as it's being operated the business meets minimum governmental requirements for businesses of its type. It makes sense for you and the seller to check with the licensing authority for each required license or permit to learn which ones can be transferred and which ones can't. And while you're at it, find out what procedures are needed to make sure the business obtains all necessary licenses under your new ownership.

You don't want to wait until the day of closing to discover that there will be a delay in transferring or obtaining a needed license or permit. For example, if you're buying a pest control business, you may need to take and pass a state license exam. Such exams may be offered infrequently—perhaps only four times a year.

An alert seller may give you a summary of licensing information like the one below.

Sample Licensing Information Summary

To Potential Buyers of Allegro Bar and Grill:

The following is a list of licenses needed to run the business.

Type of License Needed	Expiration Date	Licensing Authority	Is Permission Needed to Transfer?
Beer and wine license	December 31, 20xx	State Alcohol Board	Yes
Liquor license	June 30, 20xx	State Alcohol Board	Yes
Health license	April 30, 20xx	County Health Commission	Reinspection needed. Permits needed for renovations.
Entertainment license	September 30, 20xx	City Police Department	No
Sales tax license	November 30, 20xx	State Revenue Board	No

Intellectual Property

Depending on the business you're considering, some or even most of its value may reside in its patents, copyrights, trademarks, business names, or trade secrets. These rights are broadly referred to as intellectual property. You—and any intellectual property lawyer you consult—will want to see any documents that relate to the business's intellectual property, especially those that confirm ownership of intellectual property. These documents help you evaluate how secure this property will be if there's a legal challenge. As a practical matter, if the business has little or no intellectual property, you'll spend little or no time on this detail.

However, especially if the business is in the publishing or software fields or if its key products are protected by patents, your review will be part of a formal intellectual property audit in which you—along with the appropriate professional help—evaluate the value of the intellectual property and size up the risk of potential claims of infringement. The audit will have two stages. First, you'll obtain information from the seller on how the intellectual property was created and what's been done to protect it. This will include copies of copyright, patent, and trademark documents. Then you and your consultant will dig deeper, reviewing all subsequent registrations, agreements with authors or other creative types, and—especially as regards trade secrets—security

precautions taken by the seller to be sure that secrecy has been maintained.

Here's a brief explanation of the various types of intellectual property and a listing of documents that you and your lawyer should ask to see in each category.

Patents

A patent is a document issued by the U.S. Patent and Trademark Office (PTO) that grants a monopoly for a limited period of time on the use and development of an invention (utility patent) or on a design for a useful object (design patent). The utility patent right lasts approximately 17–18 years; the design patent right lasts 14 years. You and your lawyer will want to see:

- all patents granted by the U.S. Patent and Trademark Office
- all patent applications in process
- all documents pertaining to patent pending status
- employment and independent contractor agreements that might affect patent ownership
- preinvention assignments of rights
- assignments to the business if it acquired the patent from another company or owner
- agreements in which the business has licensed other businesses to use its patents, or in which other businesses have licensed the business to use theirs, and
- data concerning the business's ongoing supervision of patent rights.

RESOURCE

For a complete explanation of patent law, see *Nolo's Patents for Beginners,* by David Pressman and Richard Stim (Nolo).

Copyrights

A copyright is a legal right granted to the creator of a "work of authorship." In a typical small business setting, this can include such things as booklets, brochures, advertising copy, jingles, videos, and software. The owner of the copyright can stop others from copying, selling, displaying, performing, or modifying the work for a significant period of time. The copyright in works created after 1977 by individuals usually lasts for the life of the author plus an additional 70 years. The copyright in works created by employees for their employers lasts for 95 years from the date of publication, or 120 years from the date of creation, whichever occurs first.

A business acquires copyright in works it creates regardless of whether it registers the work with the U.S. Copyright Office. However, a business needs to register the work before suing someone for infringement. If the business you're investigating has copyrights that will be transferred to you as part of the sale, you and your lawyer will want to see:

- all copyright registrations
- all applications for copyright registrations
- employment and independent contractor agreements that might affect copyright ownership

- copies of the work that's copyrighted, to see if the copyright notice has been properly included
- assignments from those involved in the creation of the copyrighted material, such as an author's assignment of a copyright to the publisher
- agreements in which the business has a license to use someone else's copyrighted material, or in which another business has licensed the business to use its copyrighted material, and
- data concerning steps the business has taken to prevent infringement and/or to stop those who are infringing on the copyright.

RESOURCE

For a full explanation of copyright law and procedure, see *The Copyright Handbook: What Every Writer Needs to Know,* by Attorney Stephen Fishman (Nolo).

Trademarks and Service Marks

A trademark is a distinctive word, phrase, logo, graphic symbol, or other device that's used to identify the source of a product and to distinguish a manufacturer's or merchant's products from anyone else's. Some examples are Dell computers and Microsoft software. A service mark serves the same function as a trademark, but for a company's services rather than a particular product—for example, AOL is a service mark for America Online's services. The same law applies to both types of marks. The owner of a trademark or service mark can prevent others from using it in a way that confuses people about the products or services the owner provides or about their origin.

Business Names and Trademarks

A trade name is the formal name of a business. For example, Ford Motor Company is a trade name. A trade name is used for such things as opening bank accounts, paying taxes, ordering supplies, and filing lawsuits. A trade name can become a trademark or service mark when it's used to identify products or services (for example, a Ford car). Even if you're not sure whether or not the trade name of the business you're buying amounts to a trademark, you should treat it as such for purposes of your purchase. In other words, the seller should transfer the trade name (and any accompanying goodwill) to you. The seller should also give you any documentation that the trade name has been registered with the local county clerk or secretary of state.

As with a copyright, a business can register a trademark or service mark with the federal government, but even if it doesn't, it has substantial legal rights simply by being the first to use the mark. If the seller will be transferring trademarks to you as part of the sale of a business, you and your lawyer will want to see:

- examples of how the business has used the mark—for example, labels for products or advertisements for services
- applications for federal, state, or international registrations
- registration documents
- assignments, if the business has acquired the mark from someone else
- documents indicating steps the business has taken to protect the mark, and
- any documents relating to licensing of the mark to third parties.

Trade Secrets

A trade secret is any formula, pattern, physical device, idea, process, or compilation of information, or virtually any other information, that (1) isn't generally known or readily ascertainable by a business's competitors, (2) offers the business an actual or potential economic advantage over others, and (3) is treated by the business in a way that can reasonably be expected to prevent the public or competitors from learning about it.

Unlike valuable copyrights and patents, which many businesses don't own, almost every small enterprise owns trade secrets. Lest you consider the business you're buying to be an exception, think of its customer or client list or its roster of suppliers. These lists can be and often are trade secrets, and they're frequently a significant part of what you're paying for. Trade secrets, which are protected by state law, are not registered with any public office. To get a court order barring someone else from improperly using a trade secret, a business needs to show the material really is secret and that the business has taken reasonable precautions to keep it secret. You and your lawyer will want to see:

- any nondisclosure agreements that employees and other people have signed
- any innovations, inventions, or other documents that contain or utilize the trade secret
- assignments, if the business has acquired trade secrets from someone else
- any documents regarding licensing of trade secrets to third parties, and
- any other documents the business has (such as instructions to employees) that show the steps that have been taken to preserve trade secrets inside and outside the company.

 RESOURCE

For a complete explanation of trade secret law, see *Nondisclosure Agreements: Protect Your Trade Secrets & More*, by Richard Stim and Stephen Fishman. It's out of print, but the authors have posted it online for free, at www.ndasforfree.com.

The Role of Confidentiality Agreements

It's understandable that sellers will be cautious—or even slightly paranoid—when releasing confidential information about a business to a potential buyer. Basically, unless you're a family member, a close friend, or someone else the seller knows well and trusts totally, the seller will want to hold back information that could provide you with a competitive advantage until he or she is convinced that your character and reputation are good. While it's not the norm, there undoubtedly are dishonest folks out there who may attempt to con a seller into thinking they're sincere buyers while their real goal is to snoop into the business's affairs.

But if a deal to sell a business is going to crystallize, the seller is going to have to share confidential information with you. You're not going to pay good money for a supposedly valuable business without carefully investigating how it works. "Trust me!" won't satisfy you. Your motto must be "Show me."

Assuming that you're able to persuade the seller that it's necessary to the sale and that you are sufficiently trustworthy, the seller still will undoubtedly ask you to sign an agreement (called a confidentiality agreement or nondisclosure agreement) pledging to keep the business information confidential. The agreement creates a legal obligation for you to respect the seller's ownership of the information. You agree to use the sensitive data only to evaluate the business—and not to share it with anyone else except your lawyer or accountant.

There's another concern the seller may want to deal with if you currently compete with the seller or you may open a competitive business later: The seller may want you to agree not to hire away any of the business's employees. The concern is that long-term employees know so much about the business that their jumping ship could give you a huge competitive advantage.

The seller's twin goals of keeping information confidential and discouraging you from taking away key employees are usually accomplished by casting a confidentiality agreement in traditional contract form, but it may take the form of a letter like the one below. You or the seller can edit the sample to fit your own situation.

 FORM

Where to find the forms. If you're reading a print copy of this book, you'll find a copy of the Confidentiality Letter on the CD-ROM at the back. If you're using an ebook version, you can download the letter on the Nolo website; the link is included in Appendix A.

When you sign a copy of the confidentiality letter and return it to the seller, the letter becomes a legally binding contract.

Information to Garner From Other Sources

No doubt about it: Assembling and analyzing the data you collect from the seller is a major project, but it's an essential part of deciding whether a given business is for you—and how much you're willing to pay for it. And even after doing everything described above, your job may not be done yet. In addition to gathering information from the seller, you many also want to scrutinize information from other sources to get a fuller picture of the business you're considering. Let's look at some avenues you might go down to supplement what you've learned from the seller.

UCC Lien Check

Creditors may have a lien on some or all of the business property owned by the seller. This would be the case, for example, if the seller borrowed money from a bank, or purchased goods or services on credit, and the creditor took appropriate legal steps to create and retain a lien. To preserve its lien, a knowledgeable creditor would have filed a Uniform Commercial Code (UCC) Financing Statement with the state's secretary of state (or other designated office). Such a filing would create a public record that the creditor has a lien on the business assets—and that the creditor can seize and sell those assets if the debt isn't paid.

It's critical that you make sure that no creditor has a lien on the assets you're buying—or that if such a lien exists, the seller will promise to pay the debt and have the creditor release the lien at or before closing. Otherwise, the creditor can take the property

Sample Confidentiality Letter

November 7, 20xx

Nancy Carr   George McAndrews
2146 Oak Boulevard   616 Tamarack Circle
Granville, SD   Granville, SD

Dear Nancy and George:

As prospective purchasers of the assets of Racafrax Enterprises LLC, you've asked to see information about the business's finances, customers, suppliers, and trade secrets, as well as proprietary data about pricing and marketing practices. We are happy to share this information with you, as long as you agree to keep it confidential, as outlined below.

1. You agree that the information we provide to you is valuable and confidential.

2. You agree to maintain the confidentiality of the information we provide to you, with the exception that you may share it with your lawyer and accountant for purposes of evaluating your possible purchase of the business. You will inform these professional advisers that they too must maintain the confidentiality of the information.

3. You agree to use the confidential information only to evaluate your possible purchase of the business and for no other purpose.

4. You agree that you won't contact customers, suppliers, or employees of Racafrax without our prior written permission.

5. You agree that if you and Racafrax do not reach agreement on your purchase of the assets, you will return to us the information we provided to you and all copies and will destroy your notes and summaries.

6. You agree that you won't recruit or hire any Racafrax employees while our discussions about your possible purchase of the business are pending, and for one year afterward.

Sample Confidentiality Letter (continued)

If you agree with the above commitments, please sign and return a copy of this letter for our files.

Sincerely yours,

Racafrax Enterprises LLC

By: _Tess Woods_
       Tess Woods, Managing Member

We agree to the above terms.

Nancy Carr
Nancy Carr
Dated: _November 11, 20xx_

George McAndrews
George McAndrews
Dated: _November 11, 20xx_

away from you even though you've paid the seller for it. To protect yourself from undisclosed liens, contact the office where UCC liens are filed and ask for a lien check. For a modest fee, you'll get copies of any liens currently in effect. You can then talk to the seller about a plan to get rid of the liens.

IRS Tax Liens

If the business or its owner has failed to pay federal income taxes or employment taxes, the IRS may have placed a tax lien on business assets. As with a UCC lien, this would give the government a security interest in those assets. If the seller doesn't pay the taxes that are owed, the IRS can seize the business assets. Obviously, as with a UCC lien, this is something you want to avoid.

The IRS gives public notice of its tax liens by filing them at a county recording office where the business is located or where the taxpayer lives. Sometimes the notice gets filed in more than one county. You should ask someone in the county clerk's office to tell you which county office receives IRS lien filings. Then go to that office and ask for a search of tax liens in both the business's name and the owner's name. If a tax lien does show up, you'll need to speak to the seller about how the lien will get removed.

State and local tax collectors may also file tax liens—often in the same office as where IRS liens are filed. Check it out.

Official Status of a Corporation or LLC

If you're considering buying a corporation or an LLC in an entity sale, you need to learn whether the entity's existence and status are properly recorded with the appropriate state office—such as the secretary of state's office. Equally important, you need to make sure the entity is currently in good standing with the state. A corporate or LLC registration may lapse, for example, because the owners failed to file required annual reports or to pay required fees or taxes. A lapsed registration puts the entity into legal limbo. You wouldn't want to buy an entity until the seller has fixed any registration problems.

So before you buy a corporation or LLC, you should contact the state office where entities are registered and ask about the status of the entity. If all is well, the state office may provide a certificate of good standing for your records. Some states provide this information online.

Past and Present Lawsuits

The clerks of the county court and federal district court in the area where the business is located can tell you whether the business or its owner have been involved in any lawsuits in the past and whether any lawsuits are now pending. If there are past or present lawsuits, you can review the court files, which are public records. Court files can contain a wealth of information about a business and its relationships with customers, suppliers, employees, and the government. They can also provide insight into relationships among the owners of a business who may have become involved in legal warfare.

Any business lawsuit can give you insight into the character of the participants and whether the seller is trustworthy or somewhat shady. Be cautious if there seem to be a lot of lawsuits that indicate the seller has a tendency to get into conflict with others over business relationships—the next conflict could be yours. But most important, be especially attentive to any lawsuit in which a judgment was entered against the entity you're considering buying. You need to find out whether the seller has paid the judgment in full or whether an appeal is in the works. You don't want to buy an entity only to find out that the business must pay a huge judgment in a case that was filed long before you bought it. And pending, unresolved lawsuits pose the same kind of risk. Make sure the seller will be responsible for any judgment that comes down against the entity in the future—and that the seller has adequate resource to pay the judgment.

Seller's Credit Report

It's useful to obtain a credit report for the business and its owner. You can order a business credit report from Dun and Bradstreet at www.dnb.com. It may disclose debts or a history of slow paying that doesn't jibe with the seller's depiction of the business as highly profitable.

Similarly, if a personal credit report discloses a debt-ridden seller, you'll have reason to ponder how a seemingly successful businessperson could be struggling financially. You can order a copy of the seller's personal report from any of the three national credit reporting services: Equifax at www.equifax.com, TransUnion at www.tuc.com, or Experian at www.experian.com. Permission of the seller may be required.

Problems With Customers, Clients, and the Government

Customers and clients who have problems with a business may complain to a governmental agency that regulates such businesses, such as a state agency that issues licenses. Similarly, a governmental agency itself may have a file on a business, such as when a health department repeatedly cites a restaurant for health code violations. To the extent that such files are available for public inspection (and most are these days, thanks to freedom-of-information rules), they can reveal important information about the owner and how the business has been operated in the past. The files of the Better Business Bureau and other consumer protection agencies may contain similar information.

A business's history of dissatisfied customers or clients—or repeated problems with the authorities—should raise a warning flag for you. Sure, if you buy the business, it will be "under new management" (as the cliché goes), but its old reputation may live on in the public mind and can drag you down. It also creates a greater likelihood that there may be future problems hiding in the woodwork.

Why and How the Seller May Check You Out

One reason sellers check out buyers is to weed out time wasters, kooks, and competitors whose only intention is to mine as much confidential information as possible. Another is that the seller wants to make sure you have the skill, determination, and integrity to succeed with the business. But there are several other reasons why sellers want to look into a buyer's financial resources, business prospects, and reputation for integrity before signing a sales agreement or sharing sensitive information. Of course, the seller will probably omit the normal investigation if you're a friend or relative whom the seller trusts and whose financial status is clear.

Determining Your Ability to Close the Deal

The seller will want to make sure you have the financing it will take to buy the business. He or she won't want to waste time with someone who can't come up with the dough.

From the seller's perspective, your ability to bring the necessary money to the closing

table is a huge concern if you're buying the business for a lump sum cash payment. But it's a matter of just as great consequence if—as is more typical—you're buying on an installment basis with, say, a 25% down payment on a $700,000 sale price. The seller will still want to be sure that, come closing day, you'll be able to produce the $175,000 down payment. Understandably, the seller would find it painful to sign a contract, take the business off the market, and put time and effort into picking out a ski cabin, only to discover that you can't come up with the money.

Determining Your Ability to Pay Installments

Even if you can produce the money necessary to make the required down payment, the seller will still want to make sure that you're in strong enough financial shape that you'll make the installment payments on time. What's more, a seller who's planning to work for you as an employee or consultant after the closing will be concerned about getting paid for those services. And even if the seller won't be working for you, if the business fails because you're a subpar businessperson or you don't pay up as promised, the seller might have to take the business back in a deteriorated condition.

If an investigation leaves the seller with qualms about your ability to meet all payment commitments following the closing, you may be asked to provide additional protections. These protections might include giving the seller a lien on your home or having someone who is unquestionably financially solvent guarantee payment of the remainder of the purchase price.

Evaluating the Quality of the Seller's Future Relationship With You

A seller who will have an ongoing relationship with you after the closing will want to make sure that the two of you will get along. Or put another way, even though the sale of a business is primarily about dollars and cents, the seller won't want to ignore your personal characteristics. This will be particularly true if the seller plans to work for you for some months or years as a consultant or employee.

In addition, the seller's reputation may be at stake. Even though the business will be under new ownership, it's likely that for years after the closing, the seller will still be associated with it in the minds of many people. A buyer's lack of ethics will often reflect poorly on the seller. So especially if the seller plans to keep living in the same community or working in the same field, he or she will want to be proud to be associated with whoever buys the business.

The Seller's Investigation of You

Now that you see why the seller will want to check you out, let's look at what you might expect. The process might start

with the seller asking you to produce a financial statement, career resumé, and other documents. The seller may then move on to additional sources of information, including checking with people who know you.

Your Financial Statement

Your financial statement will show the seller what assets you own and what debts you owe. This is especially important to the seller if you'll be signing a promissory note for some of the sale price. The seller will be extending credit to you—in effect, he or she will be in the position of a bank or other conventional lender.

The assets listed on your financial statement might include cash in the bank, stocks, bonds, mutual funds, a house, and one or more cars. Debts may include credit card balances, car payments, home mortgages or deeds of trust, and home equity loans or lines of credit. Also, you may also owe money on education loans. In addition to the financial statement itself, the seller may ask for evidence that the information is accurate: a bank statement, a recent statement from your stockbroker, or a deed to your home. And the seller may want to peruse your recent tax returns.

If you already own a business, the seller may want to see a financial statement of that business in addition to your personal financial statement. And if you're buying the seller's business through a corporation or an LLC that you own, the seller will probably want to review its financial statement as well as the statements of anyone who will be guaranteeing payment of the promissory note.

Even though you may be reluctant to disclose private information to the seller, you're probably going to have to do it if you expect the seller to extend credit to you. Don't hold back any unpleasant facts; it's crucial that the information you provide be as complete and accurate as possible. If it's not, you may later be accused of misrepresentation and fraud, with costly legal consequences.

RESOURCE

You can use a bank form as a model for your financial statement. If you don't have a financial statement already prepared, you can pick up a business or mortgage loan application form at the bank where you do business. Part of the form will consist of a financial statement that you can fill in and give to the seller. That way, you'll be giving the seller the same information a bank would require in lending money to you.

Your Credit History

Lenders who make loans for home or car purchases invariably get a credit report on the borrower. Likewise, it's logical for the seller to get one on you before selling you a business. If you've been in business before, the seller may order a credit report about your previous or existing business.

RESOURCE

It pays to see your credit report in advance. You can order a copy of your personal report for free at a centralized credit reporting website, www.annualcreditreport.com. You can also call 877-322-8228, or complete the Annual Credit Report Request Form and mail it to: Annual Credit Report Request Service, P.O. Box 105281, Atlanta, GA 30348-5281. If you see data on your credit report that might put off a seller, you can take steps to fix the problem. For information on how to do this, see *Credit Repair*, by Robin Leonard, J.D., and Attorney John Lamb (Nolo).

Your Career Resumé

Whether or not the seller asks for it, you might consider submitting a career resumé listing your education and prior work experience and organizational affiliations. This will help the seller understand more about whether you're likely to succeed as an owner of the business. Your resumé should contain the names of references and prior business associates. This will enable the seller to start contacting people who are familiar with your financial position, work habits, and business ethics.

Talking to People Who Know You

People who have dealt with or observed you can help the seller understand your business experience, work habits, and reputation for integrity. In trying to put together a complete picture of you, the seller may go beyond the references you list, figuring that these people are likely to provide mostly positive feedback. So the seller may seek out people who have had business dealings with you and who are likely to provide an objective point of view. This can include, for example, your current and former landlords. In other words, the seller may want to talk to people who have no obvious reason to say only positive things about you.

EXAMPLE: Sam is trying to sell his little breakfast restaurant, The Fresh Egg. He is eagerly approached by Maria, who says she used to own a juice bar and would now love to get into the restaurant business. She makes a good first impression when she arrives well-dressed, driving a new Lexus SUV. Sam is less impressed, however, when he sees Maria's financial statement. She has only $1,200 in the bank and no other assets besides her SUV, which she will be paying for over the next three years. She also owes $20,000 in college loans and $5,000 on two credit cards. Sam decides to check some more. After talking with Maria's references—including a college roommate and a member of Maria's former rowing crew—who all say she's terrific, Sam decides to investigate further. Realizing that he has met the landlord of Maria's old juice bar, he calls her and learns that Maria was rarely on time with the rent. When Sam stops by, a nearby store owner says that while

Maria's posted hours were 7 a.m. to 6 p.m., she hardly ever opened before 9:30 a.m. and often shut down for a week at a time for vacation. Finally, a city health department inspection report shows that Maria typically had three or more reasonably serious violations whenever routine inspections were made. Although Maria assures Sam that she can borrow the 10% down payment for the restaurant from a boyfriend, Sam decides that extending credit to Maria would be a risky proposition. He tells her that if she's serious about buying the business, she'll need to bring in a guarantor or co-owner who has substantial assets.

Your Complaint Record With or Disciplinary Action by Public Agencies

If the business you're considering buying requires its owner to be licensed, the seller will want to make sure that you have a currently valid license and that this license is in good standing.

To get this information, the seller may check with the appropriate licensing agency—for example, a state agency that licenses auto repair shops or real estate brokers. The licensing authority may also furnish the seller with any information that's regularly available to the public about disciplinary action that's been taken against you, as well as consumer complaints. For example, someone selling a veterinary practice can find out if the vet who's offering to buy it has ever been suspended or reprimanded or has a history of complaints from dissatisfied customers.

Your Business Plan

If you're serious about buying a business, you may have a blueprint for the future that looks ahead to the next three to five years. The seller may inquire about whether you have such a plan and, if so, ask to see it. If you present a naïve or silly plan, the seller will not be impressed.

At the very least, be prepared to explain how you expect to run the business and finance your payments in the early months of operation.

TIP

A nervous seller may ask you about what will happen if things go wrong. You should be prepared with a sensible response. Many buyers assume they'll be making money right off the bat and will meet payments to the seller entirely out of the business profits. And things may turn out that way. But the seller may know that it's often no easy task to earn enough to make a living wage and cover payments like the installment payments you're taking on. The seller may also realize that you'll face a pile of expenses related to the change in ownership,

---

and it's possible that in the early days, the net income of the business may be less than expected. So be prepared to explain your plan for exactly what happens if costs are higher and revenue lower than expected.

With either an asset sale or an entity sale, you should have enough operating cash to carry the business for at least 90 days—if not longer. You need to be able to stay afloat during the critical early months. This means having money not only to meet the initial payments to the seller, but also for riding out the period before income starts arriving faster than bills do.

Consulting Court Records

A diligent seller may check out local court records to find out whether you've been involved in any lawsuits (though some may show up in a credit report as well). This is public information, of course. If it turns out that you've been sued a number of times, this can be a deal killer—particularly if the suits were about your alleged failure to pay bills. Similarly, finding that you've initiated a number of lawsuits—that is, you were the plaintiff rather than the defendant—can also be a go-slow signal the seller, who may fear being named as the defendant in your next litigation.

Checklist of Information to Review in Investigating the Business

Here are some of the items you may want to obtain from the seller in the process of evaluating a business:

- ☐ Business tax returns
- ☐ Business financial statements
- ☐ Detailed list of assets
- ☐ Details on accounts receivable, debts, and other liabilities
- ☐ Current lease
- ☐ The deed and title insurance policy (if you're buying real estate as part of the deal)
- ☐ Contracts with customers, suppliers, and employers
- ☐ Licenses and permits, and
- ☐ Documents pertaining to intellectual property.

Here is some information you may want to obtain from sources other than the seller:

- ☐ Existence of UCC liens
- ☐ Existence of tax liens
- ☐ Official status of the corporation or LLC (in an entity sale)
- ☐ Past and present lawsuits involving the seller
- ☐ Credit history of seller and the business, and
- ☐ Complaints by consumers and public agencies.

Drafting a Letter of Intent

Eventually, when you and the seller reach a solid understanding, you'll need to capture the terms of your deal in a sales agreement, as explained in detail in Part 3 of this book. In our view, it's best to move as quickly as possible toward reaching a final sales agreement. But sometimes, there are reasons for you and the seller to sign a preliminary document called a letter of intent before the sales agreement is completed. This chapter explains why you might want a letter of intent in some circumstances, tells how to prepare one, and highly recommends that any such letter be nonbinding. A sample letter of intent is included.

> **CAUTION**
>
> **Never sign a letter of intent if you're seriously looking at other businesses.** Signing a letter of intent—even a nonbinding one—implies that you hope to reach full agreement and ultimately close with this seller. If you're serious enough to sign such a letter, don't simultaneously negotiate with others, even if the letter doesn't prohibit it. Unless you clearly tell the seller in advance that you'll continue to have discussions with others (in which case the letter is all but meaningless), you risk an angry confrontation if the seller learns of your other negotiations. The unhappy result may be that an otherwise viable deal falls apart.

Why Use a Letter of Intent

A letter of intent summarizes the main terms that you and the seller believe will become part of a sales agreement. It can be either a legally binding and enforceable commitment to the terms listed in the letter, or simply a nonbinding recap of where you stand in your negotiations (as we recommend).

While using a letter of intent as part of the purchase of a small business is not that common, occasionally a buyer and seller will choose to prepare one. The reasons are varied, but usually involve one or both parties' concern about whether the other is serious about consummating the deal. For example, even at an early stage of negotiations you may find yourself under intense pressure from an eager seller to get something down in writing, and you may conclude that the deal may slip away if you don't cooperate. The seller, in turn, may be pushing for a letter of intent as reassurance that a deal and closing are imminent, and that there's no longer any need to continue discussions with other interested buyers.

> **EXAMPLE:** Lennie, who runs a small taxi business in a suburban city, has been negotiating to buy the business assets of Green Cab Company LLC, an outfit that operates six cabs in the same city. The deal is falling nicely into place. But

Lennie and Green Cab's owner (Ned) still have some fine points to work out, including how the sale price will be allocated among the various assets—something that can have important tax consequences for each (as explained in Chapter 3). They also need to agree on the details of Ned's covenant not to compete—its duration and geographical area—as well as how much Ned will be paid for his consulting services during the six months following the sale. Because Lennie is about to go out of town for his daughter's wedding and Ned's tax adviser is tied up with another client's IRS audit, Lennie and Ned won't be able to finalize their deal for at least ten days. Two other prospective buyers are interested in the business, but Ned is reluctant to spend time with them if it's 95% likely that he'll ultimately sell to Lennie. Still, before putting off the other buyers, Ned wants something in writing as concrete evidence that a sale to Lennie is almost certain to happen. Even though there are some crucial details to be worked out, Lennie understands the logic of Ned's request and prepares a nonbinding letter of intent capturing the high points of the agreement he and Ned are working on. After both sign this letter, Ned informs the other buyers that they should probably look elsewhere.

As a buyer, you might want to seek a letter of intent if you've been looking at two or three other businesses and would like to tell the less-appealing candidates that you're close to a deal with your leading choice. You might not want to back away from the other businesses unless you have a relatively firm commitment from the favored one.

Another reason you or the seller might consider creating a letter of intent is to reduce the chances that the other party will try to introduce new or unpalatable terms just before the closing, when there's enormous momentum to complete the transaction. Although a nonbinding letter has no legal power to prevent this, it may nevertheless be a positive moral force to encourage the other party to hold to the terms of the deal that was negotiated.

What to Put in Your Letter of Intent

The items appropriately covered in your letter of intent will depend on the nature of your purchase and the key points on which you and the seller have already agreed. There's no formula that will work for every deal, but below are some points that buyers and sellers will want to consider. Unless you've discussed and agreed on most of these substantive and procedural terms, chances are your negotiations are at such a preliminary stage that it's too soon to even consider preparing a nonbinding letter of intent.

Substantive Items

Here are some of the substantive items you might consider covering in a letter of intent:

- the sale price or how it will be determined
- whether you'll be buying the business's assets or buying the corporation, LLC, or other entity itself
- how payment will be made—full sale price at closing or installment payments
- the measures that will protect the seller in an installment sale, such as your giving the seller a security interest in the business's assets, signing a personal guarantee, or possibly imposing a lien on your home in the seller's favor
- a list of any business assets that are not part of the deal, such as a particular computer or a work of art that the seller will keep
- which accounts receivable, if any, will be transferred
- whether liabilities such as bank loans or sums owed on equipment purchases will be transferred as part of the sale or retained by the seller
- whether liabilities such as the responsibility of paying for warranty repairs on past sales items will be transferred to you

- whether a presale inventory of business property will be conducted and, if so, whether it will be done by the two of you or by an outsider
- whether you'll be taking over the current lease
- whether the seller will be signing a covenant not to compete that limits his or her right to do similar work in the future and, if so, an outline of its major terms, and
- any arrangements for the seller to do future work for you as an employee or consultant.

Procedural Items

Here are some of the procedural items you might consider covering in a letter of intent:

- whether you reserve the right to have discussions with other possible businesses or will negotiate exclusively with the seller with whom you're signing the letter of intent
- a schedule for completing negotiations and signing a sales agreement, and perhaps the date by which you expect the deal will be closed
- a list of the important issues that remain to be agreed upon
- a description of any further investigation of the business or of the seller's representations about the business that you plan to conduct
- a description of any further investigation of you that the seller plans to

conduct, such as looking into your financial status or prior business experience

- whether you and the seller will sign nondisclosure agreements to discourage the leaking or misuse of confidential information (you may have already attended to this), and
- whether the letter of intent is binding (something not recommended, for reasons explained below).

TIP

Customize your letter of intent to meet your needs. Not every item on these lists will apply to your purchase—and there may be some points you'd like to include that aren't on either list. That's fine. Your letter of intent should be crafted to reflect your particular transaction and the current state of your negotiations.

Why You Should Only Sign a Nonbinding Letter of Intent

Any letter of intent you sign should be of the nonbinding variety. In other words, you should avoid signing a preliminary document that might be treated as a binding contract. Otherwise, you face the possibility that your letter of intent will enmesh you in arguments—and perhaps even litigation— over what exactly you and the seller have committed yourselves to. Any letter of intent is by definition going to be less complete

than a definitive sales agreement. If you bind yourself, you risk finding that the general (perhaps even vague) provisions of the letter will later be interpreted by the seller in ways that surprise and disappoint you. And if a court ultimately agrees with the seller, you may be stuck with a deal you never intended to agree to. What's more, even if you win in a subsequent court action, you'll have had to cope with a huge, unproductive, and expensive headache.

Think of it this way: No letter of intent will contain crucially important fine-print terms of your purchase. If you knew those, you'd have a sales agreement already. For example, you could find yourself legally bound to buy a business from the seller at the price listed in the letter without the guarantees needed to give you effective recourse if the seller hasn't disclosed the true financial status of the business or if the seller starts to compete with the business after you buy it. While these and other details are customarily included in a sales agreement and in the closing documents referred to in the sales agreement, they may be omitted or glossed over in a preliminary letter.

TIP

If the seller insists on a binding letter of intent, get ready to stay up all night. An anxious seller may want to bind you to the purchase as quickly as possible. That's understandable. But instead of signing a binding letter of intent, make the time to promptly negotiate a full and binding sales agreement containing all necessary provisions—even if you and the seller have to sit up all night to get it done. If the seller doesn't like that approach, suggest signing a nonbinding letter of intent that includes a tight schedule for negotiating a binding sales agreement.

Format for a Letter of Intent

A letter of intent is usually just that—a letter (see the sample set out below). You write a "Dear Seller" letter to the seller or receive a "Dear Buyer" letter from the seller. If the person receiving the letter agrees that it accurately states the intent of both of you, he or she signs a copy of the letter and gives or sends the originator a copy that contains both signatures.

There's no legal rule that a letter of intent follow any particular format. Instead of using a letter, your preliminary document can as easily be prepared in the format of a traditional agreement that you both sign. If you follow the more formal approach, your document can be labeled in various ways: Memorandum of Agreement, Memorandum of Understanding, or Preliminary Sales Agreement. The key point is that any document that serves the same purpose as a letter of intent carries with it the same risks, so if you want to avoid legal complications, you need to be sure any document you sign is nonbinding.

If the seller prepares the letter of intent, it may be ambiguous as to whether or not it's legally binding. There's an easy solution. Before signing, add these words: "This is not a legally binding agreement, but simply a summary of the current status of our discussions. We will only have a legally binding agreement when we both sign a sales agreement."

To help you draft your own letter of intent, here's a sample based on a typical business purchase scenario. The seller (Fit for Life LLC) has two stores that sell exercise equipment and a third retail outlet (operating under the name The Long Run) that sells running apparel, including shoes and shorts. Marvin would like to buy The Long Run but has another almost-as-good business in mind if this deal doesn't come through. Negotiations between Marvin and Nan and Peter (Fit for Life's owners) have been going well but have been taking longer than Marvin anticipated. When Nan and Peter tell Marvin that they're going to an out-of-state trade show and will need to delay working on a sales agreement for four days, Marvin begins to wonder if the deal will really happen or whether he should follow up with the other potential seller. Confronting his need for Nan and Peter to show a definite commitment to the deal, he prepares and asks them to sign a nonbinding letter of intent confirming their understanding of the potential deal. They agree.

Sample Letter of Intent

Marvin Townsend
456 Cactus Road
Phoenix, AZ 55555

June 15, 20xx

Nan Ludwig and Peter Sutton

Fit for Life LLC
123 Sunshine Way
Phoenix, AZ 55555

Dear Nan and Peter:

This is a letter of intent concerning my proposed purchase of your running apparel business, The Long Run. Your company, Fit for Life LLC, owns The Long Run and will be selling it to me. The business I am proposing to buy is located at 789 Southwest Avenue, Smalldale.

This letter of intent is not a legally binding agreement. As we continue to work out the remaining details with you, the terms set out below may change. The purpose of this letter is simply to summarize the results of our discussions so far.

Exclusive Dealing
For the next two months, assuming that I haven't notified you of my intent to withdraw from discussions with you, I do not plan to negotiate for the purchase of any other business. Likewise, you do not plan to negotiate with any other buyers.

Terms of the Sale

Sale Price
I (or a corporation or LLC that I may form) will pay $300,000 for the business assets of The Long Run, plus an additional amount for the merchandise on hand at the time of closing. To determine the value of the merchandise, we will jointly conduct a physical inventory at that time. I will pay the wholesale price for the merchandise that The Long Run acquired in the 90 days preceding closing, and a lesser value for older merchandise as determined to be commercially reasonable by Neil Chang, regional director of the Athletic Apparel Association.

Sample Letter of Intent (continued)

Payment of Sale Price

I will make a down payment of $30,000 at closing. I will sign a promissory note for $270,000 payable in monthly installments of principal and interest (at a 7.0% annual rate). The note will be amortized so that I will make equal monthly payments of principal and interest that will pay off the note in 60 months.

Security for Sale Price

No matter how my business is legally organized, my wife and I will personally sign the promissory note. This means if I form a corporation or LLC to purchase the assets of The Long Run unit from Fit for Life, my business entity will sign the note, and my wife and I will personally guarantee payment. In addition, I will give Fit for Life a security interest in the business assets and a second mortgage on our home for the full amount of the note.

Assets

The assets to be transferred to me include all furnishings and equipment located at The Long Run store (except for the Dell notebook computer on Nan's desk), the merchandise on hand as of the date of closing, the phone number, and the business name, The Long Run. Fit for Life has not registered The Long Run as a trademark, but you'll assign to me all trademark and other legal rights that Fit for Life may have in the name. Fit for Life will keep the accounts receivable as of the date of closing (I understand you have only a few in-house accounts).

Liabilities

At closing or before, Fit for Life will pay all liabilities affecting The Long Run, including the $50,000 debt owed to First Commercial.

The Company Van

You've told me that the van with the store's logo (The Long Run) on it is leased from VanLease Associates. Fit for Life will arrange to have the lease transferred to me if I accept responsibility for future lease payments and if VanLease approves of the transfer. (Or, if I prefer, Fit for Life will keep the van and continue to pay on the lease.)

Sample Letter of Intent (continued)

Real Estate Lease

I understand that Fit for Life owns the building where The Long Run is located at 789 Southwest Avenue, Smalldale. As we discussed, Fit for Life is willing to rent it to me under a triple-net lease at $3,000 a month for five years, with an option to renew for five more years for $3,500 a month. If I do decide to rent it, I will post a security deposit equal to two months' rent.

Postsale Issues

Competition

Neither Fit for Life, nor either of you, will compete in the sports apparel business in Snow Bird County for five years from the date of closing. The two of you and Fit for Life LLC will have the right to continue your activities in the exercise equipment business, meaning that you and Fit for Life can operate a fitness center or a retail shop to sell exercise equipment. I will pay $10,000 to the company and $15,000 to each of you for your covenants not to compete.

Consultation

I will retain Nan as an independent contractor to help in the transition of the business for the first six months. I will pay Nan $3,000 a month and she will provide, under my direction, up to 30 hours a month of consultation to me on an as-needed basis. As part of the consulting, Nan will also be available to work with me on the store floor, if I desire. Peter will have no future relationship with the business after the closing.

Items Still to Be Negotiated

I know that Fit for Life still needs to complete its investigation of my financial status, including a credit report and a review of my assets and liabilities. In addition, there are remaining issues to be resolved including how I would be compensated for referring customers to your exercise equipment store. Your accountant and mine need to help us arrive at an allocation of the purchase price for tax purposes. Other issues may also come up that we will need to address.

Sample Letter of Intent (continued)

Timetable for Negotiations and Closing

I hope that all of us can work out the final details of this nonbinding agreement as soon as reasonably possible. Accordingly, let's try to have a sales agreement ready to sign by July 15. Assuming that this is agreeable to you, I would like to plan for a closing date of July 31, which would let me fully benefit from the surge in store traffic that typically precedes the Labor Day 10K Run. (By the way, let's talk about cosponsoring that event.) I am available to meet with you next week on Tuesday afternoon, Wednesday morning, or both to work with you on the final details.

Nan and Peter, I think I've hit the high points of our negotiations for me to purchase the assets of The Long Run from Fit for Life, but because this is a nonbinding agreement, no terms or conditions are final. We have some fine-tuning yet to do and some parts of this proposed deal may change, so we won't have a legally binding contract unless and until we all sign a final sales agreement.

If you agree that we have accurately summarized our discussions, please sign a copy of this letter and return it to us. I think things are moving in the right direction and hope that you do, too.

Sincerely yours,

Marvin Townsend

Marvin Townsend

Confirmation

We agree with your analysis of where we stand in our negotiations and will work with you to tie up the loose ends so we can have a solid deal.

Nan Ludwig	*Peter Sutton*
Nan Ludwig	Peter Sutton
Member/Manager	Member/Manager
Fit for Life LLC	Fit for Life LLC

Dated: *June , 20xx*

Obviously, you'll have to adapt this sample letter to reflect your own negotiations and style of writing, but do try for a tone that's direct, friendly, and optimistic, and not full of legalisms. Again, the key is to be sure that no one reading this letter can reasonably conclude that you've struck a binding deal. To this end, the opening paragraph of the sample says that it's not a legally binding agreement. And lest there be any doubt, this is repeated near the end of the letter. Whatever else you do, be sure to include that or a similar phrase in your letter of intent so that you don't find yourself unintentionally bound by it.

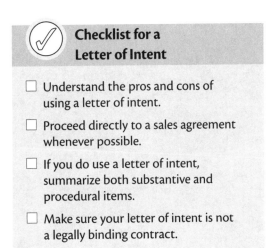

Checklist for a Letter of Intent

☐ Understand the pros and cons of using a letter of intent.

☐ Proceed directly to a sales agreement whenever possible.

☐ If you do use a letter of intent, summarize both substantive and procedural items.

☐ Make sure your letter of intent is not a legally binding contract.

P A R T

3

Preparing the Sales Agreement

Preparing the Sales Agreement and Other Legal Documents

The first half of this book explains how to analyze the tax consequences of buying a business, how to find a business that's right for you, and what terms to consider in your negotiations. Now it's time to put together the legal documents you'll need to carry out your purchase. Legal documentation and contracts will be the primary focus of the rest of this book.

This chapter provides an overview of the key documents that will be involved in the purchase of a business, including the sales agreement, the promissory note, and the seller's noncompete agreement. It explains why carefully drafted documents are so important to a successful business purchase and how to prepare them.

Overview of Your Sales Agreement

Once you've found a business you want to buy and you've come to terms with the seller, it's time to put those terms into a clearly written sales agreement. The sales agreement (or contract) is far and away the most crucial and complex document involved in the sale, because it alone captures the entire scope of your deal and reflects all of the understandings you've reached with the seller.

Because this master document dwarfs all others, a full seven chapters are devoted to it. Each chapter presents a series of sales agreement clauses, beginning with the names of the seller and buyer (Clause 1 in Chapter 12) and ending with the signatures (Clause 36 in Chapter 17).

The sales agreement is broken down into 23 basic sections, each consisting of one or more clauses. See "Guide to Sales Agreement Clauses," below, for a summary, including references to which chapter discusses which specific clause and where to find related documents.

As you review the sales agreement clauses, you'll find that a number of provisions are optional—you can use them or not, depending on what you and the seller have agreed to. This text is clearly labeled "optional." Some clauses are pretty much the same for all sales agreements except for your specific information, such as the exact sales price. For other clauses, you'll choose from several options or craft your own clause, depending on what best fits your circumstances and whether you're buying the assets of the business or the entity itself. As you read through the following chapters, the text of the book will help you choose among options where options exist.

Chapters 11 through 17 take you step by step through each clause and explain how to complete it. The clauses are all on the CD-ROM included in this book; you can use them to assemble your own sales agreement. You'll see that it's easy to delete a clause or add a new one by inserting or deleting text and renumbering the rest of the clauses. For example, if you're buying the assets of a business, you'll complete Clauses 2 and 3 (explained in Chapter 12) but not Clauses 4 and 5, which apply to entity sales. The next clause for an asset sale would be the Sale Price (Clause 6 in Chapter 13), which you would renumber Clause 4. This may sound confusing, but it will be very clear as you assemble your sales agreement electronically and follow the directions on how to use the CD-ROM in Appendix A. Also, see Appendix B for sample sales agreements that you can use as a model when preparing your own.

TIP

Feel free to innovate. The sales agreement and other documents offered in this book are carefully designed to cover the terms that apply in most business purchases—and they provide a great deal of flexibility. But you needn't be a slave to the suggested forms. Ultimately the forms should fit your deal rather than vice versa—in other words, you should never shape your deal to fit the forms. So if you need even more flexibility, don't hesitate to delete clauses, add clauses, or modify the suggested wording to reflect your understanding with the seller. If you follow the recommendation to have a lawyer review the documents before you sign them, you're unlikely to run into any serious problems.

Differences in Sales Agreements for Asset and Entity Sales

As mentioned many times throughout this book, a key point to be negotiated by you and the seller is whether you'll buy only the assets of your business or the entire entity. (If you don't fully understand this important issue, reread Chapter 8.) Many sales agreement clauses will be identical for an asset or entity sale, and the upcoming chapters specify where they differ. The specific sections where clauses will or may vary between the two types of purchases are:

- identifying the business and what's being purchased
- sale price
- security for future payment
- seller's debts and other liabilities
- seller's representations
- closing arrangements and documents, and
- risk of loss.

Appendix B includes sample sales agreements for both asset and entity sales, and the CD-ROM includes separate files for assembling your sales agreement depending on which type of sale you are involved in.

Guide to Sales Agreement Clauses			
Section and what it covers	Clauses	Where clauses are discussed	Related documents and where to find them
Names	1. Names	Chapter 12	
Identifying the business and what's being sold	**Asset Sale** 2. Sale of Business Assets (Asset Sale) 3. Assets Being Sold (Asset Sale) **Entity Sale** 4. Sale of Corporate Stock (Entity Sale—Corporation) 5. Sale of LLC Membership Interest (Entity Sale—LLC)	Chapter 12	Bill of Sale, Assignment of Lease, Assignment of Other Contracts, Assignment of Intellectual Property, and Consent to Sale of Assets: Chapter 19
Sale price	**Asset Sale** 6. Sale Price (Asset Sale) 7. Price of Inventory (Asset Sale) [*optional*] 8. Accounts Receivable (Asset Sale) [*optional*] **Entity Sale** 9. Sale Price (Entity Sale) 10. Adjustment of Sale Price (Entity Sale) [*optional*]	Chapter 13	
Deposit	11. Deposit [*optional*]	Chapter 13	
Payment at closing	12. Payment at Closing	Chapter 13	
Promissory note	13. Promissory Note [*optional*]	Chapter 13	Promissory Note: Chapter 18

Guide to Sales Agreement Clauses (continued)			
Section and what it covers	Clauses	Where clauses are discussed	Related documents and where to find them
Security for future payment	**Asset Sale** 14. Security for Payment (Asset Sale) [*optional*] **Entity Sale** 15. Security for Payment (Entity Sale) [*optional*]	Chapter 13	Security Agreements for asset and entity sales, UCC Financing Statement, Escrow Agreement for Stock Certificates, and Escrow Agreement for LLC Transfer Certificates: Chapter 18
Seller's debts and other liabilities	**Asset Sale** 16. Seller's Debts and Other Liabilities (Asset Sale) **Entity Sale** 17. Entity's Debts and Other Liabilities (Entity Sale) [*optional*]	Chapter 14	Statement Regarding Absence of Creditors: Chapter 19
Seller's representations	**Asset Sale** 18. Seller's Representations (Asset Sale) **Entity Sale** 19. Seller's Representations (Entity Sale)	Chapter 14	
Buyer's representations	20. Buyer's Representations	Chapter 14	
Covenant not to compete	21. Covenant Not to Compete [*optional*]	Chapter 15	Covenant Not to Compete: Chapter 20
Future services	22. Future Services [*optional*]	Chapter 15	Employment Contract and Independent Contractor Agreement: Chapter 20
Contingencies	23. Contingency [*optional*]	Chapter 16	

Guide to Sales Agreement Clauses (continued)			
Section and what it covers	**Clauses**	**Where clauses are discussed**	**Related documents and where to find them**
Closing arrangements and documents	24. Closing **Asset Sale** 25. Documents for Transferring Assets **Entity Sale** 26. Documents for Transferring Entity	Chapter 16	Closing Checklists for Asset and Entity Sales: Chapter 21
Dispute resolution	27. Disputes [*optional*]	Chapter 16	
Risk of loss	28. Risk of Loss (Asset Sale) 29. Risk of Loss (Entity Sale)	Chapter 16	
Entire agreement	30. Entire Agreement	Chapter 16	
Modification	31. Modification	Chapter 16	
Governing law	32. Governing Law	Chapter 16	
Severability	33. Severability	Chapter 16	
Notices	34. Notices	Chapter 16	
Other additional terms	35. Other Additional Terms [*optional*]	Chapter 16	
Required signatures	36. Required Signatures	Chapter 17	

Related Legal Documents

Here's an overview of key legal documents—in addition to the sales agreement—that you'll use in the purchase of a business, along with a description of where they appear in the rest of the book (Part 4, Chapters 18 through 20). You'll attach most of these documents to your sales agreement, but you won't sign them until the closing—the time when the business actually passes to you. See "How to Prepare Attachments to Your Sale Agreement," below.

Documents for Installment Payments

If you'll be making a down payment at closing and then paying the rest of the sale price in installments, the seller will expect you to sign documents that firmly commit you to paying the installments—and that protect the seller if you stop paying. These documents (covered in Chapter 18) include a promissory note, security agreement, and UCC Financing Statement. If you're buying a corporation or LLC, the seller may also want an escrow agreement under which a third party (escrow agent) takes physical possession of the stock certificates or LLC membership certificates and transfers them to you only after you've paid the seller in full. The escrow agreement form is also discussed in Chapter 18.

Documents for Transferring the Assets or the Entity to You

The seller will need to complete documents at the closing that will complete the actual transfer of the business to you. In an asset sale, this will include a bill of sale that lists the assets included in the sale: primarily, tangible personal property, such as machinery, inventory, supplies, and office equipment. In addition, you may need to prepare documents for the seller to assign leases and other contracts to you, and/or to transfer intellectual property such as copyrights, trademarks, and patents. And if you're buying an entity, the seller will need to formalize the transfer of shares of stock or LLC membership interests. Chapter 19 explains all these documents and how to prepare them.

Documents Dealing With Non-competition and Future Work to Be Performed by the Seller

If the seller is making a commitment to you not to compete with the business after the closing, you'll need a form called a covenant not to compete. Likewise, if the seller will be working for you after the closing, you'll want to prepare an employment contract or an independent contractor agreement. Chapter 20 provides an overview of these documents and the issues you need to consider when preparing them.

The Closing Checklist

To assure a smooth closing, you and the seller should agree on a comprehensive closing checklist as explained in Chapter 21, where you'll also find tips on where and when to hold the closing.

Well-Drafted Documents Are Crucial

To make sure you don't end up involved in costly, time-consuming legal disputes, you need carefully drafted sale documents. The courts are full of lawsuits dealing with ambiguous, incomplete, and even contradictory documents used in business purchases. Fortunately, by using well-crafted documents, you can drastically reduce the possibility of legal disputes.

Before moving on to the specifics of assembling your sales agreement and related documents, here's an overview.

Comprehensive Documents Avoid Arguments About Who Said What

With a comprehensive sales agreement, promissory note, and other documents such as those recommended in this book, you avoid the problem of oral agreements, which are notoriously unreliable. What's said simply isn't always what's heard or remembered. By capturing all the details of the deal in a written sales agreement and related documents, you and the seller can greatly reduce the likelihood of a serious dispute that ends up in court.

The Drafting Process Helps You and the Seller Cover All the Key Issues

In the process of carefully drafting comprehensive documents, you can make sure that all important legal and practical details—including some that you and the seller may never have even discussed—don't get left out. For example, you and the seller may not have talked about what will happen if business debts should surface that weren't disclosed by the seller—a point that should always be a major concern for a buyer. Or you may not have discussed the mechanics of how the inventory will be valued on the eve of closing.

As part of a careful document-drafting process, any omissions of details like these are likely to jump out at you. And, especially if you follow the thorough approach set out in this book, you'll be well-positioned to cover all key points.

Well-Drafted Documents Protect Your Interests and Limit Your Liability

You can use your sales agreement to put clear limits on your liability for any preexisting claims against the business, and you can tailor your representations (statements of fact that the seller will rely on) and warranties (guarantees to the seller) to curtail your exposure to the seller if unforeseen problems should arise. To gain this type of legal protection, however, you'll need to be forthright in what you disclose to the seller about your financial resources and credit history. If instead you distort or hide important information, no prophylactic legal language is likely to protect you.

Finely Tuned Documents Can Be a Reference Point If You Have a Dispute

Even when both seller and buyer proceed honestly and in complete good faith, a dispute can later surface over some detail of the purchase. If that happens, having comprehensive, precisely worded documents can make it easier to resolve the dispute. With those documents in hand, you and the seller may be able to speedily negotiate a satisfactory solution to the problem. Or, if you can't solve the problem without outside intervention, your written contracts will help contain the problems and the cost of solving them—whether you resolve your dispute through mediation, arbitration, or court.

Preparing Your Sales Agreement and Related Legal Documents

Now that you understand the many reasons for having clear and comprehensive documents and have a basic overview of what's in the sales agreement and how to draft one, let's consider two important practical concerns:

- Should the first draft come from you or the seller?
- What role, if any, should your lawyer play in the process?

TIP

Check your letter of intent. If you and the seller have signed a letter of intent, as described in Chapter 10, be sure to consult it as you prepare your sales agreement. It can be a good checklist of the terms to which you and the seller have agreed, at least in principle.

Preparing the First Drafts

Drafting—and, inevitably, redrafting—the sales agreement and other documents requires plenty of mental effort. And, of course, if you hire a lawyer to do the first drafts or to help you with the drafting process, it will cost you serious dollars as well. As a result, you may be tempted to let the seller or the seller's lawyer prepare the first drafts, figuring that you can just review and revise those drafts later in the process. This is a poor approach. Even in a situation where you and the seller think you've hammered out all important details, the party who does the initial drafts has considerable ability to shape the deal. If you do the first drafts, you can be sure that all key points will be covered and that you're well protected. If any nitpicking needs to be done, it will be the seller, not you, who has to employ the fine-toothed comb. An anxious seller may even hesitate to quibble, which puts you more in control of the ultimate product.

Even though you may be hesitant to draft pages of contract language, keep in mind that by sensibly crafting the first drafts, you often avoid disputes and expedite the process, and you may even gain a subtle strategic advantage. This book, complete with a CD-ROM at the back, does a lot of the work for you.

> **CAUTION**
>
> **If for any reason the seller creates the first drafts, examine them very carefully.** You need to make sure your interests are fully protected, that the terms of the deal are clearly and accurately stated, and that nothing has been left out.

Involving a Lawyer

As you know, the legal documents—especially for a business that's worth a substantial sum—need to be done right. For that reason, even if you're a dedicated self-helper, it's usually cost-effective to get at least some help from a business lawyer. (Chapter 6 discusses how to work with a lawyer and other professionals.) Just how much help will depend on a number of factors, including:

- the complexity of your particular deal
- whether you've ever bought or sold a business before

- your past experience and comfort level in dealing with legal documents
- how much time you can devote to the task of drafting your sales agreement, and
- how important the savings will be if you do some of the drafting yourself.

If you're paying a large sum for a business, a lawyer's fee may take up such a small percentage of the total dollars involved that it's not worth worrying about.

One sensible approach is to create the first drafts yourself and then have an experienced business lawyer review them before you present them to the seller. Another alternative is to have your lawyer create the sales documents based on the terms you and the seller have agreed to. If you follow this approach, be careful not to fade (or be pushed) into the background. This is your deal—not the lawyer's—and to achieve the result you want, you need to stay in the loop. It follows that before you present any lawyer-drafted documents to the seller, you need to study them carefully to make sure you understand every word and that they really do capture every nuance of your deal. If for any reason you have doubts or questions, don't hesitate to ask your lawyer to make changes. Fortunately, this task of reviewing the documents, asking questions, and suggesting changes will be infinitely easier for you after you've read the chapters in this part of the book.

TIP

It's not your lawyer's sale. Be careful not to let your lawyer hijack your deal by suggesting substantive changes to the deal itself or inserting overly complex or draconian legal provisions. This can happen for a variety of reasons, including the fact that your lawyer is more familiar with larger, more complicated transactions, or unthinkingly pulls a form out of a legal form book or—most unsettling of all—is trying to justify a high fee. In many of these situations, you may wind up with an agreement that's too long, too filled with arcane jargon, too crammed with harsh and unnecessary clauses, or all three. Good lawyers try to help make deals happen—not destroy them by causing the seller to panic.

Finally, remember that the seller's lawyer isn't in the picture to protect you, but to look out for the best interests of the seller. While this may seem obvious, it bears emphasis, since the seller's lawyer may be a friendly, fair-minded, and 100% honest individual representing a principled seller who may even be a friend or family member. That's all well and good, but it doesn't change the fact that the only people who can truly protect your financial interests are you and your own lawyer, if you choose to use one.

TIP

You may want to consult a tax professional at this stage. Ideally, you will have worked out all tax issues early in the game, well before you started the drafting process.

But if your sale is especially complex or if you didn't get tax advice early on, it's a good idea to have the documents reviewed by a tax adviser (who may be someone different from your lawyer) to make sure the language will pass IRS muster and that your purchase will have the tax consequences that you anticipate.

How to Prepare Attachments to Your Sale Agreement

You want your sales agreement itself to contain all the terms of your contract with the seller, but you don't want it to get bogged down in minutiae. If your purchase involves long detailed lists of assets and liabilities, it's better to put them in attachments to the sales agreement, rather than in the body of the agreement itself. Similarly, you should consider attaching to the sales agreement the other documents that you or the seller sign at the closing. As long as the attachment clearly refers to the sales agreement to which it is being attached, this approach is as legal as it is sensible. For example, you can attach the promissory note that you're agreeing to sign, or the seller's bill of sale, so that later there will be no quibbling over the exact wording of the documents.

To effectively attach materials to a contract, simply identify the original document (for example, the sales agreement), the names of the parties (seller and buyer), and the document's date. When preparing more than one attachment, label them consecutively—that is, Attachment A,

Attachment B, and so on. You can avoid possible confusion by using a heading like the one shown below.

FORM

Where to find the forms. If you're reading a print copy of this book, you'll find a copy of the Attachment to Sales Agreement on the CD-ROM at the back. If you're using an ebook version, you can download the attachment on the Nolo website; the link is included in Appendix A.

Steps in Finalizing Your Sales Agreement and Other Documents

If you've never bought a business before, preparing the documents and then moving toward a closing can seem daunting. These tasks will be manageable, however, if you follow the logical steps outlined below.

1. Do a rough draft of your sales agreement and related documents, using the files included with this book.

Appendix A explains how to access and use the forms.

2. Once you've got a draft sales agreement, print it out. Since you will undoubtedly be making changes along the way, based on your lawyer's review and negotiations with the seller, be sure to put the date and version number on each draft.

3. Have your attorney review your draft and help you craft clauses specific to your purchase. You may want to do the first drafts before you get your lawyer involved—this book is designed for that—or you may prefer a different working relationship.

4. Once you have a rough draft of your sales agreement and other legal documents, you're ready to submit them to the seller for review. Typically, you may have to negotiate some fine points—and occasionally some major ones as well.

5. After you and the seller reach full agreement on the wording of the documents, you can both sign

---

Attachment A to the Sales Agreement

Dated: _____

Between _____ , Seller,

and _____ , Buyer

the sales agreement, following the recommendations in Chapter 17. The other documents (such as the promissory note and noncompete agreement) don't get signed until the closing.

6. The last step is the closing itself—the occasion when final documents are signed and ownership of the business changes hands. The turnover can go amazingly smoothly if you've drafted the necessary papers well in advance and used a closing checklist as recommended in Chapter 21.

Once all that is done, congratulations! You've bought a business!

Amending Your Sales Agreement

After your sales agreement has been signed, it can be changed only if you and the seller agree to and sign an amendment. A sample amendment form is shown below and included in the forms files (see Appendix A).

Each time you make an amendment, the rest of the terms of the original Sales Agreement and any earlier amendments will remain in effect. If there's a conflict between an amendment and the original sales agreement or any earlier amendment, the terms of the most recent amendment will prevail.

An amendment to a sales agreement should be signed by the same people who signed the agreement itself. As explained in Chapter 17, this can include people other

than just you and the seller. For example, it might include spouses or guarantors.

Here's how to complete this amendment form:

(1) List the amendment number (in consecutive order by date, 1, 2, 3, and so on).

(2) List the seller and buyer names as they appear in the sales agreement.

(3) Fill in the date the sales agreement was signed.

(4) Name the business that you're buying.

(5) Describe in detail the information you want to include in your amendment in the space provided. For example, if you're deleting a clause in your agreement, your amendment might read: "Clause [*number and name of clause*] of the original sales agreement is deleted in its entirety." If you're changing a portion of your agreement—for instance, you're extending the amount of time to remove a contingency—your amendment might say: "Clause [*number and name of clause*] is amended to extend the time of closing to April 1, 20xx."

(6) All parties to the sales agreement should sign and date the amendment; it is not necessary to give the parties' addresses, however, because these are already listed in the sales agreement itself.

Amendment of Sales Agreement

Amendment Number _____ ①

_____ ② _____ (Seller)

and _____ ② _____ (Buyer)

agree to the following amendment of the Sales Agreement dated _____ ③ _____

concerning :

_____ ④ _____

_____

_____

_____

_____ ⑤ _____

_____

_____

_____

In all other respects, the terms of the original Sales Agreement and any earlier amendments will remain in effect. If there is a conflict between this amendment and the original sales agreement or any earlier amendment, the terms of this amendment will prevail.

_____ ⑥ _____

_____

_____

_____

CAUTION

Don't use amendments for multiple changes. Amendments to an existing sales agreement work fine when a couple of items are being changed, such as raising or lowering the sales price or removing certain assets from the sale. But if you're changing lots of terms in the original sales agreement, amendments can get confusing. Where changes might be extensive, it often makes sense to redo the entire sales agreement to avoid the possibility of confusion.

Who's Selling, Who's Buying—
And What Is Being Purchased

The first thing you need to do in a sales agreement is to identify the seller and buyer and state what you're buying. This section of the contract will be different depending on whether your sale is an asset or an entity sale. All buyers should read "Naming the Parties," below. If you're buying in an asset sale, read "Identifying the Business and What You're Buying in an Asset Sale," below. If not, see "Identifying the Business and What You're Buying in an Entity Sale," below.

Naming the Parties

Logically enough, your sales agreement will start off by identifying the seller and buyer: the individuals or businesses (the "parties") who are agreeing to the contract.

Naming the parties can be simple if you're an individual buying a sole proprietorship and the seller, too, is an individual. In this case, all you need to do is insert the seller's name and your name. Things can get more complicated if the buyer or seller is a business entity (a partnership, a corporation, or an LLC) rather than an individual. If that's the case, you'll need to correctly name the business, designate its legal nature, and note the state in which the business is organized.

"Format for Names in a Sales Agreement," below, will help you understand how to do this for both asset and entity sales.

 TIP

Not everyone signing the agreement has to be listed as a seller or a buyer. For example, when a corporation is a buyer or a seller, the corporate officer who will be signing the agreement on behalf of the corporation won't be named as a seller or buyer. Nor will someone who is signing the agreement as a guarantor or as the spouse of a sole proprietor in a community property state. Chapter 17 explains how to obtain the signatures of people who have the authority to legally bind a business entity that's buying or selling assets or another business entity.

Naming the Seller and Buyer in an Asset Sale

In an asset sale, each party (the seller and the buyer) can be either an individual (the operator of a sole proprietorship) or an entity (a partnership, corporation, or LLC).

When an entity is selling some or all of its assets to the buyer, you identify the seller by inserting the name of the partnership, corporation, or LLC that's selling the assets.

---

1. Names

_____ (Seller)

and _____ (Buyer) agree to the following sale.

Format for Names in a Sales Agreement

This "Names" chart will help you and the buyer correctly identify the parties at the beginning of the sales agreement. The chart gives the recommended format for completing the Names clause, depending on whether the seller or buyer is a sole proprietor, a business entity, or an individual, and whether the sale is an asset or entity sale. The two subsections under "Naming the Parties" provide examples for different types of sellers for asset and entity sales, including complicated situations when an entity (rather than an individual) owns the entity being sold.

Status of Seller or Buyer	Identification of Seller or Buyer in an Asset Sale	Identification of Seller or Buyer in an Entity Sale
Sole Proprietor. A one-owner business that is neither a corporation nor an LLC. (When a married couple owns such a business, the business is a partnership, but the couple can file tax returns as a sole proprietorship.)	*Two different styles may be used:* John Smith *[or]* John Smith doing business as Ace Diner (*The second style is preferred if the sole proprietor uses a business name separate from his or her own.*)	Not applicable for a seller; a sole proprietorship is not an entity that can be sold—only its assets can be sold. A buyer who is a sole proprietor can use the same identification format as is used in an asset sale.
Partnership. A business formed by two or more people who haven't created a corporation or an LLC.	Smith & Jones, a Michigan Partnership	A seller or buyer that's a partnership can use the same identification format as is used in an asset sale.
Corporation. A business entity owned by one or more shareholders.	Modern Textiles Inc., a Texas Corporation	A seller or buyer that's a corporation can use the same identification format as is used in an asset sale.
Limited Liability Company (LLC). A business entity owned by one or more members.	Games and Such LLC, a California Limited Liability Company	A seller or buyer that's an LLC can use the same identification format as is used in an asset sale.

Format for Names in a Sales Agreement (continued)		
Status of Seller or Buyer	Identification of Seller or Buyer in an Asset Sale	Identification of Seller or Buyer in an Entity Sale
Individual(s). Someone who is not acting on behalf of a business.	*(Normally limited to buyers—for example, people buying assets in their own names, intending to later form a corporation or an LLC.)* John Smith *[or]* John Smith and Mary Jones *(Individuals who sell the assets of their business will do so as either sole proprietors or partners. See above.)*	Individuals who are selling or buying corporate shares, LLC membership interests, or partnership interests can use the same identification format as is used by individuals in an asset sale.

When a sole proprietorship is selling its assets, the business owner (sole proprietor) is named as the seller.

Similarly, when an entity is buying some or all of the assets of a business, you identify the buyer by inserting the name of the partnership, corporation, or LLC that's buying the assets. And when a sole proprietorship is buying assets, the owner of the business (the sole proprietor) is named as the buyer.

Here are a few examples.

EXAMPLE 1: Seller Is a Sole Proprietor and Buyer Is a Corporation (Asset Sale)

> **1. Names**
> John Smith (Seller) and Modern Textiles Inc., a Texas Corporation (Buyer), agree to the following sale.

EXAMPLE 2: Seller Is a Partnership and Buyer Is an LLC (Asset Sale)

> **1. Names**
> Smith and Jones, a Michigan Partnership (Seller), and Games and Such LLC, a California Limited Liability Company (Buyer), agree to the following sale.

 TIP

Always include the business's official name to avoid any ambiguity about what entity is involved in the deal. Some corporations and LLCs use a different name (often called a fictitious business name or a "dba") to identify their business to the public. In a sales agreement, always use the official corporate or LLC name. So if the seller is an Illinois corporation called New Enterprises Corp., and that corporation does business as Kwik & Klean Laundry, you should name "New Enterprises Corp., an Illinois corporation" as the seller—although it's also okay to say "New Enterprises Corp., an Illinois corporation doing business as Kwik & Klean Laundry." And if a sole proprietor uses a business name separate from the owner's, do the same.

EXAMPLE 3: Seller Is a Corporation and Buyer Is a Sole Proprietor (Asset Sale)

> **1. Names**
> Modern Textiles Inc., a Texas Corporation (Seller), and John Smith doing business as Smith's Fabric Center (Buyer), agree to the following sale.

When two or more people or entities are buying the assets of a business, refer to them as Sellers—plural—in the sales agreement. It can get confusing to use the singular Seller to refer to several people or entities.

Naming the Seller or Sellers in an Entity Sale

The basic Names clause for an entity sale is the same as for an asset sale. The key difference is how you identify the seller or sellers. Since the entity (corporation, LLC, or partnership) is being purchased, it follows that its individual owners—not the entity itself—are the sellers.

Where small businesses are concerned, identifying the parties in an entity sale is usually quite straightforward. That's because the entity being sold (such as a corporation or an LLC) is usually owned by one or a few individuals who are selling all of their ownership interests to one or a few other individuals.

The seller or sellers will almost always be either the sole owner of the entity or a small group of owners: the partners in a partnership or the owners of corporate stock or LLC membership interests. In an entity sale, you insert the name(s) of the individual(s) who are selling their shares of corporate stock, their LLC membership interests, or their partnership interests.

When two or more owners (be they people, entities, or both) are selling their interests in an entity, refer to them as Sellers—plural—throughout the sales agreement. This avoids the linguistic awkwardness of using the singular word Seller to cover several people.

Entity sales by partnerships are extremely rare. Also, there's no such thing as an entity sale of a sole proprietorship; the sale of such a business is always an asset sale.

Here are a couple of examples of how to identify the seller or sellers in an entity sale.

EXAMPLE 1: Entity Sale of a Corporate Business Owned by Individuals. If Modern Textiles Inc.—introduced in Example 3 for an asset sale, above—were owned by David Field and Jerry Nestor and they wanted to sell their shares of Modern Textiles stock to a buyer (entity purchase), the sellers would be David and Jerry and the Names clause would read as follows:

> **1. Names**
> David Field and Jerry Nestor (Sellers) and John Smith doing business as Smith's Fabric Center (Buyer) agree to the following sale.

EXAMPLE 2: Entity Sale of a Corporate Business Owned by an LLC. If Modern Textiles Inc. were owned by Kenwood LLC and Kenwood wanted to sell its shares of Modern Textiles to a buyer (an entity sale), the seller would be Kenwood LLC and the Names clause would read as follows:

> **1. Names**
> Kenwood LLC (Seller) and John Smith doing business as Smith's Fabric Center (Buyer) agree to the following sale.

Check with your lawyer if either you or the seller has a complicated ownership structure—for example, if another business entity owns the stock of the selling or buying entity or its membership interests. In this situation, the seller or buyer will be the entity that owns the stock or membership interests.

To understand how this works, let's assume an entity sale in which the shares of Aero Corporation are being sold. Let's also assume that Fiddler LLC owns 50% of Aero Corporation, and Joe Doakes owns the other 50%. Here, the sellers would be identified as Fiddler LLC and Joe Doakes.

Remember: A corporation's shareholders can consist of individuals, other corporations, LLCs, and/or partnerships. Similarly, the members of an LLC can be individuals, other LLCs, corporations, and/or partnerships. Even some partners in a partnership can be other entities. And on the buyer's side, it's possible that an entity may purchase the entity being sold (for example, Arboretum LLC is purchasing all the shares of Aero Corporation) or that some combination of individuals and entities may buy the ownership interests in the business being sold.

Usually, it's not difficult to sort out who's selling their ownership interests in the entity being sold and who's buying those interests. If you're uncertain, however, you should get advice from a lawyer.

Identifying the Business and What You're Buying in an Asset Sale

When you have an asset sale, the next clause in the sales agreement will identify the business in which the assets have been used.

Here's how to fill in this clause:

In the first blank, insert the type of business being sold, such as an automotive supply business.

In the second blank, insert the name the seller's business has been using.

In the third blank, fill in the business's complete address (street, city, and state).

Completed, this clause might look the ones shown below.

Alternative Format for Naming the Parties in a Sales Agreement (Asset Sale)

The format for naming the parties to a sales agreement discussed above will almost always work well, and it's the one included on the CD-ROM with this book. There is, however, a second method you should consider when you're buying assets from an entity. This involves having the opening portion of the sales agreement name the owners of the selling entity as well as the entity itself. That is, depending on the entity involved, the Names clause may name the partners in a partnership, the members of an LLC, or the shareholders of a corporation. When this alternative format is used, the identification clause may look like this:

---

1. Names

Modern Textiles Inc., a Texas Corporation (Seller), Games and Such LLC, a California Limited Liability Company (Buyer), and John Smith and Mary Jones, the shareholders of Modern Textiles Inc. (Shareholders), agree to the following sale.

This alternative is most appropriate when the owners of the selling entity will personally make promises to you, as would be the case if they guarantee the accuracy of the representations made in the sales agreement. You can also have the owners accept those responsibilities at the end of the document or in a separate contract (as discussed in Chapter 14). Legally, there's no difference. Either alternative is acceptable.

Similarly, when the buyer is an entity, you can name the individual owners as well as the entity in the opening clause. You might do this, for example, where you and any co-owners of your entity are personally guaranteeing payment of the promissory note or agreeing to be personally responsible for business debts. But, again, signing at the end or in a separate contract protects the seller just as well.

EXAMPLE 1: Sale of Business With One Location

> **2. Sale of Business Assets**
>
> Seller is selling to Buyer and Buyer is buying from Seller the assets described below of the restaurant business known as Red's Rite Spot located at 123 Main Street, Berkeley, California.

EXAMPLE 2: Sale of Business With Several Locations and You're Buying the Assets Used at More Than One Location

> **2. Sale of Business Assets**
>
> Seller is selling to Buyer and Buyer is buying from Seller the assets described below of the bakery business known as Bagels and Baguettes, located at 456 State Street and 789 North Liberty, Atlanta, Georgia.

Why It's Important to Identify the Assets You're Buying

In an asset sale, you should clearly identify the assets you're buying from the seller, such as:

- goodwill of the business (Option A in Clause 3, Assets Being Sold, below). Goodwill is an intangible asset that may consist of such things as the business's reputation or its loyal customer base.
- the business lease (Option B). If you're going to occupy the same business premises, fill in details on the date of the lease, the landlord's name, and the address of the rental property.
- the inventory including any goods the business sells at retail (Option C). In an asset sale, the seller will transfer ownership of the inventory to you by using a bill of sale, as described in Chapter 19.
- furniture, fixtures, and equipment (Option D). You'll itemize these assets on a separate page (an attachment to the sales agreement), rather than in this clause.
- equipment leases such as for phone systems or copiers (Option E)
- contracts with suppliers and customers that you'll be acquiring from the seller (Option F), and

> **2. Sale of Business Assets (Asset Sale)**
>
> Seller is selling to Buyer and Buyer is buying from Seller the assets described below of the
> _____ business known as
> _____ located at
> _____ .

- intellectual property rights, such as copyrights in advertising materials or the trademarked logo of the company (Option G).

Each business is unique, but an asset clause might look like the one shown below.

You can delete those items that don't apply and add those that do, relettering the options as necessary.

At this point, you're just listing the assets you're buying. In Clause 6, Sale Price, discussed in Chapter 13, you'll allocate the sales price among these assets.

Note that accounts receivable are not included in the list of assets in this clause. They're covered separately in Clause 8, discussed in Chapter 13.

You'll notice the reference to attachments in Clause 3, Assets Being Sold. For example, rather than list all the furniture you're buying in the sales agreement itself, list the furniture on a separate sheet, which you can attach to the agreement. Chapter 11 explains how to prepare attachments and how they can streamline your sales agreement. Chapter 16 includes a clause (Clause 25, Documents for Transferring Assets) where you specify

---

3. Assets Being Sold (Asset Sale)

The assets being sold consist of:

[*choose all options that apply*]

☐ A. The goodwill of the business, including the current business name and phone number.

☐ B. The lease dated _____ between _____
_____ , Seller as Tenant, and
_____ , Landlord,
covering the premises at _____
_____ for the time period from _____ to _____ .

☐ C. The inventory of goods.

☐ D. The furniture, fixtures, and equipment listed in Attachment ____ .

☐ E. The equipment leases listed in Attachment ____ .

☐ F. The supply contract with _____ .

☐ G. Intellectual property rights as follows: _____
_____
_____ .

The following assets of the business are excluded from the sale: _____
_____
_____ .

documents, such as an assignment of the lease, that the seller will deliver to you.

While the seller may be inclined to simply say in the sales agreement that all the assets of the business are being sold to you, it's better to insist that the sales agreement be more specific. Including a list of assets in the sales agreement will remove any doubt about exactly which assets are owned by the business and being sold to you. There may be some assets that the seller plans to keep, such as cash, accounts receivable, or even a desk, and there may be some assets that you don't want to buy.

CAUTION

Important chapters to read. There are several chapters you need to read carefully before completing the clause of the sales agreement called "Assets Being Sold":

- Chapter 2 contains a discussion of the importance of clarifying what you're buying and not buying in an asset sale.
- Chapters 6 and 8 explain the important documents you'll want to see that are related to assets such as a lease or a copyright, and the major types of tangible and intangible assets you may be buying or that the seller will transfer to you.
- Chapter 9 discusses whether leases and other contracts can be transferred (assigned) to you. (Sometimes, they can't be transferred without the consent of the other party to the contract.) That chapter also discusses the transfer of

business licenses, which may be relevant if you're buying a business such as a restaurant or bar.
- Chapter 13 provides information about a business's inventory and accounts receivable.
- Chapter 19 explains how assets will be transferred to you and the documents you need to complete the transfers, including a bill of sale to transfer tangible assets such as furniture and specialized assignments to transfer intangible assets such as a lease or a copyright.

CAUTION

Contracts for the seller not to compete with you—and agreements for the seller to work for you—are not business assets. As discussed in Chapter 3, for tax and other reasons, the total amount of money that you're agreeing to pay may include several components that are not payments for assets of the business. For example, the total dollars the seller will receive from you may include compensation for the seller's agreement not to compete after the assets are transferred and for services the seller will perform for you as either a consultant (independent contractor) or as an employee. You should include clauses referring to these contracts in a later part of the sales agreement. (See Clauses 21 and 22 in Chapter 15.) You shouldn't do so in the portion of the agreement dealing with the assets being sold. And, as you'll see in Chapter 20, it's usually best to spell out the details of a noncompete agreement or an employment or consulting contract in a separate document that can be an attachment to the sales agreement.

Excluding Assets From the Sale

If you and the seller have agreed that the seller will keep some assets that are or appear to be part of the business, it's smart to list those assets in the sales agreement. Sometimes excluded items are fairly minor ones, like a cell phone or a wall hanging. However, in addition to physical assets, the seller may want to exclude other assets such as cash, accounts receivable, lawsuit claims, tax refund claims, insurance refund claims, and perhaps some business records that will be of no use to you. In some cases, the seller may want to keep such assets as luxury box seats, event tickets, and club memberships. If you are willing to exclude specific assets such as those mentioned, include a clause like the following at the end of the "Assets Being Sold" clause of your sales agreement.

EXAMPLE: Exclusion of Certain Assets in Asset Sales

> The following assets of the business are excluded from the sale:
> 1. the brown, antique wooden desk and bookcase located in the sales office
> 2. all patents
> 3. subscription to *The Wall Street Journal*, and
> 4. the sound system and CD collection.

 CAUTION

Don't overlook business insurance policies. Insurance policies are a type of contract. If your insurance agent or broker informs you that the seller's insurance policies can be transferred, and you wish to assume them, you'll want to include these policies on the asset list. But if that insurance can't be assumed, you'll need to arrange for new policies so there's no gap in coverage. Also, if the seller will be retaining a security interest in business property because you'll be paying the sale price in installments, the seller's name will have to be added to your insurance as a covered party. (In the security agreement, the seller may require that you carry insurance that covers both you and the seller until the sale price has been fully paid. See Chapter 18.)

Identifying the Business and What You're Buying in an Entity Sale

You'll take a different approach if you're buying a business entity rather than its assets. If you buy a corporate or LLC entity, you'll be buying all the ownership interests in the business—that is, all shares of stock or all LLC membership interests. Since you'll acquire the corporation or LLC that owns the assets, by definition everything the corporation or LLC owns will be transferred to you as part of the sale.

In an entity sale, you don't need to identify the assets one by one, and accordingly, the description of what you're buying can be briefer. The sales agreement may say, for example, that you're buying all shares of Acme Corporation or all membership interests in Boston Bakery LLC. You can use a clause like one of the following:

For a Corporate Business

> **4. Sale of Corporate Stock (Entity Sale Only—Corporation)**
> Seller is selling to Buyer and Buyer is buying from Seller all of the Seller's shares of stock in Modern Textiles Inc., a Texas corporation.

For an LLC Business

> **5. Sale of LLC Membership Interest (Entity Sale Only—LLC)**
> Seller is selling to Buyer and Buyer is buying from Seller all of the Seller's membership interests in Digital Services LLC , an Indiana limited liability company.

The point of an entity sale is that the corporation or LLC continues to own the business's assets after the shares or membership interests are transferred to you. It's possible, however, that you and the seller have agreed that a few assets will not be included in the sale. For example, the corporation you're buying may own a computer that the main shareholder would like to keep. If so, you'll need to include language recognizing this. Of course, before the closing, the entity will need to distribute the excluded assets to the entity's owners: the shareholders, LLC members, or partners.

EXAMPLE: Exclusion of Certain Assets If a Corporation Is Being Sold as an Entity:

> Before the closing, Seller will arrange for the corporation to transfer to Seller individually the ownership of the brown antique wooden desk and bookcase located in the sales office.

CAUTION

Certain fees should be listed separately. The sales price for an entity sale should not include any payment that the seller will receive either now or in the future for his or her covenant not to compete or for consulting or any other work the seller agrees to perform for you. Unlike an asset sale, in an entity sale, there's no need to allocate the sale price among the assets that the entity owns. That's because the seller isn't selling you the assets but, rather, shares of stock or LLC membership interests. This means that in the sales agreement, you should omit the asset allocation clause as discussed in Chapter 13. Also, make sure that the sales price doesn't include any payment the seller will receive for a covenant not to compete or for services to be rendered to you. These payments will be dealt with elsewhere in the agreement.

The Sales Price and Terms of Payment

This chapter covers the parts of the sales agreement dealing with the sale price. The first three sections cover issues relevant only in asset sales, including:

- how the sales price is allocated among the typical types of assets involved in an asset sale
- issues that come up if you're buying the business's inventory of merchandise, and
- issues that come up if you're acquiring the business's accounts receivable.

A later section covers the sale price clauses for an entity sale. Unlike an asset sale, in an entity sale, the tax laws don't require you to allocate the sales price among the assets the business owns. When you buy corporate stock, LLC membership interests, or partnership interests, you're not buying individual assets owned by the business. These assets remain the property of the entity that you're acquiring. Thus, your sales agreement needn't allocate the sale price among the assets, nor will you or the seller have to file IRS Form 8594, *Asset Acquisition Statement*.

This chapter also explains how to develop the sales agreement clauses dealing with how you pay for the business. These clauses (relevant to both asset and entity sales) cover issues such as:

- whether you'll pay a deposit when the sales agreement is signed
- how much you'll pay at closing
- the terms of the promissory note, if you'll be making installment payments after the closing, and
- arrangements for the seller to get a security interest in property of the business when the business changes hands—for example, a lien on the business assets or on your home.

Sale Price: Asset Sale

After completing Clause 3 (Assets Being Sold), discussed in Chapter 12, you're now ready to list the total sales price and allocate it to the assets being purchased, such as goodwill or equipment.

Allocating the Sale Price

In the first blank, insert the total sale price for the assets. This will be the same figure as the total at the bottom of the column. You'll then allocate this amount among the assets you're buying.

Here's a sample of how the completed Sale Price clause might look. As with all other parts of the sales agreement, you'll need to tailor the language and details of the clause to fit your transaction.

Sample Sale Price Clause

6. Sale Price (Asset Sale)

The sale price for the assets listed in this section is $_____ , and is allocated as follows:

[*choose all options that apply*]

☐ A. Goodwill $_____

☐ B. Assignment of Lease $_____

☐ C. Inventory [*List here only if you've agreed on an amount. Otherwise, use Clause 7.*] $_____

☐ D. Accounts Receivable [*List here only if you've agreed on an amount. Otherwise, use Clause 8.*] $_____

☐ E. Furniture, Fixtures, and Equipment $_____

☐ F. Equipment Leases $_____

☐ G. Assignment of Contracts $_____

☐ H. Intellectual Property Rights $_____

                Total $_____

a. Proration of Certain Items [*optional*]

The total sale price will be adjusted by prorating rent, taxes, insurance premiums, utility costs, and security deposits as of the date of closing.

b. Inventory [*optional*]

The total sale price will also be adjusted by adding the value of the inventory as covered in Clause 7 (Price of Inventory).

c. Accounts Receivable [*optional*]

The total sale price will also be adjusted by adding the value of the accounts receivable as covered in Clause 8 (Accounts Receivable).

EXAMPLE:

---

6. Sale Price (Asset Sale)

The sale price for the assets listed in this section is $250,000, and is allocated as follows:

A. Goodwill	$ 100,000
B. Assignment of Lease	5,000
C. Furniture, Fixtures, and Equipment	100,000
D. Assignment of Contract	40,000
E. Intellectual Property Rights	5,000
Total	$ 250,000

Allocating the sale price among the assets isn't a legal requirement, but it's nevertheless highly recommended for a practical reason. It gives you and the seller an agreed basis for your income tax computations, reducing the likelihood of hassles with the IRS later on. As explained in Chapter 3, when you buy business assets, how you allocate the price to different assets will affect how quickly you can deduct or depreciate the cost of the various assets. Also, from the seller's standpoint, the nature of the assets and the allocation you agree upon will affect how much of the seller's gain is taxed at ordinary income rates and how much is taxed at long-term capital gain rates.

It's crucial that you thoroughly read Chapter 3 to understand how a careful allocation of your sale price into appropriate categories (rather than simply stating a lump sum) can minimize your tax burden. Broadly speaking, in allocating the sale price, your best strategy as the buyer is to have as much as possible of the sale price allocated to assets that can quickly be written off through depreciation or as tax deductions. But you may compromise on this somewhat to meet the seller's desire for lower tax rates.

Completing Form 8594, *Asset Acquisition Statement,* is a highly technical task that is best left to an experienced tax professional. To see why this is so, check out the form and its instructions, which are reproduced in Appendix C. By referring to the allocation section of your sales agreement, your tax adviser will find it easy to complete Form 8594 for you. Chances are that you will not be buying any assets that fall into Class I, II, or III (these are cash, securities, and accounts receivable) on the IRS form. Inventory will fall into Class IV, and goodwill will be a Class VII item. In all likelihood, the other assets will fall into either Class V (tangible property) or VI (covenant not to compete or other intangible property).

 SEE AN EXPERT

Because what's best for your tax picture won't necessarily be best for the seller, too, you may need help from a tax professional in order to come to a compromise on the allocation figures. This typically involves an adjustment of the sale price to best serve both of your interests. Remember that at tax time, you and the seller will each have to file IRS Form

8594, *Asset Allocation Statement.* If you agree on the allocation of the sale price and you're reasonable about it, the IRS normally will accept your allocation. A tax professional can also help you make sure that you fill out IRS Form 8954 correctly so that it stands up to scrutiny by the government.

Prorations

Because there may be some expenses that you and/or the seller will owe each other after the closing, it makes sense to address prorations and reimbursements in the sales agreement. Clause 6a does this.

When You'll Owe Money for Prepaid Expenses

Since bills for business expenses can come due at various times during a given month, and some may even arrive on a quarterly basis, chances are the seller will have paid some expenses in advance of the closing date that will benefit you. For example, let's say you close on January 15 and the seller has paid rent to the landlord for the whole month of January. Assuming that you'll be taking over the lease and staying on in the same space, it's reasonable for you to reimburse the seller for rent for the last half of January. And if upon signing the lease the seller posted a $2,000 security deposit with the landlord that the landlord will continue to hold, it's reasonable for you to reimburse the seller for that deposit if it will ultimately be refunded to you at the end of the lease.

Similarly, the seller may have also paid in advance for property taxes, utilities, or leased equipment such as a photocopier. It is normal business practice for the sales agreement to provide for the buyer to reimburse the seller for the portion of such payments that covers any time period that falls after the closing date. The process of splitting these advance payments is called proration. Subsection a of Clause 6 in the sales agreement includes standard language on proration. Usually, by the time the closing rolls around, the seller will know the amounts of the prepaid expenses and you can make the adjustments at the closing.

When the Seller Will Owe You Money for Expenses Paid by You After the Closing

Sometimes, of course, prorations should be made in the opposite direction—that is, the seller will owe you for the seller's fair portion of utility and other bills that haven't arrived or aren't due yet but that partly cover the time when the seller still owned the business. There are a few ways to handle this:

- If the amounts are insignificant, you may simply agree that you'll pay the full cost.
- When the amounts are known at the time of closing, you can handle the proration then by adjusting the sale price in your favor.
- If the seller likely will owe you money for one or more bills but you won't know the exact amount until after closing, you'll need to get something

in writing. One option is for you to simply hold back from the first or second installment payment an amount equal to what the seller ends up owing. Or, in an all-cash deal in which the seller is likely to owe money to you a few months down the road when a certain bill arrives, you might suggest that a portion of the sale price sufficient to cover the seller's obligation be held by a third party (an escrow agent) until the bill arrives. Then, part of the money will be used to pay the seller's share of the bill, and the rest will come to the seller. A lawyer for you or the seller can be the escrow agent, or it can be anyone else you both select. For example, if you're paying cash in full when closing the purchase of a car wash, you and the seller may agree that the seller will leave some money with an escrow agent to cover the seller's share of a potentially large water bill when it arrives.

- If the bill is one that the seller has been paying for some years, and the financial information you've already seen gives you a ballpark figure of what the bill might be, you can estimate it and deduct that amount from the sale price, with an agreement that no adjustments will be made if it is higher or lower. You and the seller are each taking the risk of losing a few dollars, but you have a sale agreement that's final, with no need for adjustments later.

However you decide to deal with it, a lawyer can help you with appropriate wording for the proration part of your sales agreement.

Inventory

Unless you're buying a retail or manufacturing business, you probably won't be purchasing inventory. But if you are, there are two ways to deal with it in your sales agreement.

If you and the seller have agreed on a fixed price for the inventory, you can insert the line item "Inventory" in Clause 6, Sale Price, and specify the price. For example, if you're buying a restaurant and the value of the food on hand at any given time may fluctuate between $2,500 and $3,500, it may be easier to simply allocate $3,000 of the total purchase price to the inventory of food rather than making a physical count on the day of closing. In that case, you won't need to have a separate inventory section in your sales agreement as discussed below. Instead, you will simply list $3,000 in the line item Inventory.

If you will be acquiring inventory but you haven't set a price on it yet and you won't set a price until the closing date, you can use the optional inventory language suggested above (Clause 6b), referring to a separate Price of Inventory clause. In this case, you won't include inventory as a line item in the main part of Clause 6.

The section titled "Inventory: Asset Sale," below, explains how to complete a separate clause covering inventory in your sales agreement for an asset sale.

Accounts Receivable

As with the inventory, if you'll be acquiring the seller's accounts receivable, you can deal with this asset in Clause 6 or separately in Clause 8. You'll put the accounts receivable as a line item in Clause 6 only if you and the seller have agreed on an exact amount that you'll pay for these accounts. Otherwise, you'll use the optional wording provided in Clause 6c, above, referring to Clause 8 and an adjustment of the sale price.

Payments for Seller's Employment or Consultant Services or for a Noncompete Agreement

As noted in Chapter 12, the sale price of the assets set out above does not include any money you agree to pay the seller for signing a covenant not to compete or for services the seller may provide after the closing as either an independent contractor or an employee. (The same holds true in an entity sale, as we'll explain below.)

For example, let's say the total amount of money you'll pay as a result of your purchase is $500,000, of which $50,000 is for the seller's agreement not to compete in Del Rio County for 36 months and $100,000 is a consultant's fee the seller will receive for giving advice to the business for the next 24 months. In that situation, you'll be paying

$350,000 for the assets of the business; that's the amount that should be accounted for in the sale price portion (Clause 6) of the sales agreement. The reason for not including the entire $500,000 is that noncompete agreements or consulting agreements are not assets of a business; you'll need to cover these additional sources of money in another part of the sales agreement, with details in separate documents as explained in Chapter 15.

Inventory: Asset Sale

 SKIP AHEAD
If the business you're buying doesn't have inventory—or has inventory but won't be transferring it to you—you can skip this section. Also, you can normally skip this section if you're buying an entity rather than its assets—unless yours is one of those rare entity purchases in which the sale price of the stock or LLC membership interests is going to be adjusted to reflect fluctuations in the value of the entity's inventory.

If you're buying a retail or manufacturing business or a restaurant, you'll likely be acquiring inventory as part of the sale. (Remember that goods the seller is holding on consignment don't count as inventory.) There are a few ways to deal with this in the sales agreement. If fluctuations in the value of inventory are likely to be small in the days before the closing, you may simply want to fold the inventory into the sale price and allocate a portion of the sale price to it as one more line item, as explained above.

If, however, the value of the inventory might change considerably between the inking of the sales agreement and the closing—or if for some other reason it's hard to determine a precise value before closing—you may decide to treat the inventory separately from the sale price for the other assets. In this case you'll need to come up with an inventory clause such as Clause 7, Price of Inventory. Be sure to specify in this clause what you mean by the inventory of goods—for example, clothing or food—as well as who will do the physical inventory and when. If considerable inventory is involved—and especially if it was bought at different times and different prices—you and the seller may prefer not to handle the task yourselves, instead hiring an outside company to do the physical counting. In that case, you'll want to specify those arrangements in your sales agreement, including how the cost of having the inventory counted will be shared.

Sometimes, if the value of the inventory is especially hard to estimate in advance, you may want a cap on how much will be paid for the inventory. By the same token, the seller may want to state a minimum inventory value. Clause 7, Price of Inventory, includes optional contractual language (Options a, b, and c) that will let you and

---

7. Price of Inventory (Asset Sale) [optional]

At closing, in addition to the total sale price listed in Clause 6 above, Buyer will buy the inventory of goods consisting of [merchandise held for sale/parts and supplies/food and beverages] by paying Seller the amount Seller paid for those goods, as shown in the original invoices. A physical count of the goods will be made by [Seller and Buyer] or [list name of outside inventory company]. [Seller and Buyer will share equally the cost of having the inventory counted by list name of outside inventory company .]

The count will be made _____ days before closing and will include only unopened and undamaged goods.

a. Price Paid for Inventory [optional]

Buyer will pay no more than $_____ for the goods.

b. Minimum Price Paid for Inventory [optional]

Buyer will pay at least $_____ for the goods.

c. Minimum Price With a Cap on Maximum Price [optional]

Buyer will pay at least $_____ but no more than $_____ for the goods.

the seller accomplish either or both of these goals. Simply include whatever language applies.

As a savvy buyer, you'll want to pay for inventory that's readily saleable, so you'll want to exclude items that are damaged, obsolete, or hard to sell for some other reason. If part of the business's inventory has problems of this sort, suggest that the seller simplify the deal by running a clearance sale of the undesirable merchandise before closing. Or see about buying the distressed portion of the inventory at a steep discount, adding language to Clause 7 as shown in the following example.

EXAMPLE:

> **7. Price of Inventory**
>
> At closing, in addition to the total sale price listed in Clause 6 above, Buyer will buy the inventory of goods consisting of merchandise held for sale by paying Seller the amount Seller paid for those goods, as shown in the original invoices. However, the invoice price of goods purchased by Seller more than 12 months before the closing date will be reduced by 75%. A physical count of the goods will be made by Inventory Service Company. Seller and Buyer will share equally the cost of having the inventory counted by Inventory Service Company.
>
> The count will be made 2 days before closing and will include only unopened and undamaged goods.

Dealing With the Purchase of Accounts Receivable: Asset Sale

 SKIP AHEAD

If the business doesn't have accounts receivable—or has accounts receivable but won't be transferring them to you—you can skip this section. Also, you can normally skip this section if you're buying an entity rather than its assets—unless yours is one of those rare entity purchases in which the sale price of the stock or LLC membership is going to be adjusted to reflect fluctuations in the value of the accounts receivable.

Among its assets, the business you're buying may have customers who owe the business money for services rendered or goods purchased. These customer obligations are called accounts receivable. There are several ways to handle them:

- The simplest way to handle accounts receivable is for the seller to retain ownership of them and take responsibility for collecting the money owed to the business (Alternative A of Clause 8, Accounts Receivable, below).
- Another common approach is for the seller to retain ownership of the accounts receivable but have you collect the accounts in the normal course of business, turning the proceeds over to the seller (Alternative B, below).
- Finally, as part of the sale, the seller can simply sell you the accounts that

are relatively current—perhaps at a discount, such as 25% if some will be difficult to collect (Alternative C, below).

Each of these common approaches can be worded for your sales agreement is shown below.

 CAUTION

Avoid paying full price for all of the accounts receivable. If you do, you'll be assuming 100% of the risk that all accounts will be paid. If you agree to acquire all of the accounts, it's fair to require the seller to lop off

a reasonable percentage of the total amount owed to allow for the difficulty you'll face in collecting the more problematic accounts and the possibility that some won't be collected at all. For example, you might agree that you'll pay 75% of the total amount outstanding on bills that are no more than 90 days old and 60% of the bills that are more than 90 days old.

Sale Price: Entity Sale

In an entity sale, you will also need to cover the sale price in the agreement, but the language will differ from that used in an asset sale.

---

8. Accounts Receivable (Asset Sale) *[optional]*

[choose one of the following alternatives and edit according to your situation]

☐ A. Seller's accounts receivable as of the day of closing will remain Seller's property. Buyer will have no responsibility for collecting those accounts. Seller will have the right to collect those accounts and to keep the amounts received.

☐ B. Seller's accounts receivable as of the day of closing will remain Seller's property. Buyer will use usual reasonable efforts to collect the accounts in the course of its normal billing practices. Within ten days of receiving amounts owed to Seller, Buyer will send those funds to Seller.

☐ C. At closing, Buyer will purchase all of Seller's accounts receivable that are no more than 90 days old. Buyer will pay Seller the balances owed on these accounts less 25%. Buyer will be entitled to keep all sums collected on these accounts. The accounts receivable that Buyer is not buying will remain Seller's property. Buyer will have no responsibility for collecting those accounts. Seller will have the right to collect those accounts and to keep the amounts received.

No Allocation of Sale Price in Entity Sale

Unlike an asset sale, in an entity sale, there's no need to allocate the sale price among the assets that the entity owns. That's because you're not buying the assets but, rather, the seller's shares of stock or LLC membership interest. This means that in the sales agreement, you should not include an asset allocation clause such as Clause 6. Instead, the sale price clause for an entity sale would look like the one shown below.

---

9. Sale Price (Entity Sale)

The sale price of the [stock/LLC membership interests] is $75,000.

As with the sale price in an asset sale, be sure that the price for an entity sale doesn't include any amounts that you'll pay the seller either now or in the future for a covenant not to compete or for consulting or any other work the seller agrees to perform for you. You'll cover these as separate clauses as discussed in Chapter 15.

Adjustments to the Sale Price in Entity Sale

If the business has inventory or accounts receivable, fluctuations in the value of those items can influence how much you're willing to pay for the entity or how much the seller is willing to accept. This can be a concern if there's the possibility of large swings in

value between the time the sales agreement is signed and the closing—especially if there's a time gap of more than a few days between signing and closing. In that case, it can make sense to provide for an adjustment to reflect these changes (though such adjustments tend to be less common in an entity sale than in an asset sale). Below is an example of a clause you can use in an entity sale.

---

10. Adjustment of Sale Price (Entity Sale)
 [optional]

The sale price is based on the corporation's inventory having a value of $25,000 as shown on the original invoices. If at closing the inventory is determined to be worth less or more than that amount, the sale price will be adjusted downward by the amount the inventory is worth less than $25,000 or upward by the amount the inventory value exceeds $25,000. Likewise, the sale price is based on the corporation having accounts receivable totaling $10,000. If at closing the accounts receivable are less or more than that amount, the sale price will be adjusted downward by the amount the accounts receivable are less than $10,000 or upward by the amount the accounts exceed $10,000.

You can avoid the issue of adjustments by valuing the inventory and accounts receivable just before signing the sales agreement, factoring those values into the sale price, and then moving promptly to close the sale.

Deposit

To ensure you don't get cold feet and simply walk away from the sale at the last moment, the seller may want you to put some money down as a deposit. The thinking is that if you arbitrarily bail out, the seller has at least something to show for his or her efforts. If you and seller agree that there will be a deposit, you'll pay it when you both sign the sales agreement.

If you're giving the seller a deposit, you can use a clause like the one that follows. It will work for either an asset sale or an entity sale. You'll need to fill in the amount of the deposit and any conditions for returning it. The amount of the deposit is a matter for negotiation. Keep in mind that the seller may be able to sue you if you fail to close but, as a practical matter, the seller is more likely to simply keep the deposit rather than take you to court.

The suggested language in Clause 11 lets you get back the deposit if the seller can't or doesn't meet contractual commitments or if contingencies specified in the agreement aren't removed. An example of not meeting commitments would be if the seller did not transfer to you all of the assets listed in the sales agreement.

Contingencies are covered in Chapter 16. If your sales agreement contains contingencies, you'll want protective language along the lines of this suggested deposit clause. Let's say the current lease on the business's space is up in nine months,

and you and the seller have made your deal contingent on the landlord's granting you a five-year extension of the lease. If that extension hasn't been fully worked out with the landlord yet, you may want to insist on a clause in the sales agreement expressly stating that the sale is contingent on your getting a five-year extension of the lease from the landlord. In that case, you'll want to be sure that your deposit will be returned to you if the lease extension can't be negotiated.

---

11. Deposit [optional]
Buyer will pay Seller a deposit of $5,000 when Buyer and Seller sign this contract. This deposit will be applied toward the amount due at closing. Seller will return this deposit to Buyer if the purchase is not completed because Seller does not meet its commitments under this agreement for any reason or if the contingencies in Clause 23 are not removed. Otherwise, Seller will be entitled to retain the deposit in the event the sale is not completed.

Payment at Closing

How much money changes hands at closing will depend on whether you'll be paying cash in full or paying only a portion of the purchase price and giving the seller a promissory note for the balance in installments. You can choose one of five alternatives for Clause 12, Payment at Closing, and edit to fit your own situation.

Full Payment at Closing (Alternative A)

If you'll be paying the full purchase price in cash at closing, you can use Alternative A of Clause 12. Note that the suggested language for Alternative A allows you to pay by cashier's check or wire transfer. Sellers correctly believe that either type of payment gives them greater protection than accepting your personal check.

ALTERNATIVE A: **Full Payment at Closing**

> **12. Payment at Closing**
> At closing, Buyer will pay Seller the total of the sums referred to in Clauses 6, 7, and/or 8 [if asset sale] or Clauses 9 and 10 [if entity sale] less the deposit referred to in Clause 11 [if any]. Payment will be by cashier's check or wire transfer.

Installment Payment (Alternatives B through E)

If, as is more typical, you'll be paying only a portion of the purchase money at the closing, this, along with any deposit the seller is holding, will become the down payment, with the balance to be paid in installments. In this case, you can use Alternative B, C, D, or E and edit to fit your situation. As noted above, the seller will typically want you to pay either by a cashier's check or the wire transfer of funds into the seller's bank account.

ALTERNATIVE B: **Installment Sale—No Adjustment-of-Price Clause for Either Inventory or Accounts Receivable**

> **12. Payment at Closing**
> At closing, Buyer will pay Seller $_____ . This payment will be made by cashier's check or wire transfer and, along with Buyer's deposit of $_____ , will be applied toward the total sale price of $_____ . The balance of the sale price will be paid as described in Clause _____ .

ALTERNATIVE C: **Installment Sale—Buyer Is Buying Inventory Under an Adjustment-of-Price Clause**

> **12. Payment at Closing**
> At closing, Buyer will pay Seller $_____ plus the value of the inventory as determined under the terms of Clause _____ . This payment will be made by a cashier's check or wire transfer and, along with Buyer's deposit of $_____ , will be applied toward the total sale price. The balance of the sale price will be paid as described in Clause _____ .

ALTERNATIVE D: Installment Sale—Buyer Is Buying Accounts Receivable Under an Adjustment-of-Price Clause

---

12. Payment at Closing

At closing, Buyer will pay Seller $_____ plus the value of the accounts receivable, as determined under the terms of Clause _____ . This payment will be made by a cashier's check or wire transfer and, along with Buyer's deposit of $_____ , will be applied toward the total sale price. The balance of the sale price will be paid as described in Clause _____ .

ALTERNATIVE E: Installment Sale—Buyer Is Buying Inventory and Accounts Receivable Under an Adjustment-of-Price Clause

---

12. Payment at Closing

At closing, Buyer will pay Seller $_____ plus the value of the inventory, as determined under the terms of Clause _____ , and the value of the accounts receivable, as determined under the terms of Clause _____ . This payment will be made by a cashier's check or wire transfer and, along with Buyer's deposit of $_____ , will be applied toward the total sale price. The balance of the sale price will be paid as described in Clause _____ .

In an installment sale, the exact wording of the Payment at Closing clause depends on whether or not you're buying the inventory or accounts receivable. One of the alternatives above (B through E) may meet your needs with or without modification. Or you and the seller can work out some other formula for determining how much is to be brought to the closing. That's fine. The most important goal of the Payment at Closing clause is to state unambiguously how the down payment (for an installment plan) will be calculated.

Promissory Note

 SKIP AHEAD

If you agreed to pay the full sale price at closing, you can skip this section on promissory notes and the following ones on security for future payment.

Unless you're going to make full payment for the business at closing, the seller will want you to agree that you'll sign a promissory note at the closing, setting out the terms under which you'll pay the balance of the sale price. These terms include the amount of each payment, the interest rate, how long you have to pay, and what happens if you fail to make payments. It's best to attach the form for the actual promissory note to the sales agreement, rather than summarizing its main terms in the sales agreement. (Chapter 18 explains how to draft a promissory note and includes a sample note. Carefully read that chapter as well as Chapter 7 before completing the promissory note clause in your sales agreement.)

Even though the actual promissory note will be an attachment to your sales agreement, you should specify in your sales agreement who will sign the note. You, of course, will sign the note, but maybe you and the seller have agreed there will be cosigners or guarantors. If so, be sure to include the names of those people in the promissory note clause. See Chapter 18 for information about why sellers often insist on having cosigners or guarantors sign the promissory note. A sample promissory note clause is below.

---

13. Promissory Note [*optional*]

At closing, Buyer will sign and give to Seller a promissory note for the balance of the sale price. The promissory note will be in the form of Attachment _____ . [The following people will sign the promissory note in addition to the Buyer: *list names of others who will sign* .] Each signer will be jointly and individually liable for payment.

 TIP

Use the promissory note only for the sale price balance. Don't use it for any amount you owe the seller for a noncompete agreement. This usually isn't an issue, because you'll typically pay for the noncompete agreement by a separate check at closing.

However, if you'll be paying all or part of the noncompete compensation later, use a separate promissory note for this purpose. It will save you and the seller king-size tax and accounting headaches.

Security for Future Payment: Asset Sale

When a sale involves installment payments, the seller normally will want to retain a security interest in the business assets and, possibly, obtain an interest in other property belonging to you. That way, if you stop paying, the seller can take back the business and perhaps take possession of other assets as well. If so, your sales agreement clause for an asset sale may look like this.

---

14. Security for Payment (Asset Sale] [*optional*]

At closing, to secure payment of the promissory note referred to in Clause _____ , Buyer will sign a security agreement as shown in Attachment _____ , giving Seller a security interest in the assets that Buyer is buying. [In addition, Buyer will give Seller a security interest in *list any other assets, such as a home, that are to be pledged as additional security.*] Seller will have the right to file a UCC Financing Statement with regard to the security pledged.

As with a promissory note, it's a good idea to prepare and attach a security agreement that you'll sign, rather than describing the terms of the arrangement in your sales agreement. Chapter 18 provides sample security agreements for asset and entity sales and explains their components. Chapter 18 also explains why, following the closing, the seller will want to file a Uniform Commercial Code (UCC) Financing Statement as a public record in the appropriate governmental office.

Besides retaining a security interest in the business assets you're buying, the seller may want to retain a security interest in the lease, or even take a security interest in your home. If the seller believes that a lien on the business assets isn't sufficient, you may be asked to give the seller a mortgage or deed of trust for your home as additional security. Think long and hard before you agree to go along with such a request. You'd hate to lose everything you have if the business doesn't work out for you.

Here are some examples of how your sales agreement can address additional security requirements.

EXAMPLE 1: Security Interest in Business Lease

If the seller wants to retain a security interest in a lease that will be assigned to you, so the seller can take back possession of the business space if you don't pay as promised, your Security for Payment clause can look like this:

---

14. Security for Payment

At closing, to secure payment of the promissory note referred to in Clause _____ , Buyer will sign a security agreement giving Seller a security interest in the assets that Buyer is buying and <u>the lease that is being assigned to Buyer</u> . Seller will have the right to file a UCC Financing Statement.

EXAMPLE 2: Security Interest in the Buyer's House

For even more security, the seller may ask that you agree to a mortgage or deed of trust on your home. Again, avoid such an agreement if at all possible. But if you conclude, on balance, that the risk is worth taking, you can add language such as this:

---

14. Security for Payment

At closing, to secure the payment of the promissory note referred to in Clause _____ , Buyer will sign a security agreement as shown in Attachment _____, giving Seller a security interest in the assets that Buyer is buying. Buyer will further secure the promissory note by giving Seller a second mortgage (or deed of trust) on the home located at 123 Elm Street, Sarasota, Florida, for the loan balance. Buyer will provide to Seller, at Buyer's expense, a title insurance policy insuring the mortgage (or deed of trust). Seller will have the right to file a UCC Financing Statement.

The sample language refers to a second mortgage (or deed of trust) because most homeowners already have a first mortgage on their home. If there's no first mortgage (or deed of trust), simply substitute the word "first" for "second."

To give the seller a valid security interest in your house, all owners of the house will need to sign the mortgage or deed of trust.

Security for Future Payment: Entity Sale

The financing arrangements for the sale of an entity are similar to those for an asset sale. You probably won't pay the entire amount at closing but will make a down payment and then sign a promissory note for the balance. This means the seller may want to have the promissory note (which should be signed by you and any cosigners or guarantors) backed up with a security agreement and a UCC Financing Statement that gives the seller a lien on the entity's assets until the note is fully paid. Chapter 18 provides the necessary forms and instructions.

To make this happen, the sales agreement should provide that at closing, you'll cause the entity to give the seller a security interest in its assets, so that the seller can take back the assets if the note isn't paid. The entity, rather than you personally, will sign the security agreement, because the entity, not you, will own the assets after the closing. An entity signs documents through its president, managing member, or other authorized person. The clause dealing with this subject might read as shown below.

In an entity sale, the seller will transfer ownership of the entity by endorsing over the stock certificates to you—or, in the case of an LLC, by signing certificates assigning the membership interests to you. As an additional protection, the seller may ask you to agree that until the promissory note is fully paid, the shares of stock or the LLC membership interests can't be sold to someone else. And the seller may ask you to agree that the stock certificates or LLC membership certificates will be held in escrow by a third party and not be delivered to you until the note has been paid in full. If you agree to an escrow arrangement, you can include language (Escrow Arrangements) to this effect at the end of the Security for Payment as shown below.

---

15. Security for Payment (Entity Sale)
[optional]

At closing, to secure the payment of the promissory note referred to in Clause _____, Buyer will cause the [corporation/LLC] to sign a security agreement as shown in Attachment _____ giving Seller a security interest in the assets of the [corporation/LLC]. Seller will have the right to file a UCC Financing Statement.

Escrow Arrangements [optional]

Until the promissory note referred to in Clause _____ is fully paid, Buyer will not sell the [corporate shares /LLC membership

Clause 15 continued

interests]. The certificates representing the [corporate shares/LLC membership interests] will be held in escrow by [list name of escrow agent]. At closing, Seller and Buyer will sign an escrow agreement in the form of Attachment _____ .

See Chapter 18 for a sample form of escrow agreement you can attach to your sales agreement language. ●

Dealing With Liabilities and Representations

Almost all businesses have at least some liabilities: financial obligations that the business will or may have to pay in the future. Liabilities can take many different forms, including, for example, a debt owed to a bank, a phone bill that will come due in 30 days, lease payments on business equipment, salaries owed to employees, or a potential injury claim by someone hurt by a product that the business sold or repaired. One of the main reasons for acquiring the assets of a business rather than the corporate or LLC entity is to avoid as many liabilities as possible. As explained in Chapter 8, in an asset sale, by law you normally don't inherit the business's debts and liabilities. These remain solely the obligation of the seller unless you and the seller agree that you'll be responsible for some or all of them.

Let's assume that you're buying a business's assets and that your deal with the seller doesn't require you to take over any liabilities. The seller should be willing to have your asset sale agreement clearly say that the seller—and not you—will remain responsible for the debts and liabilities of the business. This chapter includes sample sales agreement language to cover this very common situation.

Sometimes, though, as part of the negotiations for the sale of assets, you and the seller will agree that you'll assume responsibility for certain specific liabilities or types of liabilities. In that case, the asset sale agreement will need to spell out which liabilities you'll be taking over, as also covered in this chapter.

An entity sale differs from an asset sale in terms of liabilities. In an entity sale, unless modified by the parties in the sales agreement, the business's liabilities are the sole responsibility of the corporation or LLC being purchased, and they stay with the entity. The shareholders who sell their corporate stock or the LLC members who sell their LLC interests to the buyer are not personally responsible for paying any business debts, either during their ownership of the entity or after the transfer of the entity to you. (The exceptions to this general rule are covered in the section on legal liabilities to third parties.) It is possible, however, for an entity sale to be structured so that the selling shareholders or LLC members agree to be responsible for paying certain liabilities of the entity. See the section called "Liabilities an an Entity Sale," for how to fine-tune the liabilities clause in order to place this burden on the sellers.

SEE AN EXPERT

Get legal help when it comes to liabilities. Of all the subjects covered in the sales agreement, the allocation of responsibility for debts and other liabilities may be the most complex and the most likely to require some professional help. Chapter 6 explains how to find and work with a lawyer.

Other clauses in the sale agreement are also intended to reassure the buyer or the seller. These reassurances are called representations. An example of a representation would be a statement by the seller in the sales agreement that the financial information that's been given to you is accurate. Representations must be carefully drafted to avoid adverse legal consequences. This chapter will show you how to put together the clauses that contain representations.

Liabilities in an Asset Sale

From a legal standpoint, when the assets of a business are sold, the seller or the corporate or LLC entity, or both, will remain liable for all preexisting liabilities. This means that normally you won't have to worry about getting stuck for these items. As part of the negotiations, however, you may agree to assume responsibility for some liabilities. This section covers both possibilities. It provides two alternatives (A and B) to a clause on Seller's Debts and Other Liabilities, depending on whether or not you're taking over any liabilities.

Buyer Is Not Taking Over Any Liabilities in an Asset Sale (Alternative A)

In an asset sale, you and the seller will most likely agree that at or before closing the seller will pay all known debts and claims and will remain liable for any others that may

surface later, such as a delayed bill from a supplier or a customer's demand for a refund for a defective product. In that situation, you can build a Seller's Debts and Other Liabilities clause by selecting from (and modifying if necessary) Options 1 through 3 in Alternative A of Clause 16, Seller's Debts and Other Liabilities (Asset Sale).

Alternative A of Clause 16 reassures you that the seller will be responsible for all business debts and that you don't have to worry about claims by past creditors or about the seizure of business assets to satisfy past debts.

For further assurance that there won't be any problems with past liabilities, you can include one or more of the options that are shown in in Clause 16, Alternative A. Here's how each of those options works.

Option 1: Indemnification of Buyer. Let's say that two months after the closing, a bill arrives from a supplier for goods that were sold to the business before the closing and that the seller hasn't paid for. If the supplier tries to collect from you or threatens to seize any of the assets that you bought, this clause obligates the seller to pay for any legal defense of the claims in addition to paying the debt or judgment. If the business is a corporation or LLC, use the blank space in the Indemnification of Buyer option to fill in the name of the seller. You should require this personal assurance as well as the assurance of the entity.

Option 2: Indemnification of Seller. Similarly, the seller will expect the sales agreement to include language like that found in the second option of Clause 16, Alternative A. This requires you to protect the seller from exposure to any debts that arise after you take over the business. The Indemnification of Seller language is a mirror image of what the seller undertakes to do for past debts in Option 1.

Option 3: Confirmation of Payment of Debts. This is a practical, commonsense way to deal with the bulk sales law if the business is located in one of the few states that still has such a law on the books: California, Georgia, Indiana, Maryland, Virginia, or Wisconsin. These laws are explained in Chapter 19. Basically, these laws—which apply only if you're buying the assets of a business that sells goods from a stock of merchandise—require creditors to be notified of the sale. The Confirmation of Payment of Debts option lets you and the seller avoid the cumbersome paperwork that's often required for bulk sales compliance. The method suggested here should adequately protect you from claims of creditors—but it does make sense to check whether your lawyer feels comfortable with it. If you and the seller do agree to use this option, the seller will need to pay all known debts either before the closing or out of the closing proceeds. See Chapter 19 for a form you can use for the Statement Regarding Absence of Creditors referred to in the Confirmation of Payment of Debts option of Clause 16, Alternative A.

The actual language for Alternative A and all the options discussed above is shown below.

ALTERNATIVE A: Buyer Is Not Taking Over Any Liabilities in an Asset Sale

16. Seller's Debts and Other Liabilities (Asset Sale)

Buyer is not assuming any of Seller's debts or other liabilities. Seller will pay all debts and other liabilities, whether now known or unknown, that are or may become a lien on the assets being bought by Buyer.

[*choose all options that apply*]

☐ 1. Indemnification of Buyer. Seller [and each of Seller's partners/ shareholders/members] will indemnify, defend, and save Buyer harmless from and against all debts and other liabilities arising out of the Seller's ownership or use of the assets before closing.

☐ 2. Indemnification of Seller. Buyer [and each of Buyer's partners/ shareholders/members] will indemnify, defend, and save Seller harmless from and against all debts and other liabilities arising out of the Buyer's ownership or use of the assets after closing.

☐ 3. Confirmation of Payment of Debts. At closing, Seller will confirm in a Statement Regarding Absence of Creditors (Attachment ____) that Seller has paid all known debts and other liabilities of the business. Buyer and Seller waive compliance with the bulk sales law of the state of _____ .

Buyer Is Taking Over Some or All Liabilities in an Asset Sale (Alternative B)

While somewhat unusual, it is possible that in an asset sale you'll agree to take responsibility for paying some or all of the debts and liabilities of the business in exchange for an appropriate price reduction. For example, if the assets include a telephone system that the seller is buying through installment payments and there's still a year's worth of payments to be made, you may agree to take over the monthly payments to the finance company. Or maybe a customer has suffered some minor property damage because a product that the business installed malfunctioned, but because the extent of the damage is still not certain, the claim has not been settled. You may be willing to deal with the claim and pay any settlement—within reason—as a way of keeping a good relationship with the customer. If you and

ALTERNATIVE B: **Buyer Is Taking Over Liabilities in an Asset Sale**

---

16. Seller's Debts and Other Liabilities (Asset Sale)

Buyer will pay the following debts and other liabilities of the business that arose out of Seller's ownership and use of the assets before the closing: _____

_____ .

Buyer will pay the following debts and other liabilities of the business that arose out of Seller's ownership and use of the assets before the closing: _____

_____ .

Any other debts and liabilities arising out of the Seller's ownership or use of the assets before closing will be paid by [Seller *or* Buyer].

[*choose all options that apply*]

☐ 1. Indemnification of Buyer. Seller [and each of Seller's partners/shareholders/ members] will indemnify, defend, and save Buyer harmless from and against all debts and other liabilities that Seller has agreed to pay.

☐ 2. Indemnification of Seller. Buyer [and each of Buyer's partners/shareholders/ members] will indemnify, defend, and save Seller harmless from and against all debts and other liabilities that Buyer has agreed to pay, and for all debts or liabilities arising out of the Buyer's ownership or use of the assets after closing.

☐ 3. Waiver of Bulk Sales Law Compliance. Buyer and Seller waive compliance with the provisions of the bulk sales law of the state of _____ .

---

the seller agree that you'll pay certain debts or be responsible for particular liabilities, you'll need to put appropriate language in the sales agreement.

Alternative B in Clause 16, Seller's Debts and Other Liabilities, can be a starting point when you'll be paying some of the bills. See Options 1 and 2, above, for the reasoning behind the indemnification language.

You can use a third option (Waiver of Bulk Sales Law Compliance) if the business is located in California, Georgia, Maryland, Virginia, or Wisconsin and you're buying the assets of a retail business—a business that sells goods out of a stock of merchandise. These states still have bulk sales laws, which are intended to protect business creditors. If existing debts are to be paid after the closing, the creditors must be notified of the business sale. This is a cumbersome process that can require considerable paperwork, as explained in Chapter 19.

If you believe that all bills will be paid on time, you may not have to worry much about bulk sales compliance. This is especially true if you'll owe the seller a large balance after the closing and the amounts owed to creditors are relatively small. In that case, you can pay the creditors on the seller's behalf if necessary, and deduct from the promissory note balance the amounts the seller should have paid. The Indemnification of Buyer clause (Option 1) should also ease your worries on this score. Still, in a state with a bulk sales law, your lawyer may prefer strict compliance with the law. If that

happens, you won't use Clause Option 3 (Waiver of Bulk Sale Compliance). Instead, your lawyer will need to be satisfied that the seller has followed all statutory procedures.

Liabilities in an Entity Sale

In an entity sale, the liabilities of the business belong to the corporation, LLC, or partnership and continue to be the responsibility of that entity after it's transferred to you. Still, as part of the deal, the seller may agree to personally take care of one or more existing obligations of the entity. If so, you can use a clause such as Clause 17, Entity's Debts and Other Liabilities, to deal with this issue.

Clause 17A (Payment by Seller) commits the seller to take personal responsibility for payment of a certain debt owed by the entity—for example, $30,000 that the corporation owes to a bank.

A clause such as Clause 17B (Indemnification of Buyer) helps assure you that the seller has disclosed all known debts of the entity and will be personally responsible for paying any known debts of the entity that weren't disclosed.

Regardless of what your sales agreement says, the seller may be committed to be personally liable for some debts of the entity. For example, the bank that lent money to the corporation or LLC probably required the seller to personally guarantee repayment. Similarly, a company that extended credit to the business for goods or services may have required that same kind of personal guarantee. Unless the lenders or creditors agree to release the seller, the seller will continue to be personally responsible for these debts even after the business changes hands.

You can use a clause such as Clause 17C (Buyer's Personal Guarantee of Certain Entity Debt) if you're agreeing to personally guarantee payment of a specific entity debt.

---

17. Entity's Debts and Other Liabilities (Entity Sale) [*optional*]

[*choose all options that apply*]

☐ A. Payment by Seller. Seller will pay [$_____ of] the $_____ obligation that the [corporation/LLC] owes to [*list name of creditor*].

☐ B. Indemnification of Buyer. Seller will indemnify, defend, and save Buyer harmless from and against any other debts and other liabilities of the [corporation/LLC] to the extent that such debts and other liabilities are known to Seller and Seller has failed to disclose them to Buyer.

☐ C. Buyer's Personal Guarantee of Certain Entity Debt. Buyer will personally guarantee payment to [*list name of creditor*] of the $_____ that the [corporation/LLC] owes to that creditor and will sign such documents as the creditor requires for that purpose.

Finally, you're generally entitled to a setoff for any amounts that you pay because the seller has failed to make good on his or her obligations. See "Your Right to a Setoff," below.

Representations: What They Are and Why They Matter

Your decision to buy a business will be based not only on your own investigation (discussed in Chapter 9) but, equally important, on the seller's written and oral statements about the business's past income and expenses. In addition, it's reasonable for you to assume that certain facts are true— for example, that the seller or the business entity owns the assets listed for sale, unless the seller has indicated otherwise. Similarly, from the seller's perspective—especially if you're buying on an installment basis—the decision to sell the business to you will be based to some extent on documents that document your financial position.

Traditionally, buyers and sellers capture these statements and assumptions in a part of the sales agreement called representations or, sometimes, representations and warranties.

Representations. In plain English, a representation is simply a statement of a past or existing fact. Example: "Seller represents that gross sales for the 12 months ending December 31, 2004 were $300,000."

Warranties. A warranty is a promise or guarantee that existing or future facts are or will be true. Example: "Seller warrants that

Your Right to a Setoff

Chances are good that you'll be buying the business on an installment basis and paying a major portion of the sale price over a number of months or even years. This can give you significant leverage if the seller agrees to pay certain debts and obligations of the business, but then doesn't pay. Generally, the law lets you go ahead and pay those debts and then deduct the payments from your promissory note payments. This is based on your "right of setoff," sometimes called your "right of counterclaim and setoff." This right is founded on long-standing common law (judge-made law) rather than on a statute.

You can, of course, try to include an express right of setoff in the sales agreement. This might, however, throw a monkey wrench into the negotiations, since you and the seller may not agree on how the setoff clause should be worded. You should check with your lawyer if you're concerned about this issue but, normally, a right-of-setoff clause isn't necessary, because in most situations the law provides you with the right, anyway.

Still, if you're inclined to include specific language on this point, you might try the following:

> Buyer may set off against amounts due under the promissory note any amounts which Seller is obligated to pay under Section _____ of this sales agreement and which Seller fails to pay when due. Buyer's good faith exercise of this right will not constitute a default under either the promissory note or the security agreement. This right of setoff is in addition to any other remedies that Buyer may have against Seller.

the HVAC unit will be in good condition for the 24 months following the closing."

As you can well imagine, the distinction between a representation and a warranty can get very fuzzy, so legal documents usually use the terms in tandem, as in: "Seller represents and warrants that …." That way, all the bases are covered—and the suggested clauses use that inclusive language.

Representations and warranties clauses in your sales agreement can have serious legal consequences. If it turns out that your statements aren't true—especially if you were knowingly misleading—you can be responsible to the seller for financial damages, and the seller may be able to undo the sale before or even after the closing. Similarly, the seller will be responsible to you for the truth of his or her representations and warranties.

The fact that you must normally include representations and warranties in your sales agreement again underlines why it's so crucial that you provide the seller with 100%

accurate written and oral information during the negotiation process. To accomplish this, it's key that you represent only information you personally know about, not things you're pretty sure—or hope—are true. Or put another way, if you have any doubt about any of the items you list in your representations, it's best to include the words "to the best of Buyer's knowledge" before that representation.

The next two sections provide suggested clauses you can use to build the parts of the sales agreement that include representations and warranties.

Seller's Representations

The scope and detail of the representations and warranties that you'll be able to insist on is going to depend on a number of factors, including:

- **The relative bargaining power of you and the seller.** If you're anxious to buy the business for an attractive price or because it's a great fit with your existing business, you may demand little by way of representations. By contrast, if you're paying top dollar, based on the seller's projection of a rosy future, you'll expect more extensive statements and guarantees.
- **Your ability to thoroughly investigate the business.** If you're buying a small, straightforward business and its finances and assets are relatively easy to understand, you may be content

to look at business records, ask a few questions, and require little detail in the representations clause. But if the business is more complex (it owns lots of valuable copyrights, for example) and the facts about its finances or operations are more difficult to dig out or verify, you may want the seller to make more extensive representations. You'd like to keep the seller on the hook—legally and financially—for any misstatements.

- **The nature of the business operations.** You may not be too demanding if you're buying a simple service business, like a hair salon. But if the business is more complicated—say, it manufactures, sells, and repairs potentially dangerous machinery— you'll want the seller to provide more in the way of detailed representations. For example, you'll want the seller to make representations about past and pending product liability claims, workers' compensation claims history, and possible environmental hazards.

When you're buying the assets of a corporation or LLC, it's reasonable to ask all the shareholders or members to take personal responsibility for the representations and warranties. Clause 18, Seller's Representations, provides for this. You'll also need to include appropriate language in the signature portion of the sales agreement, as explained in Chapter 18. If the representations turn out to be false or the conditions the shareholders or LLC members are guaranteeing turn out to be different, you can sue the owners personally. And if your lawsuit is successful, the owners' personal assets are at risk to satisfy the judgment. You may also be able to cancel the deal and get a full refund if a court determines that false information you received was an essential component of your decision to complete the deal.

In an asset sale, the clause dealing with the seller's representations may look like Clause 18, shown below (although, of course, you'll need to choose the options that apply to your transaction). A parallel clause for an entity sale (Clause 19) is also provided below.

Clause 18N—stating that the representations and warranties will survive (last beyond) the closing—emphasizes that two years down the road, if you discover that the seller provided inaccurate information about the business, you can sue the seller. Even without this clause, it's very likely that the seller will continue to be liable to you for false statements—at least until the applicable statute of limitations runs out.

Depending on the type of entity that's selling the business, the sales agreement should be personally signed by each partner, shareholder, or member of the entity. (See Chapter 17 for advice on the signature portion of the sales agreement.)

Clause 18 will work for an asset sale. Clause 19 will work for an entity sale.

Buyer's Representations

The seller will expect you to make representations in the sales agreement. Typically, a seller has fewer unknowns to worry about than a buyer does, so the seller is likely to require fewer representations. See Clause 20, Buyer's Representations, for language to include in your sales agreement. This clause can be used for either an asset or entity sale. The only difference is in the first option (A). In an entity sale, you need to insert the words "of the entity" in the first line as noted.

18. Seller's Representations (Asset Sale)

Seller [and each of Seller's partners/shareholders/members] represent(s) and warrant(s) that:

[*choose all options that apply*]

☐ A. Seller owns the assets being sold. At closing, the assets will be free from any claims of others.

☐ B. At closing, Seller will have paid all taxes that have then come due and that affect the business and its assets.

☐ C. To the best of Seller's knowledge, there are no judgments, claims, liens, or proceedings pending against Seller, the business, or the assets being sold, and none will be pending at closing.

☐ D. To the best of Seller's knowledge, the business and financial information in the financial statement dated _____ that Seller has given Buyer is accurate.

☐ E. Until closing, Seller will operate the business in the normal manner and will use its best efforts to maintain the goodwill of suppliers, customers, the landlord, and others having business relationships with Seller.

☐ F. Seller is (and at closing will be) a [corporation/limited liability company] in good standing under the laws of the state of _____ and has (and at closing will have) the authority to perform the obligations contained in this sales agreement.

☐ G. To the best of Seller's knowledge, the assets being sold to Buyer constitute all the assets needed to operate Seller's business.

☐ H. To the best of Seller's knowledge, the current uses of the Seller's business premises are permitted under the applicable zoning laws. To the best of Seller's knowledge, the business premises presently (and at closing will) meet all applicable health, safety, and disabled access requirements and are (and at closing will be) in good repair.

☐ I. To the best of Seller's knowledge, the tangible assets are (and at closing will be) in good repair and good operating condition.

☐ J. To the best of Seller's knowledge, all items in the inventory of merchandise are (and at closing will be) unused and of saleable quality.

☐ K. To the best of Seller's knowledge, Seller is (and at closing will be) in full compliance with all laws, ordinances, or regulations applicable to the operation of the business.

☐ L. To the best of Seller's knowledge, Seller is not (and at closing will not be) in default on any contracts.

☐ M. To the best of Seller's knowledge, Seller is (and at closing will be) in compliance with all environmental laws. To the best of Seller's knowledge, there are (and at closing will be) no hazardous materials on the business premises that may be a source of future liability under the environmental laws.

☐ N. These representations and warranties will survive the closing.

☐ O. Seller [and each of Seller's partners/shareholders/members] will indemnify, defend, and save Buyer harmless from and against any financial loss, legal liability, damage, or expense arising from any breach of the above representations and warranties.

☐ P. The total liability of the Seller [and all of the Seller's partners/shareholders/members] for all breaches of representations and warranties will not exceed $ _____ .

19. Seller's Representations (Entity Sale)

Seller(s) represent(s) and warrant(s) that:

[*choose all options that apply*]

☐ A. To the best of Seller's(s') knowledge, the entity being sold owns the assets itemized in the list dated _____ . At closing, the assets will be free from any claims of others.

☐ B. At closing, the entity being sold will have paid all taxes that have then come due and that affect the business and its assets.

☐ C. To the best of Seller's(s') knowledge, there are no judgments, claims, liens, or proceedings pending against the entity or its assets, and none will be pending at closing.

☐ D. To the best of Seller's(s') knowledge, the business and financial information concerning the entity in the financial statement dated _____ that Seller(s) has/have given Buyer is accurate.

☐ E. Until closing, the entity will operate the business in the normal manner and will use its best efforts to maintain the goodwill of suppliers, customers, the landlord, and others having business relationships with the entity.

☐ F. The entity is (and at closing will be) a [corporation/limited liability company] in good standing under the laws of the state of _____ .

☐ G. To the best of Seller's(s') knowledge, the entity owns all the assets needed to operate the entity's business.

☐ H. To the best of Seller's(s') knowledge, the current uses of the entity's business premises are permitted under the applicable zoning laws. To the best of Seller's(s') knowledge, the business premises presently (and at closing will) meet all applicable health, safety, and disabled access requirements and are (and at closing will be) in good repair.

☐ I. To the best of Seller's(s') knowledge, the tangible assets of the entity are (and at closing will be) in good repair and good operating condition.

☐ J. To the best of Seller's(s') knowledge, all items in the entity's inventory of merchandise are (and at closing will be) unused and of saleable quality.

☐ K. To the best of Seller's(s') knowledge, the entity is (and at closing will be) in full compliance with all laws, ordinances, or regulations applicable to the operation of the business.

☐ L. To the best of Seller's(s') knowledge, the entity is not (and at closing will not be) in default on any contracts.

☐ M. To the best of Seller's(s') knowledge, the entity is (and at closing will be) in compliance with all environmental laws. To the best of Seller's(s') knowledge, there are (and at closing will be) no hazardous materials on the business premises that may be a source of future liability under the environmental laws.

☐ N. The [shares/LLC interests] constitute all of the issued [shares/LLC interests] of the entity. No additional [shares/LLC interests] will be issued before the closing. At closing, the [shares/LLC interests] will be free from any claims of any persons or entities other than Seller(s).

☐ O. These representations and warranties will survive the closing.

☐ P. Seller(s) will indemnify, defend, and save Buyer harmless from and against any financial loss, legal liability, damage, or expense arising from any breach of the above representations and warranties.

☐ Q. The total liability of the Seller(s) for all breaches of representations and warranties will not exceed _____ .

20. Buyer's Representations

Buyer represents and warrants that:

[*choose all options that apply*]

☐ A. Buyer has inspected the tangible assets [*insert "of the entity" if an entity sale*] that Buyer is purchasing and the leased premises and has carefully reviewed Seller's representations regarding them. Buyer is satisfied with the physical condition of the tangible assets and the premises.

☐ B. To the best of Buyer's knowledge, the business and financial information in the financial statement dated _____ that Buyer has given Seller is accurate.

☐ C. Buyer is (and at closing will be) a [partnership/corporation/limited liability company] in good standing under the laws of the state of _____ and has (and at closing will have) the authority to perform the obligations contained in this sales agreement.

☐ D. These representations and warranties will survive the closing.

☐ E. Buyer [and each of its partners/shareholder/members] will indemnify, defend, and save Seller harmless from and against any financial loss, legal liability, damage, or expense arising from any breach of the above representations and warranties.

☐ F. The total liability of the Buyer [and all of its partners/shareholder/members] for all breaches of representations and warranties will not exceed $_____ .

How Sellers and Buyers Can Avoid Unintended Liability

In making representations in the sales agreement, there are two ways for parties to help guard against unintended liability.

The first, as mentioned above, is to qualify a statement by prefacing it with the words, "to the best of Seller's knowledge" or "to the best of Buyer's knowledge." This wording appears throughout Clauses 18, 19, and 20. If you want the seller to be responsible for a representation regardless of what he or she knows or doesn't know, you should delete the words "to the best of Seller's knowledge." This would be the case, for example, if you want the seller to absolutely guarantee that there are no environmental hazards on the premises.

The second protective technique is to list any necessary exceptions to a general representation.

EXAMPLE: Exception to Seller's Representation 18I.

To the best of Seller's knowledge, the tangible assets are (and at closing will be) in good repair and good operating condition, except for the Excelsior dishwasher and the Concord ice-maker, which are in need of repair.

Payment for Noncompete
Agreements and Consultant Deals

In the course of your negotiations, you may have agreed to pay the seller for a commitment not to compete with the business after you become the owner. (Chapter 8 introduces this issue.) Also, you and the seller may have agreed that after the closing, you'll pay the seller to work for the business as an employee or consultant (independent contractor). If so, these payments will be in addition to the money you pay the seller for the assets the business—or for the business entity itself—and will need to be addressed in the sales agreement.

The best way to do this is to have clauses in your sales agreement saying that separate documents will be signed at closing concerning these arrangements. Then attach to the sales agreement copies of the actual documents, such as an employment agreement, that will be signed at closing. Using separate, attached documents encourages you and the seller to go into more detail than you might if you simply summarized your understanding in the sales agreement. In addition, you won't have to negotiate further with the seller about wording after the sales agreement is signed.

This chapter will show you how to draft the clauses referencing your noncompete and consultant agreements. The actual documents you will complete and attach to your sales agreement are covered in Chapter 20.

SEE AN EXPERT

You must amortize over a 15-year period the payments you make to the seller for an agreement not to compete. However, as explained in Chapter 8, your payments to the seller for working for you are tax-deductible business expenses. To understand exactly how this will affect your tax picture, it makes sense to consult a tax professional. And to be on the safe side, have a lawyer review the documents that you attach to the sales agreement to make sure you're adequately protected.

Seller's Agreement Not to Compete With the Business After the Sale

It's common for a business buyer to ask the seller to agree not to start a competing business or work for a competing company, at least for a certain period of time after the purchase is complete. In exchange, the buyer pays the seller a set amount of money. There's no standard amount of compensation for a noncompete agreement—it could be a nominal $10 or a not-so-trivial $10,000. Logically, the seller would want the amount to be relatively high if he or she is giving up significant opportunities to earn a living. But cutting the other way is the fact the seller will pay tax on the payment at ordinary income rates, which are higher than long-term capital gain rates. The seller might prefer to get a higher sale price for the business (assuming that the extra amount can be assigned to capital gain items) and accept a lower amount for the agreement not to compete. From your standpoint, you'd prefer to pay a relatively low amount for the seller's covenant not to compete, because it will take you 15 years to fully deduct the amount you pay. That's likely to be much longer than the covenant itself. Get some advice from a tax professional before negotiating this point with the seller.

A noncompete agreement can serve two important functions:

- It can allay your anxiety that after the closing, the seller will start a new business that competes with the old one or will go to work for a competing business. In both instances, you want reduce the possibility that the seller will divert customers and clients away from you, infringing on the goodwill you had hoped to profit from.
- It can provide tax planning flexibility for both you and the seller, as described above. For example, depending on tax considerations, the two of you can agree that the seller will be paid a small amount for the covenant not to compete (while at the same time agreeing to a high price for the business assets), or you can agree that the seller will receive a substantial sum for the noncompetition agreement (at the same time lowering the price for the business).

Occasionally, getting a covenant not to compete from the seller will be of little concern to you. This may be the case, for example, if the seller is past retirement age, seriously ill, not likely to reenter the business world for some other reason, or moving to another part of the country. It also wouldn't be a concern if the seller is selling a business that he or she recently inherited from a parent or relative and has never participated in.

Along the same lines, if a shareholder or LLC member has always been a passive investor with career interests in another field, you may choose not to insist on a noncompete agreement from that person. In most other situations, however, it's a good idea to get a noncompete agreement from all active owners of the business, whether they're selling the assets of the business or the entity itself.

Chapter 20 includes a sample noncompete agreement that you can attach to the sales agreement. That chapter explains why it's important to carefully define the type of work and activities that are considered competitive, the geographic location that will be off limits to the seller, and the time period for which the agreement applies.

Below is sample language (Clause 21) for your sales agreement. Of course, you won't include this clause if a noncompete agreement is not part of the sale package.

You and the seller may need to negotiate exactly who will be giving a covenant not to compete, and you'll need to insert the names of those people in Clause 21. If the business is a sole proprietorship, it will usually be the seller who is signing the covenant not to compete—but you should also insist on one from the seller's spouse or any other family member who is actively involved in running the business.

And if the business is a corporation, an LLC, or a partnership, you'll want non-compete agreements from each co-owner and possibly from others (such as family members and even employees) who are closely involved in the operation of the business. There may be different noncompete agreements for different people—that is, restrictions and compensation may differ from one person to another. In that case, you'll need to attach specific noncompete agreements for each person.

Typically, you'll pay at closing for each covenant not to compete. If the amount to be paid is substantial, however, the seller may be willing to accept a promissory note. This would be unusual, but if the seller does agree to a delayed payment, use a separate promissory note rather than the one used for the balance of the sale price. Otherwise, you may run into complex tax and bookkeeping problems that can be easily avoided by doing separate notes.

A Legally Enforceable Commitment Not to Compete

You may be concerned about whether a court will enforce the seller's covenant not to compete. You may have heard that some noncompete agreements or covenants are not legally valid. It's true that the law is often suspicious of covenants not to compete that are signed by employees of a business (though this doesn't mean that they will never be enforced). This is founded on a fear that the noncompete agreement will interfere with the employee's freedom to earn a living. But when the person signing the covenant is the seller of a business, the law is much less protective. It's assumed that the seller is being adequately compensated for selling the business (even if the covenant itself lists a low dollar figure). You and the seller should expect that, if the seller violates the covenant, a court will enforce it as written by issuing an injunction and assessing money damages.

---

21. Covenant Not to Compete [*optional*]
At closing, [*insert names of those who will sign a covenant*] will sign and deliver to Buyer a covenant not to compete in the form of Attachment_____ and Buyer will pay [the/each] signer the amounts specified in the attachment.

Seller's Agreement to Work for Your Business After the Sale

As discussed in Chapter 8, you may want the seller to stay on board for a transition period of several months or maybe even a year or two. The seller can help you learn the ropes, and his or her continued presence also can be reassuring to employees, customers, and suppliers. The seller may have good reasons for wanting to work for the business after it changes hands—for example, a more gradual transition out of the income stream that the business has been providing, or wanting to have some time to adjust to the life change of giving up the business.

Legally, there are two ways you can structure the arrangements for the seller to perform future services for you:

- The seller can be an employee and work for a fixed salary or on an hourly basis, either full or part time.
- The seller can be a consultant (independent contractor) and be paid a flat fee for specific tasks or projects.

Chapter 8 covers the legal issues involved in working as an independent contractor or employee. Read that material carefully before you agree to have the seller do future work for you and before you structure an agreement. You'll need to decide whether to treat the seller as an independent contractor or an employee. You'll also need to address the seller's precise job responsibilities and, of course, compensation and termination provisions.

As with a covenant not to compete, it's a good idea to prepare a separate document covering any future work the seller agrees to do for you—either as an employee or independent contractor—and attach it to the sales agreement. Chapter 20 explains how to do this. It includes sample employment and independent contractor contracts that you can use as a model in preparing your own.

To refer to the attached employment or independent contractor agreement, include sample language such as Clause 22, Future Services, in your sales agreement.

---

22. Future Services [*optional*]
At closing, [*list names of Sellers who will work for Buyer*] and [*Buyer/the entity being sold*] will sign an [*employment/independent contractor*] agreement in the form of Attachment _____ .

In a business currently owned by multiple owners, some may work for you, while others may not. In this clause, you'll name only those who are staying on. And since different people may have different duties and compensation, you may need to draft and attach specific contracts for each. As a further refinement, keep in mind that some sellers may agree to work as employees while others may work as independent contractors. You'll need to adjust this clause to reflect those arrangements.

EXAMPLE: Some Sellers Will Work as Employees, Others as Independent Contractors

> At closing, Thomas Paley and the entity being sold (Ajax Corporation) will sign an employment agreement in the form of Attachment A, in which Thomas Paley agrees to a term of employment with Ajax Corporation after the closing. Sally Wimple and the entity being sold (Ajax Corporation) will sign an independent contractor agreement in the form of Attachment B, in which Sally Wimple agrees to perform services for Ajax Corporation as an independent contractor after the closing.

A word of explanation about "the entity being sold": Imagine an entity sale in which Carla is buying all the shares of Ajax Corporation stock from Tom and Sally. If Tom and Sally agree to work for the business after the closing, they'll technically be working not for Carla but for Ajax Corporation: the entity being sold. You need to be aware of this distinction between an entity and its owner when completing this clause and the employment and independent contractor agreements. As recommended in Chapters 8 and 20, you should review the documents with a lawyer to make sure you get it right.

Anyone who's going to sign an employment or independent contractor agreement at the closing should personally sign the sales agreement. (See Chapter 17 for information on the signature portion of the sales agreement.)

Current Employees of the Business You Are Buying

Current employees of the business who are not owners will not be involved with the Future Services clause. Normally, in an asset sale, if you want to keep current employees on the payroll, you'll need to negotiate with each of them separately; the only exception is where an employee has an employment contract that can be assigned to you—a highly unusual circumstance.

In an entity sale, current employees will remain on the company's payroll unless you terminate them; existing employment contracts will continue to bind the entity, even after it changes hands, so you need to read any employment contracts carefully. ●

Other Important Legal Language for the Sales Agreement

Chapters 12 through 15 cover the main clauses you should consider including in your sales agreement, addressing such key topics as the sales price, terms of payment, and the seller's covenant not to compete. These clauses make up the guts of a sales contract and, even without more, can constitute a legal and adequately protective agreement. But to create an optimal agreement, there's more legal ground to cover, including:

- a contingency clause
- a reference to closing arrangements and documents
- a dispute resolution clause
- technical contract clauses, such as how modifications to the contract may be made, and
- additional optional terms.

Contingency Clause

Your sales agreement may need to include a contingency clause. Similar to a contingency in a contract to sell a house, a contingency in a business sale agreement is an escape valve that lets one party or the other—most often the buyer—cancel the deal if a certain event doesn't occur or a specified condition isn't met. Typically, the sales agreement says that if you use a contingency to walk away from the deal, your deposit will be refunded. (Deposits are covered by Clause 11 in Chapter 13.)

Let's say, for example, that the business's current store lease runs out in six months. Suppose that you and the seller are ready to sign a sales agreement, but you want to keep operating from the same location, and you and the landlord haven't fully negotiated an extension to the lease or substituted a satisfactory new one. You'll probably want to be able to cancel the sale if no agreement is reached on the lease. An example of what your contingency clause might look like is shown below.

Other possible scenarios: You may want to make the deal contingent on being able to obtain funding or having a liquor license transferred. The seller, too, may have contingency needs. For example, the seller may want to cancel the sale if the bank won't release him or her from personal liability for a loan that the entity took out.

There are numerous reasons for including a contingency clause in your sale agreement. Still, in many sales agreements there are no contingencies at all. If your sales agreement does require one or more contingencies, you'll need to customize the wording to fit your deal.

Try to impose relatively short time limits for removal of each contingency—something, perhaps, in the range of 15 to 30 days. That way, if the deal falls through, you can start looking for another business to buy. But the deadline doesn't have to be absolute. If you or the seller needs more time to work on removing a contingency, you can mutually agree to extend the deadline.

---

23. Contingencies [*optional*]

This sale is contingent on [*fill in*] Buyer and the landlord negotiating and signing a five-year lease satisfactory to Buyer for the premises currently occupied by the business. If the Buyer has not signed such a lease within 30 days from the signing of this agreement, Buyer can cancel this sale by notifying Seller in writing. In that case, Seller will promptly refund Buyer's deposit of $_____ . If Buyer does not notify Seller of a cancellation within 35 days of this agreement, the agreement will remain in effect.

Note that the lease example for Clause 23, above, provides for the entire deposit to be returned to you if you cancel the deal based on a sales agreement contingency. The seller may feel that other arrangements would be more appropriate. For example, the seller might want you to agree that you'll get back only 50% of your deposit. You, of course, would want to resist such a limitation, but it will be up to you how hard you argue—and it will also depend on how likely you think it is that the contingencies won't be met.

If you have a contingency clause in your sales agreement and the sale does fall through because a contingency isn't met, it's prudent for you and the seller to sign a mutual release confirming that the deal is officially dead. This clears the deck for both of you to move ahead. Your mutual release can look like this.

EXAMPLE:

Mutual Release

Jenny Phillips (Seller) and Horace Madsen (Buyer) cancel the Sales Agreement dated July 10, 20xx for the business known as The Sandwich Shack, located at 654 Archer Road , and release each other from any and all claims with respect to that Agreement. All rights and obligations arising out of the Sales Agreement are null and void.

Buyer has received a refund of the deposit.

You'll need to add signature and date lines to your release, following the format recommended in Chapter 17.

Closing Arrangements

At the closing, you meet with the seller to sign and exchange all the documents needed to complete the purchase. This usually occurs within weeks after you sign the sales agreement. You should provide in your sales agreement details as to when and where the closing takes place, using language such as that shown above.

Chapter 21 offers suggestions for when and where to hold the closing. Look ahead to those suggestions before completing your own closing clause. As explained in Chapter 21, to help assure an orderly closing, you and the seller should agree on a customized closing checklist so you know that all the bases will be covered and you won't miss anything at the closing.

Chapter 17 discusses when the seller's or buyer's spouse—and possibly other people—need to sign closing documents. Consult that discussion to see who to specify in this clause in addition to you and the seller.

---

24. Closing

The closing will take place:

Date: <u>August 31, 20xx</u> Time: <u>9:00 a.m.</u>
Location: <u>654 Archer Road, Chicago</u>

At closing, Buyer [and Buyer's spouse] and Seller [and Seller's spouse] will sign the documents specified in this contract and all other documents reasonably needed to transfer the business assets to Buyer. Buyer will pay Seller the amounts required by this contract and Seller will transfer to Buyer [*the business assets/the Seller's stock/the Seller's LLC interests*].

Documents for Transferring Assets

At the closing of an asset sale, the seller will need to sign and give you documents that legally transfer the business assets to you, as well as other documents called for in the sales agreement. These typically include a bill of sale, along with assignments of the lease, other contracts, and intellectual property. These documents were discussed in Chapter 12 and the forms themselves are included in Chapter 19. Clause 25, Documents for Transferring Assets, below, shows what a

typical sales agreement clause covering that subject might look like. Obviously, not all of these options will fit your situation, so edit according to the particular documents you will be providing at closing. Make sure that you list all the documents needed to transfer the assets listed in Clause 3, Assets Being Sold, as discussed in Chapter 12.

---

25. Documents for Transferring Assets (Asset Sale)

At closing, Seller will deliver to Buyer these signed documents:

[*choose all options that apply*]

☐ A. A bill of sale for the tangible assets being sold, including a warranty of good title.

☐ B. An assignment of the lease at [*fill in property address*], with the landlord's consent.

☐ C. An assignment of the other contracts that are being transferred to Buyer, with the written consent of the other contracting person, if such consent is required.

☐ D. Assignments of all intellectual property contracts, including trademarks, patents, and copyrights, that are part of this purchase.

Seller will also deliver to Buyer at closing all other documents reasonably needed to transfer the business assets to Buyer, including _____

_____ .

Depending on the kind of assets the business owns and will be transferring, there are other documents you may want to list in the last sentence of the transfer-of-assets clause. The sales agreement may describe these assets this way:

Transfer of Vehicles

> Assignments of the cars and trucks owned by the business, in the form required by the Department of Motor Vehicles.

Transfer of a Liquor License

> Assignment of the Class C liquor license owned by the business, in the form required by the Alcoholic Beverages Commission.

Transfer of Real Estate

> A warranty deed for the real estate being sold, along with a title insurance policy guaranteeing that Buyer is receiving a marketable title.

Documents for Transferring Entity

When you're buying an entity rather than the assets of a business, the seller will be transferring his or her interest in the entity to you. You won't need to worry about having individual assets transferred to you. Clause 26, Documents for Transferring Entity, may be appropriate in your sales agreement. Choose the alternative that applies (A or B) and edit according to your situation.

As explained in Chapter 18, if you're buying an entity on an installment payment plan, you and the seller may agree that the documents transferring ownership will held by a third party—an escrow agent—until the seller has received full payment. In that case, your clause might read like the second alternative (Clause 26B), below.

A. Documents Delivered to Buyer (Entity Sale)

> **26. Documents for Transferring Entity**
>
> At closing, Seller will deliver to Buyer [endorsed stock certificates for the corporation being sold/signed membership certificates transferring all interests in the LLC being sold].

B. Documents Delivered to Escrow Agent (Entity Sale)

> **26. Documents for Transferring Entity**
>
> At closing, Seller will deliver to [*list name of escrow agent*] [endorsed stock certificates for the corporation being sold/signed membership certificates transferring all interests in the LLC being sold] in accordance with an Escrow Agreement in the form of Attachment ____ .

Dispute Resolution Clause

You'd like to believe that once a comprehensive sales agreement has been signed, everything will go smoothly between you and the seller, but the sad reality is that disputes can and do arise. They can relate to relatively minor matters such as how to apply your proration formula to a specific bill that arrived after the closing. Or they can be major matters such as your claim that the seller misrepresented key financial information.

Ideally, you'd like to be able to negotiate a settlement of any dispute directly with the seller. This is the quickest, least costly way to put disagreements behind you. Unfortunately, once you and the seller become involved in a spat, it can often be difficult to negotiate a mutually agreeable settlement.

It's no secret that when negotiations fail, a lawsuit is usually the worst way to resolve a business problem. Not only is litigation typically expensive, prolonged, and emotionally draining but, worst of all, the results are at least to some degree unpredictable. That's why you'll normally want your sales agreement to provide that any disputes be resolved through one of two tried-and-true alternative means:

- Mediation, in which you and the seller try to achieve a voluntary settlement with the help of a neutral third party (the mediator) who uses an efficient step-by-step process to help you craft your own solution. As compared to a court fight, mediation is inexpensive, quick, and confidential—and it's effective the vast majority of the time. The mediator doesn't have the power to make decisions, so no resolution will

be imposed on you; you and the seller are in control of how to resolve your dispute.

- Arbitration, in which you and the seller ask a neutral third party (the arbitrator) to listen to both sides and then make a decision that will resolve the dispute. As with mediation, the process is almost always cheaper and speedier than having a trial, and it's confidential. And also, just like mediation, there's a minimum of paperwork and formality.

In your sales agreement, you and the seller can agree that you'll submit any dispute to mediation. Then, if the mediation doesn't lead to a settlement, the dispute will get submitted to arbitration or either party can go directly to court, depending on how your disputes clause is worded. If you choose the arbitration option, the arbitrator will make a final decision, and that decision will be enforced by a court, if necessary.

With the clause below, Clause 27, Disputes, you and the seller can name the mediator and arbitrator now or agree on them when the need arises. Another possibility is to name an organization such as the American Arbitration Association, which will provide a trained mediator when needed. This clause assumes that you and the seller will share the cost of the dispute resolution equally and that if the dispute is not resolved within 60 days, you'll either move on to arbitration or go directly to court. In either case, mediation will be attempted first.

27. Disputes [*optional*]

If a dispute arises concerning this agreement or the sale, Seller and Buyer will try in good faith to settle it through mediation conducted by [*list name of specific mediator or mediation group/a mediator to be mutually selected*].

Seller and Buyer will share the cost of the mediator equally. Seller and Buyer will cooperate fully with the mediator and will attempt to reach a mutually satisfactory resolution of the dispute.

If the dispute is not resolved within 60 days after it is referred to the mediator, Seller and Buyer agree that

[*choose alternative that applies*]

☐ the dispute will be arbitrated by [*list name of specific arbitrator or arbitration group/an arbitrator to be mutually selected*]. Judgment on the arbitration award may be entered in any court that has jurisdiction over the matter. Costs of arbitration, including lawyers' fees, will be allocated by the arbitrator.

[*or*]

☐ either party may take the matter to court.

If you're not sold on the merits of either mediation or arbitration, and you prefer the traditional route of going to court to deal with problems, do not include Clause 27, Disputes, in your sales agreement.

RESOURCE

For lists of professional mediators and extensive information on mediation, see the Mediation Information and Resource Center at www.mediate.com. To learn more about arbitration and find an arbitrator, see the American Arbitration Association's website at www.adr.org or the website of the Association for Conflict Resolution at www.acrnet.org.

Technical Contract Clauses

If you were to look at a pile of contracts for the sale of a business—or, in fact, for a wide variety of business transactions—you'd find that many of them include a similar set of clauses, usually near the end. Typically, these technical clauses (called "boilerplate") cover such issues as:

- whether the parties intend the contract to be modified in writing only
- how each party will communicate with the other regarding the contract
- what will happen to the rest of the contract if a judge decides that one part of it isn't legal, and
- which state's law will govern the contract.

This section covers the most common technical clauses.

Risk of Loss

There's always a possibility that the assets you're buying will be damaged or destroyed before the closing. You'd like reassurance that if there's a loss, the seller will replace the lost or damaged assets or pay for their replacement. If the seller is following prudent business practices and carrying adequate insurance, that shouldn't be a problem, though should assets be destroyed, the seller will have to pay for any deductible under the business's insurance policy.

A clause to consider using in an asset sale might look like this:

> **28. Risk of Loss**
> Seller will replace or pay for the replacement of any assets that are destroyed or damaged before the closing.

In an entity sale, you can use a slightly different version of this clause:

> **28. Risk of Loss**
> Seller will cause [the corporation/the LLC] being sold to replace or pay for the replacement of any of its assets that are destroyed or damaged before the closing.

Entire Agreement

Before you sign your agreement, you and the seller will have discussed and probably negotiated dozens of issues, from the sale price and terms of payment, to how to physically count the inventory and how long the seller will work for you as a consultant. Ideally, all the relevant points that you

agree on will end up in your contract. But it's also possible that you and the seller may have talked about additional issues but not reached a conclusion and, for that reason, left them out of the final agreement. For example, you and the seller may have talked about the possibility of the seller receiving a 25% discount on goods or services that he or she may later buy from you. To avoid the problem that one of you might later claim that your deal also includes a certain oral agreement, your sales agreement should say that only what's written in it (not anything else you discussed before) is part of your deal. Although no legal language is absolutely foolproof, including an "Entire Agreement" clause in your sales agreement will go a long way to prevent the seller from later successfully claiming in arbitration or court that you agreed to something that's missing from (or conflicts with something in) the contract.

Similarly, you and the seller may have negotiated your contract by sending letters, emails, faxes, or other written documents back and forth—or may have even written a letter of intent, as discussed in Chapter 10, before working on a more formal contract. Again, the purpose of an "Entire Agreement" clause such as Clause 29 is to prevent those previous writings from being considered part of your contract should either party later try to claim that one or more of them constitutes an inadvertently omitted part of your agreement.

> **29. Entire Agreement**
> This is the entire agreement between the parties. It replaces and supersedes any oral agreements between the parties, as well as any prior writings.

Modification

After you've signed your sales agreement but before the closing, you and the seller may talk about making one or more written changes to its provisions. But you absolutely don't want a casual conversation with the seller to somehow turn into a modification of your agreement. To prevent this possibility, a "modification" clause such as Clause 30 simply requires that any amendment to the agreement be in writing and signed by both of you.

> **30. Modification**
> This agreement may be modified only by a written amendment signed by both parties.

Chapter 11 explains how to modify a signed sales agreement and includes an amendment form for doing so.

Governing Law

Although the chances are small that you and the seller will end up in court or in arbitration over the sale, it makes sense to designate which state's law will apply to the sale before you get into a dispute. Usually,

you and the seller will be in the same state as the business, so you'll just fill in that state.

If you and the seller are located in different states, designating the governing law is more important, though it may take more negotiation. Although contract law is very similar from state to state, there can be small but significant differences. If you don't choose which state's law will govern your agreement, you could spend precious time fighting over that issue later instead of attending to the actual dispute. It's usually advantageous for you to have the laws of your home state govern, because this is the law that you and your lawyer will probably be most familiar with. And, of course, using the courts in your own state will be more convenient and less expensive than if you have to travel elsewhere for litigation.

Use Clause 31, Governing Law, to address this issue.

> **31. Governing Law**
> This agreement will be governed by and interpreted under the laws of the state of _____, and any litigation regarding this agreement or its attachments will be brought in the courts of that state.

Severability

There's always a possibility, however remote, that you'll get into a dispute with the seller and that a judge or arbitrator will need to interpret your sales agreement.

And, once this happens, there's also at least a theoretical possibility that the judge or arbitrator will rule that a provision of your agreement is unenforceable or invalid. If your agreement isn't properly worded, what happens next is iffy. The risk is that some judges or arbitrators, upon discovering an unenforceable or invalid clause, may void the entire agreement.

To prevent this, Clause 32, Severability, says that if a court or arbitrator finds that any part of your sales agreement is not enforceable, the unenforceable material should simply be discarded (severed), leaving the rest of the agreement intact.

---

32. Severability

If a court or arbitrator determines that a provision in this agreement is invalid or not enforceable, that determination will affect only that provision. The provision will be modified only to the extent needed to make it valid and enforceable. The rest of the agreement will be unaffected and all other clauses will remain valid and in force.

Notices

Because you and the seller may not see each other frequently, it makes sense to formally exchange mailing addresses and agree on how you'll send each other any written communications required by the sales agreement. For example, you may need to send the seller a notice concerning a bill that the seller has agreed to pay, and the seller may need to send you a legal notice, such as a warning that you're in breach of the contract for failing to make payments on time. Generally, as recommended in Clause 35 in Chapter 17, you'll fill in the respective addresses following the signatures at the end of the sales agreement. A clause like Clause 33, Notices, can be helpful.

This clause applies to notices—not to installment payments. Typically, the address where you send the seller the monthly installment payments can be inserted in the promissory note, and first-class mail will suffice, as explained in Chapter 18.

---

33. Notices

All notices must be sent in writing. A notice may be delivered to a person at the address that follows the person's signature or to a new address that the person designates in writing. A notice may be delivered:

 A. in person

 B. by certified mail, or

 C. by overnight courier.

Additional Optional Clauses

For many sales agreements, the clauses discussed above and in the preceding chapters will be all you need. But it's possible that your sale won't fit the typical mold and that you'll need to address some additional issues and terms. Given the reality that there are thousands of different types of businesses, and that every small enterprise is somewhat unique, no book can present every contractual possibility. So if your purchase includes some features not anticipated by the clauses suggested here, you'll need to do some drafting on your own. In most instances, you can simply add sensible language to capture additional needed details, although if the extra material is complicated or lots of money is at stake, you'll be well advised to work with your lawyer.

There are many kinds of special terms you may need to add to your agreement. For example, perhaps you and the seller have agreed that for six months following the closing, the seller can continue to use his or her current office within the business premises at no charge. Or maybe you and the seller have agreed that you'll hire the seller's son or daughter as a clerk. Or maybe the seller will have the right to buy back certain assets at a discounted price if you should decide to sell the business or its assets. There's no telling what you and the seller may come up with.

---

34. Other Additional Terms [optional]
[For the first six months following the closing, Buyer will allow Seller to occupy Seller's current office at no charge. Seller will also be allowed to use the telephone and the equipment in the office at no charge.]

Signatures on a Sales Agreement

Don't be surprised if the seller isn't completely satisfied with your first draft of the sales agreement. Typically, the two of you will have to spend a little time—maybe even a lot of time—discussing and revising the wording. You may go through a number of drafts before you reach a meeting of the minds.

Once you and the seller have ironed out your differences over substance and language, however, the sales agreement will of course need to be signed before it is legally binding. Usually you and the seller will sign the agreement several days or weeks before the closing. You can specify the closing date and location in Clause 24 (Closing), which is discussed in Chapter 16. And see Chapter 21, which covers details of the closing, including checklists of other legal documents that may need to be signed to complete the sale.

Signing a sales agreement seems like a simple and obvious task, but it can involve some important legal subtleties, which are explained in this chapter. The first is that the signature format will vary, based on whether a person is signing as an individual or on behalf of a business entity. There are also differences based on the type of business entity buying or selling the business.

Chapter 12 explains how to identify the seller and buyer at the beginning of the sales agreement. It points out that the proper naming of the parties will depend on whether you're describing a sole proprietorship, partnership, corporation, or LLC. To best understand the following discussion

of signatures, it may help to review that material.

> **CAUTION**
>
> **In addition to signing the sales agreement, consider some sensible precautions.** To keep important clauses from getting lost in the shuffle, make sure you number the pages. Then, you and the seller should initial each page when you sign the agreement. This is a safeguard against modified pages being inserted—either by accident or as part of a scam.

Required Signatures for Sole Proprietors on a Sales Agreement

For a sales agreement to be legally binding, it must be signed by the people who have authority to legally bind the seller and buyer. This section explains who signs for a sole proprietorship. The next section, below, provides an overview of who signs for an entity such as a corporation or an LLC. The following section covers the issue of spouses signing the sales agreement.

A seller who is a sole proprietor will sign the sales agreement personally, using the one of the sole proprietor signature formats suggested in the section called "Typical Formats for Signing a Sales Agreement," below. In addition, if the sole proprietor is married and lives in a community property state, his or her spouse should sign as well, for the reasons discussed in the section called "A Spouse's Signature on the Sales Agreement," below.

If you (the buyer) are a sole proprietor, you'll also sign the sales agreement personally —again, using one of the signature formats suggested below. And in some cases, your spouse should sign the sales agreement, as discussed below.

Required Signatures for an Entity on a Sales Agreement

When a seller or a buyer is not a person but an entity—a partnership, corporation, or LLC— things can get more complicated. Basically, the people who have legal authority to bind an entity must sign the sales agreement on behalf of that entity. Who these people might be depends on whether yours is an asset sale or an entity sale. In addition to the people with legal authority, in some circumstances spouses must also sign the sales agreement, as discussed in the section called "A Spouse's Signature on the Sales Agreement," below.

Asset Sale by an Entity

Here's an overview of how to deal with signatures on a sales agreement when a partnership, corporation, or LLC is selling assets but the entity isn't being sold.

You'll certainly want the sales agreement to be signed by the person or people who have authority to bind the entity—for example, the president and secretary of the corporation. But that may not be enough.

To be on the safe side, require that all the partners, shareholders, or LLC members of the entity sign.

Similarly, if you have a partnership, corporation, or LLC that's buying the assets of a business, the agreement must be signed by the people with authority to bind the entity. But also, to avoid problems resulting from dissension among any co-owners, you'll wisely ask for the signatures of all partners, shareholders, or members of your entity.

Sale of an Entity by Its Owners

If the owners of an entity are selling you their interests in that entity, each co-owner will sign the sales agreement. No one will sign on behalf of the entity, because, in this case, the entity is not the seller. You'll probably be buying the entity interest as an individual—perhaps along with other individuals who will become co-owners. You and any cobuyers should each sign the sales agreement. However, if you've formed an entity of your own to buy and own the entity being sold, the people with legal authority to bind your entity will need to sign—and the seller will probably want to have all owners of your entity sign, if they're not the same as the people with authority to bind the entity.

Guidelines on Who Signs the Sales Agreement for an Entity

Here are some general guidelines to help you sort out who is eligible to sign the sales agreement on behalf of an entity. These guidelines apply when an entity is a seller, a buyer, or a guarantor in either an asset sale or an entity sale.

Partnership

The basic rule is that any general partner has the legal power to sign a contract on behalf of a partnership, meaning the other party can rely on just one general partner's signature. The main exception to this rule is where the partners have agreed among themselves in a written partnership agreement that only certain partners have the power to sign contracts, or that more than one signature is needed. In that case, and if the other party is informed of this limitation in advance, the assumed authority of each partner to bind the partnership will no longer be in effect. This means, for example, that if you've been informed that only one specific partner has authority to sign on behalf of the partnership or that all partners must sign, your sales agreement won't bind the partnership if you don't follow the partnership's internal rules.

If you receive information orally or in writing that the partners have modified the normal rule that any general partner can bind the partnership, your only prudent course is to require all partners to sign the sales agreement.

Corporation

A corporation determines which of its officers have the authority to sign agreements on behalf of the business. This is usually stated in the bylaws or a board of directors' resolution. The corporation's president usually is an authorized signer, but other officers may also have authority.

Limited Liability Company (LLC)

In most situations, the same rule that applies to a partnership also applies to an LLC: Any member (owner) can sign on behalf of the LLC. But if the members have agreed that not all members have this power and the other party is told about it, the signature of someone who lacks the authority won't be binding. The exception to this rule is for LLCs where one or more members are given the title of manager. In that situation, only a manager can bind the LLC.

Avoid Disputes by Having All Owners Sign the Sales Agreement

So much for the general legal guidelines. To be 100% certain about whether a particular person has the legal power to sign an agreement for the sale of an entity's assets, you'd need to see the entity's organizational records—and, in the case of a corporation, probably its board of directors' resolutions as well. But there's usually a simpler and equally effective way to proceed. Since the selling or buying entity involved in a small business sale will usually have a limited number of owners—partners, shareholders, or LLC members—you can have all of the owners sign the sales agreement to indicate that they approve of the sale and its terms. This heads off any later challenge from an owner who may object to the sale.

If you follow this suggestion and decide to get the signatures of all owners, then in addition to providing a spot for the signature of someone acting on behalf of the entity, you can include an entity owners' approval section like the one shown at the end of the section called "Typical Formats for Signing a Sales Agreement," below.

 TIP

Ask to see the organizational documents if you can't get all the signatures. If for some reason all partners or owners can't sign, it would be prudent to ask to see the organizational documents that give authority to one or more partners or owners to bind the entity or that limits their ability to do so. You may already have a copy of these documents if you were given them as part of the disclosure process—if so, check to make sure that the right people are signing the sales agreement.

A Spouse's Signature on the Sales Agreement

There are a few situations in which it may be prudent to include the signature of a seller's or buyer's spouse on the sales agreement. Let's look at each of them.

Community Property Basics

Nine states follow the community property system: Arizona, California, Idaho, Louisiana, Nevada, New Mexico, Texas, Washington, and Wisconsin. In these states, and in the absence of a marriage contract providing otherwise, a married couple's property accumulated after marriage is usually community—or jointly owned—property regardless of the names in which it's held. (Exceptions include property received by inheritance or gift.) This means that a married couple's community property normally includes at least a partial interest in any sole proprietorship business that either spouse owns—even one that was owned by one spouse prior to marriage. Legally, it's also true that in a community property state, if you pay a fair price to purchase business assets from a sole proprietor whose spouse plays no role in running the business, the law doesn't absolutely require that you get the consent of the owner's spouse. Still, because it's almost impossible to determine with certainty how much a business is worth and an uncommitted spouse could always disagree, it's always a good idea in a community property state to require the spouse of a sole proprietor seller to sign the sales agreement and closing documents.

Signature of Seller's Spouse

If the seller is married, lives in a community property state (listed below in "Community Property Basics"), and is selling the assets of a sole proprietorship, you'll definitely want to have the seller's spouse cosign the sales agreement. That will eliminate any risk that the seller's spouse will later claim an interest in the business assets under community property law and prevent your full use of the assets.

There may be other situations in which you or the seller will feel more comfortable if the seller's spouse signs the sales agreement, such as if the seller is getting divorced or if the sellers' spouse has a property interest in some of the business assets—or if he or she has been working closely with the seller in running a sole proprietorship, creating the impression that the business legally is a partnership rather than a sole proprietorship.

See below for suggested language for requiring the signature of a seller's spouse on a sales agreement.

Signature of Buyer's Spouse

In an installment sale where you—and perhaps others—are buying the business as individuals, you (and any cobuyers) will personally sign the promissory note that covers the balance of the sale price after you've made the down payment. If you've formed an entity to buy the business, the seller will probably want all the co-owners of your entity to personally guarantee the promissory note.

Even then, the seller may feel that a personal guarantee will be of little value if it's your spouse who has the deep pockets, or if your bank accounts and other assets are held in the name of you and your spouse. For that reason, the seller may request that your spouse sign the promissory note as well. If you go along with this request, your jointly owned property as well as your spouse's paychecks will be on the line if the note payments aren't made. The seller may also want to make sure that your spouse—and the spouses of any cobuyers—don't refuse to sign the promissory note when it comes time to close. For that reason, the seller may also ask that spouses agree in the sales agreement that they'll cosign the promissory note.

Signature Formats

Here is suggested language for the signature of a spouse on a sales agreement.

Consent of Seller's Spouse

You can use the following wording when the seller's spouse will be signing:

> I am married to the Seller. I consent to the sale described above, and I waive any interest I might otherwise have in the [business assets/entity ownership interests], whether under the community property laws or otherwise.

Consent of Buyer's Spouse

You can use the following wording when the buyer's spouse will be signing the promissory note in an installment sale:

> I am married to [the Buyer/one of the owners of the buying entity/the owner of the buying entity]. In consideration of Seller extending credit to Buyer for the purchase of the [business assets/entity ownership interests] described above, I agree to cosign or personally guarantee the promissory note to be given by Buyer to Seller.

Signature Clause in a Sales Agreement

It's time to create the clause you'll use in your sales agreement to indicate who will be signing. Here is a general signature clause you can adapt to fit your particular sale.

> **35. Required Signatures**
> This agreement is valid only if signed by Seller [*and Seller's spouse/all owners of the selling entity*] and Buyer [and Buyer's spouse/ all owners of the buying entity].
>
> *Optional*
> [and by the following additional person/ people: _____
> _____.]

You'll use the phrase "and Seller's spouse" if the seller is a person, whose spouse will also be signing. You'll use the phrase "all owners of the selling entity" if the seller is a partnership, corporation, or LLC.

Likewise, you'll use the phrase "and Buyer's spouse" if the buyer is a person, and his or her spouse will be signing. And you'll use the phrase "all owners of the buying entity" if the buyer is a partnership, corporation, or LLC.

The optional line about additional signers can be used for situations not fully covered by the main clause, such as when a relative or friend of yours will be guaranteeing the promissory note. Normally, however, the add-on line won't be necessary in the Required Signatures clause.

Typical Formats for Signing a Sales Agreement

The section above explains how to draft a clause (Clause 35, Required Signatures) listing everyone who must sign your sales agreement to make it a legally binding document. Now you need to finish off the sales agreement by providing a place for everyone to sign. This section covers the formats for signatures.

 TIP
Use these formats on other legal documents as well. The signature formats suggested here for the sales agreement are also appropriate for other documents described in this book (Chapters 18 through 20), such as promissory notes and security agreements.

General Signature Format

The elements for the signature section when someone is acting on behalf of a business entity are:

- (1) the name of the company

- (2) the state where the company is legally established

- (3) the type of legal entity

- (4) a place for an authorized person to sign on behalf of the company.

- (5) the printed name of the signer

- (6) the signer's title

- (7) the address of the entity

- (8) the date when the person is signing the sales agreement

For a corporation it would look like this (for a sole proprietor you'll simplify it as set out in "Signature Lines on a Sales Agreement," below):

---

(1) The Coffee Cup Inc.

(2) A New York (3) Corporation

By: _____ (4)

(5) Alice Appleby

(6) President

(7) 123 Chesterfield Boulevard

White Plains, New York

Dated: _____ (8)

Where an individual (such as a shareholder of a corporation) is agreeing to guarantee the accuracy of the representations of a party or agreeing to indemnify the other party (as described later in this chapter), the signature format can be simplified as follows:

Bert Becker

Bert Becker

56 Dennison Place

White Plains, New York

Dated: _____

Signature Lines on a Sales Agreement

This chart shows how you can deal with signatures in a variety of situations. I recommend that you include the address of the business or signer as well, as in the "General Signature Format," above.

Individual	*John Smith* John Smith
Sole Proprietorship *(either style can be used)*	*John Smith* John Smith doing business as Ace's Diner [*or*] Ace's Diner A Sole Proprietorship By: *John Smith* John Smith, Owner
Partnership	Smith & Jones A Michigan Partnership By: *Mary Jones* Mary Jones, Partner
Corporation	Modern Textiles Inc. A Texas Corporation By: *Mary Jones* Mary Jones, President
Limited Liability Company	Games and Such LLC A California Limited Liability Company By: *Mary Jones* Mary Jones, [Member/Manager]

When an entity is a seller or buyer, you can have the owners of that entity confirm in the signature portion of the agreement that they consent to the sale. Suggested language to insert immediately before the signatures is provided below.

Owner's Consent When the Seller Is an Entity

When the seller is an entity owned by more than one person, insert the following language before the seller's signature:

> We are all of the Seller's [partners/shareholders/members]. Each of us approves of and consents to the sale described in the above agreement.

When the seller is a corporation or an LLC owned by just one person, the following language would work:

> I am the sole [shareholder/member] of the Seller. I approve of and consent to the sale described in the above agreement.

Owner's Consent When the Buyer Is an Entity

When the buyer is an entity owned by more than one person, insert the following language before the lines for the owners' signatures:

> We are all of the Buyer's [partners/shareholders/members]. Each of us approves of and consents to the purchase described in the above agreement.

When the buyer is a corporation or an LLC owned by just one person, the suggested insertion would read as follows:

> I am the sole [shareholder/member] of the Buyer. I approve of and consent to the sale described in the above agreement.

This will work if the owners don't intend to accept personal responsibility for commitments contained in the sales agreement—that is, they are signing only on behalf of the entity, but not individually, and by doing so are preserving their normal immunity from liability for the entity's obligations. If they do intend to accept personal responsibility, use the language suggested under "Accepting Personal Responsibility for Commitments in a Sales Agreement," below.

Commitment of Outside Guarantor

In some situations, you might agree to ask someone other than your entity owner or your spouse to guarantee the promises you are making in an installment sale. You can use the following wording when an outsider will be guaranteeing your promissory note:

> In consideration of Seller extending credit to Buyer for the purchase of the [business assets/entity ownership interests] described above, I agree to cosign or personally guarantee the promissory note to be given by Buyer to Seller.

Accepting Personal Responsibility for Commitments in a Sales Agreement

When the seller or buyer is an individual rather than an entity, that person is automatically liable for the commitments that he or she makes in the sales agreement. It's a different story, however, if the seller or buyer is a corporation, an LLC, or a partnership. In that case, the owners of the entity aren't personally responsible (legally liable) unless one or all of them signs the sales agreement as an individual and specifically agrees to be liable.

You and the seller will be particularly concerned about this legal point if your sales agreement calls for the owners of an entity to accept personal responsibility for commitments made in the agreement. Let's say that the seller, an individual, is selling assets to your corporation on an installment payment basis. And let's assume, too, that the owners (shareholders) of the buying corporation will be guaranteeing the promissory note that your corporation will be signing. The seller likely will want you

and the co-owners of your entity not only to indicate that you'll agree with the purchase of assets, but also that you'll sign the promissory note as guarantors—and comply with any other portions of the agreement that make you personally responsible. Similarly, the owners of a selling entity may be personally guaranteeing the payment of certain entity debts.

In drafting an appropriate signature section, you'll need to carefully review the clauses of your sales agreement to see exactly what, if any, personal commitments it contemplates. Your agreement may say, for example, that the owners of the seller's entity will personally:

- indemnify the buyer against certain liabilities (Clause 16, Chapter 14)
- stand behind the seller's representations and warranties (Clause 18, Chapter 14)
- not compete with the buyer (Clause 21, Chapter 15), and
- sign an employment or consulting contract (Clause 22, Chapter 15).

Or your agreement may say, for example, that the owners of the buyer's entity will personally:

- cosign or personally guarantee the promissory note for the balance of the purchase price (Clause 13, Chapter 13)
- indemnify the seller against certain liabilities (Clause 17, Chapter 14), and
- stand behind the buyer's representations and warranties (Clause 20, Chapter 14).

The previous section provides language you can use in the signature portion of the sales agreement allowing owners of an entity to confirm that they consent to the sale. The following sections provide additional language you can use to confirm that entity owners not only consent to the sale but also agree to assume personal responsibility. You'll need to modify the language to fit your needs and insert it just before the signature lines for the owner or owners.

We are all of the Seller's [partners/shareholders/members]. Each of us approves of and consents to the sale described in the above agreement.

In addition, in consideration of Buyer entering into this agreement with Seller, each of us agrees to:

1. Indemnify, defend, and save Buyer harmless from and against the debts and other liabilities which, under this agreement, are the responsibility of Seller.

2. Indemnify, defend, and save Buyer harmless from and against any loss, liability damage, or expense arising from any breach of the above representations and warranties made by Seller.

3. Honor the noncompete provisions of this agreement and sign any noncompete document required by this agreement.

4. Honor the [employment/consulting] terms of this agreement and sign any [employment/consulting] document required by this agreement.

Personal Responsibility for a Selling Entity's Commitments

You can adapt the language shown below when owners of a selling entity will be accepting personal responsibility for commitments in a sales agreement.

When the seller is a corporation or an LLC owned by just one person, the beginning of the suggested insertion would read as follows:

I am the sole [shareholder/member] of the selling entity. I approve of and consent to the sale described in the above agreement.

In addition, in consideration of Buyer entering into this agreement with Seller, I agree to: [insert the four points from the box above]

Personal Responsibility for a Buying Entity's Commitments

You can adapt the following language when owners of a buying entity will be accepting personal responsibility for commitments in a sales agreement.

> We are all of the Buyer's [partners/share-holders/members]. Each of us approves of and consents to the purchase described in the above agreement.
>
> In addition, in consideration of Seller entering into this agreement with Buyer, each of us agrees to:
>
> 1. Cosign or personally guarantee the promissory note to be given by Buyer to Seller under this agreement.
> 2. Indemnify, defend, and save Seller harmless from and against the debts and other liabilities which, under this agreement, are the responsibility of Buyer.
> 3. Indemnify, defend, and save Seller harmless from and against any loss, liability damage, or expense arising from any breach of the above representations and warranties made by Buyer.

When the buyer is a corporation or an LLC owned by just one person, the beginning of the suggested insertion would read as follows:

> I am the sole [shareholder/member] of the Buyer. I approve of and consent to the sale described in the above agreement.
>
> In addition, in consideration of Seller entering into this agreement with Buyer, I agree to: [*insert the four points from the box above*]

Signing the Sales Agreement

If you've followed all the information in this book about negotiating and preparing a sales agreement—and you and the seller are satisfied with the final draft—signing it should be a breeze. But here are few pointers to help you as you enter the home stretch.

Timing the Signing

Usually, a seller and buyer sign the sales agreement as soon as all the kinks have been worked out and there's a solid deal. Occasionally, the parties wait to sign until the day of closing. The problem with this second method is that you might spend significant time getting ready to acquire the business, only to learn, at the last minute, that the seller has had a change of heart. When the outcome is uncertain, you understandably may be reluctant to meticulously prepare for the closing, as recommended in Chapter 21.

It's preferable, and more common, to sign the sales agreement days or weeks before the closing—because it gives both you and the seller adequate time to arrange for an orderly transition.

Multiple Originals

It makes sense to sign at least two originals of the sales agreement. That way, there's one for you and one for the seller—and perhaps enough for lawyers, bankers, or anyone else close to the deal who'd like to have an agreement that contains original signatures. By the way, this idea of signing multiple originals applies to many of the documents that will be signed at closing, but not to the promissory note, since you don't want to have more than one original in circulation. See the discussion of promissory notes in Chapter 18.

Dating the Sales Agreement

While dating an agreement is not a legal requirement, it makes good business and practical sense to do so. The simplest way is to insert a date for each signer, following the name and address information, as shown in the earlier example. This allows people to sign on different dates, perhaps because they can't all be available to do so on the same day. The agreement will be effective when the last required signature has been obtained.

Notaries and Witnesses

There's no practical or legal need to have the signatures on your sales agreement notarized or witnessed. Documents that pertain to real estate ownership—deeds and mortgages, for example—must be notarized. Wills and a few other documents must be signed in the presence of a witness. But very few other legal papers need this level of authentication.

Modification

Occasionally, your sales agreement will need to be modified—either just before it gets signed or at some point between signing and the closing. See Chapter 11 for suggestions on how best to accomplish this. ●

P A R T

4

Preparing the Promissory Note and Other Sales Documents

Promissory Notes and Other Installment Payment Documents

SKIP AHEAD

When to skip ahead. This chapter covers documents related to installment sales. If you'll be paying the full sale price up front, you can skip ahead to the next chapter.

Chapters 11 through 17 showed you how to create the sales agreement, the main document involved in the purchase of a business. But you'll need additional documents to carry out the terms of the sales agreement and actually have the business transferred to you. Chapters 18 (this one) through 20 will help you prepare a dozen documents you're most likely to need, including a promissory note, bill of sale, and assignment of lease.

You and the seller should prepare the sale documents as early in the sales process as possible so that both of you know in advance the exact wording of the main papers you'll sign at the closing. Chapter 21 explains how to create a closing checklist to reduce the possibility that necessary paperwork may get overlooked.

Because it's likely that you'll buy the business on an installment basis—that is, you'll pay for it over time, rather than in one lump sum—this chapter will focus on the four documents you'll need for an installment sale:

- Promissory Note
- Security Agreement
- UCC Financing Statement, and
- Escrow Agreement for an Entity Sale.

The first three documents can be used in either an asset sale or an entity sale. The fourth—the escrow agreement—applies only to an entity sale. The seller will want these documents to help make sure that you'll pay all the money you've agreed to pay for the business.

FORM

Where to find the forms. If you're reading a print copy of this book, you'll find copies of the Promissory Note, security agreements, and escrow agreements on the CD-ROM at the back. If you're using an ebook version, you can download these forms on the Nolo website; the links are included in Appendix A.

The Promissory Note

Typically, at closing, you'll make a down payment and sign a promissory note that sets out the terms under which you'll pay the seller the remainder of the sale price. A promissory note says, in effect, "Buyer promises to pay Seller $_____ plus interest of ____%," and then it describes how and when you're to make the payments. The promissory note usually covers the following points:

- when you'll make installment payments
- the amount of each payment
- what rate of interest you'll pay, and
- what happens if you don't pay as promised.

To increase the odds that you'll make all the payments called for in the promissory note, the seller may want to have your sales agreement provide that the promissory note will be guaranteed by the owners of your legal entity (shareholders or LLC members), the spouse of each owner, and perhaps other people. Assuming that you've agreed to such guarantees, your promissory note should include a place for those guarantors to sign, as explained below.

See Chapter 13, Clause 13, for sales agreement language describing the promissory note. As with other key documents to be signed at closing, the form for the note should be attached to the sales agreement so that the exact wording is known to both you and the seller well in advance.

Understanding Promissory Notes

A promissory note is a binding legal contract. As with all contracts, something of value is exchanged between two parties. In this case, you receive the assets of the seller's business or the ownership of a corporate, LLC, or partnership entity. In exchange, the seller receives your promise to pay the balance owed on the sale price—usually with interest—at specified dates.

If you don't meet the payment terms, the seller can sue you and any cosigners or guarantors and get a judgment for the amount owed plus court costs and possibly all or part of the lawyer's fee for obtaining the judgment. With a judgment in hand, the seller can then collect the money owed from your assets, including bank accounts, securities, vehicles, and even real estate.

Interest

The promissory note will state the annual interest rate that you'll pay on the principal balance. Unless otherwise specified in the note, interest is paid at the end of the borrowing interval—not in advance. So, for example, if you sign the note on January 1 and agree to make monthly payments that include interest, the February 1 payment will include interest on the balance owed for the month of January.

Because interest rates often move up and down with the health of the economy and rate of inflation, there's no single recommended number. One reasonable approach is to look at the interest the seller would receive if, instead of extending credit to you, he or she received cash and stuck the money in a relatively safe investment such as a mutual fund that specializes in government and high-grade corporate bonds. The seller might want to add a premium to that rate to account for the fact that you're a riskier creditor. For example, if a conservative bond fund pays interest at a rate of 4%, the seller might want to charge at least 8%. But if bonds are earning 7%, the seller might want to charge 10% or more, assuming your state's usury laws allow it.

State usury laws may cap the rate of interest that a lender can charge—often in the range of 10% to 20%. (Some states let a lender charge a higher interest rate when credit is extended to a business rather than to an individual, and some impose no limit on loans to an LLC or a corporation.) If a lender charges more than the rate allowed by the state's usury law, generally the excess amount won't be collectible, and there may be other financial penalties.

But as long as the interest rate doesn't exceed your state's limit, you and the seller can negotiate any rate that's acceptable to both of you. As a practical matter, you and the seller will need to check the usury law of your state only if the anticipated interest rate exceeds 10%.

Your accountant or bank may be able to tell you your state's usury rules. Or, to research the law yourself, check your state statutes under the words "usury," "interest," "credit," or "loans."

Signers and Guarantors

You, of course, will sign the promissory note, but you and the seller may agree that others will sign as guarantors to give the seller extra assurance that the debt will be fully paid. As noted above, a person who signs a note, or guarantees it, is personally liable for repaying it, meaning that his or her personal assets are at risk if the note isn't paid. So if you're a sole proprietor, you'll sign the note and be personally liable for paying it. The same is true when you've formed a partnership and all the partners sign. But if you've formed a corporation or an LLC to buy the business, only the entity is liable for repayment—not the shareholders or LLC members who own the entity.

You and the seller may agree that for additional security, nonowners will sign or guarantee the note. Here is a list of the most likely candidates:

- **The spouse of a person who is signing a note.** This allows the seller to reach joint or community property of the couple if payment isn't made, or even to reach the separate property of the spouse who is making the guarantee.
- **The owners of the corporation or LCC that's buying the business.** Unless these shareholders or LLC members personally guarantee the note, they won't be personally responsible for repaying it. Without their guarantee the seller can only look to the entity and its assets to satisfy the debt.
- **A signer's deep-pocket friend or relative who's willing to help out.** The seller may find this useful if the signer has limited financial means or a checkered credit history.

In Clause 13 (Promissory Note) of your sales agreement (described in Chapter 13), you should list the names of everyone who will be required to sign or guarantee the promissory note. Also, see Chapter 8 for additional discussion of these issues.

Security Interest

To further assure the seller that the debt you owe will be fully paid, you can agree that the seller will retain a security interest (lien) on your property. This typically consists of a security interest in the assets of the business, created by using a security agreement and UCC Financing Statement as described below. The security interest will allow the seller to take or sell the property that's been pledged as security if the debt isn't paid as promised.

The security agreement and UCC Financing Statement won't work for real estate. To create a lien on real estate, you'll need to give the seller a mortgage or deed of trust, which the seller will then record with the appropriate land records office. A seller will be especially interested in getting a lien on real estate if you're buying a service business that doesn't have much in the way of tangible personal property that would otherwise be meaningful security.

Real estate in which the seller acquires a security interest doesn't have to be owned or used by the business. It can, for example, be your home—though in that case, the lien is likely to take the form of a second mortgage or second deed of trust. Because of variations in state laws and the need to meet subtle technical requirements, you and the seller should consult a lawyer or title insurance company for guidance on creating a valid real estate lien.

See Chapter 13, Clauses 14 and 15 (Security for Payment), for information on how to provide in your sales agreement for the granting of a security interest.

 TIP

The seller may suggest that you provide term life insurance as a backup. This would involve your taking out a term life insurance policy that will cover the promissory note in case you die before paying off the debt. Whether this is a reasonable request depends on how much such insurance would cost you.

Acceleration Clause

Most sellers expect to include an acceleration clause in the promissory note. An acceleration clause states that if you don't make a required payment within a specified number of days after it becomes due, the seller can immediately demand payment of the entire remaining balance (in other words, accelerate the due date of the note). And if you still don't pay, the seller can sue right away for the full amount owed.

Without an acceleration clause, the seller would have to sue you each time an installment payment was missed or wait until all payments were missed and then sue for the full amount. Either would be burdensome for the seller. The promissory note form in this book contains an acceleration clause. If you want to see whether you can get away without one, you can try leaving it out of your first draft of the promissory note and see how the seller responds.

CAUTION

You may have to pay for the seller's legal help if you default. The promissory note says that you'll pay the seller's court costs and lawyer's fees if the seller has to sue you to collect the note—see the clause called Collection Costs (Attorney Fees). Costs and legal fees can quickly add up, which means that you can be find yourself even more deeply in debt if you fail to make the payments on time. You can try deleting this clause, but the seller will probably balk.

Installment Payment Plans

Typically, you'll agree to pay the seller the same amount each month for a specified number of months, with part of each payment going to interest and the rest to reducing the amount owed (principal). This is the same way most people pay off a home mortgage, except that in a business sale the seller will probably want a shorter repayment term than most mortgages, such as three to five years. When you make the last payment, the note's principal and interest are fully paid. In legal and accounting jargon, this type of loan is said to be fully amortized over the period that the payments are made. Amortization calculators, available online and in numerous software packages, can quickly determine how much you must pay each month and for how long, under various payment scenarios.

The promissory note in this book provides for amortized monthly payments. Repayment plans other than the amortization method are also available—though they're used less often, because sellers and buyers generally prefer regular monthly payments. See "Alternative Repayment Methods," below, for details.

SEE AN EXPERT

When to use a professional. As with other key documents used in the sale of a business, it's prudent to have a lawyer or tax professional review the form of the promissory note, especially if the terms of the note are unusual or you're not sure about the legal or tax effect of the language you're using.

Promissory Note Form

Below is a sample promissory note form that provides for amortized monthly payments.

FORM

Where to find the forms. If you're reading a print copy of this book, you'll find a copy of the Promissory Note on the CD-ROM at the back. If you're using an ebook version, you can download the note on the Nolo website; the link is included in Appendix A.

Instructions for Promissory Note

Here's are instructions referring to each of the numbered paragraphs in the promissory note explaining how to complete the note.

Promissory Note
(Amortized Monthly Payments)

1. Names
Buyer: _Georgetown West, Inc., a Florida Corporation_

Seller: _Burgundy Associates LLC, a Florida Limited Liability Company_

2. Promise to Pay
For value received, Buyer promises to pay Seller $ _50,000_ and interest at the
yearly rate of _8_ % on the unpaid balance as specified below. Payments will be
made to Seller at _123 Center Street, Miami, Florida_
or such other place as Seller may designate.

3. Monthly Installments
Buyer will pay _36_ monthly installments of $ _1,566.82_ each.

4. Date of Installment Payments
Buyer will make an installment payment on the _first_ day of each month
beginning _April 1, 20xx_ , until the principal and interest have been paid in
full, which will be no later than _March 1, 20xx_ .

5. Application of Payments
Payments will be applied first to interest and then to principal.

6. Prepayment
Buyer may prepay all or any part of the principal without penalty.

7. Loan Acceleration
If Buyer is more than _30_ days late in making any payment, Seller may
declare that the entire balance of unpaid principal is due immediately, together with
the interest that has accrued.

8. Security
(a) Buyer agrees that until the principal and interest owed under this promissory note
are paid in full, this note will be secured by a security agreement and Uniform
Commercial Code Financing Statement giving Seller a security interest in the
equipment, fixtures, inventory, and accounts receivable of the business known as
Gold Star Bakery .

(b) Buyer also agrees that until the principal and interest owed under this promissory note are paid in full, this note will be secured by a mortgage covering the real estate commonly known as _345 Wilson Road, Miami, Florida_

_____ and more fully described as follows: _Lot 35, Tyler and Williams Subdivision, City of Miami, Dade County, Florida_ .

9. Collection Costs (Attorney Fees)

If Seller prevails in a lawsuit to collect on this note, Buyer will pay Seller's costs and lawyers' fees in an amount the court finds to be reasonable.

10. Governing Law

This note will be governed by and construed in accordance with the laws of the state of _____Florida_____ .

Buyer

Georgetown West, Inc.

a _Florida Corporation_

By: _George Allen_

Printed name: _George Allen_

Title: _President_

Address: _789 Main Street, Miami,_

Florida

Dated: _March 1, 20xx_

Guarantors

We personally guarantee payment of the above note, jointly and severally.

Signature: _Jeffery Peterson_   Signature: _Angie Mason_

Printed name: _Jeffery Peterson_   Printed name: _Angie Mason_

Address: _678 Elwood Blvd._   Address: _234 Arrow Court_

Miami, Florida   _Miami, Florida_

Dated: _March 1, 20xx_   Dated: _March 1, 20xx_

1. Names

Insert the names and addresses of the buyer (first blank) and seller (second blank). See Chapter 12 for a discussion of how to identify the seller and buyer in the sales agreement and related documents.

2. Promise to Pay

In the first blank, insert the principal amount that's owed. You may have to fill in the amount on the day of closing if the promissory note balance will be affected by price adjustments described in your sales agreement. In the second blank, fill in the annual interest rate. In the third blank, fill in the address where the buyer is to send payments.

The phrase "For value received" in this paragraph is legal jargon meaning that you have received something from the seller in exchange for your promise to pay money—a legal requirement in every promissory note.

3. Monthly Installments

Insert the number of monthly payments you'll make to repay the loan and the amount of each installment. If you know the principal amount, the interest rate, and the number of years that payments will be made, you can consult an amortization calculator or schedule to arrive at the monthly payment. Use Intuit's *Quicken* program, or any similar program, to quickly calculate the amount of each installment. Computer-generated amortization schedules

can also tell you what portion of a payment is principal and what portion is interest. At the beginning of the loan repayment period, the interest portion will be relatively high, but it will decline as you continue to make payments.

4. Date of Installment Payments

Insert the day of the month when payments will be made, the date the first payment is due, and the date by which the principal and interest must be repaid in full. For example, if the business is sold on July 15, 2008, you might provide for payments to be made on the 15th of each month, with the first payment due on August 15, 2008.

5. Application of Payments

You don't need to insert anything here. Each payment automatically goes to pay accrued interest first. The rest goes toward the remaining principal.

6. Prepayment

You don't need to insert anything here. This clause allows you to prepay the money owed —that is, pay all or part of the principal in advance. By prepaying, you can cut down on the total amount of interest to be paid.

7. Loan Acceleration

It's typical in a promissory note to provide that if a payment is late by more than a specified number of days, the lender can declare the entire unpaid balance due. As discussed above, this is called an "acceleration clause." Fill in the number of days after the payment due date that will trigger acceleration. Thirty days is often appropriate, but you may be able to negotiate a longer period.

Alternative Repayment Methods

In certain circumstances, you and the seller may opt for a repayment plan that's different from the typical amortization method. For example, if you're anxious to preserve cash during the early days of taking over the business, you may propose one of the following repayment methods:

- **Equal monthly payments—large final balloon payment.** You make equal but relatively modest monthly payments of principal and interest for a set period of time, such as three to five years. These payments are not enough to pay off (or fully amortize) the note. Instead, after making the last monthly payment, you must still make one final larger payment, called a balloon payment, to pay off the balance. This type of plan may seem appealing but, after getting used to making relatively modest payments, you may find it hard to suddenly come up with a large payment. Anticipating this, a seller may be reluctant to accept a balloon payment note.

- **Payments of interest only—large final balloon payment of principal.** To keep monthly payments even lower, you pay interest only (no principal) at specified intervals, such as monthly. At the end of the loan term, you make a very large balloon payment to cover the entire principal and any remaining interest. The seller is likely to see this as even chancier and less advisable than a plan of equal monthly payments with a balloon payment.

- **Single payment of principal and interest.** You make no monthly payments, but instead pay off the note at a specified date in one payment that includes the entire principal amount and the accrued interest. Most sellers prefer receiving installment payments—and most buyers prefer paying over time, rather than having the balloon payment looming over their heads.

8. Security

This portion of the promissory note is related to the security (lien) arrangements that you and the seller have agreed to.

Delete both paragraphs (a) and (b) if the note is unsecured, meaning that you haven't given the seller a lien on or security interest in any property.

Retain the first paragraph (a) if you're giving the seller a security interest in business property. Insert the name of the business. You can use one of the Security Agreement forms found later in this chapter. Then the seller should complete a Uniform Commercial Code (UCC) Financing Statement, which can be recorded (filed) with the appropriate state or county office. When you pay off the note, the seller must give you an official discharge of the Financing Statement to file at the same place where the Financing Statement was filed.

Retain the second paragraph (b) if you're giving the seller a lien on real estate. Indicate whether this will be done by a mortgage or a deed of trust. (The practice varies from state to state.) Finally, insert the address and the legal description of the real estate as found in your deed or title insurance policy.

SEE AN EXPERT

Have a lawyer prepare the mortgage or deed of trust. Because of the technical intricacies of real estate titles, it's best to have an expert draft the mortgage or deed of trust that will secure the promissory note. After the note has been signed, the seller will record the mortgage or deed of trust at the appropriate land records office. When the note is paid, the seller should remove the lien (security interest) by giving you a discharge of the mortgage or deed of trust, to be recorded where the original document was recorded.

9. Collection Costs (Attorney Fees)

Nothing needs to be filled in here. This clause requires you to pay the seller's reasonable costs and attorney fees if the seller takes you to court to collect on the note and wins the lawsuit. As suggested above, you can try deleting this clause from the first draft, and see if the seller insists on it.

10. Governing Law

Insert the name of the state where the business is located. For details on this standard clause, see Chapter 16.

11. Signature and Guarantee

Only you and the guarantors, if any, sign the promissory note. The seller does not sign it. See Chapter 17 for suggested signature formats for documents such as a promissory note.

As noted above, if you're a sole proprietor or partner and sign the note, you'll be personally liable for repaying it. But if the buyer is a corporation or an LLC, you and any owners of the entity won't be personally liable. For that reason, the seller may insist on guarantors signing the promissory note. See the earlier discussion of guarantors, and also Chapter 13, which covers guarantees by entity owners, spouses, and others.

The Security Agreement

In addition to getting your personal promise and possibly the promise of guarantors to make payments under a promissory note, the seller will likely want to keep a lien (security interest) on the assets of the business, such as equipment and inventory. This will allow the seller to take back those assets if you start to miss the agreed payment dates. You and the seller can use a security agreement, like the ones that follow, to give the seller a lien. There are two different security agreements shown here—one for an asset sale and one for an entity sale.

These security agreements are separate from your sales agreement, but the sales agreement should refer to them and state generally what your arrangements are. These arrangements are covered in Clause 14 or 15 as described in Chapter 13.

> **CAUTION**
>
> **You can't use a security agreement to place a lien on real estate.** For that you'll need a mortgage or deed of trust, and this book does not cover those forms of security. If you're granting the seller a lien on real estate, you'll definitely want to see a lawyer for help.

Security Agreement Form for Asset Sale

Here is a form of security agreement you can use for an asset sale.

 FORM

Where to find the forms. If you're reading a print copy of this book, you'll find a copy of the Security Agreement (Asset Sale) on the CD-ROM at the back. If you're using an ebook version, you can download the agreement on the Nolo website; the link is included in Appendix A.

Instructions for Security Agreement (Asset Sale)

These instructions, and the form above, are for a security agreement used in an asset sale.

1. Names and Secured Property

Insert the names of the buyer (first blank) and seller (second blank). See Chapter 12 for a discussion of how to identify the parties in the sales agreement and related documents.

In the form, "Secured Property" means the property as to which the seller is obtaining a lien. The language in the form is merely a suggestion. The scope of the property covered by the lien is a matter of negotiation between you and the seller. The seller, of course, would like a broad lien but, at the very least, will probably expect a lien on the tangible personal property that you're buying. You can use an attachment like the

Security Agreement for Asset Sale

1. Names and Secured Property

Georgetown West Inc., a Florida Corporation , Buyer, grants to

Burgundy Associates LLC, a Florida Limited Liability Company , Seller,

a continuing security interest in the following property (the "Secured Property"),
which consists of:

  A. The property listed in Attachment _A_ , and

  B. Any additional tangible personal property that Buyer now owns or later
     acquires in connection with Buyer's business, including replacement inventory.

2. Security for Promissory Note

Buyer is granting this security interest to secure performance of a promissory note
that Buyer executed on _March 1, 20xx_ as partial payment for certain business
assets. The promissory note obligates Buyer to pay Seller $ _50,000_ with
interest at the rate of _8_ % a year, on the terms stated in the promissory note.

3. Financing Statement and Other Documents

Concurrently with the execution of this Security Agreement, Seller will have the right
to file a UCC Financing Statement. Buyer will sign any other documents that Seller
reasonably requests to protect Seller's security interest in the Secured Property.

4. Use and Care of the Secured Property

Until the promissory note is fully paid, Buyer agrees to:

  A. Keep the Secured Property at _456 Charlotte Street, Miami, Florida_
     and use it only in the operation of the _Georgetown Donut Shop_
     business.

  B. Maintain the Secured Property in good repair.

  C. Not sell, transfer, or release the Secured Property unless Seller consents.
     Buyer may sell inventory in the ordinary course of Buyer's business but will
     reasonably renew and replenish inventory to keep it at its current level.

  D. Pay all taxes on the Secured Property as taxes become due.

  E. Insure the Secured Property against normal risks, with an insurance policy
     that names Buyer and Seller as beneficiaries.

  F. Deliver to Seller a copy of the insurance policy insuring the Secured Property
     and provide to Seller annual proof that Buyer has paid the premiums on the
     policy.

G. Allow Seller to inspect the Secured Property at any reasonable time.

5. Buyer's Default

If Buyer is more than ___ten___ days late in making any payment required by the promissory note or if the Buyer fails to correct any violations of Clause ___4___ within ___ten___ days of receiving written notice from Seller, Buyer will be in default.

6. Seller's Rights

If Buyer is in default, Seller may exercise the remedies contained in the Uniform Commercial Code for the State of _____Florida_____ and any other remedies legally available to Seller. Seller may, for example:

   A. Remove the Secured Property from the place where it is located.

   B. Require Buyer to assemble the Secured Property and make it available to Seller at a place designated by Seller that is reasonably convenient to Buyer and Seller.

   C. Sell or lease the Secured Property, or otherwise dispose of it.

7. Notice to Buyer

Seller will give Buyer at least ___ten___ days' notice of when and where the Secured Property will be sold, leased, or otherwise disposed of. Any notice required here or by statute will be deemed given to Buyer if sent by first-class mail to Buyer at the following address: _789 Main Street, Miami, Florida_____.

8. Entire Agreement

This is the entire agreement between the parties concerning Seller's security interest in the Secured Property. It replaces and supersedes any and all oral agreements between the parties, as well as any prior writings on that subject.

9. Successors and Assignees

This agreement binds and benefits the heirs, successors, and assignees of the parties.

10. Governing Law

This agreement will be governed by and construed in accordance with the laws of the State of _____Florida_____.

11. Modification

This agreement may be modified only by a written amendment signed by both parties.

12. Waiver

If either party waives any provision of this agreement at any time, that waiver will only be effective for the specific instance and purpose for which that waiver was given. If either party fails to exercise or delays exercising any of its rights or remedies under this agreement, that party retains the right to enforce that term or provision at a later time.

13. Severability

If a court determines that a provision in this agreement is invalid or not enforceable, that determination will affect only that provision. The provision will be modified only to the extent necessary to make it valid and enforceable. The rest of the agreement will be unaffected.

Seller	Buyer
Burgundy Associates LLC	Georgetown West, Inc.
a Florida Limited Liability Company	a Florida Corporation
By: _Cheryl Jackson_	By: _George Allen_
Printed name: Cheryl Jackson	Printed name: George Allen
Title: Member	Title: President
Address: 123 Center Street	Address: 789 Main Street
Miami, Florida	Miami, Florida
Dated: March 1, 20xx	Dated: March 1, 20xx

one suggested for a Bill of Sale (Chapter 19) to list those assets.

The lien may cover furniture, fixtures, equipment, supplies, inventory, and even accounts receivable. It can cover not only what you receive from the seller, but also other property that you now own or later acquire in connection with the business. Depending on what you and seller agree to, you can expand the suggested language of the form and the attachment. A broad description of the "Secured Property" could, for example, look like this in your security agreement:

> All of Buyer's goods, equipment, fixtures, inventory, accounts receivable, and general intangibles, whether currently owned by Buyer or acquired later.

2. Security for Promissory Note

In the first blank, fill in the date you're signing the promissory note. Then insert the amount of the promissory note and the interest rate.

3. Financing Statement and Other Documents

You don't need to insert anything in this paragraph. It confirms that the seller has the right to file a Uniform Commercial Code form (called Form UCC-1) with the appropriate governmental agency in your state to let the public know that the business assets are subject to the seller's lien. Anyone

checking the public records—a bank's loan department, for example—will learn that the seller has a lien on the property described in the notice.

4. Use and Care of the Secured Property

Fill in the location where the secured property will be kept and the name of the business that will be using it. This paragraph of the security agreement also requires you to keep the secured property in good repair and to retain ownership of it. You also agree to pay taxes on the secured property and keep it insured.

5. Buyer's Default

This paragraph says that you'll be in default (that is, out of compliance with the security agreement) if you don't make the required payments or don't promptly correct any violation of the requirements listed in the preceding clause. The sample form says the default begins ten days after the seller sends written notice to you, but you can change this to some other number of days if you wish. When you're in default, the seller can exercise certain rights under Clause 6 (Seller's Rights), including selling the secured property.

6. Seller's Rights

This summarizes the seller's rights under the Uniform Commercial Code in the event you default on the security agreement obligations. Basically, the seller can seize the secured property and sell it to pay off your debt.

Fill in the name of the state where the property is located.

7. Notice to Buyer

This clause says that the seller will give you at least ten days' notice of when and where the secured property will be sold or otherwise disposed of if you default. Fill in the address where the seller should send that notice.

8-13. Standard Clauses

The remainder of the agreement contains standard clauses (technical contract clauses) —most of which are similar to those suggested for inclusion in the sales agreement. See Chapter 16 for an explanation of standard clauses.

The language about successors and assignees (Clause 9) means that if an individual buyer or seller dies, his or her heirs will be bound by the security agreement but will also get the benefit of its provisions. Similarly, if someone steps into the shoes of either party—whether the party is an individual or an entity—those newcomers (successors and assignees) will be bound by and get the benefits of the agreement.

The waiver provision (Clause 12) means that if the seller doesn't declare a default immediately if you're late on a payment or two, it won't be held against the seller, who will still be allowed to declare a default for late payments that occur in the future.

The only thing you'll need to fill in for the standard clauses is the name of the state whose law will apply to the contract in Clause 10.

Signatures

The seller and the buyer will both sign the security agreement. See Chapter 17 for suggested formats for the signature part of documents such as security agreements.

Security Agreement Form for Entity Sale

A security agreement for an entity sale will vary slightly from the suggested form shown above for an asset sale. Here's a form you can use as a starting point.

 FORM

Where to find the forms. If you're reading a print copy of this book, you'll find a copy of the Security Agreement (Entity Sale) on the CD-ROM at the back. If you're using an ebook version, you can download the agreement on the Nolo website; the link is included in Appendix A.

Instructions for Security Agreement (Entity Sale)

These instructions are for the security agreement used in an entity sale.

Security Agreement for Entity Sale

1. Names and Secured Property

_____ Pepper Pots and Pans Inc., a Florida Corporation _____ , the Company, the stock

of which has been sold to _____ Mildred Parsons _____ ,

Buyer, grants to _____ Mitchell Heath _____ , Seller, a continuing

security interest in the following property (the "Secured Property"), which consists of:

A. The property listed in Attachment __1__ , and

B. Any additional tangible personal property that the Company now owns
or later acquires in connection with its business, including replacement
inventory.

2. Security for Promissory Note

The Company is granting this security interest to secure performance of a promissory

note that Buyer executed on _____ September 1, 20xx _____ as partial payment for the

_____ shares of stock _____ of the Company. The promissory note

obligates Buyer to pay Seller $_____ 50,000 _____ with interest at the rate of __8__ %

a year, on the terms stated in the promissory note.

3. Financing Statement and Other Documents

Concurrently with the execution of this Security Agreement, Seller will have the right
to file a UCC Financing Statement. The Company will sign any other documents that
Seller reasonably requests to protect Seller's security interest in the Secured Property.

4. Use and Care of the Secured Property

Until the promissory note is fully paid, the Company agrees to:

A. Keep the Secured Property at _1250 West End Avenue, San Jose, California_
and use it only in the operation of the _____ kitchen supply _____
business.

B. Maintain the Secured Property in good repair.

C. Not sell, transfer, or release the Secured Property unless Seller consents. The
Company may sell inventory in the ordinary course of the Company's business
but will reasonably renew and replenish inventory to keep it at its current
level.

D. Pay all taxes on the Secured Property as taxes become due.

E. Insure the Secured Property against normal risks, with an insurance policy
that names the Company and Seller as beneficiaries.

    F. Deliver to Seller a copy of the insurance policy insuring the Secured Property and provide to Seller annual proof that the Company has paid the premiums on the policy.

    G. Allow Seller to inspect the Secured Property at any reasonable time.

5. Buyer's Default

If Buyer is more than __ten__ days late in making any payment required by the promissory note or if the Company fails to correct any violations of Clause 4 within __ten__ days of receiving written notice from Seller, the Company will be in default.

6. Seller's Rights

If the Company is in default, Seller may exercise the remedies contained in the Uniform Commercial Code for the State of _____California_____ and any other remedies legally available to Seller. Seller may, for example:

    A. Remove the Secured Property from the place where it is located.

    B. Require the Company to assemble the Secured Property and make it available to Seller at a place designated by Seller that is reasonably convenient to the Company and Seller.

    C. Sell or lease the Secured Property, or otherwise dispose of it.

7. Notice to the Company

Seller will give the Company at least __ten__ days' notice of when and where the Secured Property will be sold, leased, or otherwise disposed of. Any notice required here or by statute will be deemed given to the Company if sent by first-class mail to the Company at the following address: __620 Fillmore Circle,__ ____San Jose, California_____ .

8. Entire Agreement

This is the entire agreement between the parties concerning Seller's security interest in the Secured Property. It replaces and supersedes any and all oral agreements between the parties, as well as any prior writings on that subject.

9. Successors and Assignees

This agreement binds and benefits the heirs, successors, and assignees of the parties.

10. Governing Law

This agreement will be governed by and construed in accordance with the laws of the State of __California__ .

11. Modification

This agreement may be modified only by a written amendment signed by both parties.

12. Waiver

If either party waives any provision of this agreement at any time, that waiver will only be effective for the specific instance and purpose for which that waiver was given. If either party fails to exercise or delays exercising any of its rights or remedies under this agreement, that party retains the right to enforce that term or provision at a later time.

13. Severability

If a court determines that a provision in this agreement is invalid or not enforceable, that determination will affect only that provision. The provision will be modified only to the extent necessary to make it valid and enforceable. The rest of the agreement will be unaffected.

The Company

Pepper Pots and Pans Inc.

a   Florida Corporation

By: Charles Pepper

Printed name: Charles Pepper

Title: President

Address: 620 Fillmore Circle

San Jose, California

Dated: September 1, 20xx

Buyer

a

By: Mitchell Heath

Printed name: Mitchell Heath

Title:

Address: 891 South Central Avenue

San Jose, California

Dated: September 1, 20xx

1. Names and Secured Property

In an entity sale (in which one or more people are selling their shares of corporate stock or their membership interests in an LLC), the seller will probably ask you for an escrow agreement, as described later in this chapter. In addition, the seller may want a security agreement. If so, you'll need to use a slightly different security agreement form from the one provided for asset sales, because the entity itself, which owns the assets of the business, will be granting the security interest to the seller.

In the opening paragraph, you'll need to insert the names of the entity that's being sold (the corporation or the LLC—for which the form uses the generic term "the Company") and the buyer and the seller. See Chapter 12 for a discussion on how to insert names at the beginning of a document.

In the form, "Secured Property" means the property as to which the seller is obtaining a lien. The language in the form is merely a suggestion. The scope of the property covered by the lien is a matter of negotiation between you and the seller. The seller, of course, would like a broad lien but, at the very least, will probably expect a lien on the tangible personal property owned by the entity at the time ownership of the entity is transferred to you. You can use an attachment like the one suggested for a Bill of Sale (Chapter 19) to list those assets.

The lien can cover all of the entity's furniture, fixtures, equipment, supplies, inventory, and even accounts receivable. It can also cover any property that the entity acquires later. Depending on what you and seller agree, you can expand the suggested language of the form and the attachment. A broad description of the Secured Property could, for example, look like this in your security agreement:

> All of the Company's goods, equipment, fixtures, inventory, accounts receivable, and general intangibles, whether now owned by the Company or acquired later.

2. Security for Promissory Note

The seller may want the entity to sign a security agreement so that if you fail to pay for the stock or LLC membership interest as promised, the seller can take back the assets of the entity. In the first blank, fill in the date the promissory note is being signed. In the next blank, fill in "shares of stock" if the entity is a corporation, or "membership interests" if the entity is an LLC. Then insert the amount of the promissory note and the interest rate.

3-13. Remaining Clauses

See above for a discussion of clauses for a security agreement for an asset sale.

Signatures

The seller and the entity that's being sold will both sign the security agreement. See Chapter 17 for suggested formats for the signature part of a document such as a security agreement.

The UCC Financing Statement

The security agreement is your acknowledgment that the seller has a lien on the business assets until the promissory note is paid in full. But the seller may be worried that, despite that acknowledgment, you may sell the business assets to some outsider who doesn't know about the lien. Although you will have violated your contract, the seller would probably be out of luck so far as regaining control of the assets is concerned, since the outsider had no knowledge that the seller still had an ownership interest in the assets.

To avoid that problem, in addition to the security agreement, the seller will surely want to prepare a UCC Financing Statement, and file it with the appropriate public agency in your state (often a division of the secretary of state's office). The lien then becomes a matter of public record, and third parties are assumed to know of its existence. If that seems confusing, think of it this way: The UCC Financing Statement serves the same function as the mortgage or deed of trust on your house, which is filed at a public office and lets everyone know that your lender has a lien on your house. A prudent third party buying business assets will do a UCC lien check, discover the seller's lien, and decline to buy the assets. If the third party fails to do this and acquires the assets, the seller's lien will be legally intact because it's a public record, and the seller can recover the assets from the third party as long as you still owe the seller money.

You'll find blank copies of the UCC Financing Statement and Addendum and instructions for completing them Appendix C and the CD-ROM at the back of this book, in case you have some reason to provide them for the seller—but it is the seller's responsibility to prepare and file the UCC statement.

Escrow Agreement for Entity Sale

In an entity sale, there's another technique the seller may want to use to protect himself or herself from a default on the promissory note. The seller may ask for an escrow agreement in which a third party—the escrow agent—hangs on to the stock certificates or LLC membership documents until the full sales price has been paid. This makes it easier for the seller to reclaim ownership of the business entity if you start to miss payments. Under this arrangement, if you default, the seller gets back the transfer documents from the escrow agent.

A real estate title company that routinely performs escrow services will usually be willing to act as the escrow agent for a modest fee. But you may not need a company to handle the job. You and the seller are free to choose anyone you feel is trustworthy. If one of you has a lawyer willing to perform the function, that person may be a good choice.

Below are sample escrow agreements you can use in an entity sale. If you're buying corporate shares, use the Escrow Agreement

Escrow Agreement for Stock Certificates

1. Names

_____ (Seller),

_____ (Buyer), and

_____ (Escrow Agent)

agree to the following escrow arrangements.

2. Delivery of Stock Certificates

Seller will deliver to Escrow Agent the following stock certificates for _____

_____ , a(n)

_____ corporation, endorsed in blank for transfer:

Certificate Number	Name of Transferor
_____	_____
_____	_____
_____	_____

3. Establishment of Escrow

Escrow Agent will accept and hold the stock certificates according to the terms of this agreement.

4. Delivery of Stock Certificates by Escrow Agent as Directed by Buyer and Seller, or by Court Order

Seller and Buyer agree that Buyer will be entitled to receive the stock certificates when all payments have been made to Seller under the promissory note that Buyer signed today in connection with purchase of the business. If Buyer defaults on that note, Seller will be entitled to a return of the stock certificates.

Escrow Agent, however, will not deliver the stock certificates to either Seller or Buyer except as directed by a distribution letter from both, or by a final arbitration award or court order as described below.

If Buyer and Seller furnish a signed distribution letter to Escrow Agent, Escrow Agent will deliver the stock certificates as the letter directs.

Similarly, Escrow Agent will deliver the stock certificates as directed by a final arbitration award or court order that is no longer subject to appeal or stay.

After delivery of the stock certificates to the Seller or Buyer, the party not receiving the stock certificates will have no further rights to them.

5. Rights When Buyer Is Not in Default

While the stock certificates are on deposit with Escrow Agent and as long as Buyer is not in default under the promissory note and security agreement signed by Buyer today, Buyer will have the full right to operate the business of the company but may not sell it or encumber its assets.

6. No Judgment to Be Exercised by Escrow Agent

The Escrow Agent will make no independent judgment about whether or not Buyer is in default.

7. Restrictions on Buyer

As long as any of Buyer's obligations stated in the promissory note or security agreement remain unsatisfied, the Buyer will not permit the corporation to participate in a merger or consolidation, or to issue any additional shares of stock or grant any stock option.

8. Termination of Escrow

The escrow will end when Escrow Agent no longer holds the stock certificates and the parties have paid Escrow Agent all amounts for which they are responsible. The parties will share equally Escrow Agent's fees.

9. Conduct of Escrow Agent

Escrow Agent will:

    A. Not be liable for any action taken by Escrow Agent in good faith and without negligence.

    B. Be able to refrain from any action under this agreement if Escrow Agent knows of a disagreement between the parties regarding any material facts or the happening of any event contemplated by this agreement.

10. Additional Documents

The parties will, at the request of any other party, sign any agreements or documents consistent with this agreement that are necessary to consummate the transactions contemplated in this agreement.

11. Notices

Any required or permitted notice will be deemed given to a party if sent by first-class mail to the party at the address following the party's signature.

12. Successors and Assignees

This agreement binds and benefits the heirs, successors, and assignees of the parties.

13. Governing Law

This agreement will be governed by and construed in accordance with the laws of the State of _____Ohio_____ .

14. Modification

This agreement may be modified only by a writing signed by all parties.

15. Waiver

If any party waives any provision of this agreement at any time, that waiver will only be effective for the specific instance and purpose for which that waiver was given. If any party fails to exercise or delays exercising any of its rights or remedies under this agreement, that party retains the right to enforce that term or provision at a later time.

16. Severability

If a court determines that any provision of this agreement is invalid or unenforceable, any invalidity or unenforceability will affect only that provision. Such provision may be modified, amended, or limited only to the extent necessary to make it valid and enforceable.

Seller

Theodore Burger

Printed name: __Theodore Burger__

Address: __234 Pepper Pike__

__Cleveland, Ohio__

Dated: __October 2, 20xx__

Buyer

Sandra Mason

Printed name: __Sandra Mason__

Address: __67 Trenton Road__

__Cleveland, Ohio__

Dated: __October 2, 20xx__

Escrow Agent

Phyllis Chung

Printed name: __Phyllis Chung__

Address: __One Newton Tower__

__Cleveland, Ohio__

Dated: __October 2, 20xx__

Escrow Agreement for LLC Transfer Certificates

1. Names

Theodore Burger _____ (Seller),

Sandra Mason _____ (Buyer), and

Phyllis Chung _____ (Escrow Agent)

agree to the following escrow arrangements.

2. Delivery of LLC Transfer Certificates

Seller will deliver to Escrow Agent the following LLC transfer certificates for _____

Green Tree LLC _____ , a(n)

Ohio _____ limited liability company:

Certificate Number	Name of Transferor
101	Theodore Burger

3. Establishment of Escrow

Escrow Agent will accept and hold the LLC transfer certificates according to the terms of this agreement.

4. Delivery of LLC Transfer Certificates by Escrow Agent as Directed by Buyer and Seller, or by Court Order

Seller and Buyer agree that Buyer will be entitled to receive the LLC transfer certificates when all payments have been made to Seller under the promissory note that Buyer signed today in connection with purchase of the business. If Buyer defaults on that note, Seller will be entitled to a return of the transfer certificates.

Escrow Agent, however, will not deliver the transfer certificates to either Seller or Buyer except as directed by a distribution letter from both, or by a final arbitration award or court order as described below.

If Buyer and Seller furnish a signed distribution letter to Escrow Agent, Escrow Agent will deliver the transfer certificates as the letter directs.

Similarly, Escrow Agent will deliver the transfer certificates as directed by a final arbitration award or court order that is no longer subject to appeal or stay.

After delivery of the transfer certificates to the Seller or Buyer, the party not receiving the transfer certificates will have no further rights to them.

5. Rights When Buyer Is Not in Default

While the LLC transfer certificates are on deposit with Escrow Agent and as long as Buyer is not in default under the promissory note and security agreement signed by Buyer today, Buyer will have the full right to operate the business of the company but may not sell it or encumber its assets.

6. No Judgment to Be Exercised by Escrow Agent

The Escrow Agent will make no independent judgment about whether or not Buyer is in default.

7. Restrictions on Buyer

As long as any of Buyer's obligations stated in the promissory note or security agreement remain unsatisfied, the Buyer will not permit the limited liability company to participate in a merger or consolidation, or to issue any additional member or ownership interests, or grant any option for the purchase of such membership or ownership interests.

8. Termination of Escrow

The escrow will end when Escrow Agent no longer holds the LLC transfer certificates and the parties have paid Escrow Agent all amounts for which they are responsible. The parties will share equally Escrow Agent's fees.

9. Conduct of Escrow Agent

Escrow Agent will:

A. Not be liable for any action taken by Escrow Agent in good faith and without negligence.

B. Be able to refrain from any action under this agreement if Escrow Agent knows of a disagreement between the parties regarding any material facts or the happening of any event contemplated by this agreement.

10. Additional Documents

The parties will, at the request of any other party, sign any agreements or documents consistent with this agreement that are necessary to consummate the transactions contemplated in this agreement.

11. Notices

Any required or permitted notice will be deemed given to a party if sent by first-class mail to the party at the address following the party's signature.

12. Successors and Assignees

This agreement binds and benefits the heirs, successors, and assignees of the parties.

13. Governing Law

This agreement will be governed by and construed in accordance with the laws of the State of _____Ohio_____ .

14. Modification

This agreement may be modified only by a writing signed by all parties.

15. Waiver

If any party waives any provision of this agreement at any time, that waiver will only be effective for the specific instance and purpose for which that waiver was given. If any party fails to exercise or delays exercising any of its rights or remedies under this agreement, that party retains the right to enforce that term or provision at a later time.

16. Severability

If a court determines that any provision of this agreement is invalid or unenforceable, any invalidity or unenforceability will affect only that provision. Such provision may be modified, amended, or limited only to the extent necessary to make it valid and enforceable.

Seller

Theodore Burger

Printed name: _____Theodore Burger_____

Address: _____234 Pepper Pike_____

_____Cleveland, Ohio_____

Dated: _____October 2, 20xx_____

Buyer

Sandra Mason

Printed name: _____Sandra Mason_____

Address: _____67 Trenton Road_____

_____Cleveland, Ohio_____

Dated: _____October 2, 20xx_____

Escrow Agent

Phyllis Chung

Printed name: _____Phyllis Chung_____

Address: _____One Newton Tower_____

_____Cleveland, Ohio_____

Dated: _____October 2, 20xx_____

for Stock Certificates form. If you're buying LLC membership interests, use the Escrow Agreement for LLC Transfer Certificates.

FORM

Where to find the forms. If you're reading a print copy of this book, you'll find copies of the two escrow agreements on the CD-ROM at the back. If you're using an ebook version, you can download the agreements on the Nolo website; the links are included in Appendix A.

Instructions for Escrow Agreements for Entity Sale

These instructions apply to both escrow agreements for stock certificates and for LLC transfer certificates.

1. Names

Insert the names of the seller, buyer, and escrow agent. For more information on how to designate the parties at the beginning of an agreement, see Chapter 12.

2. Delivery of Certificates to Escrow Agent

In the first space, insert the name of the company. In the second space, insert the state in which the company was formed. Then, for each certificate being turned over to the escrow agent, list the certificate number and the name of the current owner of the interest represented by the certificate —in other words, the person who is selling

that interest. This person is referred to as the transferor.

3. Establishment of Escrow

Nothing needs to be inserted in this section. It establishes that the escrow agent will serve under the terms of the agreement.

4. Delivery of Certificates by Escrow Agent

This clause says that you can get the certificates when all payments have been made. Otherwise, the certificates are to be returned to the seller. The escrow agent will release the certificates only as directed in a letter signed by the seller and buyer, or in response to a court order or arbitration award. Nothing needs to be inserted in this section.

5. Rights When Buyer Is Not in Default

Even though you don't have the certificates yet, this section gives you the right to operate the business while you're not in default. You cannot, however, sell the business or allow a lien to be placed on its assets (other than any lien the seller already has). Nothing needs to be inserted in this section.

6. No Judgment to Be Exercised by Escrow Agent

This section says that the escrow agent will not determine whether or not you're in default. That's up to the parties, a judge, or an arbitrator. Nothing needs to be inserted in this section.

7. Restrictions on Buyer

This section says that until the promissory note is paid, you can't allow the company to be part of a merger or consolidation. Also, the company can't issue any more ownership interests (stock or LLC memberships) or grant any option for such additional interests. Nothing needs to be filled in here.

8. Termination of Escrow

This section says that the escrow arrangements will end when the escrow agent has delivered the certificates and been paid. The buyer and seller agree to split the escrow agent's fees. Nothing needs to be inserted in this section.

9. Conduct of Escrow Agent

This clause says that the escrow agent can be liable for actions taken negligently or in bad faith, but not otherwise. It also says the escrow agent won't act if the agent knows of a disagreement between the buyer and the seller relating to the escrow arrangements. Nothing needs to be inserted here.

10. Additional Documents

In this section, the parties agree that they'll sign any additional documents that are needed. Nothing needs to be inserted here.

11-16. Standard Clauses

The rest of the sections are standard contract clauses—most of which are explained in Chapter 16. In Clause 13 (Governing Law), you'll need to fill in the state where the business is located.

Signatures

See Chapter 17 for information about how to list the parties in the signature part of a document, such as an escrow agreement. ●

Bill of Sale, Lease Assignment, and Other Documents for Transferring the Business

I n this chapter, you'll find the documents you'll need to legally transfer ownership of business assets (in an asset sale) or to transfer ownership of an entity (in an entity sale) from the seller to you. Some of these documents will be mentioned in your sales agreement—especially in Clauses 24, 25, and 26.

The first five sections of this chapter cover the transfer of assets and the documents needed to do this. Because the business may own several different types of assets, you may need to use more than one document to fully accomplish this task, including:

- **Bill of Sale.** Normally, the seller will sign a bill of sale to transfer ownership of most tangible assets, such as furniture, equipment, and inventory. This chapter provides a sample bill of sale and instructions on how to complete one. It also lists property that can't be transferred by a bill of sale, including vehicles and real estate.

- **Statement Regarding Absence of Creditors.** As explained in Chapter 14, a handful of states still have bulk sales laws designed to assure the buyer of some types of retail and wholesale businesses that the assets are free from any claims of the seller's creditors. In this chapter, you'll find a practical way to verify that the seller has complied with any applicable bulk sales provisions.

- **Assignments.** In addition to transferring tangible assets, the business may need to transfer intangible assets such as leases, employment contracts, and agreements with customers and suppliers, as well as intellectual property such as trademarks, patents, and copyrights. If so, having the seller sign a bill of sale won't be sufficient. Specialized contracts—called assignments—are typically used to transfer such property. You'll find examples in this chapter.

This chapter also discusses documents needed for transferring ownership of an entity—a corporation or an LLC. This involves transferring the stock or LLC membership interests to you. In contrast to an asset sale, assignments of contracts usually are not needed in an entity sale. This chapter concludes with consent forms you can use if you have an entity that's acquiring a business.

Unlike the promissory note and other closing documents covered elsewhere, the documents described in this chapter normally won't be attached to the sales agreement. For the most part, these documents will be prepared after the sales agreement is signed, and then signed at the closing. The only exceptions are the consent documents discussed below; ideally, these consent documents should be prepared and signed before the sales agreement is signed.

FORM

Where to find the forms. If you're reading a print copy of this book, you'll find blank copies of the Bill of Sale, Statement Regarding

Absence of Creditors, Lease Assignment, and consent forms approving an entity's sale of assets on the CD-ROM at the back. If you're using an ebook version, you can download the forms on the Nolo website; the links are included in Appendix A. Samples are in the different sections below.

Bill of Sale: Asset Sale

SKIP AHEAD

When to skip ahead. If you're buying the stock of a corporation rather than its assets, or you're buying the membership interests in an LLC, you won't need a bill of sale. The entity will continue to own the business assets. You can skip ahead to the section called "Bulk Sales Compliance."

This section explains the various uses of a bill of sale and includes a sample form and instructions for completing it. The bill of sale is used in an asset sale to transfer owner-ship of assets to you. It is used primarily for tangible personal property (business equip-ment, for example), but in a few instances, it can include some intangible property such as a customer list. Your Sales Agreement, Clause 2, Sale of Business Assets (discussed in Chapter 12), describes the assets you're buying, and Clause 25, Documents for Transferring Assets (discussed in Chapter 16), may specifically call for the seller to provide a bill of sale.

Transfer of Tangible Property

By definition, in an asset sale, the business will transfer property (assets) to you. The seller can sign a bill of sale to transfer ownership of most types of tangible property, such as:

- furniture
- trade fixtures
- equipment and machinery
- artwork
- inventory
- signs, and
- supplies.

A bill of sale can also be used to transfer ownership of customer lists or the right to a phone number, even though, technically speaking, these constitute intangible property.

Transfer of Vehicles

A bill of sale can't be used to transfer ownership of cars, trucks, airplanes, and, in some states, larger boats, because these vehicles require registration. The seller will need to use a state-prescribed form to transfer ownership of vehicles—though there's no harm in also listing vehicles in the bill of sale so that you have a complete list. In that case, it's a good idea to have the bill of sale specify that the seller will also be signing state-required forms to transfer ownership of vehicles.

RESOURCE

Check your state department of motor vehicles for the custom and law in your state for transferring ownership of vehicles. To find the website for your state department of motor vehicles, look up your state's home page at www.statelocalgov.net.

Transfer of Land and Buildings

Occasionally, an asset sale of a small business will include the sale of real estate owned by the business and used for its operation—for example, the building in which a dry cleaner or print shop is located. A bill of sale can't be used to legally transfer real estate (land and buildings), because a bill of sale works only for tangible personal property. Land and buildings—while they may be tangible—are classified as real property (or real estate) and require special treatment.

Transferring real estate will require the seller to sign a deed that you record (file) at a designated county office to make it a matter of public record. You should also require the seller to provide a title insurance policy so it's clear that you're receiving clear title that isn't subject to any liens. The seller should also give you a recent survey so you can make sure there aren't any encroachments. And to meet your concerns about hidden environmental problems, you should require the preparation of at least a Phase I environmental review. (See Chapter 9 for more information about how to investigate these issues.)

The inclusion of real estate in an asset sale makes the sale more complicated and introduces elements of state law and local procedure that are not covered in depth in this book.

SEE AN EXPERT

See a lawyer or a real estate title company for help in having buildings and land transferred to you. Transferring real estate isn't difficult, but it is technical in that it typically requires a title search and the preparation and recording of a deed. Unless you have a great deal of experience in local real estate matters, you'll need professional help.

Transfer of Business Licenses and Permits

To complete your acquisition of the business, the seller may need to transfer a business license or permit to you or assist you in arranging for such a transfer or even the issuance of a new license or permit. Liquor stores, bars, and restaurants, for example, need licenses issued by a state or local regulatory agency. Since licenses and permits are a matter of state law and local ordinances, and because there's considerable variation from business to business and from place to place, this book provides no forms for this purpose. You and the seller will need to consult the agencies that issue any necessary licenses and permits for advice on what to do when you're buying a business. If you have trouble navigating the bureaucracy on your own, a lawyer may be able to cut through the red tape. See Chapter 9 for an overview of issues involving the sale of a business that requires a license or permit.

Bill of Sale Form

Below is a sample bill of sale form the seller can sign to transfer ownership of the assets of the business to you.

 FORM

Where to find the forms. If you're reading a print copy of this book, you'll find a copy of the Bill of Sale for Business Assets on the CD-ROM at the back. If you're using an ebook version, you can download the form on the Nolo website; the link is included in Appendix A.

Instructions for Completing a Bill of Sale for Business Assets

Here's how to complete the bill of sale.

1. Names

Insert the names of the seller and buyer as they appear in the sales agreement. See Chapter 12 for a discussion of how to identify the parties in the sales agreement.

2. Acknowledgment of Payment

If you won't owe part of the sale price after the closing (that is, you're making full payment for your business at the closing), omit the bracketed material dealing with the promissory note and security interest. Otherwise, retain the bracketed material. Chapter 18 covers promissory notes and security agreements.

3. Warranty of Ownership

This clause contains a warranty (guarantee) that the seller owns the assets that are being sold. This assures you that no one else has any rights, such as a partial ownership interest or a security interest, in the assets being transferred. If it later turns out that another person or company does have rights in the property, you can sue the seller for breaching the warranty and can get a judgment allowing you to collect money for any damages you suffer as a result of the breach.

If you won't be giving the seller a security interest in the assets, omit the bracketed material dealing with the security interest. Otherwise, retain the bracketed material. Chapter 18 covers security agreements.

Signatures

See Chapter 17 for suggested formats for signatures on contracts and other documents. The buyer does not sign the bill of sale. The seller does, and if the seller is a sole proprietorship in a community property state, his or her spouse should also sign. Where an entity is selling its assets and the owners are personally guaranteeing the warranty of Clause 3, they too should sign.

Bill of Sale for Business Assets

1. Names

Burgundy Associates LLC, a Florida Limited Liability Company , Seller, transfers to
Georgetown West, Inc. a Florida Corporation Buyer,
full ownership of the property listed in Attachment _____ to this Bill of Sale.

2. Acknowledgment of Payment

Seller acknowledges receiving payment for this property in the form of a cashier's
check [*optional:* and a promissory note secured by a security interest in the
property].

3. Warranty of Ownership

Seller warrants that Seller is the legal owner of the property and that the property is
free of all liens and encumbrances [*optional:* except for the security interest granted
today by Buyer to Seller].

Seller

Burgundy Associates LLC,

a _Florida Limited Liability Company_

By: _Cheryl Jackson_

Printed name: _Cheryl Jackson_

Title: _Member_

Address: _123 Center Street,_

Miami, Florida

Dated: _February 18, 20xx_

Attachment to Bill of Sale

Clause 1, Names, refers to a separate attachment for details on the property being transferred. Use a separate sheet (or sheets) of blank paper to list and clearly identify all tangible items being transferred. This attachment then is part of the bill of sale. See Chapter 11 for advice on preparing attachments.

List the names of the seller and buyer on the attachment exactly as they appear in the bill of sale. Next, clearly describe all of the property you are transferring to the buyer. The description of the assets should be as detailed as possible. It should include:

- a list of any furniture, fixtures, or equipment; in the case of equipment, it's often appropriate to include make, model, and serial number
- the amount of and detailed description of any inventory, and
- a full description of any other tangible assets the seller is transferring to the buyer.

Here are a couple of examples to get you started.

EXAMPLE 1: Attachment to Bill of Sale Describing Some of the Business Assets of a Small Restaurant

---

Attachment A to Bill of Sale
Dated _____

From _____ , Seller, to

_____ , Buyer

1 15-foot Polar Bear walk-in freezer, serial
no. 8526422

Attachment continued

---

1 Polar Bear reach-in freezer, serial no. 44986743

1 15-foot Polar Bear walk-in refrigerator, serial no. 883390E

1 Viking gas range, serial no. JUVS4590222

2 Cutlets Select meat slicers, serial nos. JCRO882 and JCR0883.

EXAMPLE 2: Attachment to Bill of Sale Describing Some of the Business Assets of a Small Used Bookstore

---

Attachment A to Bill of Sale
Dated _____

From _____ , Seller, to

_____ , Buyer

1. The inventory of books located in the store at 789 Howard Street
2. Two maple desks, chairs, and two lamps
3. Dell computer system (including printer, monitor, and software)
4. Sony telephone system
5. Panasonic fax machine
6. Office supplies
7. 26 maple book cases
8. Electronic cash register and credit card reader
9. Two window signs
10. Maple counter
11. One forklift
12. Three wall hangings
13. Three easy chairs in customer area
14. Two 16' x 20' oriental rugs
15. The customer list
16. All rights to the current phone number of the business.

You and the seller should initial the attachment to the bill of sale.

To make sure the property hasn't deteriorated between the time the parties sign the purchase agreement and the time of closing, you may want to make a final inspection of the property just before closing the sale.

Bulk Sales Compliance

A handful of states have bulk sales laws that require creditors to be notified of a business sale. (See "States With Bulk Sales Laws," below.) These are designed to prevent sellers from ordering large amounts of goods on credit, selling the business, and leaving the buyer—and the creditors—holding the bag.

Most states that still have a bulk sales law set a specific procedure to be followed that will assure the buyer that the seller's creditors won't have continuing claims against the assets after they're transferred. Usually, someone selling a business must give the buyer a list (sworn to under penalty of perjury) of all business creditors and the amount each is owed. Then, several days before the sale is closed—the exact number of days is specified in the state law—the buyer must send a notice to creditors so they know the business is changing hands and can arrange to have their claims paid at or before closing. If a proper notice is sent, the buyer knows that, after the closing, purchased goods are free from old claims by creditors of the seller.

Although bulk sales notices are not conceptually difficult, their preparation is governed by fussy state laws, and the notices must be sent (and in some states, published) in very precise ways. In California, for example, a seller needs to notify creditors by (1) filing notice of the sale at the county recorder's office, and (2) publishing notice of the sale in a general circulation newspaper in the county where the assets are located. The filing and publication must be done at least 12 days before the closing. Because the details differ from state to state, you'll need to check the relevant statutes where your transaction is taking place.

States With Bulk Sales Laws

Here is a list of states with bulk sales laws. For details, check your state statutes under "bulk sales" or "Uniform Commercial Code." See Chapter 2 for advice on doing legal research.

California	Maryland
Georgia	Virginia

Only buyers living in these states and buying a business with an inventory of goods will need to worry about bulk sales laws, so most likely these rules won't affect you. But if it turns out that your purchase is or may be covered, there's a simple, practical way that you may be able to avoid the cumbersome paperwork that's often required for compliance with a bulk sales statute. Here's how.

Step 1: Provide in your sales agreement that the seller will pay all outstanding debts of the business before closing or out of the closing proceeds. (See Chapter 14, Clause 16, Seller's Debts and Other Liabilities, for sales agreement language that requires the seller to pay all outstanding debts.)

Step 2: The seller pays the debts, as agreed.

Step 3: At closing, the seller signs a statement such as the Statement Regarding Absence of Creditors, shown below, and gives it to the buyer. With this assurance, you have less concern that the seller may not give notice to creditors to comply with the bulk sales requirements of your state's laws (if any). As noted above, there's some variation from state to state regarding the degree of formality that's needed when a seller verifies in writing at the closing that all debts and liabilities of the business have been paid. By getting the statement in the form of an affidavit—a written statement signed under oath in the presence of a notary public—the seller will almost certainly meet the formal requirements of every state.

SEE AN EXPERT

If you're in a state that still has a bulk sales notice requirement, check with a lawyer. Find out whether the seller's affidavit

will protect you. There may be legal reasons why the lawyer may recommend that other procedures be followed.

Statement Regarding Absence of Creditors Form

Here is a written statement the seller can give you verifying that all debts and liabilities of the business have been paid.

 FORM

Where to find the forms. If you're reading a print copy of this book, you'll find a copy of the Statement Regarding Absence of Creditors on the CD-ROM at the back. If you're using an ebook version, you can download the statement on the Nolo website; the link is included in Appendix A.

Instructions for Completing Statement Regarding Absence of Creditors

Here's how to complete the Statement Regarding Absence of Creditors form.

1. Sale of Business Assets

Fill in the name of the seller and the buyer. Chapter 12 offers suggested formats for naming the parties at the beginning of a legal document. Also, insert the name of the business being sold.

2. No Security Interests

Nothing needs to be inserted here. The seller is affirming that the assets being sold are not subject to any security interests or other liens.

3. No Creditors

Here the seller is affirming that all debts and liabilities of the business have been paid. If the business is an entity and not a sole proprietorship, the seller can also affirm that the owners of the business entity have no debts or liabilities that affect the assets or the right of the seller to transfer the assets. Simply insert one of the indicated choices, depending on the type of entity.

4. No Claims

Here the seller affirms that there are no claims against the seller that affect the assets or the seller's right to transfer the assets to you. If the business is an entity and not a sole proprietorship, the seller can make the same affirmation regarding the owners by inserting one of the indicated choices, depending on the type of entity.

5. Indemnification

Nothing needs to be inserted here. This clause says that if there are any liabilities or claims, the seller will make sure that you won't suffer any loss.

Signatures

If the seller is a sole proprietor, he or she will sign this form. If the seller is an entity, one of the owners will sign on behalf of the entity. Chapter 17 contains suggested formats for the signature portion of a document such as this.

The Statement Regarding Absence of Creditors form should be signed in the presence of a notary public who's authorized to notarize documents in your state.

Notarization

The form contains notarization language that helps protect you against a forgery. The notary will want proof of the seller's identity, such as a driver's license that bears a photo and signature. The notary can help the seller complete this section of the form and can make any changes needed to comply with local law and practice.

Finding a notary public shouldn't be a problem; many advertise in the yellow pages. Banks, real estate offices, title companies, and mail and shipping companies usually have notary services.

Assignments in an Asset Sale

In any sale, there may be contracts or rights that the seller assigns (transfers) to the buyer. The procedures for such assignments are different for asset sales and entity sales. This section deals with assignments in asset sales; the subsequent section deals with assignments in entity sales.

Statement Regarding Absence of Creditors

1. Sale of Business Assets

I make this statement in connection with the sale by _Burgundy Associates, LLC,_ _a Florida limited liability company_ , Seller, to _Georgetown West, Inc., a Florida corporation_ , Buyer, of the assets of the business known as _Gold Star Bakery_ .

2. No Security Interests

The assets that Seller is transferring to Buyer today by a Bill of Sale are free of all security interests and other liens and encumbrances, except for the security interest granted today by Buyer to Seller.

3. No Creditors

Seller has paid all debts and liabilities of Seller's business. There are no debts or liabilities of ☐ the Seller ☑ Seller's partners ☐ Seller's members ☐ Seller's shareholders that affect Seller's assets or the right of Seller to transfer the assets to Buyer.

4. No Claims

There are no claims or liens either disputed or undisputed against Seller, [*optional:* or ☐ the Seller's partners ☑ the Seller's members ☐ the Seller's shareholders] that affect Seller's assets or the right of Seller to transfer the assets to Buyer.

5. Indemnification

If, contrary to Clauses 2, 3, or 4 of this Statement there are any security interests or other liens, debts, liabilities, or claims that affect the assets, Seller will immediately remove the encumbrances or liens; pay the debts, liabilities, or claims; and indemnify, defend, hold harmless, and protect Buyer from any loss or liability arising out of such security interest, lien, debt, liability, or claim.

Burgundy Associates LLC,

a _Florida Limited Liability Company_

By: _Cheryl Jackson_

Printed name: _Cheryl Jackson_

Title: _Member_

Address: _123 Center Street, Miami, Florida_

Dated: _February 18, 20xx_

Certificate of Acknowledgment of Notary Public

State of _____

County of _____ ss }

On _____ , before me, _____

_____ , a notary public in and for said state, personally

appeared _____ , personally known to

me (or proved to me on the basis of satisfactory evidence) to be the person whose

name is subscribed to the within instrument, and acknowledged to me that he or she

executed the same in his or her authorized capacity and that by his or her signature

on the instrument, the person, or the entity upon behalf of which the person acted,

executed the instrument.

WITNESS my hand and official seal.

_____

Notary Public for the State of _____

My commission expires _____

[NOTARY SEAL]

Assignment of a Lease

Particularly in the sale of a small retail business, restaurant, or service business that caters to a walk-in trade, you'll probably want to continue operating the business at the same location. As part of your deal, you and the seller may have agreed that the seller will assign (transfer) the current lease to you.

If you're buying the assets of a business and you want to keep the lease, list the lease as an asset in Clause 2 (Sale of Business Assets) of your sales agreement. (See Chapter 12.) Then, at closing, the seller will need to assign the lease to you. As discussed in more detail in Chapter 9, this usually means that the seller will need to get the landlord's consent to assign the lease. In Clause 25 (Documents for Transferring Assets), you can list the lease assignment.

You can use the Assignment for Lease form shown below for assigning a lease and getting the landlord's consent. The form says that you'll be taking over the lease and that you'll pay rent and fulfill the other obligations of the seller under the lease. It also provides that the landlord will consent to the assignment (Clause 8) and provides a place for the landlord to sign at the end.

FORM

Where to find the forms. If you're reading a print copy of this book, you'll find a copy of the Assignment of Lease on the CD-ROM at the back. If you're using an ebook version, you can download the assignment on the Nolo website; the link is included in Appendix A.

Most of the clauses in this form are self-explanatory. Here's advice on completing some specific clauses.

In Clause 1, Names, insert the names of the seller, the buyer, and the landlord. See Chapter 12 for suggested formats for naming parties at the beginning of a document.

In Clause 2, Assignment, insert the date of your sales agreement, the date of the lease (which you should attach to the assignment), and the address of the premises the business leases.

In Clause 3, Effective Date, insert the date that you'll take possession of the leased space—probably the date of the closing.

Clause 6, Landlord's Certification, deals with the status of rent payments, the security deposit, and that fact the lease is still in effect. You'll need to fill in the date on which rent is paid and the amount of any security deposit held by the landlord.

Many of the remaining clauses are standard contract clauses as explained in Chapter 16.

For suggested formats for the signature portion of the assignment, see Chapter 17.

Assignment of Other Contracts

A lease may not be the only type of contract that you'll take over. The business may have contracts with customers, suppliers, employees, and service providers that the seller will be transferring to you as part of the sale. (See the discussion in Chapters 9, 12, and 19.)

When you're buying the assets of a business, it's always appropriate for the seller to make a written assignment of the business's contracts to you, because whoever signed the contract on behalf of the business you're buying (the entity or a sole proprietor) will no longer be involved. But before the seller assigns a contract, you and the seller will need to read it carefully to see whether there are any conditions, such as getting the other party's agreement to the assignment. You may even find that a contract states that it can't be assigned. In that case, you and the seller will need to see whether the other party is willing to waive that prohibition and allow an assignment anyhow. It's fairly routine to ask for this type of accommodation, but don't be surprised if the other party asks for something in return—for example, if a manufacturing company that you're buying has signed a contract in which it's agreed to sell widgets to a certain customer at $5.00 a unit and the contract prohibits assignment, the customer may agree to an assignment if the price is lowered to $4.50.

In preparing your sales agreement for an asset sale, you can refer to the contracts

Assignment of Lease

1. Names

This lease assignment is made by _____Frederico Ricci_____ ,
Seller, and _____Hal Morgan_____ , Buyer,
with the consent of _____Commercial Management LLC_____ ,
Landlord.

2. Assignment

For valuable consideration (as set forth in the Sales Agreement between the parties
dated _____January 15, 20xx_____), Seller assigns to Buyer all of Seller's rights in the
attached lease dated _____May 11, 20xx_____ , which covers the premises
located at _____123 Dolphin Avenue, Portland, Oregon_____ .

3. Effective Date

This assignment will take effect on _____February 15, 20xx_____ .

4. Acceptance

Buyer accepts this assignment and assumes the lease and all its terms. From the
effective date of this assignment, Buyer will pay the rent to Landlord and will perform
all of Seller's other obligations under the lease.

5. Condition of Premises

Buyer has inspected the premises and will accept possession of the premises in
as-is condition, subject to Landlord's maintenance obligations under the lease and
prevailing law.

6. Landlord's Certification

Landlord certifies that:

    A. Seller has paid all rent through _____March 1, 20xx_____ .

    B. Landlord is holding a security deposit of $_____5,000_____ , which Landlord
       will now hold for Buyer under the lease terms.

    C. Seller is not currently in default in performing any obligations under the lease.

    D. The lease has not been modified and it remains in full effect as written.

7. Reimbursement

Buyer will immediately reimburse Seller for the security deposit and any rent or other amounts that Seller has paid in advance under the lease for the period following the effective date of this assignment.

8. Landlord's Consent

Landlord consents to this assignment and to Buyer taking over all Seller's rights and obligations under the lease.

9. Release

Landlord releases Seller from liability for the payment of rent and from the performance of all other lease obligations from the effective date of this assignment.

10. Successors and Assignees

This agreement binds and benefits the heirs, successors, and assignees of the parties.

11. Governing Law

This agreement will be governed by and construed in accordance with the laws of the State of _____Oregon_____.

12. Modification

This agreement may be modified only by a writing signed by the party against whom such modification is sought to be enforced.

13. Waiver

If any party waives any provision of this agreement at any time, that waiver will only be effective for the specific instance and purpose for which that waiver was given. If any party fails to exercise or delays exercising any of its rights or remedies under this agreement, that party retains the right to enforce that term or provision at a later time.

14. Severability

If a court determines that any provision of this agreement is invalid or unenforceable, any invalidity or unenforceability will affect only that provision. Such provision shall be modified, amended, or limited only to the extent necessary to make it valid and enforceable.

Seller

Frederico Ricci

Printed name: Frederico Ricci

Name of Business: D/B/A Ricci Auto Repair

Address: 123 Dolphin Ave.

Portland, Oregon

Dated: January 22, 20xx

Buyer

Hal Morgan

Printed name: Hal Morgan

Name of Business: D/B/A Hal's Speedy Service

Address: 345 Central Street

Portland, Oregon

Dated: January 22, 20xx

Landlord

Commercial Management LLC

An Oregon Limited Liability Company

By: _Sherry Martin_

Printed name: Sherry Martin

Title: Manager

Address: One Barclay Plaza

Portland, Oregon

Dated: January 22, 20xx

being assigned in Clause 2, Sale of Business Assets (see Chapter 12), listing each contract on an attachment if there are more than a few. You can also put the Assignment of Contracts on your list in Clause 25, Documents for Transferring Assets. (See Chapter 16.) Where the consent of the other party to the contract being assigned is needed, you or the seller may make getting that consent a contingency in Clause 23, Contingencies. (See Chapter 16.) The Assignment of Contracts gets signed at the closing.

You can use an Assignment of Contracts form like the one shown below when there's no need to obtain the consent of the other party. If consent is required, you can you use a simple Consent to Assignment of Contract form such as the one shown just after the assignment form.

 FORM

Where to find the forms. If you're reading a print copy of this book, you'll find blank copies of the Assignment of Contracts and Consent to Assignment of Contract forms on the CD-ROM at the back. If you're using an ebook version, you can download the forms on the Nolo website; the links are included in Appendix A.

Most of the clauses in the Assignment of Contracts form are self-explanatory. Here's advice on completing some specific clauses.

In Clause 1 (Names), insert the names of the seller and the buyer. See Chapter 12 for suggested formats for naming parties at the beginning of a document.

In Clause 2 (Assignment), insert the date of your sales agreement. Use an attachment to describe each of the contracts that the seller is assigning to you. See Chapter 11 for information on preparing attachments.

In Clause 3 (Effective Date), insert the date that the assignment takes effect— probably the date of the closing.

Many of the remaining clauses are standard contract clauses as explained in Chapter 16.

For suggested formats for the signature portion of the assignment, see Chapter 17.

Assigning a contract doesn't automatically relieve the seller from obligations under the contract. To avoid continuing liability, the seller may be able to convince the other contracting party to agree to place additional language, such as the following, in the Consent to Assignment:

> Arco releases Frederico Ricci from all further liability regarding the contract.

If this language is included, the seller will no longer have to worry about continuing to be liable once the contract has been assigned to you.

Assignment of Intellectual Property

The assets you're buying may include intellectual property such as copyrights, patents, trademarks, service marks, and trade

Assignment of Contracts

1. Names

This assignment of contracts is made by _____Frederico Ricci_____,
Seller, and _____Hal Morgan_____,
Buyer.

2. Assignment

For valuable consideration (as set forth in the Sales Agreement between the parties
dated ___January 15, 20xx___), Seller assigns to Buyer all of Seller's rights in
the contracts listed in Attachment __A__ to this assignment.

3. Effective Date

This assignment will take effect on ___February 15, 20xx___.

4. Acceptance

Buyer accepts this assignment and assumes the benefits and obligations of the
contracts. From the effective date of this assignment, Buyer will meet all of Seller's
obligations under the contracts.

5. Successors and Assignees

This agreement binds and benefits the heirs, successors, and assignees of the parties.

6. Governing Law

This agreement will be governed by and construed in accordance with the laws of the
State of ___Oregon___.

7. Modification

This agreement may be modified only by a writing signed by the party against whom
such modification is sought to be enforced.

8. Waiver

If either party waives any provision of this agreement at any time, that waiver will
only be effective for the specific instance and purpose for which that waiver was
given. If either party fails to exercise or delays exercising any of its rights or remedies
under this agreement, that party retains the right to enforce that term or provision at
a later time.

9. Severability

If a court determines that any provision of this agreement is invalid or unenforceable, any invalidity or unenforceability will affect only that provision. Such provision shall be modified, amended, or limited only to the extent necessary to make it valid and enforceable.

Seller	**Buyer**
Frederico Ricci	*Hal Morgan*
Printed name: Frederico Ricci	Printed name: Hal Morgan
Name of Business: D/B/A Ricci Auto Repair	Name of Business: D/B/A Hal's Speedy Service
Address: 123 Dolphin Ave. Portland, Oregon	Address: 345 Central Street Portland, Oregon
Date: January 22, 20xx	Date: January 22, 20xx

Consent to Assignment of Contract

With regard to the ___automotive parts___

contract dated ___May 15, 20xx___ between ___Frederico Ricci___

___(Customer) and ___Arco Auto Products Inc.___

___(Supplier), ___Arco___

___consents to Customer's assignment of the contract to

Hal Morgan d/b/a Hal's Speedy Service. ___.

Arco Auto Products Inc.___

a(n) ___Oregon Corporation___

By: ___Todd Williams___

Printed name: ___Todd Williams___

Title: ___President___

Address: ___654 Oakdale Street___

___Portland, Oregon___

Dated: ___January 25, 20xx___

---

secrets. In an asset sale, the seller will need to assign these intellectual property rights to you, using a form like the one included in this book. You should specify in Clause 2 of your sales agreement (Sale of Business Assets; see Chapter 12) that intellectual property is among the assets being sold, and then list the specifics in an attachment to your sales agreement. You can list Assignment of Intellectual Property in Clause 25 (Documents for Transferring Assets in Chapter 16) as one of the documents to be signed at closing.

Since most small businesses are likely to have minimal intellectual property among their assets, a simple assignment like the one shown below should suffice.

 FORM

Where to find the forms. If you're reading a print copy of this book, you'll find a copy of the Assignment of Intellectual Property on the CD-ROM at the back. If you're using an ebook version, you can download the assignment on the Nolo website; the link is included in Appendix A.

RESOURCE

Businesses with extensive intellectual property need more specific assignment documents. If the assets you're buying include a significant amount of intellectual property, you'll need to create more specific assignment documents. In that case, consult either *Profit From Your Idea: How to Make Smart Licensing Deals* (for patents and trade secrets) or *Getting Permission* (for copyrights and trademarks), both by Richard Stim (Nolo). It also makes sense to confer with an intellectual property lawyer.

Most of the clauses in the Assignment of Intellectual Property form are self-explanatory. Here's advice on completing some specific clauses.

In Clause 1, Names, insert the names of the seller and buyer. See Chapter 12 for suggested formats for names at the beginning of a document.

In Clause 2, Assignment of Rights, insert the date of your sales agreement.

Note that Clause 4, Additional Documents, refers to an attachment. Use your best efforts to create as complete a list as you can of the intellectual property that you're buying.

Only the seller signs the assignment. See Chapter 17 for suggested formats for the signature portion of a document, such as an assignment.

The Assignment of Intellectual Property form includes a spot for notarization, which is optional. There is no requirement that copyright, trademark, or patent assignments be notarized. However, you may want to require that formality as an assurance that the seller's signature's is authentic.

RESOURCE

Transferring the right to use a fictitious name. In an asset sale, you may be taking over a business name that's not a trademark or service mark. If so, the seller has probably registered the name as a fictitious or assumed name. In that case, you'll need to check with the state or county office where the name was registered. Chances are they'll have a form the seller can use to cancel the registration. This should free up the name, making it available for you to pick up using a fresh registration form.

Transferring an Entity

If you're buying a corporation or LLC as an entity, the seller needs to transfer the entity to you at closing. This transfer doesn't require a bill of sale or the other transfer documents that are described above for an asset sale, because the entity continues to own the assets; transferring the entity gives the new owner full control over those assets. Typically, less paperwork is required to transfer ownership of an entity than to transfer assets in an asset sale.

This discussion of transferring ownership of a corporation or LLC assumes that all the owners of the entity have signed the sales

Assignment of Intellectual Property

1. Names

This Assignment of Intellectual Property is made by __Burgundy Associates LLC,__ __a Florida limited liability company__ , Seller, to __Georgetown West Inc., a__ __Florida Corporation__ , Buyer.

2. Assignment of Rights

For valuable consideration (as set forth in the Sales Agreement between the parties dated __February 15, 20xx__), Seller assigns to Buyer all of Seller's rights, title, and interest in any and all copyrights, patents, trademarks, service marks, trade secrets, and other related proprietary rights (the Intellectual Property) that constitute business assets of Seller, except for any Intellectual Property specifically excluded in the Sales Agreement.

3. Scope of Transferred Rights

This transfer of rights includes, but is not limited to, all registered, unregistered, or pending registrations, derivatives of the Intellectual Property, term extensions, renewals, or foreign rights associated with the Intellectual Property. For any trademark or service mark rights that are being assigned, Seller also transfers to Buyer any goodwill associated with such marks.

4. Additional Documents

Seller has made a good faith effort to list in Attachment 1 the Intellectual Property being transferred. To the extent that Seller has failed to list such Intellectual Property, Seller will cooperate with Buyer to sign further papers to accomplish the transfer of rights. Seller will also cooperate with Buyer in the processing of any Intellectual Property applications, registrations, or prosecutions and will sign any further papers required to evidence this assignment.

__Burgundy Associates LLC__

a __Florida Limited Liability Company__

By: _Cheryl Jackson_

Printed name: __Cheryl Jackson__

Title: __Member__

Address: __123 Center Street, Miami, Florida__

Dated: __February 22, 20xx__

agreement and that all of them are selling their entire interests in the business to you. This is the situation in the vast majority of small business sales. If this description doesn't apply to your purchase, you and the seller will need to carefully check any buy-sell agreement, shareholders' agreement, or operating agreement affecting the entity's owners to see if there are any limits on the sale of stock or LLC interests. Hopefully, you attended to this critical detail long before you signed the sales agreement to make sure that all necessary parties have consented to the deal.

Transferring Ownership of a Corporation

Very likely, when the corporation was created, stock certificates were issued to the owners (shareholders) as evidence of their ownership. If so, on the back of each certificate there should be a transfer clause. The shareholders should sign the back of the certificates in the indicated spot and deliver the certificates to you—or perhaps to an escrow agent to hold until you make all the required installment payments. It's possible, however, that in the rush to set up the corporation, no stock certificates were issued. In that case, the seller can take care of this step before closing. Through a written consent or resolution, the corporation's directors can authorize the issuance of shares and provide for the signing of stock certificates, which can then be transferred to you at the closing.

RESOURCE

For full information on corporate consents and resolutions, see *The Corporate Records Handbook,* by Anthony Mancuso (Nolo).

Transferring Ownership of an LLC

Transferring ownership of an LLC is similar to transferring ownership of a corporation. If the LLC has issued membership certificates that resemble stock certificates, each LLC member can sign the transfer clause. Otherwise, the seller needs to prepare a separate document called Assignment of LLC Membership Interests. Whichever method of transfer is used, make sure that the language specifically transfers full economic and membership rights.

RESOURCE

For more on LLC documentation, see *Form Your Own Limited Liability Company* and *Your Limited Liability Company,* both by Anthony Mancuso (Nolo).

After the Transfer

Once ownership of the corporation or LLC has been transferred to you, you have the right to select new corporate directors and officers, or new LLC managers, and to remove the current ones. Still, as part of the changing of the guard, it's appropriate at closing for current officeholders to give their written resignations to you. If the seller is going to work for the entity after the closing, the arrangements should be covered in an employment agreement or independent contractor agreement, as described in Chapter 20.

Finally, it's a good idea for you to change the entity's registered agent. The name and address of a corporation's or LLC's registered agent are kept on file at the state office where corporations and LLCs are registered (often the secretary of state's office). The idea is that there's a specific person authorized to accept notices and legal documents for the business. Chances are that when the corporation or LLC was set up, one of the owners was listed as the company's registered agent. Once you've bought the entity, you'll want to list yourself or a co-owner as the official contact person. Check with your state's business registration office for a form to use in changing the registered agent. The form may be available online at the office's website. You can locate the appropriate website by going to www.statelocalgov.net.

For more information on recommended procedures after an entity is transferred to you, see Chapter 22.

Assignments in an Entity Sale

Normally, you won't need a separate document to transfer an entity's contracts and intellectual property to you. These rights of the entity stay with the entity, and it will continue to get the benefit of those rights. But let's take a closer look at this subject.

Assignment of Lease

If you're buying a corporation, LLC, or partnership business entity, you usually won't need any special paperwork to transfer an existing lease. That's because the entity is already named as the tenant in the lease. But occasionally, a lease will say that if ownership of the entity changes, the landlord's consent is required for the entity to continue to occupy the premises. In that case, of course, you and the seller will need to arrange for the landlord to consent in writing.

Assignment of Other Contracts

With the sale of an entity (a corporation or an LLC), the seller ordinarily won't need to make a written assignment of business contracts as would be required in an asset sale. That's because the contracts are already in the name of the business entity. After the sale, the corporation or LLC will get the benefit of the contracts—and be bound by the contractual obligations—without any new documents being signed. But there can be an exception in a situation where a contract with the entity contains a clause that says that the consent of the other party must be obtained if the entity is sold. In that case, you and the seller obviously will need to honor that clause by getting the other party's consent. Assuming the consent is given, the contract won't need to be assigned, because the entity itself (the corporation or LLC) remains a party to the contract.

Another exception that will require additional written documentation involves contracts for a particular person to provide future services. For example, suppose that an ad agency has a contract saying that the owner will personally supervise a certain account. If that owner will no longer be on the entity's payroll after the business is sold, you and the seller will need to get the other party's consent to the continuation of the contract. (See Chapter 9 for more on the issue of transferring contracts in an entity sale.)

Assignment of Intellectual Property

An assignment for intellectual property owned by the company you're buying isn't normally needed in an entity sale, since the ownership of the intellectual property will remain in the corporation or entity that's being sold.

Your Entity's Approval of a Business Purchase

SKIP AHEAD

You can skip this section if the buyer is not an existing entity.

In either an asset sale or an entity sale, the buyer may be an existing entity. This would be the case, for example, if you've been doing business as a corporation, LLC, or partnership, and your company is now buying another business. It's also possible that you've created a new entity for the very purpose of acquiring the assets of another business or the ownership interests in that business. Generally, there's no legal requirement that the owners of your entity approve the purchase of another business— although there's the highly remote chance that your corporate bylaws, LLC operating agreement, or partnership agreement may require such approval.

Still, it's a good idea to have the owners of your entity formally approve the proposed sales agreement (in addition to having them sign the sales agreement itself). What's more, in the case of a buyer that's a corporation, it's also a good idea to have the board of directors formally approve the proposed agreement. Buying a business is a major event for any small entity, so it's good practice to proceed with a high degree of formality.

You can document the directors' approval of a sales agreement by having them sign a simple written consent. This avoids the need for a formal meeting where a vote is taken. Similarly, you can document the owners' approval through a simple written consent.

Here are some written consents that you can use, depending on the kind of entity you have. The consent form should be prepared and signed before your entity signs the sales agreement. It will not be attached to the sales agreement but should be kept with your entity's official records. Some of the sample sales agreements in Appendix B also have consents included at the end of the agreement that demonstrate slightly more detailed consent formats.

Directors' Consent to the Corporation's Purchase of a Business

We are all of the directors of _____ ,
a(n) [*list name of state*] corporation. We consent to the corporation's purchase of the
[business assets/entity ownership interests] of [*list name of business being purchased*]
on the terms stated in the attached sales agreement.

    The corporation's president is authorized to sign the sales agreement on behalf
of the corporation and to take such actions as the president deems necessary or
appropriate to carry out the terms of the sales agreement.

Dated: _____   Date: _____

Printed name: _____   Printed name: _____

Printed name: _____   Printed name: _____

Printed name: _____   Printed name: _____

Printed name: _____   Printed name: _____

Shareholders' Consent to the Corporation's Purchase of a Business

We own all of the stock of _____ ,
a(n) [*list name of state*] corporation. We consent to the corporation's purchase of the
[business assets/entity ownership interests] of [*list name of business being purchased*]
on the terms stated in the attached sales agreement.

    The corporation's president is authorized to sign the sales agreement on behalf
of the corporation and to take such actions as the president deems necessary or
appropriate to carry out the terms of the sales agreement.

Dated: _____   Date: _____

Printed name: _____   Printed name: _____

Printed name: _____   Printed name: _____

Printed name: _____   Printed name: _____

Printed name: _____   Printed name: _____

LLC Members' Consent to the Company's Purchase of a Business

We own all of the membership interests in _____,
a(n) [_list name of state_] limited liability company. We consent to the company's
purchase of the [business assets/entity ownership interests] of [_list name of business
being purchased_] on the terms stated in the attached sales agreement.
_____ is authorized
to sign the sales agreement on behalf of the company and to take such actions as
☐ he ☐ she deems necessary or appropriate to carry out the terms of the sales
agreement.

Dated: _____   Date: _____

Printed name: _____   Printed name: _____

Printed name: _____   Printed name: _____

Printed name: _____   Printed name: _____

Printed name: _____   Printed name: _____

Partners' Consent to the Partnership's Purchase of a Business

We are all of the partners in _____,
a(n) [_list name of state_] partnership. We consent to the partnership's purchase of the
[business assets/entity ownership interests] of [_list name of business being purchased_]
on the terms stated in the attached sales agreement.
_____ is authorized
to sign the sales agreement on behalf of the partnership and to take such actions
as ☐ he ☐ she deems necessary or appropriate to carry out the terms of the sales
agreement.

Dated: _____   Date: _____

Printed name: _____   Printed name: _____

Printed name: _____   Printed name: _____

Printed name: _____   Printed name: _____

Printed name: _____   Printed name: _____

RESOURCE

For more information on written consents, see *The Corporate Records Handbook* and *Your Limited Liability Company,* both written by Anthony Mancuso (Nolo).

FORM

Where to find the forms. If you're reading a print copy of this book, you'll find blank copies of the Directors' Consent to the Corporation's Purchase of a Business, Shareholders' Consent to the Corporation's Purchase of a Business, LLC Members' Consent to the Company's Purchase of a Business, and Partners' Consent to the Partnership's Purchase of a Business forms on the CD-ROM at the back. If you're using an ebook version, you can download the forms on the Nolo website; the links are included in Appendix A. ●

Documents for Noncompete and Future Work Commitments

When you negotiate with a seller for the purchase of a business, your discussions will very likely include the question of whether the seller will continue to have a future working relationship with the business, and the issue of the seller's agreement (covenant) not to compete with you. These topics are covered in detail in Chapters 8 and 15, and this chapter gives you the practical tools to document the agreements you make.

If the seller agrees to sign a noncompete, employment, or independent contractor agreement, you'll include language in your sales agreement referring to these agreements. Chapter 15 covers the basic functions of noncompete, employment, and independent contractor agreements and includes specific clauses stating that relevant documents will be signed at closing concerning these arrangements, with copies of the actual documents attached to the sales agreement. You may want to go back and reread Chapter 15 now, paying special attention to Clauses 21 (Covenant Not to Compete) and 22 (Future Services).

It's best to prepare any noncompete or future work agreement at the same time that you craft the sales agreement. Then there can be no doubt about what needs to be signed at closing to cover these important topics. These documents can be attachments to the sales agreement. See Chapter 11 for information about attachments.

SEE AN EXPERT

Get legal help with noncompete agreements and contracts covering the seller's future relationship with the business. As with the other important documents discussed in this book, have a lawyer look over all agreements dealing with noncompetition and future services. These documents may govern your relationship with the seller for years to come, so you want to make sure that they're as clear as possible and can be enforced if need be.

Covenant Not to Compete

It's quite possible that you won't want to buy a certain business unless the seller agrees not to compete with you for a certain period after the sale. A covenant not to compete, also known as a noncompete agreement, usually requires the owners of the business being sold (and sometimes their spouses who work in the business) to refrain from competing against the buyer (typically, for one to three years) in the geographic area where the buyer conducts business. Without a covenant not to compete, you take the risk that the seller will pocket your money and open up a competing business down the street, significantly reducing the value of your purchase.

This chapter explains how to prepare a covenant not to compete and includes a sample agreement. In working on the covenant, you and the seller will need to consider carefully:

- the kinds of work the seller can and can't do

- the geographic areas that are off limits
- the length of time the agreement applies, and
- how much you'll pay the seller for the covenant.

Limits on the Seller's Competitive Activities After the Sale

If the seller plans to remain active in the same line of work, he or she will want to tightly limit any covenant not to compete. For example, the seller may be willing to agree not to compete within ten miles of the business location—or perhaps within the same county or state—for two years after the sale. By contrast, you might prefer that the seller sign a five-year commitment prohibiting competitive activities in a ten-state area. The seller may balk at your suggestion, finding it too restrictive. You'll need to negotiate the details to arrive at a compromise.

Obviously, if the seller is retiring for good, planning to move to a different part of the country, or entering a completely different line of work, the terms of the covenant not to compete will not be contentious. But what if the seller's future plans are uncertain? The seller may want to keep open the possibility of doing some related work that may not really threaten the profitability of the business you're buying. For example, someone selling you a tile-laying business might want to later open a showroom that sells imported tile to professional installers.

You may conclude that the seller's opening of such a showroom, while related to the current business, would be essentially non-competitive.

The challenge, then, is to carefully define the type of work that will be off limits so that the seller has reasonable flexibility and you're adequately protected.

There are two broad ways to do this: One is to narrowly define the work that would constitute prohibited competition. The other is to start with a broad definition of the competitive work that's off limits, but then carve out an exception for the work the seller may want to do in the future.

To better understand these two approaches, let's look at the case of Len, who is selling his court reporting business to Consolidated Court Reporting LLC. As you may know, court reporters such as Ken generally use their stenographic skills in one or more of the following ways:

- They create a written record (transcript) of trials and other courtroom hearings.
- They create a written record of pretrial discovery depositions in which lawyers question the parties and witnesses who are expected to testify in court.
- They create closed-caption accounts of TV news broadcasts or real-time transcripts of speeches and lectures—typically displayed on an auditorium screen, on television, or on notebook computers. This work is intended primarily for the benefit of hearing-impaired people.

Let's now assume that Ken wants to keep open the possibility that after the closing, he can earn money by doing closed-captions and related work. Assuming the buyer is primarily interested in court and other legal-system-related parts of Ken's business, the noncompetition language can be approached in two different ways, as illustrated below.

Specifying the Prohibited Competition

> For five years following the closing, Seller will not, within Adams County, prepare transcripts of lawsuit depositions, trials, or other legal proceedings.

Under this formulation, Ken is free to do closed-caption and related work—as well as any other type of stenographic work that may become available in the future, as long as it doesn't involve legal proceedings.

Carving Out an Exception

> For five years following the closing, Seller will not, within Adams County, provide any court reporting or public stenographic services, except that he may without limitation provide closed-caption accounts for television programs and real-time transcripts of speeches, lectures, and similar events.

Although this formulation specifically identifies the work Ken can do after closing, it may in fact be a bit more restrictive, because it defines what Ken can do without violating the noncompete agreement but it does not

cover other possibilities. In the real world, the difference between the two approaches may be insignificant, but in theory at least, the first approach (specifying the prohibited competitive activities) could possibly open up some additional opportunities for Ken to earn money.

The clause illustrated above could be broadened a bit and afford more flexibility to Ken by adding a few more words:

> For five years following the closing, Seller will not, within Adams County, provide any court reporting or public stenographic services, except that he may without limitation provide closed-caption accounts for television programs and real-time transcripts of speeches, lectures, and similar events, and he may provide similar services that are unrelated to specific court cases.

If the seller is clear about his or her goals, as in the case described above, there may be situations in which you're willing to agree to the seller's plan to earn a living in a related, but not directly competitive, field of work. For example:

- If you're buying a restaurant, you may feel that it's okay for the seller to go into the catering business or to work as a chef for someone else in the area.
- If you're buying a business that helps companies set up and maintain internal computer networks or intranets, you may have no objection to the seller operating a business that

helps design websites for companies that plan to market products directly to the public or starting a business installing wireless networks in homes, coffee shops, and other locations.

- If you're buying a small manufacturing business, you may have no problem with the seller owning or working in a service business in the same field, especially if the seller agrees to feature your products.

The point is that even though the seller may want to do work that's somewhat related to the business you're buying—and even though the work would be done in the same geographical area as the business you're buying—it may not cut into your profits. You may be able to accommodate the seller to a reasonable extent.

RESOURCE

Allowing the seller to go into a related business sometimes can be a benefit to you. Let's say you're buying a restaurant, and the seller—following the closing—wants to open a bakery with a small café. You might be amenable to this if the seller agrees that the bakery will supply bread and pastries to the restaurant at a very favorable price.

Covenant Not to Compete Form

A sample Covenant Not to Compete form that you can use as a starting point is shown below.

 FORM

Where to find the forms. If you're reading a print copy of this book, you'll find a copy of the Covenant Not to Compete on the CD-ROM at the back. If you're using an ebook version, you can download the form on the Nolo website; the link is included in Appendix A.

Instructions for Preparing a Covenant Not to Compete

Here's how to complete a Covenant Not to Compete form.

1. Names

Fill in the seller's name, the name of the business, and the buyer's name as they appear in the sales agreement.

2. Background

In the first blank, choose the status that best represents the seller's association with the business being sold: owner, if the business is a sole proprietorship; shareholder, if the business is a corporation; or member, if the business is an LLC.

Then indicate whether the buyer is buying the assets or the business entity.

3. Payment

Fill in the amount of money you're paying the seller for the covenant not to compete. Remember that this payment is separate from the sale price. If you're signing a promissory note for all or part of the amount

Covenant Not to Compete

1. Names

I, _____ (Seller),

make this covenant not to compete with the business known as _____

_____ (the Business), which has

been purchased by _____ (Buyer).

2. Background

I have been ☐ an owner ☐ a shareholder ☐ a member ☐ of the Business.
Concurrently with my signing of this covenant, the Buyer is buying ☐ the assets of
the business ☐ the business entity.

3. Payment

I make this covenant in consideration of that purchase and of the further payment of

$ _____ that I have received from Buyer.

4. Noncompetition

For the next _____ years, I will not directly or indirectly participate in a

_____ business within

_____ miles of the current location of the Business named above. This

includes participating in my own business or acting as a co-owner, director, officer,

consultant, independent contractor, employee, or agent of a competing business.

In particular, I will not:

(a) solicit or attempt to solicit any business or trade from actual or prospective
customers or clients of the Business

(b) employ or attempt to employ any employee of the Business

(c) divert or attempt to divert business away from the Business, or

(d) encourage any independent contractor or consultant to end a relationship
with the Business.

5. Permitted Activities

It will not be a breach of this covenant for me to engage in any of the following

activities: _____

_____

_____ .

6. Breach

I acknowledge and agree that if I breach or threaten to breach any of the terms of this covenant, Buyer and the Business will sustain irreparable harm and will be entitled to obtain an injunction to stop any breach or threatened breach.

7. Governing Law

I agree that this covenant will be governed and construed in accordance with the laws of the State of _____ .

Signature: _____   Dated: _____

---

you owe for the seller's covenant, make it a separate promissory note—not part of the one for the balance of the sale price.

CAUTION

For the seller's agreement not to compete to be legally binding, you must pay the seller something of value in exchange for that promise. In legal parlance, this is known as consideration. As little as a few dollars will meet this technical requirement. In negotiating the figure, don't lose sight of the tax implications. You won't be able to deduct the payment immediately as a business expense; you'll have to spread the deduction over a 15-year period, even though the the covenant itself may not last anywhere near that long. For that reason, you'll usually prefer to keep the payment for the covenant as low as possible. But this is a complicated area of tax law, so check with your tax adviser to see how the tax rules apply to your particular situation. And see Chapter 3 for general information on the tax consequences of buying a business.

4. Noncompetition

Fill in the specific details of your agreement, including the type of business the seller is agreeing not to participate in and the geographic location (such as a particular metropolitan area) or scope, such as number of miles. You'll need to modify this if miles or geographic scope is not relevant—as might be the case with an Internet business, for example.

In some service or manufacturing businesses, one way to craft a noncompete agreement is to specify certain customers or clients who are off limits to the seller.

Also, in Clause 4 (Noncompetition), indicate the length of the agreement, such as three years. Ordinarily, you'll want the seller to agree not to compete for at least one year. Restricting the seller's ability to compete for up to three years is common. A court may invalidate a longer period unless it's truly necessary to protect your business. That can be hard to prove.

5. Permitted Activities

Spell out activities that the seller can engage in. If you're buying a bakery, for example, you might be willing to allow the seller to work for a company that distributes baking ovens and related equipment. It's part of the baking industry, but the seller's work wouldn't be a competitive threat to you.

Delete this clause if the seller has no plans to work in a related business and is unlikely to ever want to.

6. Breach

You do not need to insert anything here. This clause allows you to seek an injunction—an order that someone has to do something or refrain from doing something—if the seller violates the agreement or seems to be about to do so.

7. Governing Law

Usually, you'll fill in the name of the state where the business is located. See Chapter 16 for more information on Governing Law clauses.

Signatures

Only the seller will sign this covenant. See Chapter 17 for a suggested format to use when someone signs a document as an individual. Although you'll attach a copy of the covenant to your sales agreement, the seller won't sign it until the closing.

Contract for Employment

If the seller will be working for you as an employee, you'll probably want to prepare an employment contract and attach it to your sales agreement, as discussed in Clause 22, Future Services. (See Chapter 15.) The employment contract gets signed at the closing.

The basic terms of an employment agreement include the job duties, the duration of employment, the payment amount and schedule, benefits (such as health insurance), and a termination policy. Chapter 8 explains the legal ins and outs of employment agreements, including how they compare with an independent contractor relationship. The following sample employment contract shows many of the topics that can be addressed in an employment contract.

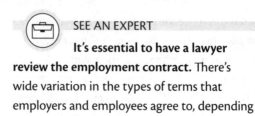 SEE AN EXPERT

It's essential to have a lawyer review the employment contract. There's wide variation in the types of terms that employers and employees agree to, depending

Sample Employment Contract

1. Names

This contract is between Vintage Valley LLC, an Illinois Limited Liability Company, Employer, and Marla Fenby, Employee.

2. Job Duties

Employer hires employee for the position of bookkeeper. Employee agrees to perform the following services for Employer: maintenance of all of Employer's income and expense records and preparation of reports and tax returns in consultation with the Certified Public Accountant retained by Employer.

3. Duration of Employment

The employment will begin on May 1, 2011 and end on April 30, 2012, unless terminated sooner as specified in this contract.

4. Compensation

Employer will pay Employee $5,000 each month.

5. Other Benefits

Employer will provide the following additional benefits to Employee:
Two weeks' paid vacation each year, and medical and health insurance as described in the Vintage Valley Employee Handbook.

6. Employer's Policies

Employee accepts Employer's policies as contained in the Vintage Valley Employee Handbook, which Employee acknowledges receiving.

7. Termination

If Employee does not satisfactorily perform the job duties described in Paragraph 2 of this contract or substantially violates Employer's policies as set forth in its Employee Handbook, Employer may terminate Employee's employment.

8. Confidential Information

Employee will not disclose or use at any time, except as part of the employment with Employer, any confidential information pertaining to the business of Employer. This includes, but is not limited to, Employer's sales and profit figures; its customer lists; its trade secrets; its relationship with its contractors, customers, or suppliers; and opportunities for new or developing business. Employee acknowledges the unique and confidential nature of this information and the irreparable harm that will be caused to Employer by its unauthorized use or disclosure.

9. Entire Agreement

This contract contains the entire agreement between the parties on the subject of employment. Any amendments require the written agreement of both parties.

10. Governing Law

This agreement will be governed by and construed in accordance with the laws of the State of Illinois.

11. Waiver

If any party waives any provision of this agreement at any time, that waiver will only be effective for the specific instance and purpose for which that waiver was given. If any party fails to exercise or delays exercising any of its rights or remedies under this agreement, that party retains the right to enforce that term or provision at a later time.

12. Severability

If a court determines that any provision of this agreement is invalid or unenforceable, any invalidity or unenforceability will affect only that provision. Such provision may be modified, amended, or limited only to the extent necessary to make it valid and enforceable.

Employer	**Employee**
Vintage Valley LLC	*Marla Fenby*
An Illinois Limited Liability Company	Marla Fenby
By: *Felice Randall*	678 Morton Blvd.
Felice Randall, Manager	Unit No. 2
345 Placid Road	Evanston, Illinois
Chicago, Illinois	
Dated: April 1, 2011	Dated: April 1, 2011

Personal Guarantee

In consideration of Employee agreeing to work for Vintage Valley LLC, I personally guarantee performance of all of the Employer's obligations in the above agreement.

Felice Randall

Felice Randall

on many factors, including the industry and the employee's position. Also, employment law continues to grow ever more complex. As a result, an employment contract needs to be a highly customized document. You want to make sure you don't overlook some subtlety that could cause a problem down the road. Be sure to get solid legal advice before you prepare and sign an employment contract.

CAUTION

If you're buying an entity (a corporation, an LLC, or a partnership), the entity will be the seller's employer. The seller may want you to personally guarantee payment of the wages promised in the employment contract. A guarantee provision is included at the end of the sample employment contract shown below. Just remember that if you sign such a guarantee, you place your personal assets at risk if the entity runs out of money.

Contract for an Independent Contractor

As part of the negotiations for selling your business, you and the seller may have agreed that after the closing, the seller will work for you as an independent contractor rather than as an employee. If so, you'll want to prepare an independent contractor agreement and attach it to your sales agreement. (See Clause 22, Future Services, in Chapter 15.) You'll sign the independent contractor agreement at the closing of your sale.

The differences between an employment relationship and an independent contractor relationship are explained in Chapter 8. One key difference is that if someone works for you as an independent contractor, you don't withhold income taxes from that person's pay. And you're not responsible for withholding or paying any part of the Social Security and Medicare taxes. Taxes are solely the independent contractor's responsibility.

RESOURCE

Recommended reading on independent contractors. For in-depth coverage of this subject, see *Consultant & Independent Contractor Agreements*, by Stephen Fishman (Nolo). The book contains numerous agreements covering different situations.

SEE AN EXPERT

Work with a lawyer to develop your independent contractor agreement. As with an employment agreement, the law can be complicated. You don't want to leave out anything that can be important to you—or phrase something in a way that can cause big problems later. So make sure you get an experienced lawyer involved in the drafting process.

Independent Contractor Agreement Form

A sample Independent Contractor Agreement form that you can use as a starting point is shown below.

FORM

Where to find the forms. If you're reading a print copy of this book, you'll find a copy of the Independent Contractor Agreement on the CD-ROM at the back. If you're using an ebook version, you can download the agreement on the Nolo website; the link is included in Appendix A.

Instructions for Completing the Independent Contractor Agreement

Here's how to complete the independent contractor agreement.

1. Names

Fill in your company's name (the Client) and the seller's name (the Contractor). See Chapter 12 for suggested formats to use in naming the parties at the beginning of an agreement.

2. Services to be Performed

Provide a detailed description of the services the contractor will be providing.

> **EXAMPLE:**
>
> Contractor will advise Client's manager on the ordering of new products and will assist in the placement of products in the store. Contractor will also keep the inventory software updated as needed to meet industry standards.

Basically, you'll insert a plain-English description of the kind of work the contractor will be doing.

3. Time Commitment

If the contractor is making a commitment to work a certain number of hours or within a certain range of hours, you can supply that information here.

4. Payment

The sample agreement assumes that you'll pay the contractor by the hour. If so, you can insert the hourly rate. If you'll be paying on any other basis, such as a monthly fee or a per-project basis, you can revise the wording to reflect that.

5-17. Additional Clauses

You don't need to insert anything in most of Clauses 5 through 17. They include statements that:

- The contractor will give you invoices for the services performed (Clause 5).
- The contractor will have independent contractor status (Clause 6).
- The contractor retains the right to work for other people (Clause 7).
- The contractor may hire assistants to help do his or her work (Clause 8).
- The contactor will be responsible for his or her own equipment, tools, and supplies necessary to perform the work and all expenses except where noted (Clause 9).

Independent Contractor Agreement

1. Names

This contract is between _Vintage Valley LLC, an Illinois Limited Liability Company_ , Client, and _____ Marla Fenby _____ , Contractor.

2. Services to be Performed

Contractor agrees to perform the following services for Client: _maintenance all of Client's income and expense records and preparation of reports and tax returns in consultation with the Certified Public Accountant retained by Client._ .

3. Time Commitment

Contractor will spend _____ between 15 and 25 hours per week _____ performing the services.

4. Payment

Client will pay Contractor at the rate of $_____ 40 per hour _____ .

5. Invoices

Contractor will submit invoices to Client for all services performed.

6. Independent Contractor Status

The parties intend Contractor to be an independent contractor in the performance of the services. Contractor will have the right to control and determine the methods and means of performing the contractual services.

7. Other Clients

Contractor retains the right to perform services for other clients.

8. Assistants

Contractor, at Contractor's expense, may employ assistants as Contractor deems appropriate to carry out this agreement. Contractor will be responsible for paying these assistants, as well as any expense attributable to them including income taxes, unemployment insurance, and Social Security taxes. Contractor will maintain workers' compensation insurance for all of its employees.

9. Equipment and Supplies

A. Contractor, at Contractor's expense, will provide all equipment, tools, and supplies necessary to perform the contractual services, except for the following which will be provided by Client: _____

    _a computer and bookkeeping software_____ .

B. Contractor will be responsible for all expenses required for the performance of the contractual services, except for the following which will be paid for by Client:

    _stationery and bookkeeping supplies_____

_____ .

10. Local, State, and Federal Taxes

Contractor will pay all income taxes and Social Security and Medicare taxes incurred while performing services under this agreement. Client will not:

- withhold Social Security and Medicare taxes from payments to Contractor or pay such taxes on Contractor's behalf
- make state or federal unemployment compensation contributions on Contractor's behalf, or
- withhold state or federal income tax from payment to Contractor.

11. Intellectual Property

Contractor assigns to Client all patent, copyright, and trade secret rights in anything created or developed by Contractor for Client under this Agreement.

12. Duration of Agreement

This agreement will remain in effect until ___April 30, 2013___ .

13. Entire Agreement

This contract contains the entire agreement between the parties on the subject of services to be rendered by Contractor for Client. Any amendments require the written agreement of both parties.

14. Governing Law

This agreement will be governed by and construed in accordance with the laws of the State of ___Illinois___ .

15. Modification

This agreement may be modified only by a written amendment signed by all parties.

16. Waiver

If any party waives any provision of this agreement at any time, that waiver will only be effective for the specific instance and purpose for which that waiver was given. If any party fails to exercise or delays exercising any of its rights or remedies under this agreement, that party retains the right to enforce that term or provision at a later time.

17. Severability

If a court determines that any provision of this agreement is invalid or unenforceable, any invalidity or unenforceability will affect only that provision. Such provision may be modified, amended, or limited only to the extent necessary to make it valid and enforceable.

Client	**Contractor**
Vintage Valley LLC	*Marla Fenby*
An Illinois Limited Liability Company	Marla Fenby
By: *Felice Randall*	678 Morton Blvd.
Felice Randall, Manager	Unit No. 2
345 Placid Road	Evanston, Illinois
Chicago, Illinois	
Dated: April 1, 2011	Dated: April 1, 2011

- The contractor will be responsible for paying his or her own income, Social Security, and Medicare taxes and unemployment compensation contributions (Clause 10).
- The contractor will have all intellectual property rights in what he or she produces under the agreement— though this language can be modified if that's not what you want (Clause 11).

- The agreement will be in effect until a fixed date (Clause 12).

Clauses 13 through 17 are standard contract clauses and are explained in Chapter 16.

Signatures

You and the contractor will sign this agreement at the closing. See Chapter 17 for suggested formats for the signature portion of an agreement such as this one. ●

Closing the Deal

Preparing for a Smooth Closing

To complete the transfer of the business after you and the seller have signed the sales agreement, you'll have a meeting, called the closing. At this meeting you'll pay the seller the sale price or the agreed down payment. If it's an asset sale, you'll sign documents such as a promissory note and security agreement. In exchange, to turn ownership over to you, the seller signs a bill of sale for the business assets—or, in an entity sale, the seller signs stock certificates or LLC documents. When you walk out the door, you're the new owner of the business.

You may find that your closing is simultaneously a joyous and a terrifying moment—especially if you've never owned a business before. True, you'll be excited about being self-employed and having the chance to give free rein to your entrepreneurial zeal. But you'll also be faced with the uncertainties that lie ahead and the fact that you may not have much of a safety net if you run into rough times. So you're likely to come into the closing with mixed and even contradictory feelings.

In anticipation of what may be an emotional event, it's smart to use the sales agreement to help assure that the closing is conducted efficiently. Your sales agreement can be the starting point for a checklist of the documents that need to be signed at the closing. You can go on to construct a more comprehensive checklist several days before the closing and review it with the seller before the closing.

The first section of this chapter helps you plan for the details of the closing. Later sections will help you make sure that your checklist is as complete as possible, and help you prepare for any last-minute glitches.

The checklists below give an overview of documents and tangible items that may need to change hands at the closing. Use it to ensure a smooth transition.

Where and When to Hold the Closing and Who Should Attend

Your sales agreement should say where and when the closing will take place. See Chapter 16, Clause 24, Closing, for suggested language.

Who Attends the Closing

Sometimes, only the seller and the buyer will attend the closing, but often others need to attend as well. Plan carefully so that all necessary people can be on hand to sign the required papers.

Spouses, for example, may need to attend the closing. Let's say the seller is married, lives in a community property state, and is selling the assets of a sole proprietorship business. In that situation, the seller's spouse should sign the transfer documents. Similarly, it may be necessary for your spouse to be present to sign documents, such as a promissory note. If spouses or other necessary signers (such as guarantors) won't be able to attend the closing in person, you and the seller will have to get their signatures in advance or have them sign a power of attorney authorizing someone else to sign papers in their behalf.

If you've never bought a business before—and even if you have—your lawyer's presence at the closing can be reassuring; it helps you know that you're doing everything correctly.

Chapter 17 discusses the format that individuals and entities should use to sign the sales agreement and other legal documents. Review your sales agreement to see who is committed to signing documents at the closing. Also, look at the documents you've attached to your sales agreement for other indications about who needs to sign.

When to Hold the Closing

It's best to schedule your closing on a weekday, because governmental offices, banks, and title companies are sure to be open and you may need to transact some final business with them on the day of closing. And morning is better than later in the day because it gives you time to work out problems if something unexpected comes up.

If the last day of a month falls on a weekday, that can be a good time for a closing, since it makes it easier to prorate (divide) expenses such as rent and taxes. For example, rent is typically due on the first day of a month. By closing on the last day of a month, you and the seller won't have to fuss over how to allocate a month's rent. But, of course, you want to keep the importance of easy arithmetic in perspective. If you and the seller are ready to close on the tenth of the month, it won't make sense to hold off for three weeks.

Where to Hold the Closing

If either you or the seller plans to have a lawyer at the closing, you may be inclined to schedule the closing at the lawyer's office—if for no other reason than to avoid the cost of paying the lawyer to travel across town. Usually that's okay, but sometimes there are good reasons to hold the closing at the business location, assuming there's a quiet office there large enough to accommodate several people and easy access to computers, copiers, and fax machines. If, for example, you'll be participating in a physical count of the inventory on the day of the closing or for some reason want to have the seller's business records at hand, the business can be the best location.

If no lawyer will be involved in the closing, and the business location is not a good choice, find an alternate place that's quiet, private, and has a computer, printer, copier, and fax so you can easily tweak documents on the spot or, if necessary, even redraft some. FedEx Kinko's—the nationwide copy service—has excellent conference room facilities available at many locations. One of these can be an ideal place to close, since any needed business equipment is right there. Some hotel chains as well as many local chambers of commerce offer similar facilities. The cost is usually reasonable.

Documents for Transferring Assets

You and the seller should agree on a customized closing checklist so you know that all the bases are covered. The items on a checklist will vary somewhat from business to business. The sales agreement should have addressed many—perhaps most—of them. For example, if you're buying the assets of a business on an installment plan, you'll find that Clause 13 refers to a promissory note and Clause 14 refers to a security agreement and UCC Financing Statement. Both clauses are discussed in Chapter 13. Likewise, if the seller is planning to work for you after the closing, you'll see that Clause 22, Future Services, discussed in Chapter 15, refers to a consulting agreement or an employment contract. Also, look at Clause 25, Documents for Transferring Assets, in Chapter 16, which lists additional documents that will need to be signed.

Because no two sales are exactly alike, your closing checklist will be unique to your sale. Still, while it helps to see a master list of items that may be required for your closing, such as the Closing Checklist for an Asset Sale, below, remember that no compilation can be exhaustive.

If you're buying an entity rather than its assets, see the section called "Documents for Transferring an Entity," below, for a similar checklist.

FORM

Where to find the forms. If you're reading a print copy of this book, you'll find a copy of the Closing Checklist for an Asset Sale on the CD-ROM at the back. If you're using an ebook version, you can download the checklist on the Nolo website; the link is included in Appendix A.

Many of the items in the master checklist are covered in detail elsewhere in this book and some items need no explanation, but there are a few that may not be familiar to you.

Insurance Certificates for the Policy Covering Secured Assets. The Security Agreement (discussed in Chapter 18) usually requires that the buyer carry property insurance that protects the seller's interest in the secured assets. At closing, the seller will want to see evidence that such insurance is in place.

Name Change Certificate for Assumed Name. The seller may have registered an assumed name or fictitious name for the business with a state or local official. If your sales agreement calls for the seller to transfer the name to you, you or the seller will need to get a form from the registry clerk that you can use to list the proper person or entity now entitled to use the name.

New Signature Cards for Bank Accounts. Occasionally, a sales agreement will call for bank accounts to be transferred to the buyer. If so, you or the seller will need to get forms from the bank to remove the seller's name as

Closing Checklist for an Asset Sale

[Check all those items that apply to your sale]

Items That Are Relatively Common

☐ Bill of Sale

☐ Cashier's Check

☐ Promissory Note

☐ Security Agreement

☐ UCC Financing Statement

☐ Asset Acquistion Statement (IRS Form 8594)

☐ Consent of Entity Owners to Sale of Assets

☐ Covenant Not to Compete

☐ Employment Contract

☐ Consulting Contract (Independent Contractor Agreement)

☐ Insurance Certificates for the Policy Covering Secured Assets

Items That Are Less Common

☐ Statement Regarding Absence of Creditors

☐ Assignment of Lease

☐ Assignment of Contracts

☐ Assignment of Intellectual Property

☐ Escrow Agreement for Post-Closing Adjustments

☐ Motor Vehicle Transfer Documents

☐ License Transfer Documents

☐ Real Estate Transfer Documents

☐ Title Insurance Commitment

☐ Mortgage or Deed of Trust

☐ Name Change Certificate for Assumed Names

☐ New Signature Cards for Bank Accounts

☐ Name Change Documents for Utility and Tax Bills

☐ Powers of Attorney for Absent Signers

Other Items

☐ Customer Lists

☐ Supplier Lists

☐ Trade Secrets

☐ Keys to Premises

☐ Alarm Codes

☐ Safe Combinations

☐ Computer Access Codes

☐ Keys to File Cabinets

☐ Keys to Vehicles

☐ Owner's Manuals for Equipment

a signer on the account and to list you or your managers as signers.

Name Change Documents for Utility and Tax Bills. Utility companies and tax officials need to know where to send bills in the future. Find out what documents they need to make the change, and have those documents available at the closing.

Documents for Transferring an Entity

As with asset sales, no two entity sales are exactly alike, so your closing checklist will be unique to your sale. The Closing Checklist for an Entity Sale, below, is a compilation of items that may be required for your closing though, understandably, this checklist is not exhaustive. The most common items are listed first, followed by items that are less likely to be on your personalized checklist.

FORM

Where to find the forms. If you're reading a print copy of this book, you'll find a copy of the Closing Checklist for an Entity Sale on the CD-ROM at the back. If you're using an ebook version, you can download the checklist on the Nolo website; the link is included in Appendix A.

A few of the items on the master list may need a bit of explanation.

Corporate or LLC Record Book. Most corporations maintain an official record book (typically in a loose-leaf binder) that contains the articles of incorporation, the corporate bylaws, corporate resolutions and minutes, stock certificate records, and shareholder agreements. An LLC may have a similar record book or may have only a folder containing the articles of organization and the operating agreement. You'll undoubtedly want these records and, of course, you are entitled to them. The seller may want to retain a photocopy in case legal questions come up later.

New Signature Cards for Bank Accounts. Unless your sales agreement excludes them, entity bank accounts remain the property of the entity. You'll need to get forms from the bank to remove the seller's name as a signer on the account and to list you and perhaps other managers as signers.

See the section called "Documents for Transferring Assets," above, for an explanation of insurance certificates.

Handling Last-Minute Problems

Rarely is the closing process perfect. Even with the most thorough preparation, it's common for some fine-tuning of the closing documents to occur at the closing table. For example, a tax bill may not arrive until the last minute; at the closing, you may have to allocate the bill between you and the seller as required by the sales agreement. Or the seller may have agreed in the sales contract to pay off some business debts out of the closing proceeds. In that case, the unpaid bills need

Closing Checklist for an Entity Sale

[Check all those items that apply to your sale]

Items That Are Relatively Common

- ☐ Stock Certificates or LLC Membership Certificates
- ☐ Cashier's Check
- ☐ Promissory Note
- ☐ Security Agreement
- ☐ UCC Financing Statement
- ☐ Corporate or LLC Record Book
- ☐ Escrow Agreement for Stock Certificates or LLC Membership Certificates
- ☐ Change of Registered Agent
- ☐ Resignation of Directors and Officers
- ☐ Covenant Not to Compete
- ☐ Employment Contract
- ☐ Consulting Contract (Independent Contractor Agreement)
- ☐ Insurance Certificate for Policy Covering Secured Assets

Items That Are Less Common

- ☐ Mortgage or Deed of Trust to Secure Payment of Promissory Note
- ☐ New Signature Cards for Bank Accounts
- ☐ Powers of Attorney for Absent Signers
- ☐ Lease
- ☐ Contracts With Customers and Suppliers
- ☐ Landlord's Consent If Required by Lease

Other Items

- ☐ Customer Lists
- ☐ Supplier Lists
- ☐ Trade Secrets
- ☐ Keys to Premises
- ☐ Alarm Codes
- ☐ Safe Combinations
- ☐ Computer Access Codes
- ☐ Keys to File Cabinets
- ☐ Keys to Vehicles
- ☐ Owner's Manuals for Equipment

to be examined, the amounts accounted for, and checks actually written and sent to the creditors at the closing so that you're sure it happens.

And if the sale price is based in part on the value of the inventory as of the day of closing, you and the seller may need to make arrangements for the taking of a physical inventory—either right before or sometimes even during the closing.

Looking Ahead

So the closing has been completed. You did it: You actually bought a business. Now it's time to come up to speed on the fine points of being a business owner. Chapter 22 introduces you to the main legal principles you should know about when you take over a business. ●

Running a Small Business: Some Legal and Tax Basics

So you've closed on your business purchase and are in the driver's seat. Now you face the day-to-day challenges of running the business efficiently, producing a decent profit—and avoiding legal and tax problems. This chapter will introduce you to some legal and tax concepts that every small business owner needs to understand, including: entity concerns, safe business practices for your corporation or LLC, tax basics, insuring your business, and negotiating a favorable lease.

RESOURCE

Because this book is about buying a business and not about running it, this chapter only hits the highlights of these important subjects. But fortunately, you can consult a host of other Nolo books and electronic products that go into much greater depth on the topics introduced here, as well as other aspects of running a small business. Here's a partial list of recommended titles:

- *Legal Guide for Starting & Running a Small Business*, by Fred S. Steingold
- *Legal Forms for Starting & Running a Small Business*, by Fred S. Steingold
- *Hiring Your First Employee*, by Fred S. Steingold
- *Tax Savvy for Small Business*, by Frederick W. Daily
- *How to Run a Thriving Business: Strategies for Success & Satisfaction*, by Ralph Warner
- *How to Write a Business Plan*, by Mike McKeever

- *Form Your Own Limited Liability Company*, by Anthony Mancuso
- *Your Limited Liability Company: An Operating Manual*, by Anthony Mancuso
- *Incorporate Your Business: A Legal Guide to Forming a Corporation in Your State*, by Anthony Mancuso
- *The Corporate Records Handbook: Meetings, Minutes & Resolutions*, by Anthony Mancuso
- *Form a Partnership: The Complete Legal Guide*, by Denis Clifford and Ralph Warner
- *Business Buyout Agreements: A Step-by-Step Guide for Co-Owners*, by Anthony Mancuso and Bethany Lawrence
- *The Employer's Legal Handbook*, by Fred S. Steingold
- *Working With Independent Contractors*, by Stephen Fishman, and
- *Negotiate the Best Lease for Your Business*, by Janet Portman and Fred S. Steingold

For a complete list of Nolo business books, ebooks, and software, go to www.nolo.com.

Entity Concerns

Earlier, you learned about the types of business entities typically used by small businesses. You'll recall that they are the sole proprietorship, the partnership, the corporation, and the limited liability company. Technically speaking, a sole proprietorship is not a separate entity; for legal and tax purposes, the owner and the business are the same.

Let's look at some paperwork concerns that you should address—or at least think about—after you've bought a business.

You'll Be Running the Business as a Sole Proprietorship

The paperwork burdens for a sole proprietorship are simple and straightforward. Here are some suggestions.

Set up a separate bank account for your business. This isn't a legal requirement, but keeping your business and personal finances separate will save you numerous accounting and tax headaches. And there are excellent software packages available, such as Intuit's *QuickBooks*, to help you manage your sole proprietorship finances with little or no professional assistance.

Register your assumed or fictitious name. If you'll be using a business name and not just your own name, state law typically requires you to register the name with a designated county office. This lets the public know who is behind the business name. If the prior owner of the business used the same business name, his or her name registration will need to be cancelled before the business name becomes available to you.

Consider obtaining a federal Employer Identification Number (EIN). This isn't an IRS requirement—as a sole proprietor, you're free to use your Social Security number for federal tax filings. But many sole operators prefer to get a separate tax number for their business—and some banks require it as a condition of opening a business account.

Obtain any needed license or permit. The requirements will depend on state and local law. Most likely, you will have taken care of this as part of the purchase process. But if not, make sure you deal with it right away.

Buy business insurance. At the very least, you need liability insurance (in case you injure someone or damage their property) and property insurance (in case your property is damaged by flood, fire, or windstorm).

You'll Be Running the Business as a Partnership

The paperwork for a partnership is only slightly more burdensome than for a sole proprietorship. Having a partnership means you and one or more other people will own the business, and you won't operate as a corporation or an LLC. Most likely, you and the other owners bought the assets of the business you're purchasing; it's quite rare to buy a partnership as an entity. Assuming that that's your situation, here are some suggestions.

Sign a partnership agreement. This isn't a legal requirement, but it's highly desirable. Without a written agreement, state law will define the partners' rights and obligations. The default provisions of the law may work just fine—but, then again, they may be different from what you and your partners really want. Besides, going through the process of discussing management rules, income withdrawals, and potential exit strategies can help assure you that you and your partners are on the same page. It's far better to resolve major issues now than when you're five or ten years down the road.

File a certificate of partnership. State law typically requires that you file a certificate at a county office so that the public can learn who is behind the partnership name.

Open a bank account for the partnership. The law doesn't require this, but it makes sound business sense to separate partnership finances from those of the individual partners.

Get a federal Employer Tax Identification Number (EIN). Your partnership won't have to pay a federal income tax (recall that it's a "pass-through" entity), but it will have to file an information return that reports each partner's share of profit or loss. You'll need the tax ID number for this purpose.

Obtain any needed license or permit. The requirements will depend on state and local law.

Buy business insurance. Doing business can be risky. Insurance will help shield you from financial disaster.

You'll Be Running the Business as a New Corporation or LLC (Asset Purchase)

You may have bought the assets of a business with the idea that you—and any cobuyers—would form a corporation or an LLC and run a business using the purchased assets. The steps you should take following the

closing will depend in part on what has happened so far. Under one scenario, you may have formed your corporation or LLC early on and had it sign the sales agreement as the buyer. Under another scenario, you and perhaps others may have bought the assets as individuals, intending to form an entity later. Either way, you may find the following list helpful. Just remember that under the first scenario, you probably have already attended to many items on the list.

File papers creating the entity. File articles of incorporation (for a corporation) or articles of organization (for an LLC) with the appropriate state agency—often the secretary of state's office.

Prepare and sign an owners' agreement. This will be a shareholders' agreement (for a corporation) or an operating agreement (for an LLC). This document will cover how you and the other owners will run the business, handle profits and losses, and deal with the transfer of shares or LLC membership interests.

Create your corporate hierarchy. Using minutes or a written consent, the incorporator or the shareholders should adopt bylaws. The shareholders should elect a board of directors (a single director may sometimes suffice), which in turn will elect corporate officers, such as a president, secretary, and treasurer. Most LLCs opt for a simplified structure, so they can avoid this step.

Issue stock certificates or LLC membership certificates. This is the official evidence of entity ownership.

Obtain a federal Employer Identification Number (EIN). Most entities need one. The exception is a single-member LLC, which can use its owner's Social Security number.

Make sure the entity owns the assets. This won't be a problem if your corporation or LLC bought the assets. By contrast, if you bought the assets as an individual, you'll need to transfer them to the entity by a bill of sale or other transfer documents.

Open an entity bank account. As part of the process, you'll designate who can sign checks on behalf of the entity.

Make federal tax elections. A corporation is automatically a C corporation, which is a taxable entity. If like many small businesses you prefer to have S corporation status (income and losses are passed through to the shareholders), you'll need to file IRS Form 2553, *Election by a Small Business Corporation.* An LLC is automatically treated as a pass-through entity and pays no taxes. In the rare case in which you'd prefer to have your LLC taxed like a C corporation, you'll need to file IRS Form 8832, *Entity Classification Election.* See a tax pro for guidance.

You've Purchased a Corporation or an LLC Which You'll Continue to Run (Entity Purchase)

When you purchase an entity, you'll probably discover that the previous owners have already taken care of most of the procedural steps. If so, you'll be focusing on the transition—that is, shaping the entity

to your own needs. Here are some checklist items to consider.

Change the name of the registered agent, and the names of signers on entity bank accounts. If the business requires permits or licenses in the names of individuals, make those name changes as well.

Issue new stock certificates or LLC membership certificates to the new owners. Of course, if the old certificates are being held in escrow until the sale price is fully paid, you'll have to delay this step until later.

Review the entity documents to make sure they are consistent with the way you and your co-owners want to run the business. For a corporation, these documents include the articles of incorporation, the bylaws, and any shareholders' agreement or buy-sell agreement. For an LLC, look at the articles of organization and operating agreement. Make any amendments you feel are appropriate.

Put your own crew in charge. If you've bought a corporation, your shareholders will need to elect a new board of directors, and the directors will need to choose corporate officers, such as a president, secretary, and treasurer. If you've bought an LLC, and it's to be run by one or more managers, you'll need to designate who those people are.

Safe Business Practices for Your Corporation or LLC

As you know, businesspeople form or buy corporations and LLCs to limit their personal liability. They want to avoid some of the risks of doing business as a sole proprietorship or partnership. The key to getting as much protection as possible is to keep in mind that your corporation or LLC is a legal entity separate from its owner or owners as individuals.

Forgetting this basic principle can be risky. If you're careless about maintaining the separation between the entity and yourself, you can jeopardize your freedom from personal liability. While it's rare for a judge to impose personal liability on a corporate shareholder or LLC member, it does happen. And when it does, it's almost always in a small business where the owners have allowed the line between the entity and the owners to get very fuzzy or disappear.

Still, doing business as a corporation or LLC needn't be dangerous. There are several simple steps you can take to preserve your entity status so that you don't have to lie awake nights worrying about personal liability. These steps are not time-consuming—and they make good business sense.

Make sure your entity has enough money and other assets to meet your foreseeable business requirements. The amount, of course, varies from business to business. Get a recommendation from your accountant or someone in the same business. If you're going to give or lend money to the entity, transfer funds into the entity's account and then pay expenses—don't pay them directly from your personal accounts.

Insure against obvious risks. Determine whether there's a substantial risk of

customers or others being injured in the course of your business operations. If there is, it's wise to obtain a reasonable amount of liability insurance. There have been some cases—not many—in which a judge has felt that the failure of a small corporation or LLC to buy insurance that was reasonably available was so reckless that it was a factor that could lead to the owners being held personally liable.

Observe entity formalities. This is especially important if you have a corporation; LLCs can operate with fewer legal formalities. With a corporation, keep a record book in which you preserve meeting minutes and written consents. Hold annual meetings as required by state law, and file any annual reports that are mandatory.

Separate your personal finances from those of the entity. At the very least, this means maintaining a separate bank account for the entity. Don't use the entity bank account to pay your personal expenses. Have the entity give you salary checks on a regular basis (deducting employee withholding taxes). Deposit the paychecks in your personal account; then use the funds to pay your own bills.

Document all transactions between you and the entity. If the entity leases property from you, sign a lease. If the entity borrows money from you, sign a promissory note. Do the same thing you would do if it were a transaction between strangers.

Use the correct entity name, including suffixes such as Inc. or LLC. If you want to use a less-formal designation, your entity can get an assumed or fictitious name for the informal version.

Sign documents on behalf of your entity rather than as an individual. For example, you should use a format such as the following when signing letters, contracts, and other documents:

For a Corporation

> Jones Bakery Inc.
>
> A Texas Corporation
>
> By: _____
>
>   William Jones, President

For a Limited Liability Company

> Smith Bindery LLC
>
> By: _____
>
>   Lucy Smith, Member

Tax Basics

To guard against having to pay interest and penalties on tax deficiencies, you need to know what tax forms to file and when to file them. And by being aware of the fine points of the tax laws, you can legally save a bundle of money—not to mention aggravation. For example, having a clear picture of what the IRS regards as a proper business expense will allow you to take deductions that otherwise might not occur to you.

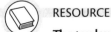

RESOURCE

The tax laws are vast and compli-cated. There's much more for you to learn beyond what you'll find here. For starters, see *Tax Savvy for Small Business*, by Frederick W. Daily (Nolo), and the IRS website at www.irs.gov. You may want to hire an accountant to help set up your books and prepare—or at least review— your business tax returns.

This section provides a few highlights of federal tax requirements. You also need to be aware of your state's tax scheme as it relates to small businesses. Contact your state's taxing authority to get detailed information.

Employer Identification Number

Even if your business has no employees, you must get an Employer Identification Number (EIN) from the IRS if your business is:

- a partnership
- an S corporation
- a C (regular) corporation
- an LLC with two or more members, or
- a single-member LLC that you've chosen to have taxed as a corporation.

Technically, if you're a sole proprietor or the sole member of an LLC that is not being taxed as a corporation, you can use your personal Social Security number instead of an EIN. Still, you may decide to get an EIN to differentiate between your personal and business finances.

At the IRS website (www.irs.gov), you'll find Form SS-4, *Application for Employer Identification Number*, along with detailed instructions. You can fill in the blanks using your computer and submit the form electronically.

Business Taxes in General

Three main categories of federal business taxes may apply to your business:

- income taxes
- employment taxes, and
- self-employment taxes.

Get IRS Publication 509, *Tax Calendars,* to see when to file returns and make tax payments.

Excise taxes. Besides the three main business taxes, the federal government imposes excise taxes on a few specialized transactions and products. These taxes are almost never of concern to small businesses. For more information, see IRS Publication 334, *Tax Guide for Small Business.*

Income Tax

Here are the forms you'll use to report your business income.

Type of Legal Entity	IRS Form
Sole Proprietorship	Schedule C (Form 1040)
Partnership	Form 1065
Regular Corporation (C Corporation)	Form 1120
S Corporation	Form 1120-S
LLC	Form 1065 or 1120 (or Schedule C if you have a single-member LLC and you haven't elected to be taxed as a corporation)

Remember that partnerships, S corporations, and most LLCs don't pay federal income tax. They simply report the income or losses of their owners.

Federal Payroll Taxes

There are several types of employment-related taxes the federal government exacts from business.

Federal Income Tax Withholding (FIT). You must withhold income taxes from employees' paychecks based on each one's IRS Form W-4. IRS Circular E tells you how much to withhold.

Social Security Tax (FICA). You must withhold the employee's share of the Social Security tax and Medicare tax. You must also pay the employer's share of those taxes. The amounts change annually. Consult the latest edition of Circular E.

Federal Unemployment Tax (FUTA). You must report and pay the federal unemployment tax (FUTA). This tax is *not* withheld form the employee's pay. Use IRS Form 940 or 940EZ to report this tax. Sole proprietorships and partnerships don't pay the FUTA on the owners' compensation.

You must periodically deposit the withheld income tax and the employer's and employee's share of Social Security and Medicare taxes at an authorized institution—usually a bank. The IRS sends you coupons to use in making these deposits. A typical small business makes these deposits monthly.

CAUTION

Deposit these taxes on time.
There are substantial penalties if you don't.
And if you're an owner of a small business and personally involved in its management, you can be held personally liable for these taxes and the additional penalties, even if the business has the funds to pay them.

Self-Employment Tax

The self-employment tax applies to income you receive from actively working in your business when you're not treated as an employee of the business. If you're a sole proprietor or a partner—or, in many situations, an LLC member—you must pay the federal self-employment tax in addition to regular income tax. The tax is equal to the employer's and employee's portions of the Social Security and Medicare taxes that you and your employer would pay on your compensation if you received it as an employee. Compute this tax each year on Schedule SE, which you attach to your personal Form 1040.

TIP

You may not owe the full self-employment tax on all of your business earnings. If you have income from another job that's subject to withholding, the income from your other job will reduce the tax base for your self-employment tax.

Business Deductions

The general formula for business income taxes is that you first figure out your gross profit: your gross receipts or sales less returns and allowances and the cost of goods sold. Then you subtract your other business expenses to find the net income or loss of your business. For an in-depth analysis of what business expenses can be deducted, see IRS Publications 535, *Business Expenses.*

To be deductible, a business expense must be ordinary and necessary—something that's common in your type of business, trade, or profession. If you have an expense that's partly for business and partly personal, you must separate the personal from the business part. Only the business part is deductible.

Among the many types of expenses you can deduct are advertising, bad debts, car and truck expenses, depreciation, employee benefit programs, insurance, professional services, rent, utilities, and wages. Depreciation is the term that applies to business property—such as machinery and equipment—that has a useful life longer than one year. The idea is that usually the deduction for this property must be spread out over several years. The IRS rules are fairly complicated, dealing with such concepts as straight-line depreciation and accelerated depreciation. But you'll be pleased to learn that a special tax law provision (called the Section 179 capital expense election) allows you to write off a generous amount of depreciable property in the year of purchase.

Using this special provision, you may even be able to immediately deduct the full cost of any equipment you acquire.

Insuring Your Business

A well-designed insurance program can protect your business from many types of perils. It's best to work with a single insurance agent or broker for all your business needs so the various types of coverage can be coordinated.

Here are some types of insurance to consider.

Property insurance. This insurance covers damage to buildings, including permanently installed fixtures and equipment, and outdoor features (such as light poles). You'll also want coverage for business personal property such as furniture, equipment, and inventory. Your insurance agent can help you understand the differences among the three types of property insurance: Basic Form, Broad Form, and Special Form. Make sure the policy you settle on is a good match for your specific business. And opt for a policy that pays full replacement cost rather than just the current fair market value of damaged property.

Liability insurance. You need liability insurance in case someone is injured or their property damaged as a result of your business operations. But general liability policies don't insure against all risks. You may need separate policies—or riders—for product liability coverage or vehicle accidents. And

most states require workers' compensation insurance for workers who are injured on the job. State law may allow your business to self-insure for worker injuries, but you probably won't have the type of cash reserves that the law requires.

Other insurance. There are many other types of insurance available—some of which may be appropriate for your business, for example:

- bonds covering employee theft and embezzlement
- crime coverage, covering thefts and robberies by people who aren't employees
- business interruption insurance, covering lost income if your business is closed because of fire, windstorm, or flood damage, and
- industry-specific packages based on your type of business.

Negotiating a Favorable Lease

Many small businesses are located in leased premises. Because rent can be a major expense, the lease terms are very important. Even if you've taken over an existing lease, sooner or later you'll need to negotiate a new one—either for the current premises or for space located elsewhere. The more you know about leases, the better deal you'll be able to strike.

When you talk to the landlord, you'll probably be shown a typed or printed lease prepared by the landlord or the landlord's lawyer. Because the terms typically favor the landlord, consider it no more than the starting point. Chances are excellent that you'll be able to negotiate at least some significant improvements. Here are some common lease terms and how you might approach them.

Personal Guarantee

If your business is a corporation or LLC, the landlord's lease may provide that you'll personally guarantee payment of the rent and other charges. This means, of course, that you'll be personally liable and that your personal assets will be at risk if the business falls on hard times. You'd like to avoid guaranteeing payment at all, but there is room for compromise. You might suggest, for example, that you'll only guarantee up to three months of rent and that the guarantee will end if the business has paid its rent on time during the first two years of the lease.

Defining the Space You're Leasing

The lease should identify the space you'll be occupying. If you're leasing the whole building, that's easy: Simply give the street address. If you're leasing less than the whole building, specify your space more precisely. One way is to refer to building or floor plan drawings. For example, you might say "Suite 2 of the Commerce Building as shown on the attached drawing" or "The south half of the first floor of the Enterprise Plaza."

Don't overlook the common areas: space you'll be sharing with other tenants. This often includes hallways, restrooms, elevators, storage space, and parking. Spell out in your lease that your business (and your customers) can use these additional spaces and facilities.

Because commercial space is often priced by the square foot, find out what method the landlord is using to compute square footage. Sometimes it's measured from the exterior of the walls or from the middle of walls' thickness. If this is the case, you'll be paying for some space that's not really usable. That's not necessarily bad—but you need to find out about it in advance. Square footage calculations affect rent negotiations and comparisons with other space you may be considering.

An Option to Renew

You can often bargain for a clause that gives you the right to renew or extend your lease when its term ends. Let's say you're negotiating a four-year lease. You like the location, the rent is favorable, and you'd like the right to stay for an extended period if your business is doing well. But at the same time, you're nervous about signing a four-year lease in case your business doesn't prosper. A two-year lease that contains an option to stay for two more years may be ideal.

Typically, you exercise an option to stay by giving your landlord written notice a set number of days or months before the lease expires. The amount of notice is negotiable.

Rent

Leases usually state the rent on a monthly basis, for example, $1,000 per month, and indicate when payment is due—typically the first of the month in advance. The lease may also say that the rent for your two-year lease is $24,000 payable in monthly installments of $1,000 per month on the first day of the month. Sometimes there's a late charge if you're more than a few days late.

This isn't the only way to compute rent. Depending on the type of building and local custom, here are the main ways a lease may deal with rent.

Gross leases. These require the tenant to pay a flat monthly amount. The landlord pays for all operating costs for the building: taxes, insurance, repairs, and utilities. Under one common variation, the tenant pays for its own electricity, heat, and air conditioning.

Net leases. You pay a monthly base rent plus some or all of the real estate taxes. If you sign this kind of lease, make sure the portion of taxes allocated to your space is fair.

Net-net leases. This type of lease goes farther and requires you to pay the base rental amount plus real estate taxes and the landlord's insurance on the space you occupy.

Net-net-net ("triple net") leases. You pay the base rental amount plus the landlord's operating costs, including taxes, insurance, repairs, and maintenance.

Percentage leases. These leases are used most commonly for retailers in a shopping mall. You pay base rent plus a percentage of gross income.

Read the lease carefully to make sure you understand everything you'll be required to pay.

Improvements by the Landlord

The landlord may be willing to refurbish your space. If the improvements are somewhat unique to your business, however, the landlord will want you to sign a long-term lease—and the cost of the improvements may be factored into the rent. Still, it can be a good deal, since the landlord may be able to get the work done at a lower cost than you can, and you don't have to come up with a large payment up front. Your lease should be as specific as possible about the improvements the landlord is agreeing to make. You can attach the plans and specifications to your lease.

Compliance With the ADA

The federal Americans with Disabilities Act (ADA) makes both you and your landlord responsible for ensuring the premises are accessible to disabled people. You can work out the details in your lease. Here are some suggestions on how to proceed:

- Ask the landlord to state (lawyers say "warrant") that the building complies with the ADA, based on an ADA survey or audit performed by an engineer or architect.

- If the landlord will be making improvements, see if the landlord will agree to pay for fully complying with the ADA.
- Make sure that the costs of bringing common areas into compliance aren't passed along to you as part of "CAM" (common area maintenance) charges.
- To comply with the ADA, you or the landlord may need to provide accessible parking and install ramps, wide entry doors, and specially designed restrooms. Since some of these improvements may be costly, you'd like the landlord to foot as much of the bill as possible.

CAUTION

Your obligations don't end with access to the building. To meet ADA requirements, you may have to redesign your interior space to provide improved access for disabled customers and employees. For example, you may need to widen aisles so that people using wheelchairs, walkers, and electric scooters have ample room to maneuver, and you may need to lower service counters for ease of access. For more information, check the U.S. Department of Justice website, www.usdoj.gov, where you can download several helpful publications.

The Fine Print in Your Lease

Study the lease thoroughly so that you're sure your responsibilities and those of the landlord are clear and reasonable. In addition to the major items already discussed, make sure the lease deals acceptably with costs, including any of the following that concern you.

Real estate taxes. If nothing is mentioned in the lease, this is normally the landlord's responsibility.

Utilities—water, electricity, natural gas, heating oil, etc. These are usually the tenant's responsibility if not specifically mentioned in the lease.

Maintenance of the building and of your premises. Without a lease provision to the contrary, the landlord must pay for maintaining the building, while you pay for maintaining your own space. If you're leasing an entire building, you are normally responsible for all maintenance unless the lease specifies otherwise.

Repair and maintenance of the interior walls, ceiling, and floors in your space. This is normally the tenant's problem in the absence of a lease provision.

Repair of malfunctioning plumbing, electrical, and mechanical systems (heating, ventilation, and air conditioning—commonly called HVAC). Without a lease provision, payment responsibilities are debatable. Generally, the landlord is responsible for systems that affect the entire building—although the opposite is usually true if you lease the entire building. When you rent less

Fine Print in Your Lease (continued)

than an entire building, the responsibility for mechanical or electrical facilities within the four walls of your space isn't always clear; you could find yourself arguing over who must pay for replacing a defective light fixture or a thermostat that goes haywire if the lease doesn't cover it.

Janitorial services. These are normally the tenant's responsibility unless the lease says otherwise. Landlords usually provide janitorial services for bathrooms and other areas used in common by several tenants.

Window washing. Without specific lease language, the landlord normally doesn't have to wash windows. In smaller buildings, leases usually leave window washing to the tenant, with the possible exception of windows serving common areas such as hallways, entryways, and storage areas. In larger, multistoried buildings, the landlord usually accepts responsibility—at least for the exterior of the windows.

Trash removal. Without lease language to the contrary, this is the tenant's chore.

Landscape care and snow removal. This is generally the landlord's duty unless you lease the entire building, in which case the burden

shifts to you. It's always wise to address this issue in the lease—particularly if you're a tenant in a professional or other building where projecting the right image is important.

Parking lot maintenance. This is something the landlord usually must pay for unless the whole parking lot is under your control, in which case it's usually your job unless the lease provides otherwise. In addition to maintenance, be sure the lease is clear regarding the landlord's duty to make a certain number of spaces available, keep the lot or garage open during normal business hours, and provide security.

On service items such as janitorial services and window washing, specify how often this will be done. If the landlord is responsible for heating and air conditioning, will these services be available weekends and at night? If your business keeps long hours, you want your space to be comfortable at all times.

Regarding repairs, you and your landlord may find it convenient to allow you to make certain minor repairs not exceeding a fixed sum (say $300) and to deduct those outlays from your next month's rent.

The Road to Success

In the world of business, nothing stays the same for very long. To succeed, you'll need to keep abreast of market trends in your industry and track the legal and tax developments that affect your business. Make sure you stay involved in trade associations, and keep up to date by checking updates to Nolo small business publications at www.nolo.com. From time to time you may also want to consult professional advisers.

And always remember, you're not alone. Other business owners can be amazingly generous in providing advice and support, and there are lots of resources out there for most types of small businesses. Make use of them.

Being in business for yourself is enormously challenging and can be deeply rewarding. Here at Nolo we sincerely hope that the business you've bought brings you financial rewards and personal satisfaction.

●

Using the Interactive Forms

The forms in this book are available on the CD-ROM and online at **www.nolo.com/back-of-book/BUYBU3.html**. To use the files, your computer must have specific software programs installed. Here is a list of types of files provided by this book, as well as the software programs you'll need to access them:

- **RTF.** You can open, edit, print, and save these form files with most word processing programs such as Microsoft Word, Windows WordPad, and recent versions of WordPerfect.
- **PDF.** You can view these files with Adobe Reader, free software from www.adobe.com. Government PDFs are sometimes fillable using your computer, but most PDFs are designed to be printed out and completed by hand.

TIP

Note to Macintosh Users. These forms were designed for use with Windows. They should also work on Macintosh computers; however, Nolo cannot provide technical support for non-Windows users.

Editing RTFs

Here are some general instructions about editing RTF forms in your word processing program. Refer to the book's instructions and sample agreements for help about what should go in each blank.

- **Underlines.** Underlines indicate where to enter information. After filling in the needed text, delete the underline. In most word processing programs you can do this by highlighting the underlined portion and typing CTRL-U.
- **Bracketed and italicized text.** Bracketed and italicized text indicates instructions. Be sure to remove all instructional text before you finalize your document.
- **Optional text.** Optional text gives you the choice to include or exclude text. Delete any optional text you don't want to use. Renumber numbered items, if necessary.
- **Alternative text.** Alternative text gives you the choice between two or more text options. Delete those options you don't want to use. Renumber numbered items, if necessary.
- **Signature lines.** Signature lines should appear on a page with at least some text from the document itself.

Every word processing program uses different commands to open, format, save, and print documents, so refer to your software's help documents for help using your program. Nolo cannot provide technical support for questions about how to use your computer or your software.

List of Forms

The following files are in RTF:

Form Title	File Name
Confidentiality Letter	Confidentiality.rtf
Attachment to Sales Agreement	Attachment.rtf
Amendment of Sales Agreement	Amendment.rtf
Promissory Note	PromissoryNote.rtf
Security Agreement for Asset Sale	AssetSecurity.rtf
Security Agreement for Entity Sale	EntitySecurity.rtf
Escrow Agreement for Stock Certificates	StockEscrow.rtf
Escrow Agreement for LLC Transfer Certificates	LLCEscrow.rtf
Bill of Sale for Business Assets	BillSale.rtf
Statement Regarding Absence of Creditors	CreditorsStatement.rtf
Assignment of Lease	LeaseAssignment.rtf
Assignment of Contracts	ContractsAssignment.rtf
Consent to Assignment of Contract	AssignmentConsent.rtf
Assignment of Intellectual Property	IPAssignment.rtf
Directors' Consent to the Corporation's Purchase of a Business	DirectorConsent.rtf
Shareholders' Consent to the Corporation's Purchase of a Business	ShareholderConsent.rtf
LLC Members' Consent to the Company's Purchase of a Business	MemberConsent.rtf
Partners' Consent to the Partnership's Purchase of a Business	PartnerConsent.rtf
Covenant Not to Compete	Noncompete.rtf
Independent Contractor Agreement	ICAgreement.rtf
Closing Checklist for an Asset Sale	AssetChecklist.rtf
Closing Checklist for an Entity Sale	EntityChecklist.rtf
Asset Sale Agreement	AssetSale.rtf
Entity Sale Agreement	EntitySale.rtf

The following files are in PDF:

Form Title	File Name
IRS 8594, Asset Acquisition Statement	f8594.pdf
Instructions, IRS 8594, Asset Acquisition Statement	i8594.pdf
UCC Financial Statement and Addendum	ra_9_ucc-1.pdf

CAUTION

In accordance with U.S. copyright laws, the forms provided by this book are for your personal use only. ●

Sample Sales Agreements

Sample # 1

Asset Sale of a Restaurant by One Sole Proprietor to Another

Sales Agreement

1. Names

Peter Hanson doing business as Pete's Place (Seller) and Martha Wentworth (Buyer) agree to the following sale.

2. Sale of Business Assets

Seller is selling to Buyer and Buyer is buying from Seller the assets described below of the restaurant business known as Pete's Place located at 234 Morley Circle, Chesterfield, Ohio.

3. Assets Being Sold

The assets being sold consist of:

A. The goodwill of the business, including the current business name and phone number.

B. The lease dated July 1, 20xx between Seller as Tenant, and Property Central LLC, Landlord, covering the premises at 234 Morley Circle, Chesterfield, Ohio, for the time period from July 1, 20xx to June 30, 20xx.

C. The inventory of food and beverages.

D. The furniture, fixtures, and equipment listed in Attachment A.

E. The equipment leases listed in Attachment B.

F. The supply contract with Western Ohio Provision Company.

G. Intellectual property rights, as follows: rights to all menus and all advertising materials of the business, including all copyrights in those items; the trademarked logo of the business; and the complete recipe file.

The following assets of the business are excluded from the sale:

1. The computer located in the office area.

2. Accounts receivable.

3. The sound system and CD collection.

4. Sale Price

The sale price for the assets listed in this section is $25,000.00, and is allocated as follows:

A. Goodwill	$ 5,000.00
B. Furniture, Fixtures, and Equipment	15,000.00
C. Assignment of Equipment Leases	1,000.00
D. Assignment of Supply Contract	1,500.00
E. Intellectual Property Rights	2,500.00
Total	$ 25,000.00

The total sale price will be adjusted by prorating rent, taxes, insurance premiums, utility costs, and security deposits as of the date of closing.

The total sale price will also be adjusted by adding the value of the inventory as covered in Clause 5.

5. Price of Inventory

At closing, in addition to the total sale price listed in Clause 4 above, Buyer will buy the inventory of food and beverages by paying Seller the amount Seller paid for the food and beverages, as shown in the original invoices. A physical count of the food and beverages will be made by Seller and Buyer one day before closing. Buyer will pay no more than $4,000.00 for the food and beverages.

6. Accounts Receivable

Seller's accounts receivable as of the day of closing will remain Seller's property. Buyer will have no responsibility for collecting those accounts. Seller will have the right to collect those accounts and to keep the amounts received.

7. Deposit

Buyer will pay Seller a deposit of $1,000.00 when Buyer and Seller sign this contract. This deposit will be applied toward the amount due at closing. Seller will return this deposit to Buyer if the purchase is not completed because Seller cannot or does not meet his commitments under this agreement for any reason or if the contingencies in Clause 15 are not removed. Otherwise, Seller will be entitled to retain the deposit in the event the sale is not complete.

8. Payment at Closing

At closing, Buyer will pay Seller 20% of the adjusted sale price. The deposit referred to in Clause 7 will be applied toward the 20% payment. The rest of the closing payment will be made by cashier's check or wire transfer. The balance of the sale price will be paid as described in Clause 9.

9. Promissory Note

At closing, Buyer will sign and give to Seller a promissory note for the balance of the sale price. The promissory note will be in the form of Attachment C. The following person will sign the promissory note along with Buyer: Buyer's husband, Jack Wentworth. Each signer will be jointly and individually liable for payment.

10. Security for Payment

At closing, to secure payment of the promissory note referred to in Clause 9, Buyer will sign a security agreement as shown in Attachment D giving Seller a security interest in the assets that Buyer is buying. Seller will have the right to file a UCC Financing Statement with regard to the security pledged.

Buyer will further secure the promissory note by giving Seller a second mortgage on the home located at 123 Oak Street, Chesterfield, Ohio, for the loan balance. Buyer will provide to Seller, at Buyer's expense, a title insurance policy insuring the mortgage.

11. Seller's Debts and Other Liabilities

Buyer is not assuming any of Seller's debts or other liabilities. Seller will pay all debts and other liabilities, whether now known or unknown, that are or may become a lien on the assets being bought by Buyer.

Seller and his wife, Emily Hanson, will indemnify, defend, and save Buyer harmless from and against all debts and other liabilities arising out of the Seller's ownership or use of the assets before closing.

Buyer and her husband, Jack Wentworth, will indemnify, defend, and save Seller harmless from and against all debts and other liabilities arising out of the Buyer's ownership or use of the assets after closing.

At closing, Seller will confirm in a Statement Regarding Absence of Creditors (Attachment E) that Seller has paid all known debts and other liabilities of the business.

12. Seller's Representations

Seller represents and warrants that:

A. Seller owns the assets being sold. At closing, the assets will be free from any claims of others.

B. At closing, Seller will have paid all taxes that have then come due and that affect the business and its assets.

C. To the best of Seller's knowledge, there are no judgments, claims, liens, or proceedings pending against Seller, the business, or the assets being sold, and to the best of the Seller's knowledge, none will be pending at closing.

D. To the best of Seller's knowledge, the business and financial information in the financial statement dated June 30, 20xx that Seller has given Buyer is accurate.

E. Until closing, Seller will operate the business in the normal manner and will use his best efforts to maintain the goodwill of suppliers, customers, the landlord, and others having business relationships with Seller.

F. To the best of Seller's knowledge, the current uses of the Seller's business premises are permitted under the applicable zoning laws. To the best of Seller's knowledge, the business premises presently (and at closing will) meet all applicable health, safety, and disabled access requirements and are (and at closing will be) in good repair.

G. To the best of Seller's knowledge, the tangible assets are (and at closing will be) in good repair and good operating condition.

These representations and warranties will survive the closing.

Seller and his wife Emily Hanson will indemnify, defend , and save Buyer harmless from and against any financial loss, legal liability, damage, or expense arising from any breach of the above representations and warranties.

13. Buyer's Representations

Buyer represents and warrants that:

A. Buyer has inspected the tangible assets that Buyer is purchasing and the leased premises and has carefully reviewed Seller's representations regarding them. Buyer is satisfied with the physical condition of the tangible assets and the premises.

B. To the best of Buyer's knowledge, the business and financial information in the financial statement dated June 30, 20xx that Buyer has given Seller is accurate.

These representations and warranties will survive the closing.

Buyer and her husband, Jack Wentworth, will indemnify, defend, and save Seller harmless from and against any loss, legal liability, damage, or expense arising from any breach of the above representations and warranties.

14. Covenant Not to Compete

At closing, Seller will sign and deliver to Buyer a covenant not to compete in the form of Attachment F, and Buyer will pay Seller the amounts specified in the attached covenant not to compete.

15. Contingencies

This sale is contingent on Buyer and the landlord negotiating and signing a five-year lease satisfactory to Buyer for the premises currently occupied by the business. If Buyer has not signed such a lease within 15 days from the signing of this agreement, Buyer can cancel this sale by notifying Seller in writing. In that case, Seller will promptly refund the deposit to Buyer. If Buyer does not notify Seller of a cancellation within 20 days from the signing of this agreement, the agreement will remain in effect.

This sale is further contingent on the Ohio Liquor Board's approving a transfer of Seller's liquor license to Buyer. If within 21 days from the signing of this agreement the Board does not approve the transfer, Buyer can cancel this sale by notifying Seller in writing. In that case, Seller will promptly refund the deposit to Buyer. If Buyer does not notify Seller of a cancellation within 23 days from the signing of this agreement, the agreement will remain in effect.

16. Closing

The closing will take place:

> Date: Thursday, September 30, 20xx
> Time: 9:00 a.m.
> Location: The restaurant premises at 234 Morley Circle

At closing, Buyer and Buyer's husband, Jack Wentworth, and Seller and Seller's wife, Emily Hanson, will sign the documents specified in this contract and all other documents reasonably needed to transfer the business assets to Buyer. Buyer will pay Seller the amounts required by this contract and Seller will transfer the business assets to Buyer.

17. Documents for Transferring Assets

At closing, Seller will deliver to Buyer these signed documents:

A. A bill of sale for the tangible assets being sold, including a warranty of good title.

    B. An assignment of the supply contract with the written consent of the other contracting person, if such consent is required.

    C. Assignments of all copyrights that are part of this purchase, and all other intellectual property.

    D. Assignment of the Class C liquor license in the form required by the Alcoholic Beverages Commission.

Seller will also deliver to Buyer at closing all other documents reasonably needed to transfer the business assets to Buyer.

18. Disputes

If a dispute arises concerning this agreement or the sale, Seller and Buyer will try in good faith to settle it through mediation conducted by a mediator to be mutually selected. Seller and Buyer will share the cost of the mediator equally. Seller and Buyer will cooperate fully with the mediator and will attempt to reach a mutually satisfactory resolution of the dispute.

If the dispute is not resolved within 60 days after it is referred to the mediator, it will be arbitrated by an arbitrator to be mutually selected. Judgment on the arbitration award may be entered in any court that has jurisdiction over the matter. Costs of arbitration, including lawyers' fees, will be allocated by the arbitrator.

19. Risk of Loss

Seller will replace or pay for the replacement of any assets that are destroyed or damaged before the closing.

20. Entire Agreement

This is the entire agreement between the parties. It replaces and supersedes any oral agreements between the parties, as well as any prior writings.

21. Modification

This agreement may be modified only by a written amendment signed by both parties.

22. Governing Law

This agreement will be governed by and interpreted under the laws of the State of Ohio, and any litigation will be brought in the courts of that state.

23. Severability

If a court or arbitrator determines that a provision in this agreement is invalid or not enforceable, that determination will affect only that provision. The provision will be modified only to the extent needed to make it valid and enforceable. The rest of the agreement will be unaffected.

24. Notices

All notices must be sent in writing. A notice may be delivered to a person at the address that follows the person's signature or to a new address that the person designates in writing. A notice may be delivered:

    A. in person,

    B. by certified mail, or

    C. by overnight courier.

25. Required Signatures

This agreement is valid only if signed by Seller, Buyer, and their respective spouses.

Seller:

_____

Peter Hanson doing business as
Pete's Place
234 Morley Circle
Chesterfield, Ohio

Dated: _____

Buyer:

_____

Martha Wentworth
241 Argo Drive
Chesterfield, Ohio

Dated: _____

Consent of Spouses:

I am married to the Seller. I consent to the sale described above, and I waive any interest in the business assets. I agree to the indemnity provisions of Clauses 11 and 12.

_____

Emily Hanson

I am married to the Buyer. In consideration of Seller extending credit to Buyer for the purchase of the business assets described above, I agree to cosign or personally guarantee the promissory note to be given by Buyer to Seller. I agree to the indemnity provisions of Clauses 11 and 13.

_____

Jack Wentworth

Sample #2

Entity Sale of a Bookstore by the Two Shareholders to an Individual

Sales Agreement

1. Names

Nora Romano and Eileen Nordby (Sellers) and Karl Brandon (Buyer) agree to the following sale.

2. Sale of Corporate Stock

Sellers are selling to Buyer and Buyer is buying from Sellers all of the Sellers' stock of The Reader's Corner Inc., a Pennsylvania corporation.

3. Sale Price

The sale price of the stock is $75,000.

4. Adjustment of Sale Price

The day before the closing, a physical count of the inventory will be made by Inventory Service Associates, with the cost of the count being shared equally by Seller and Buyer. The sale price is based on the corporation's inventory having a wholesale value of $40,000 as shown on the original invoices. If the count discloses that the inventory is worth more or less than that amount, the sale price will be adjusted downward by the amount the inventory is worth less than $40,000 or upward by the amount the inventory value exceeds $40,000.

Likewise, the sale price is also based on the corporation having accounts receivable totaling $10,000. If at closing the accounts receivable are more or less than that amount, the sale price will be adjusted downward by the amount the accounts receivable are less than $10,000 or upward by the amount the accounts exceed $10,000.

5. Corporate Debts and Liabilities

Sellers will pay the $3,000 obligation that the corporation owes to Keystone Cabinetry.

Sellers will indemnify, defend, and save Buyer harmless from and against any other debts and liabilities of the corporation to the extent that such debts and other liabilities are known to Sellers and Sellers have failed to disclose them to Buyer.

6. Deposit
Buyer will pay Sellers a deposit of $5,000 when Buyer and Sellers sign this contract. This deposit will be applied toward the amount due at closing. Sellers will return this deposit to Buyer if the purchase is not completed because Sellers cannot or do not meet their commitments for any reason. Otherwise, Sellers will be entitled to retain the deposit in the event the sale is not completed.

7. Payment at Closing
At closing, Buyer will pay Sellers 20% of the adjusted sale price. The deposit referred to in Clause 6 will be applied toward the 20% payment. The rest of the closing payment will be made by a cashier's check or wire transfer. The balance of the sale price with be paid as described in Clause 8

8. Promissory Note
At closing, Buyer will sign and give to Sellers a promissory note for the balance of the sale price. The promissory note will be in the form of Attachment A. The following person will sign the promissory note in addition to Buyer: Buyer's wife, Felicia Brandon. Each signer will be jointly and individually liable for payment.

9. Security for Payment
At closing, to secure payment of the promissory note, Buyer will cause the corporation to sign a security agreement as shown in Attachment B. Sellers will have the right to file a UCC financing statement giving Sellers a security interest in the assets of the corporation.

Buyer will further secure the promissory note by giving Sellers a second mortgage on the home located at 123 Trail Wood Road, Terrance, Pennsylvania. Buyer will provide to Sellers, at Buyer's expense, a title insurance policy insuring the mortgage.

Until the promissory note referred to in Clause 8 is fully paid, Buyer will not sell the corporate shares. The certificates representing the shares will be held in escrow by Pine Trust Company. At closing, Sellers and Buyer will sign an escrow agreement in the form of Attachment C.

10. Lease of Business Premises
Sellers own the building at 345 Allerton, Terrance, Pennsylvania, in which the business of the corporation is currently located. At closing, Sellers and Buyer will sign a

Lease with Option to Purchase in the form of Attachment D. Buyer's wife, Felicia Brandon, will cosign the lease.

11. Seller's Representations

Sellers represent and warrant that:

A. The entity is (and at closing will be) a corporation in good standing under the laws of the state of Pennsylvania.

B. The shares being sold constitute all of the issued shares of the entity. No additional shares will be issued before the closing. At closing, the shares will be free from any claims of any persons or entities other than Sellers.

C. At closing, the corporation will have paid all taxes that have then come due and that affect the business and its assets.

D. To the best of Sellers' knowledge, there are no judgments, claims, liens, or proceedings pending against the corporation or its assets being sold except for those already disclosed to Buyer, and to the best of the Sellers' knowledge, there will be no others pending at closing.

E. To the best of Sellers' knowledge, the business and financial information in the financial statement dated June 30, 20xx that Sellers have given Buyer is accurate.

F. Until closing, Sellers will operate the corporation in the normal manner and will use their best efforts to maintain the goodwill of suppliers, customers, and others having business relationships with the corporation.

G. To the best of Sellers' knowledge, the current uses of the corporation's business premises are permitted under the applicable zoning laws. To the best of Sellers' knowledge, the premises presently (and at closing will) meet all applicable health, safety, and disabled access requirements and are (and at closing will be) in good repair.

H. To the best of Sellers' knowledge, the tangible assets of the corporation are (and at closing will be) in good repair and good operating condition.

I. To the best of Sellers' knowledge, the corporation is (and at closing will be) in compliance with all environmental laws. To the best of Sellers' knowledge, there are (and at closing will be) no hazardous materials on the business premises that may be a source of future liability under the environmental laws.

These representations and warranties will survive the closing.

Sellers will indemnify, defend, and save Buyer harmless from and against any financial loss, legal liability, damage, or expense arising from any breach of the above representations and warranties.

12. Buyer's Representations

Buyer represents and warrants that:

    A. Buyer has inspected the tangible assets of the corporation that Buyer is purchasing and the leased premises and has carefully reviewed Sellers' representations regarding them. Buyer is satisfied with the physical condition of the tangible assets and the premises.

    B. To the best of Buyer's knowledge, the business and financial information in the financial statement dated June 30, 20xx that Buyer has given Sellers is accurate.

These representations and warranties will survive the closing.

Buyer and his wife, Felicia Brandon, will indemnify, defend, and save Sellers harmless from and against any financial loss, legal liability, damage, or expense arising from any breach of the above representations and warranties.

13. Covenant Not to Compete

At closing, each Seller will sign and deliver to Buyer a covenant not to compete in the form of Attachment E, and Buyer will pay each Seller the amounts specified in the covenant not to compete.

14. Future Services

At closing, Seller, Nora Romano, and the corporation will sign an employment agreement in the form of Attachment F, and Buyer, Karl Brandon, and the corporation will sign an independent contractor (consulting) agreement in the form of Attachment G.

15. Closing

The closing will take place:

        Date: Thursday, September 30, 20xx

        Time: 9:00 a.m.

        Location: The bookstore premises at 345 Allerton

At closing, Buyer and Buyer's wife, Felicia Brandon, and the Sellers will sign the documents specified in this contract and all other documents reasonably needed to transfer the corporate shares assets to Buyer. Buyer will pay Sellers the amounts required by this contract and Sellers will place the share certificates with the escrow agent as provided in Clause 9 above.

16. Closing Documents

At closing, Sellers will deliver to Buyer these signed documents:

    A. Stock certificates endorsed in blank, along with the escrow agreement.

    B. The Lease With Option to Purchase.

    C. The corporate record book.

    D. Resignations of corporate officers.

Sellers will also deliver to Buyer at closing all other documents reasonably needed to transfer the entity to Buyer.

17. Disputes

If a dispute arises concerning this agreement or the sale, Sellers and Buyer will try in good faith to settle it through mediation conducted by a mediator to be mutually selected. Sellers and Buyer will share the cost of the mediator equally. Sellers and Buyer will cooperate fully with the mediator and will attempt to reach a mutually satisfactory resolution of the dispute.

If the dispute is not resolved within 60 days after it is referred to the mediator, it will be arbitrated by an arbitrator to be mutually selected. Judgment on the arbitration award may be entered in any court that has jurisdiction over the matter. Costs of arbitration, including lawyers' fees, will be allocated by the arbitrator.

18. Risk of Loss

Sellers will replace or pay for the replacement of any corporate assets that are destroyed or damaged before the closing.

19. Entire Agreement

This is the entire agreement between the parties. It replaces and supersedes any oral agreements between the parties, as well as any prior writings.

20. Modification

This agreement may be modified only by a written amendment signed by all parties.

21. Governing Law

This agreement will be governed by and interpreted under the laws of the State of Pennsylvania, and any litigation will be brought in the courts of that state.

22. Severability

If a court or arbitrator determines that a provision in this agreement is invalid or not enforceable, that determination will affect only that provision. The provision will be modified only to the extent needed to make it valid and enforceable. The rest of the agreement will be unaffected.

23. Notices

All notices must be sent in writing. A notice may be delivered to a person at the address that follows the person's signature or to a new address that the person designates in writing. A notice may be delivered:

    A. in person,

    B. by certified mail, or

    C. by overnight courier.

24. Required Signatures

This agreement is valid only if signed by Sellers, Buyer, and their respective spouses.

Sellers:

_____

Nora Romano
567 Hartley Way
Terrance, Pennsylvania

Dated: _____

_____

Eileen Nordby
654 McKinley Parkway
Terrance, Pennsylania

Dated: _____

Buyer:

_____

Karl Brandon
351 Barton Pike
Terrance, Pennsylvania

Dated: _____

Consent of Spouses:

I am married to Nora Romano, one of the Sellers. I consent to the sale described above, and I waive any interest in the corporate shares.

_____

Timothy Romano

I am married to Eileen Nordby, one of the Sellers. I consent to the sale described above, and I waive any interest in the corporate shares.

_____

Jeffrey Nordby

I am married to the Buyer. In consideration of Sellers extending credit to Buyer for the purchase of the corporate shares described above, I agree to cosign or personally guarantee the promissory note to be given by Buyer to Sellers, and to cosign the lease. I agree to the indemnity provisions of Clause 12.

_____

Felicia Brandon

Sample #3
Asset Sale of a Landscaping Business by a Single-Owner LLC to a Partnership

Sales Agreement

1. Names

Martin Services LLC, a Colorado Limited Liability Company, doing business as Custom Green (Seller), and Boulder Enterprises, a Colorado Partnership (Buyer), agree to the following sale.

2. Sale of Business Assets

Seller is selling to Buyer and Buyer is buying from Seller the assets described below of the landscaping business known as Custom Green located at 345 Manchester Drive, Boulder, Colorado.

3. Assets Being Sold

The assets being sold consist of:

A. The goodwill of the business, including the business name, Custom Green, and the company's current phone number.

B. The furniture, fixtures, and equipment listed in Attachment A.

C. The ongoing customer contracts listed in Attachment B.

D. The lease dated September 1, 2011 between Seller as Tenant, and Commercial Associates Inc. as Landlord, for the premises at 345 Manchester Drive, Boulder, Colorado, for the time period from September 1, 2011 to August 30, 2013.

E. Intellectual property rights, as follows: All rights to the copyrighted booklets "What Every Homeowner Should Know About Landscaping" and "What Every Commercial Property Owner Should Know About Landscaping"; all rights to the patented "Kwik Green-Up System" described in Attachment C; and the trademarked logo of the business.

4. Sale Price

The sale price for the assets listed in this section is $200,000.00, and is allocated as follows:

A. Goodwill	$ 50,000.00
B. Furniture, Fixtures, and Equipment	100,000.00
C. Assignment of Equipment Leases	5,000.00
D. Assignment of Supply Contract	35,000.00
E. Intellectual Property Rights	10,000.00
Total	$200,000.00

The total sale price will be adjusted by prorating rent, taxes, insurance premiums, utility costs, and security deposits as of the date of closing.

The total sale price will also be adjusted by adding the value of the accounts receivable as covered in Clause 5.

5. Accounts Receivable

At closing, Buyer will purchase all of Seller's accounts receivable. Buyer will pay Seller the balances owed on these accounts (as jointly determined by Buyer and Seller) less 35%. Buyer will be entitled to keep all sums collected on these accounts.

6. Deposit

Buyer will pay Seller a deposit of $10,000.00 when Buyer and Seller sign this contract. This deposit will be applied toward the amount due at closing. Seller will return this deposit to Buyer if the purchase is not completed because Seller cannot or does not meet its commitments under this agreement for any reason. Otherwise, Seller will be entitled to retain the deposit in the event the sale is not completed.

7. Payment at Closing

At closing, Buyer will pay Seller 30% of the adjusted sale price. The deposit referred to in Clause 6 will be applied toward the 30% payment. The rest of the closing payment will be made by cashier's check or wire transfer. The balance of the sale price will be paid as described in Clause 8.

8. Promissory Note

At closing, Buyer will sign and give to Seller a promissory note for the balance of the sale price. The promissory note will be in the form of Attachment D. The following people will sign the promissory note in addition to Buyer: each partner of Boulder Enterprises along with their spouses. Each signer will be jointly and individually liable for payment.

9. Security for Payment

At closing, to secure the payment of the promissory note, Buyer will sign a security agreement as shown in Attachment E giving Seller a security interest in the assets that Buyer is buying. Seller will have the right to file a UCC financing statement with regard to the security pledged.

10. Seller's Debts and Other Liabilities

Buyer will pay the following debts of the business that arose out of Seller's ownership and use of the assets before the closing:

- The $10,000 balance owed to First Finance Associates for the Durango truck.
- The $5,000 balance owed to First Finance Associates for the tree-trimming machine.

Any other debts and liabilities arising out Seller's ownership or use of the assets before closing will be paid by Seller.

Seller and its owner, Larry T. Martin, will indemnify, defend, and save Buyer harmless from and against all debts and other liabilities that Seller has agreed to pay.

Buyer and each of its partners will indemnify, defend, and save Seller harmless from and against all debts and other liabilities that Buyer has agreed to pay, and any debts or liabilities arising out of the Buyer's ownership or use of the assets after closing.

11. Seller's Representations

Seller represents and warrants that:

A. Seller owns the assets being sold. At closing, the assets will be free from any claims of others.

B. At closing, Seller will have paid all taxes that have then come due and that affect the business and its assets.

C. To the best of Seller's knowledge, except for the liens of First Finance Associates in connection with the equipment balance specified in Clause 10, there are no judgments, claims, liens, or proceedings pending against assets being sold, and to the best of the Seller's knowledge, none will be pending at closing.

    D. To the best of Seller's knowledge, the business and financial information in the financial statement dated June 30, 20xx that Seller has given Buyer is accurate.

    E. Until closing, Seller will operate the business in the normal manner and will use his best efforts to maintain the goodwill of suppliers, customers, the landlord, and others having business relationships with Seller.

    F. To the best of Seller's knowledge, the tangible assets are (and at closing will be) in good repair and good operating condition.

    G. Seller is (and at closing will be) a limited liability company in good standing under the laws of the state of Colorado and has (and at closing will have) the authority to perform the obligations contained in this sales agreement.

These representations and warranties will survive the closing.

Seller and its owner, Larry T. Martin, indemnify, defend, and save Buyer harmless from and against any financial loss, legal liability, damage, or expense arising from any breach of the above representations and warranties.

12. Buyer's Representations

Buyer represents and warrants that:

    A. Buyer has inspected the tangible assets that Buyer is purchasing and the leased premises and has carefully reviewed Seller's representations regarding them. Buyer is satisfied with the physical condition of the tangible assets and the premises.

    B. To the best of Buyer's knowledge, the business and financial information in the financial statement dated June 30, 20xx that Buyer has given Seller is accurate.

These representations and warranties will survive the closing.

Buyer and its two partners will indemnify, defend, and save Seller harmless from and against any financial loss, legal liability, damage, or expense arising from any breach of the above representations and warranties.

13. Covenant Not to Compete

Following the closing, Seller will no longer engage in the landscaping business in the state of Colorado. At closing, Larry T. Martin will sign and deliver to Buyer a covenant not to compete in the form of Attachment F, and Buyer will pay him the amounts specified in the covenant.

14. Future Services

At closing, Buyer and Larry T. Martin will sign an independent contractor agreement in the form of Attachment G.

15. Contingencies

This sale is contingent on Seller providing Buyer with written confirmation from the Boulder Parks and Recreation Board that the Centennial Square contract is fully transferable to Buyer. If Seller has not proved such confirmation to Buyer within 15 days from the signing of this agreement, Buyer can cancel this sale by notifying Seller in writing. In that case, Seller will promptly refund the deposit to Buyer. If Buyer does not notify Seller of a cancellation within 20 days from the signing of this agreement, the agreement will remain in effect.

16. Closing

The closing will take place:

> Date: Thursday, September 30, 20xx
> Time: 9:00 a.m.
> Location: The offices of Seller's lawyers (Bryant and Chodak) at 567 Commerce Drive

At closing, Buyer and Buyer's partners, Seller and Seller's owner, Larry T. Martin, will sign the documents specified in this contract and all other documents reasonably needed to transfer the business assets to Buyer. Buyer will pay Seller the amounts required by this contract and Seller will transfer the business assets to Buyer.

17. Documents for Transferring Assets

At closing, Seller will deliver to Buyer these signed documents:

A. A bill of sale for the tangible assets being sold, including a warranty of good title.

B. Motor vehicle transfer documents for all registered vehicles being transferred.

C. An assignment of the customer contracts with the written consent of the other contracting person, if such consent is required.

D. An assignment of the lease at 345 Manchester Drive and of all accounts receivable.

E. Assignments of all copyrights and patents that are part of this purchase, and all other intellectual property.

Seller will also deliver to Buyer at closing all other documents reasonably needed to transfer the business assets to Buyer.

18. Disputes

If a dispute arises concerning this agreement or the sale, Seller and Buyer will try in good faith to settle it through mediation conducted by the Boulder Mediation Center.

Seller and Buyer will share the cost of the mediator equally. Seller and Buyer will cooperate fully with the mediator and will attempt to reach a mutually satisfactory resolution of the dispute. If the dispute is not resolved within 60 days after it is referred to the mediator, either party may take the matter to court.

19. Risk of Loss

Seller will replace or pay for the replacement of any assets that are destroyed or damaged before the closing.

20. Entire Agreement

This is the entire agreement between the parties. It replaces and supersedes any oral agreements between the parties, as well as any prior writings.

21. Modification

This agreement may be modified only by a written amendment signed by both parties.

22. Governing Law

This agreement will be governed by and interpreted under the laws of the State of Colorado, and any litigation will be brought in the courts of that state.

23. Severability

If a court or arbitrator determines that a provision in this agreement is invalid or not enforceable, that determination will affect only that provision. The provision will be modified only to the extent needed to make it valid and enforceable. The rest of the agreement will be unaffected.

24. Notices

All notices must be sent in writing. A notice may be delivered to a person at the address that follows the person's signature or to a new address that the person designates in writing. A notice may be delivered:

    A. in person,

    B. by certified mail, or

    C. by overnight courier.

25. Required Signatures

This agreement is valid only if signed by Seller; its owner, Larry T. Martin; Buyer; Buyer's partners; and the spouses of each partner.

Seller:

Martin Services LLC

A Colorado Limited Liability Company

By: _____

    Larry T. Martin, Member
    987 Sky High Avenue
    Boulder, Colorado

Dated: _____

Buyer:

Boulder Enterprises

A Colorado Partnership

By: _____

    Norris Kwan, Partner
    765 Dexter Avenue
    Boulder, Colorado

Dated: _____

Consent of Seller's Owner:

I am the Seller's sole member. I approve of and consent to the sale described in the above agreement.

In addition, in consideration of Buyer entering into this agreement with Seller, I agree to:

1. Indemnify, defend, and save Buyer harmless from and against the debts and other liabilities which, under this agreement, are the responsibility of Seller.

2. Indemnify, defend, and save Buyer harmless from and against any loss, liability, damage, or expense arising from any breach of the above representations and warranties made by Seller.

3. Sign the noncompete document required by this agreement.

4. Sign and honor the consulting document required by this agreement.

_____

Larry T. Martin

Consent of Buyer's Owners:

We are all of the Buyer's partners. Each of us approves of and consents to the purchase described in the above agreement.

In addition, in consideration of Seller entering into this agreement with Buyer, each of us agrees to:

1. Cosign or personally guarantee the promissory note to be given by Buyer to Seller under this agreement.

2. Indemnify, defend, and save Seller harmless from and against the debts and other liabilities which, under this agreement, are the responsibility of Buyer.

3. Indemnify, defend, and save Seller harmless from and against any loss, liability, damage, or expense arising from any breach of the above representations and warranties made by Buyer.

_____

Norris Kwan

_____

Nina Costanides

Consent of Spouses:

I am married to Larry T. Martin. I consent to the sale described above, and I waive any interest in the business assets, whether under the community property laws or otherwise. I agree to the indemnity provisions of Clauses 10 and 11.

_____

Mindy Martin

I am married to Norris Kwan, one of the Buyer's partners. In consideration of Seller extending credit to Buyer for the purchase of the business assets described above, I agree to cosign or personally guarantee the promissory note to be given by Buyer to Seller.

_____

Estelle Kwan

I am married to Nina Costanides, one of the Buyer's partners. In consideration of Seller extending credit to Buyer for the purchase of the business assets described above, I agree to cosign or personally guarantee the promissory note to be given by Buyer to Seller.

_____

Peter Costanides

Forms

Form **8594** (Rev. February 2006) Department of the Treasury Internal Revenue Service	**Asset Acquisition Statement** **Under Section 1060** ▶ Attach to your income tax return. ▶ See separate instructions.	OMB No. 1545-1021 Attachment Sequence No. **61**

Name as shown on return	Identifying number as shown on return

Check the box that identifies you:
☐ Purchaser ☐ Seller

Part I **General Information**

1 Name of other party to the transaction	Other party's identifying number

Address (number, street, and room or suite no.)

City or town, state, and ZIP code

2 Date of sale	3 Total sales price (consideration)

Part II **Original Statement of Assets Transferred**

4 Assets	Aggregate fair market value (actual amount for Class I)	Allocation of sales price
Class I	$	$
Class II	$	$
Class III	$	$
Class IV	$	$
Class V	$	$
Class VI and VII	$	$
Total	$	$

5 Did the purchaser and seller provide for an allocation of the sales price in the sales contract or in another written document signed by both parties? . . . . ☐ Yes ☐ No

If "Yes," are the aggregate fair market values (FMV) listed for each of asset Classes I, II, III, IV, V, VI, and VII the amounts agreed upon in your sales contract or in a separate written document? . . . . . . ☐ Yes ☐ No

6 In the purchase of the group of assets (or stock), did the purchaser also purchase a license or a covenant not to compete, or enter into a lease agreement, employment contract, management contract, or similar arrangement with the seller (or managers, directors, owners, or employees of the seller)? . . . . . ☐ Yes ☐ No

If "Yes," attach a schedule that specifies **(a)** the type of agreement and **(b)** the maximum amount of consideration (not including interest) paid or to be paid under the agreement. See instructions.

For Paperwork Reduction Act Notice, see separate instructions. Cat. No. 63768Z Form **8594** (Rev. 2-2006)

Form 8594 (Rev. 2-2006)   Page **2**

| Part III | **Supplemental Statement**—Complete only if amending an original statement or previously filed supplemental statement because of an increase or decrease in consideration. See instructions. |

7 Tax year and tax return form number with which the original Form 8594 and any supplemental statements were filed.

8 Assets	Allocation of sales price as previously reported	Increase or (decrease)	Redetermined allocation of sales price
Class I	$	$	$
Class II	$	$	$
Class III	$	$	$
Class IV	$	$	$
Class V	$	$	$
Class VI and VII	$	$	$
Total	$		$

9 Reason(s) for increase or decrease. Attach additional sheets if more space is needed.

_____
_____
_____
_____
_____
_____
_____
_____
_____
_____
_____
_____
_____
_____
_____
_____
_____
_____
_____

Instructions for Form 8594
(Rev. December 2008)

Department of the Treasury
Internal Revenue Service

(For use with the February 2006 revision of Form 8594)
Asset Acquisition Statement Under Section 1060

Section references are to the Internal Revenue Code unless otherwise noted.

General Instructions

Purpose of Form

Both the seller and purchaser of a group of assets that makes up a trade or business must use Form 8594 to report such a sale if goodwill or going concern value attaches, or could attach, to such assets and if the purchaser's basis in the assets is determined only by the amount paid for the assets.

Form 8594 must also be filed if the purchaser or seller is amending an original or a previously filed supplemental Form 8594 because of an increase or decrease in the purchaser's cost of the assets or the amount realized by the seller.

Who Must File

Generally, both the purchaser and seller must file Form 8594 and attach it to their income tax returns (Forms 1040, 1041, 1065, 1120, 1120S, etc.) when there is a transfer of a group of assets that make up a trade or business (defined below) and the purchaser's basis in such assets is determined wholly by the amount paid for the assets. This applies whether the group of assets constitutes a trade or business in the hands of the seller, the purchaser, or both.

If the purchaser or seller is a controlled foreign corporation (CFC), each U.S. shareholder should attach Form 8594 to its Form 5471.

Exceptions. You are not required to file Form 8594 if any of the following apply.
● A group of assets that makes up a trade or business is exchanged for like-kind property in a transaction to which section 1031 applies. If section 1031 does not apply to all the assets transferred, however, Form 8594 is required for the part of the group of assets to which section 1031 does not apply. For information about such a transaction, see Regulations sections 1.1031(j)-1(b) and 1.1060-1(b)(8).
● A partnership interest is transferred. See Regulations section 1.755-1(d) for special reporting requirements. However, the purchase of a partnership interest that is treated for federal income tax purposes as a purchase of partnership assets, which constitute a trade or business, is subject to section 1060. In this case, the purchaser must file Form 8594. See Rev.

Rul. 99-6, 1999-6, I.R.B. 6, available at http://www.irs.gov/pub/irs-irbs/irb99-06.pdf.

When To File

Generally, attach Form 8594 to your income tax return for the year in which the sale date occurred.

If the amount allocated to any asset is increased or decreased after the year in which the sale occurs, the seller and/or purchaser (whoever is affected) must complete Parts I and III of Form 8594 and attach the form to the income tax return for the year in which the increase or decrease is taken into account.

Penalties

If you do not file a correct Form 8594 by the due date of your return and you cannot show reasonable cause, you may be subject to penalties. See sections 6721 through 6724.

Definitions

Trade or business. A group of assets makes up a trade or business if goodwill or going concern value could under any circumstances attach to such assets. A group of assets can also qualify as a trade or business if it qualifies as an active trade or business under section 355 (relating to distributions of stock in controlled corporations).

Factors to consider in determining whether goodwill or going concern value could attach include:
● The presence of any section 197 or other intangible assets (but the transfer of such an asset in the absence of other assets will not be a trade or business);
● Any excess of the total paid for the assets over the aggregate book value of the assets (other than goodwill or going concern value) as shown in the purchaser's financial accounting books and records; or
● A license, a lease agreement, a covenant not to compete, a management contract, an employment contract, or other similar agreements between purchaser and seller (or managers, directors, owners, or employees of the seller).

Consideration. The purchaser's consideration is the cost of the assets. The seller's consideration is the amount realized.

Fair market value. Fair market value is the gross fair market value unreduced by mortgages, liens, pledges, or other liabilities. However, for determining the

seller's gain or loss, generally, the fair market value of any property is not less than any nonrecourse debt to which the property is subject.

Classes of assets. The following definitions are the classifications for deemed or actual asset acquisitions.

Class I assets are cash and general deposit accounts (including savings and checking accounts) other than certificates of deposit held in banks, savings and loan associations, and other depository institutions.

Class II assets are actively traded personal property within the meaning of section 1092(d)(1) and Regulations section 1.1092(d)-1 (determined without regard to section 1092(d)(3)). In addition, Class II assets include certificates of deposit and foreign currency even if they are not actively traded personal property. Class II assets do not include stock of target affiliates, whether or not actively traded, other than actively traded stock described in section 1504(a)(4). Examples of Class II assets include U.S. government securities and publicly traded stock.

Class III assets are assets that the taxpayer marks-to-market at least annually for federal income tax purposes and debt instruments (including accounts receivable). However, Class III assets do not include:
● Debt instruments issued by persons related at the beginning of the day following the acquisition date to the target under section 267(b) or 707;
● Contingent debt instruments subject to Regulations sections 1.1275-4 and 1.483-4, or section 988, unless the instrument is subject to the noncontingent bond method of Regulations section 1.1275-4(b) or is described in Regulations section 1.988-2(b)(2)(i)(B)(2); and
● Debt instruments convertible into the stock of the issuer or other property.

Class IV assets are stock in trade of the taxpayer or other property of a kind that would properly be included in the inventory of the taxpayer if on hand at the close of the taxable year, or property held by the taxpayer primarily for sale to customers in the ordinary course of its trade or business.

Class V assets are all assets other than Class I, II, III, IV, VI, and VII assets.

Note. Furniture and fixtures, buildings, land, vehicles, and equipment, which constitute all or part of a trade or business (defined earlier) are generally Class V assets.

Class VI assets are all section 197 intangibles (as defined in section 197) except goodwill and going concern value. Section 197 intangibles include:
● Workforce in place;
● Business books and records, operating systems, or any other information base, process, design, pattern, know-how, formula, or similar item;
● Any customer-based intangible;
● Any supplier-based intangible;
● Any license, permit, or other right granted by a government unit;
● Any covenant not to compete entered into in connection with the acquisition of an interest in a trade or a business; and
● Any franchise, trademark, or trade name (however, see exception below for certain professional sports franchises).

See section 197 (d) for more information.

The term "section 197 intangible" does not include any of the following:
● An interest in a corporation, partnership, trust, or estate;
● Interests under certain financial contracts;
● Interests in land;
● Certain computer software;
● Certain separately acquired interests in films, sound recordings, video tapes, books, or other similar property;
● Interests under leases of tangible property;
● Certain separately acquired rights to receive tangible property or services;
● Certain separately acquired interests in patents or copyrights;
● Interests under indebtedness;
● Professional sports franchises acquired before October 23, 2004; and
● Certain transactions costs.

See section 197(e) for more information.

Class VII assets are goodwill and going concern value (whether or not the goodwill or going concern value qualifies as a section 197 intangible).

Allocation of consideration. An allocation of the purchase price must be made to determine the purchaser's basis in each acquired asset and the seller's gain or loss on the transfer of each asset. Use the residual method for the allocation of the sales price among the amortizable section 197 intangibles and other assets transferred. See Regulations section 1.1060-1(c). The amount allocated to an asset, other than a Class VII asset, cannot exceed its fair market value on the purchase date. The amount you can allocate to an asset also is subject to any applicable limits under the Internal Revenue Code or general principles of tax law.

Consideration should be allocated as follows.

1. Reduce the consideration by the amount of Class I assets transferred.
2. Allocate the remaining consideration to Class II assets, then to

Class III, IV, V, and VI assets in that order. Within each class, allocate the remaining consideration to the class assets in proportion to their fair market values on the purchase date.
3. Allocate consideration to Class VII assets.

If an asset in one of the classifications described above can be included in more than one class, choose the lower numbered class (e.g., if an asset could be included in Class III or IV, choose Class III).

Reallocation after an increase or decrease in consideration. If an increase or decrease in consideration that must be taken into account to redetermine the seller's amount realized on the sale, or the purchaser's cost basis in the assets, occurs after the purchase date, the seller and/or purchaser must allocate the increase or decrease among the assets. If the increase or decrease occurs in the same tax year as the purchase date, consider the increase or decrease to have occurred on the purchase date. If the increase or decrease occurs after the tax year of the purchase date, consider it in the tax year in which it occurs.

For an increase or decrease related to a patent, copyright, etc., see *Specific Allocation,* later.

Allocation of increase. Allocate an increase in consideration as described under *Allocation of consideration.* If an asset has been disposed of, depreciated, amortized, or depleted by the purchaser before the increase occurs, any amount allocated to that asset by the purchaser must be properly taken into account under principles of tax law applicable when part of the cost of an asset (not previously reflected in its basis) is paid after the asset has been disposed of, depreciated, amortized, or depleted.

Allocation of decrease. Allocate a decrease in consideration as follows.

1. Reduce the amount previously allocated to Class VII assets.
2. Reduce the amount previously allocated to Class VI assets, then to Class V, IV, III, and II assets in that order. Within each class, allocate the decrease among the class assets in proportion to their fair market values on the purchase date.

You cannot decrease the amount allocated to an asset below zero. If an asset has a basis of zero at the time the decrease is taken into account because it has been disposed of, depreciated, amortized, or depleted by the purchaser under section 1060, the decrease in consideration allocable to such asset must be properly taken into account under the principles of tax law applicable when the cost of an asset (previously reflected in basis) is reduced after the asset has been disposed of, depreciated, amortized, or depleted. An asset is considered to have been disposed of to

the extent the decrease allocated to it would reduce its basis below zero.

Patents, copyrights, and similar property. You must make a specific allocation (defined below) if an increase or decrease in consideration is the result of a contingency that directly relates to income produced by a particular intangible asset, such as a patent, a secret process, or a copyright, and the increase or decrease is related only to such asset and not to other assets. If the specific allocation rule does not apply, make an allocation of any increase or decrease as you would for any other assets as described under *Allocation of increase* and *Allocation of decrease.*

Specific allocation. Limited to the fair market value of the asset, any increase or decrease in consideration is allocated first specifically to the patent, copyright, or similar property to which the increase or decrease relates, and then to the other assets in the order described under *Allocation of increase* and *Allocation of decrease.* For purposes of applying the fair market value limit to the patent, copyright, or similar property, the fair market value of such asset is redetermined when the increase or decrease is taken into account by considering only the reasons for the increase or decrease. The fair market values of the other assets are not redetermined.

Specific Instructions

For an original statement, complete Parts I and II. For a Supplemental Statement, complete Parts I and III.

Enter your name and taxpayer identification number (TIN) at the top of the form. Then check the box for purchaser or seller.

Part I—General Information

Line 1. Enter the name, address, and TIN of the other party to the transaction (purchaser or seller). You are required to enter the TIN of the other party. If the other party is an individual or sole proprietor, enter the social security number. If the other party is a corporation, partnership, or other entity, enter the employer identification number.

Line 2. Enter the date on which the sale of the assets occurred.

Line 3. Enter the total consideration transferred for the assets.

Part II—Original Statement of Assets Transferred

Line 4. For a particular class of assets, enter the total fair market value of all the assets in the class and the total allocation of the sales price. For Classes VI and VII, enter the total fair market value of Class VI and Class VII combined, and the total portion of the sales price allocated to Class VI and Class VII combined.

Line 6. This line must be completed by the purchaser and the seller. To determine the maximum consideration to be paid, assume that any contingencies specified in the agreement are met and that the consideration paid is the highest amount possible. If you cannot determine the maximum consideration, state how the consideration will be computed and the payment period.

Part III—Supplemental Statement

Complete Part III and file a new Form 8594 for each year that an increase or decrease in consideration occurs. See *Reallocation after an increase or decrease in consideration,* on page 2, and *When To File,* on page 1. Give the reason(s) for the increase or decrease in allocation. Also, enter the tax year(s) and form number with which the original and any supplemental statements were filed. For example, enter "2006 Form 1040."

Paperwork Reduction Act Notice. We ask for the information on this form to carry out the Internal Revenue laws of the United States. You are required to give us the information. We need it to ensure that you are complying with these laws and to allow us to figure and collect the right amount of tax.

You are not required to provide the information requested on a form that is subject to the Paperwork Reduction Act unless the form displays a valid OMB control number. Books or records relating to a form or its instructions must be retained as long as their contents may become material in the administration of any Internal Revenue law. Generally, tax returns and return information are confidential, as required by section 6103.

The time needed to complete and file this tax form will vary depending on individual circumstances. The estimated burden for individual taxpayers filing this form is approved under OMB control number 1545-0074 and is included in the estimates shown in the instructions for their individual income tax return. The estimated burden for all other taxpayers who file this form is shown below.

Recordkeeping	11 hr.
Learning about the law or the form	2 hr., 34 min.
Preparing and sending the form to the IRS	2 hr., 52 min.

If you have comments concerning the accuracy of these time estimates or suggestions for making this form simpler, we would be happy to hear from you. You can write to the IRS at the address listed in the instructions for the tax return with which this form is filed.

UCC FINANCING STATEMENT
FOLLOW INSTRUCTIONS (front and back) CAREFULLY

A. NAME & PHONE OF CONTACT AT FILER [optional]

B. SEND ACKNOWLEDGMENT TO: (Name and Address)

THE ABOVE SPACE IS FOR FILING OFFICE USE ONLY

1. DEBTOR'S EXACT FULL LEGAL NAME - insert only <u>one</u> debtor name (1a or 1b) - do not abbreviate or combine names

1a. ORGANIZATION'S NAME					
OR 1b. INDIVIDUAL'S LAST NAME		FIRST NAME	MIDDLE NAME		SUFFIX
1c. MAILING ADDRESS		CITY	STATE	POSTAL CODE	COUNTRY
1d. <u>SEE INSTRUCTIONS</u>	ADD'L INFO RE ORGANIZATION DEBTOR	1e. TYPE OF ORGANIZATION	1f. JURISDICTION OF ORGANIZATION	1g. ORGANIZATIONAL ID #, if any	☐ NONE

2. ADDITIONAL DEBTOR'S EXACT FULL LEGAL NAME - insert only <u>one</u> debtor name (2a or 2b) - do not abbreviate or combine names

2a. ORGANIZATION'S NAME					
OR 2b. INDIVIDUAL'S LAST NAME		FIRST NAME	MIDDLE NAME		SUFFIX
2c. MAILING ADDRESS		CITY	STATE	POSTAL CODE	COUNTRY
2d. <u>SEE INSTRUCTIONS</u>	ADD'L INFO RE ORGANIZATION DEBTOR	2e. TYPE OF ORGANIZATION	2f. JURISDICTION OF ORGANIZATION	2g. ORGANIZATIONAL ID #, if any	☐ NONE

3. SECURED PARTY'S NAME (or NAME of TOTAL ASSIGNEE of ASSIGNOR S/P) - insert only <u>one</u> secured party name (3a or 3b)

3a. ORGANIZATION'S NAME				
OR 3b. INDIVIDUAL'S LAST NAME	FIRST NAME	MIDDLE NAME		SUFFIX
3c. MAILING ADDRESS	CITY	STATE	POSTAL CODE	COUNTRY

4. This FINANCING STATEMENT covers the following collateral:

5. ALTERNATIVE DESIGNATION (if applicable): ☐ LESSEE/LESSOR ☐ CONSIGNEE/CONSIGNOR ☐ BAILEE/BAILOR ☐ SELLER/BUYER ☐ AG. LIEN ☐ NON-UCC FILING

6. ☐ This FINANCING STATEMENT is to be filed [for record] (or recorded) in the REAL ESTATE RECORDS.   Attach Addendum [if applicable] | **7.** Check to REQUEST SEARCH REPORT(S) on Debtor(s) [ADDITIONAL FEE] [optional] ☐ All Debtors ☐ Debtor 1 ☐ Debtor 2

8. OPTIONAL FILER REFERENCE DATA

International Association of Commercial Administrators (IACA)

FILING OFFICE COPY — UCC FINANCING STATEMENT (FORM UCC1) (REV. 05/22/02)

UCC FINANCING STATEMENT ADDENDUM
FOLLOW INSTRUCTIONS (front and back) CAREFULLY

9. NAME OF FIRST DEBTOR (1a or 1b) ON RELATED FINANCING STATEMENT

OR

9a. ORGANIZATION'S NAME

9b. INDIVIDUAL'S LAST NAME | FIRST NAME | MIDDLE NAME,SUFFIX

10. MISCELLANEOUS:

THE ABOVE SPACE IS FOR FILING OFFICE USE ONLY

11. ADDITIONAL DEBTOR'S EXACT FULL LEGAL NAME - insert only one name (11a or 11b) - do not abbreviate or combine names

OR

11a. ORGANIZATION'S NAME

| 11b. INDIVIDUAL'S LAST NAME | FIRST NAME | MIDDLE NAME | SUFFIX |

| 11c. MAILING ADDRESS | CITY | STATE | POSTAL CODE | COUNTRY |

| 11d. SEE INSTRUCTIONS | ADD'L INFO RE ORGANIZATION DEBTOR | 11e. TYPE OF ORGANIZATION | 11f. JURISDICTION OF ORGANIZATION | 11g. ORGANIZATIONAL ID #, if any | | NONE |

12. ☐ ADDITIONAL SECURED PARTY'S or ☐ ASSIGNOR S/P'S NAME - insert only one name (12a or 12b)

OR

12a. ORGANIZATION'S NAME

| 12b. INDIVIDUAL'S LAST NAME | FIRST NAME | MIDDLE NAME | SUFFIX |

| 12c. MAILING ADDRESS | CITY | STATE | POSTAL CODE | COUNTRY |

13. This FINANCING STATEMENT covers ☐ timber to be cut or ☐ as-extracted collateral, or is filed as a ☐ fixture filing.

14. Description of real estate:

16. Additional collateral description:

15. Name and address of a RECORD OWNER of above-described real estate (if Debtor does not have a record interest):

17. Check only if applicable and check only one box.

Debtor is a ☐ Trust or ☐ Trustee acting with respect to property held in trust or ☐ Decedent's Estate

18. Check only if applicable and check only one box.

☐ Debtor is a TRANSMITTING UTILITY

☐ Filed in connection with a Manufactured-Home Transaction

☐ Filed in connection with a Public-Finance Transaction

International Association of Commercial Administrators (IACA)

FILING OFFICE COPY — UCC FINANCING STATEMENT ADDENDUM (FORM UCC1Ad) (REV. 05/21/09)

Instructions for UCC Financing Statement (Form UCC1)

Please type or laser-print this form. Be sure it is completely legible. Read all Instructions, especially Instruction 1; correct Debtor name is crucial. Follow Instructions completely.

Fill in form very carefully; mistakes may have important legal consequences. If you have questions, consult your attorney. Filing office cannot give legal advice.

Do not insert anything in the open space in the upper portion of this form; it is reserved for filing office use.

When properly completed, send Filing Office Copy, with required fee, to filing office. If you want an acknowledgment, complete item B and, if filing in a filing office that returns an acknowledgment copy furnished by filer, you may also send Acknowledgment Copy; otherwise detach. If you want to make a search request, complete item 7 (after reading Instruction 7 below) and send Search Report Copy, otherwise detach. Always detach Debtor and Secured Party Copies.

If you need to use attachments, you are encouraged to use either Addendum (Form UCC1Ad) or Additional Party (Form UCC1AP).

A. To assist filing offices that might wish to communicate with filer, filer may provide information in item A. This item is optional.

B. Complete item B if you want an acknowledgment sent to you. If filing in a filing office that returns an acknowledgment copy furnished by filer, present simultaneously with this form a carbon or other copy of this form for use as an acknowledgment copy.

1. **Debtor name**: Enter <u>only one Debtor name in item 1</u>, an organization's name (1a) <u>or</u> an individual's name (1b). Enter Debtor's <u>exact full legal name</u>. Don't abbreviate.

1a. <u>Organization Debtor</u>. "Organization" means an entity having a legal identity separate from its owner. A partnership is an organization; a sole proprietorship is not an organization, even if it does business under a trade name. If Debtor is a partnership, enter exact full legal name of partnership; you need not enter names of partners as additional Debtors. If Debtor is a registered organization (e.g., corporation, limited partnership, limited liability company), it is advisable to examine Debtor's current filed charter documents to determine Debtor's correct name, organization type, and jurisdiction of organization.

1b. <u>Individual Debtor</u>. "Individual" means a natural person; this includes a sole proprietorship, whether or not operating under a trade name. Don't use prefixes (Mr., Mrs., Ms.). Use suffix box only for titles of lineage (Jr., Sr., III) and not for other suffixes or titles (e.g., M.D.). Use married woman's personal name (Mary Smith, not Mrs. John Smith). Enter individual Debtor's family name (surname) in Last Name box, first given name in First Name box, and all additional given names in Middle Name box.

For both <u>organization and individual Debtors</u>: Don't use Debtor's trade name, DBA, AKA, FKA, Division name, etc. in place of or combined with Debtor's legal name; you may add such other names as additional Debtors if you wish (but this is neither required nor recommended).

1c. An address is always required for the Debtor named in 1a or 1b.

1d. Reserved for Financing Statements to be filed in North Dakota or South Dakota <u>only</u>. If this Financing Statement is to be filed in North Dakota or South Dakota, the Debtor's taxpayer identification number (tax ID#) — social security number or employer identification number must be placed in this box.

1e,f,g. "Additional information re organization Debtor" is always required. Type of organization and jurisdiction of organization as well as Debtor's exact legal name can be determined from Debtor's current filed charter document. Organizational ID #, if any, is assigned by the agency where the charter document was filed; this is different from tax ID #; this should be entered preceded by the 2-character U.S. Postal identification of state of organization if one of the United States (e.g., CA12345, for a California corporation whose organizational ID # is 12345); if agency does not assign organizational ID #, check box in item 1g indicating "none."

Note: If Debtor is a trust or a trustee acting with respect to property held in trust, enter Debtor's name in item 1 and attach Addendum (Form UCC1Ad) and check appropriate box in item 17. If Debtor is a decedent's estate, enter name of deceased individual in item 1b and attach Addendum (Form UCC1Ad) and check appropriate box in item 17. If Debtor is a transmitting utility or this Financing Statement is filed in connection with a Manufactured-Home Transaction or a Public-Finance Transaction as defined in applicable Commercial Code, attach Addendum (Form UCC1Ad) and check appropriate box in item 18.

2. If an additional Debtor is included, complete item 2, determined and formatted per Instruction 1. To include further additional Debtors, attach either Addendum (Form UCC1Ad) or Additional Party (Form UCC1AP) and follow Instruction 1 for determining and formatting additional names.

3. Enter information for Secured Party or Total Assignee, determined and formatted per Instruction 1. To include further additional Secured Parties, attach either Addendum (Form UCC1Ad) or Additional Party (Form UCC1AP) and follow Instruction 1 for determining and formatting additional names. If there has been a total assignment of the Secured Party's interest prior to filing this form, you may either (1) enter Assignor S/P's name and address in item 3 and file an Amendment (Form UCC3) [see item 5 of that form]; or (2) enter Total Assignee's name and address in item 3 and, if you wish, also attaching Addendum (Form UCC1Ad) giving Assignor S/P's name and address in item 12.

4. Use item 4 to indicate the collateral covered by this Financing Statement. If space in item 4 is insufficient, put the entire collateral description or continuation of the collateral description on either Addendum (Form UCC1Ad) or other attached additional page(s).

5. If filer desires (at filer's option) to use titles of lessee and lessor, or consignee and consignor, or seller and buyer (in the case of accounts or chattel paper), or bailee and bailor instead of Debtor and Secured Party, check the appropriate box in item 5. If this is an agricultural lien (as defined in applicable Commercial Code) filing or is otherwise not a UCC security interest filing (e.g., a tax lien, judgment lien, etc.), check the appropriate box in item 5, complete items 1-7 as applicable and attach any other items required under other law.

6. If this Financing Statement is filed as a fixture filing or if the collateral consists of timber to be cut or as-extracted collateral, complete items 1-5, check the box in item 6, and complete the required information (items 13, 14 and/or 15) on Addendum (Form UCC1Ad).

7. This item is optional. Check appropriate box in item 7 to request Search Report(s) on all or some of the Debtors named in this Financing Statement. The Report will list all Financing Statements on file against the designated Debtor on the date of the Report, including this Financing Statement. There is an additional fee for each Report. If you have checked a box in item 7, file Search Report Copy together with Filing Officer Copy (and Acknowledgment Copy). Note: Not all states do searches and not all states will honor a search request made via this form; some states require a separate request form.

8. This item is optional and is for filer's use only. For filer's convenience of reference, filer may enter in item 8 any identifying information (e.g., Secured Party's loan number, law firm file number, Debtor's name or other identification, state in which form is being filed, etc.) that filer may find useful.

Instructions for UCC Financing Statement Addendum (Form UCC1Ad)

9. Insert name of first Debtor shown on Financing Statement to which this Addendum relates, exactly as shown in item 1 of Financing Statement.

10. Miscellaneous: Under certain circumstances, additional information not provided on Financing Statement may be required. Also, some states have non-uniform requirements. Use this space to provide such additional information or to comply with such requirements; otherwise, leave blank.

11. If this Addendum adds an additional Debtor, complete item 11 in accordance with Instruction 1 of Financing Statement. To include further additional Debtors, attach either an additional Addendum (Form UCC1Ad) or Additional Party (Form UCC1AP) and follow Instruction 1 of Financing Statement for determining and formatting additional names.

12. If this Addendum adds an additional Secured Party, complete item 12 in accordance with Instruction 3 of Financing Statement. To include further additional Secured Parties, attach either an additional Addendum (Form UCC1Ad) or Additional Party (Form UCC1AP) and follow Instruction 1 of Financing Statement for determining and formatting additional names. In the case of a total assignment of the Secured Party's interest before the filing of this Financing Statement, if filer has given the name and address of the Total Assignee in item 3 of Financing Statement, filer may give the Assignor S/P's name and address in item 12.

13-15. If collateral is timber to be cut or as-extracted collateral, or if this Financing Statement is filed as a fixture filing, check appropriate box in item 13; provide description of real estate in item 14; and, if Debtor is not a record owner of the described real estate, also provide, in item 15, the name and address of a record owner. Also provide collateral description in item 4 of Financing Statement. Also check box 6 on Financing Statement. Description of real estate must be sufficient under the applicable law of the jurisdiction where the real estate is located.

16. Use this space to provide continued description of collateral, if you cannot complete description in item 4 of Financing Statement.

17. If Debtor is a trust or a trustee acting with respect to property held in trust or is a decedent's estate, check the appropriate box.

18. If Debtor is a transmitting utility or if the Financing Statement relates to a Manufactured-Home Transaction or a Public-Finance Transaction as defined in the applicable Commercial Code, check the appropriate box.

Index

A

Accelerated depreciation, 47

Acceleration clause, 107–108, 275, 280

Accountant's services, 85–86, 95–97, 185

Accounts receivable
  asset class for, 51, 52
  in asset sales, 199, 209, 211–212
  in entity sales, 213
  reviewing paperwork, 142–143

ADA (Americans with Disabilities Act)
  compliance, 366–367

Advertising, finding a business through,
  70–73

Allocating the purchase price, 45, 50–56,
  204, 206–207, 213

Amendments, sales agreement, 251

Amortization, 104, 238, 276, 279, 280

Appraiser, valuation by, 86

Arbitration, 248–249, 251–252

Articles of incorporation/organization,
  143, 358

Asbestos cases, 39

Assets
  excluded from sale, 164, 201
  negotiating over, 23
  as part of down payment, 103
  prior liens on, 36
  security interests in, 107
  tangible *vs.* intangible, 117–118

two ways to transfer, 118–119
  valuation based on, 81–82

Asset sales
  bill of sale, 303–308
  Closing Checklist for, 350–352
  contract assignment, 142, 313, 317–320
  employment contracts in, 129
  vs. entity sales, 28–29, 117–122
  intellectual property assignment, 317,
    320–322
  lease assignment, 137–138, 312–316
  liability in, 29, 30, 38–39, 49, 222
  preferred by buyers, 30–31
  professional fees in, 55–56
  purchase price allocation, 45, 50–56,
    204, 206–207, 213
  sales agreement overview, 32–33, 177
  sales agreement signatures, 257
  sample sales agreements, 376–383,
    391–399
  security agreement for, 217–219,
    282–287
  sole proprietorship purchases as, 28, 32,
    49, 118
  tax-saving strategies, 48–50

Asset sales, sales agreement clauses
  document for transferring assets,
    246–247
  identifying the business and assets sold,
    196, 198–201

Preliminary sales agreement. *See* Letter of
intent
Product liability, successor liability laws
and, 38–39, 120
Professional advice, 90–98
accountants, 95–97
business brokers, 97–98
checklist on, 98
lawyers, 91–95
need for ongoing, 90
understanding the limits of, 18
Professional fees, added to tax basis, 55–56
Profit and loss data, 133–136
Promissory note, 272–282
acceleration clauses, 107–108, 275, 280
in asset sales, 29
basics of, 272–276
defaulting on, 34–36, 276
instructions for completing, 276,
279–282
interest rate on, 40, 104–105, 273–274
for noncompete agreements, 240
repayment of, 34, 104, 276, 279, 280
right of setoff, 228
sales agreement clause on, 102, 216–217
sample form, 277–278
security for payment, 217–219, 274–275,
281
seller risk reduction methods, 35–36,
105–108
signers and guarantors, 260, 264–265,
274, 281–282
See also Installment purchases
Property depreciation periods, 46
Property insurance, 364

Property tax proration, 207
Prorations, 207–208, 349
Public agency complaint records, on buyer,
158–159
Publishing business valuation, 84–85
Purchase price allocation, 45, 50–56, 204,
206–207, 213
Purchase-related expense deductions,
55–57

R

Real estate
allocation class for, 51, 52, 53
depreciation of, 46
liens on, 281, 282
security interests in, 107, 275
seller's paperwork, 138–139
taxes on leased, 367
transfer of, 41, 93, 247, 304
Recapture of depreciation, 45
References, buyer's, 157–158
Registered agent changes, 324, 359
Relative of seller, noncompete agreement
with, 240
Relatives, buying a business from, 62–63
Relatives, financing and, 111–112, 274
Rent, 366
Repairs to leased property, 367–368
Representations and warranties, 227–236
in bill of sale, 305
buyer's, 230, 235
overview on, 223, 227–229
seller's, 229–234

NOLO *Keep Up to Date*

1 Go to Nolo.com/newsletters to sign up for free newsletters and discounts on Nolo products.

- **Nolo Briefs.** Our monthly email newsletter with great deals and free information.

- **Nolo's Special Offer.** A monthly newsletter with the biggest Nolo discounts around.

- **BizBriefs.** Tips and discounts on Nolo products for business owners and managers.

- **Landlord's Quarterly.** Deals and free tips just for landlords and property managers, too.

2 Don't forget to check for updates. Find this book at **Nolo.com** and click "Legal Updates."

Let Us Hear From You

3 Register your Nolo product and give us your feedback at Nolo.com/book-registration.

- Once you've registered, you qualify for technical support if you have any trouble with a download or CD (though most folks don't).

- We'll also drop you an email when a new edition of your book is released—and we'll send you a coupon for 15% off your next Nolo.com order!

BUYBU3

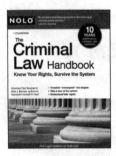

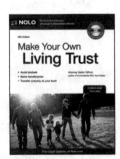